The Russell House Companion to

Working with Young People

Edited by
Fiona Factor, Vipin Chauhan and John Pitts

Russell House Publishing

First published in 2001 by:

Russell House Publishing Ltd.

4 St. George's House

Uplyme Road

Lyme Regis

Dorset DT7 3LS

Tel: 01297-443948

Fax: 01297-442722

e-mail: help@russellhouse.co.uk

British Library Cataloguing-in-publication Data:

A catalogue record for this book is available from the British Library.

ISBN: 1-898924-52-X

Typeset by The Hallamshire Press Limited, Sheffield

Printed by Bath Press, Bath

Russell House Publishing

Is a group of social work, probation, education and youth and community work practitioners and academics working in collaboration with a professional publishing team. Our aim is to work closely with the field to produce innovative and valuable materials to help managers, trainers, practitioners and students. We are keen to receive feedback on publications and new ideas for future projects.

Contents

Section One : The Context of Practice

Section Two : The Practice of Youth Work

Section 3 : Work with Young People

Introduction

Undoubtedly ambitious, this book has taken two years to complete. Its inspiration was a recognition that there exists no standard reader for practitioners working with young people or students on youth and community training courses like those available to other professional groups. Moreover, the recent plethora of new policy initiatives, innovative forms of practice, service delivery and management together with the subsequent reconfiguration of youth services in many areas made such a publication timely.

About This Book

The Russell House Companion attempts to draw together the key issues and current debates for practitioners working with young people and their communities and to illustrate the ways in which the profession of youth and community work can respond to these new challenges. In this respect, the book represents a partial snapshot of the contemporary map of youth and community work and is a contribution to the wider body of existing knowledge and professional debate. Beyond this, *The Russell House Companion* aims to help practitioners to reflect upon their roles as educators, enablers and empowerers within an inclusive, anti-oppressive framework.

This book should be considered as a tool or reference point for practitioners working in varied settings. A number of other areas and issues were originally identified for inclusion in the publication, but because it was not possible to secure the appropriate contributors, some of these issues do not appear. That is not to say that the editorial team does not think that they were of sufficient priority. *The Russell House Companion* reflects the key elements of legislation and government policy that inform today's practice, whilst allowing practitioners in those fields the rare opportunity to document their experiences, and provide an insight for others about to be or already engaged in the work.

Intended to be helpful, but not prescriptive, the book considers the diversity of young people's lives and richness of the contexts, styles and methods within which the work is located. All contributors have also identified key points and questions that practitioners need to address when developing their practice. This should allow for the reader to identify the significant messages from the text, whilst inspiring their enthusiasm to research the area further. References and where appropriate, contact agencies are identified also.

The Russell House Companion is divided into three sections, each with an introductory reader's guide. The sections are:

- The context of practice.
- The practice of youth work.
- Work with young people.

All sections encompass the underlying principles of sound youth work practice: education, equality, empowerment, and participation (NYA, 1999), intentions now embraced by a variety of professional groups.

The organisation of the text in this way allows for and encourages the reader to consider the implications of policy imperatives as well as acting as a reminder of the core principles of their practice and how such tensions can be resolved at the point of service delivery.

New Labour has turned the spotlight on young people, with a welter of new laws and policies like the Crime and Disorder Act 1998, the Learning and Skills Act 2000, and the Children (Leaving Care) Act 2000, which are destined to have a profound impact upon the delivery of inclusive and effective services for young people. The establishment of the Government's Social Exclusion Unit (1998), and the cross departmental review of young people at risk as part of the Spending Review in 2000 has led to the creation of the new Children and Young People's Unit based at the DfEE and supervised by a Cabinet Committee chaired by Gordon Brown, Chancellor of the Exchequer. This long overdue focus on young people whilst encompassing extremely positive intentions, undoubtedly runs the risk of abstracting the problems faced by young people from a social, political and economic context in which a polarisation of wealth and power brought about by economic re-structuring in the late 20th century has caused several commentators to observe that 'social exclusion' is largely a problem experienced by the young (Macdonald, 1997).

In the years since the 1997 election of New Labour, the notion of 'social exclusion' has been steadily re-described. Now, rather than a social phenomenon occasioned by economic globalisation and exacerbated by neo-liberal economic and social policies, 'social exclusion' is presented as a product of the values, beliefs, attitudes and behaviour of the 'excluded' themselves. Increasingly, 'social exclusion' serves as a kind of moral self-exclusion. Although the rhetoric of 'emancipation' remains, the targets for intervention and the professional strategies and techniques for their achievement are correctional, both in tone and intent. Not only do many youth workers recognise that much of this work departs from the values and goals to which a professional youth service once aspired, the young people on the receiving end of the new government initiatives recognise it too.

The shocking murder of Stephen Lawrence, and the subsequent enquiry into the police's handling of the investigation, the *Macpherson Report* (1999), bears witness to the existence of institutionally racist practices within the Police Service. Yet it is not just here that we find institutional racism. The failure of many service providers across the spectrum to respond appropriately and adequately to the needs of Black and minority ethnic clients places a duty on professionals and communities to re-examine their values and discriminatory practices, declare their intentions and engage in social change. Therefore throughout *The Russell House Companion* we have emphasised the implications of such change for Black and minority ethnic young people.

Whether it is school exclusion, teenage pregnancy or youth offending, a consistent emphasis of Government has been the importance of the 'joined up' response, considering all aspects of a young person's life when looking for some resolution. For youth and community workers this should of course be a fundamental tenet of best practice.

This has spawned a renewed emphasis upon, and in some cases a demand for inter-disciplinary responses and multi-agency co-operation, not only in terms of the old style consultation, but more recently in the joint design and delivery of services. This has forced many professionals to critically review existing provision for young people, and in doing so, many have found it wanting.

The contributors to *The Russell House Companion* have all had youth and community work experience, as have the editors, although many are no longer working in the more traditional youth and community service settings. That they are operating in a wide variety of fields exemplifies the worth and broad applicability of the skills, knowledge and values of youth and community work. The growing recognition of the success of such interventions by other professional groups, and their part in establishing effective relationships with disadvantaged young people, is to be applauded, and if youth work philosophies and methods enhance the service delivery to young people and their communities, there can be no complaint.

However, this dissemination of youth and community work into new areas of practice at the expense of a dedicated youth and community service has created a tension. New Labour's youth strategy has had a profound impact upon such services. Youth and community work in one guise or another, is now seen as the main mode of intervention commended in the areas of economic regeneration, youth training, unemployment counselling, drugs education, community safety and juvenile justice. However the increased centrality of professional youth and community work to these endeavours parallels the continuing decline of the youth service, as resources are withdrawn from generic provision in which aims and objectives are negotiated with young 'service users'. Now resources are directed into time-limited government initiatives in which the roles to be played by youth and community workers, the problems to be addressed, the target groups for intervention, and the methods of intervention, primarily individual mentoring and programmes of cognitive-behavioural change, are prescribed and are emphatically, not subject to any re-negotiation. Moreover, as was the case in the early years of its development, this expansion of youth and community work is paralleled by the introduction of a more intrusive and punitive juvenile justice system which is consigning larger numbers of young people to residential and custodial institutions and placing more young people under formal surveillance in the community (Pitts, 2001).

Thus, we may argue that the apparent reversal of the decline in youth and community work in the UK has been achieved at the cost of the development of an 'adequate' youth and community service at a national level, the erosion of youth work professionalism, and the closer incorporation of youth work and youth workers into both surreptitious and overt strategies of youth control. These new forms of youth work are 'problem-oriented', and now describe the moment at which the young person 'buys into' the particular programme and chooses to co-operate with it. Along the way, the link between the structural social and economic changes of the past 25 years and the worsening predicament of young people becomes ever more tenuous.

Such a recognition of the skills of youth and community work practitioners whilst welcomed in some arenas, is also viewed as a *poaching* of staff by other social welfare agencies. This development inevitably leads to the further dilution of a professional service that has struggled for years to be acknowledged and given the more unequivocal statutory basis it deserved and campaigned for. Additionally, the development of *National Occupational Standards* (1999) and the establishment of PAULO, as a National Training Organisation, brings into further question the future validity of the Joint Negotiating Committee (JNC) qualification for youth and community workers. Such developments also raise a fundamental political issue: if the skills and attributes of youth and community workers are valued then why is there not similar acknowledgement of the locations in which these skills have been rehearsed, practised and developed?

For many youth and community service providers up and down the country, such severe erosion of the funding base over the last twenty years, and the high expectations of, but undelivered pre-election commitments from New Labour, has meant that skeletal provision for young people exists, recovery from which would require massive investment in both buildings and staffing levels. This is unlikely to occur. Often covertly, resources are now targeted at those young people seen as 'problematic', and who are often demonised by the media. The acknowledgement of the preventative and educational focus of youth work has been sacrificed to the knee-jerk reactions of government ministers attempting to appease 'middle England'.

The onset of the new managerialism in youth and community services has led to a greater bureaucratisation of the work and the increased requirement to generate statistics and paperwork is seen as a burden rather than an enabling activity. Subsequently there has been an increased reliance upon part-time and volunteer staff to deliver face to face work with young people whilst full time qualified workers carry out administrative and management roles. This has contributed to a sharp demarcation of such roles and brings into question the viability of a cohesive youth and community service at local levels.

Additionally, over the last decade the youth and community service has witnessed the erosion of effective equal opportunities and anti-discriminatory practices, perhaps symbolised by the disdain for the 70s and 80s style of issue-based work. It is noticeable that there is an increasing de-politicisation of the service, its functions and activities and the question that still remains valid is, in the era of New Labour, what is the profession doing about structural inequality, oppression and discrimination? There appears to be an air of collusion, complicity and complacency rather than one of challenge, commitment and controversy. Without challenge, one of the erstwhile bedrocks of the profession, there can be little hope for young people and their communities who, despite needing advocates and enablers, often just survive in despair. Without challenge, the scope for long term social change becomes futile and all that the profession of youth and community work will do is to massage the collective egos of those in power rather than question the status quo.

Finally, we also hope that *The Russell House Companion* celebrates the immense challenge and pleasure of working with young people growing up in contemporary Britain.

Fiona Factor, Vipin Chauhan and John Pitts
April 2001

References

Department of Education (2000). *Learning and Skills Act 2000.* London: HMSO.

Department of Health (2000). *Children (Leaving Care) Act 2000.* London: HMSO.

Home Office (1998). *Crime and Disorder Act 1998.* London: HMSO.

Macdonald, R. (Ed.) (1997). *Youth, the Underclass and Social Exclusion.* London: Routledge.

Macpherson, Sir W. (1999). *The Stephen Lawrence Enquiry*, Cm. 4262-1. London: HMSO.

NYA (1999). *National Occupational Standards for Youth Work.* Draft for Consultation. Leicester: NYA.

Pitts, J. (2001). *The New Politics of Youth Crime: Discipline or Solidarity.* Basingstoke: Palgrave.

Acknowledgements

With a publication of this size, it would be impossible to mention all of those who were supportive in its development. Many have been invited to contribute, were unable, but recommended others. For the quality of their work and patience demonstrated by the many contributors, our appreciation is incalculable and we hope that you are as delighted with the final product as we are. Geoffrey Mann and his colleagues at Russell House Publishing were continuously enthusiastic and helpful. Colleagues from within the University of Luton and in the field of youth and community work across the country have given endless encouragement, personal commitment and inspiration. Special thanks are due to Sue Christie who provided invaluable input and administrative support throughout the process and more latterly to Ruth Crump in the management of the text.

To all the young people who have been on the receiving end of numerous interventions, we hope that their valuable contribution to developing effective practice and shaping service delivery is adequately reflected within the text.

The Editors

Fiona Factor is Course Director of the Youth and Community Studies programme at the University of Luton. A qualified youth worker with over 15 years experience, she has worked in a variety of settings with young people, however much of her work has been as a detached youth work practitioner, managing a variety of street based and multi-agency initiatives, working with marginalised young people. Prior to joining the University of Luton in 1998 she was a trainer in Hertfordshire Youth Service. Her particular teaching and research interests include: youth policy development (including European/International perspectives); citizenship; youth justice and the Crime and Disorder Act 1998; mentoring; effective interventions with young people who are deemed to be socially excluded; accrediting young people's learning; and the design, delivery and effectiveness of the Connexions Service. She has worked in a consultancy capacity for numerous youth work providers and agencies across both the voluntary and statutory sector, focusing upon management practice, detached youth work, anti-discriminatory practice and multi-agency partnerships. Her recent research experience includes *Young People: Our Stake in the Future*, a three nation EU funded project, in which she undertook the role of external evaluator, identifying lessons for effective interventions in young people's lives. She has written in the area of youth crime and youth work interventions. Her most recent publication is *From Emancipation to Correctionalism? UK Youth Work and the Third Way* (with Pitts, J.). Andropov, Y. (Ed.) (2000). *Youth in the Baltic Region*. Joensuu University Press.

Vipin Chauhan is the Principal Partner of Lotus Management Consultancy, an independent practice that works in the voluntary, independent and public sectors. He is a skilled and experienced trainer and consultant and has been working in the field of youth and community work for a number of years. He has worked at a national level for over ten years and has an established reputation for his work on Black young people, professional training standards, quality assurance, the Black voluntary sector, Global youth work, poverty and social exclusion and management and organisational development. Vipin is a trained family and marriage counsellor and a half time Senior Lecturer in the School of Health and Community Studies at the University of Derby. Vipin is the author of *Beyond Steelbands 'n' Samosas: Black Young People in the Youth Service* (1989). Leicester: National Youth Bureau. He has recently co-authored the report *Developing Black Services*, London: Alcohol Concern, on the provision of alcohol services for the Black community and is in the process of writing another on Black perspectives in global youth work. His current research and consultancy interests include: youth and community work with Asian young people; multi-disciplinary team approaches to community development; regeneration initiatives; Black voluntary sector relations and business planning for community organisations.

John Pitts is Vauxhall Professor of Socio-legal Studies at the University of Luton. He has worked as a school teacher, detached and club-based youth worker, youth justice development officer and group worker in a Young Offender Institution. His research includes studies of the system-careers of black and white young offenders, an Anglo-French comparison of responses to young people in trouble, the relationship between school exclusion and youth offending and a three nation study of socially excluded young peoples' experience of professional help. He is author of several books and articles including, *The Politics of Juvenile Crime*, Sage (1988), *Working with Young Offenders*, Macmillan (1990 and 1999), and *The New Politics of Youth Crime: Discipline or Solidarity*, Palgrave (2001).

The Contributors

Janet Adams is a Senior Lecturer in Youth and Community Studies in the Department of Applied Social Studies at the University of Luton. She has over 30 years experience of working in youth work both within statutory and voluntary sector organisations. Her particular interests lie in the areas of participative and experiential learning, equal opportunities, group work and evaluation processes.

Paul Adams is a qualified youth worker with over 15 years experience of work with young people in the voluntary and statutory sector. He is currently National Youth Officer for the Development Education Association. He and David Land (see below) have worked together on a nationally distributed resource pack for young carers.

Lucy Ashby is a teacher and youth worker based in Norwich. She currently works at *Stand Out* a youth group for lesbian, gay and bisexual young people.

Joan Bailey has over 20 years experience working with young people in club-based, outreach and detached work, both in the UK and abroad, having spent eight years in the USA. Currently she is the Manager of the Luton Youth Inclusion Programme, a national initiative funded by the Youth Justice Board working with young people who are offending or at risk of offending. Her particular areas of interest are young people, drugs and community safety, and she has been involved in a range of projects that use peer-led approaches to address drugs and community safety.

Sajid Butt is the Policy and Information Officer at the Black Training and Enterprise Group (BTEG), with a particular interest in New Deal for Communities and Welfare to Work. He is the author of three major reports, *New Deal: Ensuring Black Communities Benefit, Closing the Gap between Black and White: An assessment of TEC Equal Opportunity Strategies* and *Championing Race Equality in Regeneration: Local Ownership in a Regional Agenda* (August 2000). Sajid represents BTEG on a number of key policy bodies, such as the National Partners Network for New Deal, Race Equality Steering Group for New Deal for Communities and TEC National Council Equal Opportunities Advisory Committee. In 1998, Sajid was a gold standard winner at the British Diversity Awards for the article, *New Deal in Danger of Failing Black Unemployed.*

Liam Cairns has been Durham's *Investing in Children* Co-ordinator since 1997. Prior to this he worked with children and their families in a variety of social work settings including child protection, youth justice, residential care and policy development for five local authorities.

Laurence Chester is Director of Social Welfare at the Roselodge Group, an organisation accommodating asylum seekers across Britain. He is a qualified social worker with over 20 years experience in working with young people. For over ten years he worked for local authorities where his work included supporting unaccompanied minors seeking asylum.

Alan Dearling has been involved in some form of work with young people for about thirty years. This includes working in, and managing, the largest youth club in 1970s Europe, in Harlow; street work with punks and Rastafarians in London and the outskirts of Glasgow; and rural youth work and training in Dorset, East Lothian and the Borders. His special interest these days is work with Travellers and members of what has become known as the 'DiY' world counter-culture. He has been a research fellow at QUT, Brisbane, Cardiff, Brunel and Luton universities and is currently senior research consultant for the Chartered Institute of Housing. He has written and edited 24 books to date, many on youth work, including the near-legendary *New Youth Games Book* with Howie Armstrong.

Kathy Edmonds is a Senior Lecturer on the BA/Dip HE Youth and Community Programme at the North East Wales Institute. She is a qualified youth and community worker with 22 years experience in a variety of settings. She is dedicated to tackling the problems caused by rural exclusion and in using youth and community work as a means of continuing education and lifelong learning.

Sacha Kaufman is the co-ordinator of Camden Detached Project. She has been a detached worker for eight years in an inner city environment. More recently her work has focused upon multi-agency interventions in the areas of crime reduction, girls work and giving young people a voice in their communities.

Parminder Kuar Puar has been a youth worker for Leicestershire County Council for four years. A Youth Tutor since January 1998 for Leicester City Council, she is currently based at Sir Johnathan North Community College, a secondary school for young women between the ages of eleven and sixteen.

Jude Kutner has a fifteen year background in youth and community work both in the statutory and voluntary sector. She is currently a freelance consultant in the field of social inclusion. Her recent focus has been in working with staff supporting asylum seekers.

David Land is a volunteer youth worker and a Development Worker with Hertfordshire County Young Carers. He is currently co-ordinating the development of multi-agency support services for young carers. He and Paul Adams have worked together on a nationally distributed resource pack for young carers.

Margaret Melrose is a Research Fellow in the Department of Applied Social Studies at the University of Luton. For a number of years now her work has been centrally concerned with issues of poverty and in particular with marginalised and vulnerable young people. She has published in the areas of child prostitution and young people and drug use in Britain. Her latest book, *Fixing It? Young People, Drugs and Disadvantage* was published in 2000.

Gerard Murray worked in the criminal justice field until 1999 specialising in the field of youth, drugs and crime. He currently works as a care manager for substance misuse with emphasis on parent and child rehabilitation.

Paul Oxborough is a member of the Staff Development and Training Team for Milton Keynes Council's Leisure Youth and Community Dept. His role focuses upon establishing new and innovative ICT training programmes for staff and young people. Prior to this he was a school-based youth worker.

David Porteous is a Lecturer in Applied Social Research and a member of the Vauxhall Centre for the Study of Crime at the University of Luton. His recent and current research has encompassed youth violence, school exclusion, remand management and bail support, mentoring and drug abuse. He is co-editor with Brigitte Volond of *Working with Young People in Europe* and with John Pitts of *Reducing Youth Violence in Schools and Neighbourhoods* (both forthcoming).

Sybil Qasir works as a Family Project Worker for the Turnaround Project, Family Support and Mediation Services run by NCH Action for Children. She works with young runaways aged between twelve and sixteen years old in London.

Rory Reynolds is a qualified social worker, a practising Child and Adolescent Therapist at Bedford Family Consultation Clinic and a lecturer on child and adolescent mental health at the University of Luton. Rory is also a theatre actor and stage director.

Pam Rogers is an Area Manager for the Youth Programmes Unit in Hertfordshire, managing the delivery of Key Stage 4 for young people who cannot complete their education in school. Pam has worked as a centre-based and detached youth worker and has experience of managing service delivery across rural and urban communities.

Julie Scurfield currently works with the County Durham Youth Offending Service as a Community Safety Officer for Young People. Her past experience with Hertfordshire Youth Service included the estab-lishment and development of the *Time Out Project* for Young Women with Children in the Broxbourne area, which she co-worked with Sue Stevens.

Baljeet Gill Singh is currently employed as a Youth Service Development Worker by Warwickshire County Council, based in Warwick. He has worked with young men on issues of masculinity since 1982 in Rochdale, Lancashire and in other education authorities on a consultancy basis.

Karen Shillitoe qualified as a community psychiatric nurse in 1986 and worked for Addictions for a number of years. She is currently engaged as a consultant in the studies of complementary therapies.

Sue Stevens is currently an Area Manager with the Youth Programmes Unit in North Hertfordshire, co-ordinating the provision for young people on alternative programmes to mainstream school in Key Stage 4. Her past experience with Hertfordshire Youth Service included the establishment and development of the Time Out Project for Young Women with Children in the Broxbourne area, which she co-worked with Julie Scurfield.

Jo Steward is a qualified social worker, currently employed by the Waltham Forest and Redbridge Health Authority at *Face to Face*, a young people's project. Her experience includes working with homeless young people; individual and group work with young women, and is currently engaged in one to one work with young people in a range of settings.

Gersh Subhra is a Senior Lecturer in youth, community and social work at the University of Derby. He is involved in and has completed a number of research and consultancy projects, including an evaluation of a national grants programme, a bail supervision project, as well as needs assessment work with small community organisations. He has recently completed a report about the Black and minority ethnic sector in Derby. He retains an active involvement in the voluntary sector as a member of various management committees at a local and national level.

Caroline Tippen is an Area Manager in the Youth Service in Hertfordshire. She is also trained as a counsellor. She has led a number of international youth exchanges between Hertfordshire and countries within both Europe and the Commonwealth. Caroline is currently a committee member of *Connect Youth International*, part of the British Council.

Tracie Trimmer manages the operations department at *London Youth*, a pan-London youth work charity. Tracie began her career in formal education and has been a youth worker for fifteen years.

Dr Annmarie Turnball is currently Director of Policy and Development for the National Centre for Volunteering. Previously she has held posts in higher education, teaching, community development and local authorities where she managed education and social services. She has long-standing research interests in women's history and the history of voluntary action.

Janet Watson is currently working as the first National Policy Officer for the National Forum for the Development of Rural Youth Work, an independent voluntary organisation she helped to found 15 years ago. Its aim is to raise, develop and maintain an awareness of issues affecting young people and those who work with them in rural areas of England and Wales. She has over 25 years youth and community experience in a variety of settings, and her involvement in rural initiatives has been extensive at local, county and national levels.

Mark Webb is a Senior Lecturer in Applied Community Studies at Manchester Metropolitan University. He is a Director and Trustee for the Bibini Centre for Black young people, an independent non-profit making organisation. From 1996 to 1998 he worked on a research project with young people in the Moss Side district in Manchester. He is committed to making post-colonial theories and questions of race and representation integral to youth and community work and social work training and research.

Howard Williamson is a Senior Research Associate in the School of Social Sciences at Cardiff University and a practising youth worker. He is Vice-Chair of the Welsh Youth Agency. He was a member of the Social Exclusion Unit's Policy Action Team on Young People and is a member of the UK New Deal Taskforce Advisory Group. He is closely involved with youth policy development in Wales, the UK and the European Union.

Leona White has been a youth tutor for the last eight years working for both Leicestershire County Council and now Leicester City Council. She is currently based at Judgemeadow Community College, a secondary school, working with young people in the 11–16 year age range.

Bisi Williams is the Youth Manager with ActionAid, an agency that works in over 30 countries in Africa and Latin America. Bisi has been a youth worker for fifteen years.

Cindy Writing works for Northamptonshire developing and providing mentoring services and life skills programmes for young people. She has worked with young people for over 15 years. Most of this experience has involved the face to face provision, management and development of information, advice and counselling services for young people in London and Northamptonshire.

Reader's Guide

The first section explores the settings and context within which youth and community practice is delivered. It is a reminder also of the profession's commitment to the delivery of inclusive services, anti-discriminatory practice and the nature and needs of the client groups with whom practitioners regularly engage. It includes a reflection of the greater incorporation of youth work methods into new arenas, and the shifts in policy emphasis with regard to the organisation of services.

Inclusive Practice: Disability

Designing services in order to ensure the accessibility of provision forms the theme of the contribution from Jude Kutner and Fiona Factor. Using disability issues as their focus, the authors offer insights into why such issues are so often marginalised and how strategies can be developed to avoid this common failure of service delivery. The social model of disability is identified as the most appropriate form of professional response, and the implications for service providers of the Disability Discrimination Act 1995 are also highlighted. The broader application of their inclusive message is evident.

Black Young People

Mark Webb presents a strong case for a review of the current discourse surrounding targeted provision and the inclusion of Black young people in the mainstream of contemporary British society. Making the reader aware of the dangers of collusion with the negative overtones incorporated in the reactive rhetoric and strategies of the exclusion debate, the author offers practitioners models to analyse the historic development of provision for Black young people. How such services should be designed in the future to ensure appropriate, inclusive and holistic responses are clearly identified.

Working with Lesbian, Gay and Bisexual Young People

The isolation experienced by, and the lack of support available to lesbian, gay and bisexual young people is well documented here in Lucy Ashby's contribution. She identifies the key issues for young people coming out and the staff supporting them. Locating her contribution within the context of separate provision, Lucy also highlights the issues for staff within the generic youth work setting. Staffing, venues, ground rules and programme content provide the reader with a clear framework from which to develop appropriate support for these young people who are so often ignored by service providers.

Work with Boys and Young Men

Tracing the historical development of services for young men, Baljeet Singh Gill revisits the professional tension created by the conflict between welfare and education versus the societal expectations of containing and policing youthful excess. He supports the delivery of young mens' work being most effective within a residential setting, whilst also acknowledging the integration of appropriate interventions within generic provision and the difficulties for some male practitioners in challenging the status quo.

Work with Girls and Young Women

Jo Steward recounts how a project targeting young women deemed vulnerable was able to encompass the best practice drawn from the history of work with girls and young women, whilst also responding positively to local research identifying this particular need. The struggle for work with girls and young women to be resourced and valued equally with other service provision, is also a reminder to readers of how threatening such work has been regarded.

Youth Work and Regeneration

Sajid Butt's critical analysis of the development of regeneration initiatives exposes the lack of meaningful consultation with those groups which such interventions are designed to assist. Readers are offered an explanation of government priorities in this area of work and strategies are offered for the effective involvement of young people in such developments.

Youth Work and Young People in Rural Areas

Rural isolation, issues of identity and access to appropriate resources and facilities are not new issues of concern for practitioners advocating on behalf of young people. Janet Watson reminds readers of the need for creativity in the delivery of effective services to young people disadvantaged by virtue of their rural surroundings, and highlights the dangers of mass migration from such communities.

School Based Youth Work

Attempting to deliver social education via youth work methods on a school site has always generated tensions between the school ethos and youth and community work principles. Here,

Parminder Kuar Puar and Leona White identify the struggle for recognition as well as celebrating the complimentary benefits of the delivery of informal education within a formal setting and its potential for enhancing the entire school community.

Community Safety: Involving Young People

Documenting how the *Morgan Report* (1991) informed the shaping of multi-agency community safety strategies, Joan Bailey describes the subsequent requirements of the Crime and Disorder Act 1998 to involve young people in the consultation, design, delivery and evaluation of community safety plans. Her contribution documents the achievements of this initiative in Luton.

Reclaiming the Evaluation Agenda

The need for practitioners to evidence the impact and value of the work they do is well established. Gersh Subhra offers a framework for re-claiming the evaluation agenda which incorporates a shared approach that encompasses the very best of the values, underpinning philosophies and methods that inform the work.

1 Inclusive Practice: Disability

Jude Kutner and Fiona Factor

Key Points

1. Commitment to accessible youth work should not be based upon adherence to legislation, but on an underlying commitment to the rights of the individual and groups.

2. Youth workers do not require 'special' skills to promote an inclusive environment in their youth project: inclusion is a process and youth workers will consolidate their learning through evolving their practice.

3. The difference between a model of integration and a model of inclusion is that integration focuses on whether the young person is 'ready' to become involved in mainstream youth provision and inclusion starts from the perspective that youth provision is accepting of all young people and should ensure that everyone has a sense of ownership and belonging.

4. Don't:
   - be afraid to ask for help and assistance, no-one is expected to have all the answers.
   - try to second guess people's needs—ask.

5. Inter-agency collaboration is essential in providing and maintaining an inclusive environment. It will help enhance learning by sharing knowledge and ideas and may provide additional resources. Costs incurred in making the project inclusive, should not be seen as a blockage to developing practice and provision; instead these should be taken into account at the initial design stage of the project and not seen as an add on.

6. The costs in making the project inclusive **are** the costs of the project.

7. It is the right of young people to be able to fully access and take part in youth provision.

Introduction

Good youth work practice is about working towards providing an environment that is inclusive, where all young people have the opportunity to take part and be involved at an equal level. Additionally, such provision is often supported by separate provision for targeted groups for whom automatic and easy access may be deemed problematic by the young people themselves.

Young people may feel excluded for a variety of different reasons. Perhaps they are shy and find it difficult to make new friends or join in group activities, or perhaps English is not their first language and they may have a difficulty in understanding instructions for a game or activity. Youth workers work with young people who have different needs all the time and often find simple strategies to assist particular young people in becoming more involved in their youth projects. For

example, in the case of a child who finds making new friends difficult, a peer buddying system could be set up and activities could be used that encourage team work and communication. For most youth workers, at one level, providing an inclusive environment is second nature, so why, when it comes to making youth provision inclusive to young people with disabilities, do we find it so difficult?

Historically, *disabled* young people have been referred to as having 'special needs'. Indeed, note the use of language: the word disabled refers to society disabling people from having full access to facilities, rather than referring to their specific needs. This has often had the effect of preventing youth workers involving themselves in inclusive practice, as there has been a tendency to assume that working with young people with 'special needs' requires 'special' skills. In reality, all young people have differing needs, and good youth work provision needs to work towards meeting those individual and collective needs.

In terms of inclusion into youth service provision disabled young people are likely to experience discrimination in a variety of different ways, the most obvious being access to the physical environment. However, unhelpful attitudes towards disability may not be as overt but can be just as disempowering.

Ensuring young people have equal access to provision is not about treating all young people the same, but having a flexible enough service to meet the changing needs of those for whom the service is provided.

We intend to consider key issues that youth workers will need to address, together with principles for good practice, borne out of our experience of engaging with anti-discriminatory practice as the basic tenet of our youth work. This will be underpinned by outlining the debates in current models of disability particularly the medical versus the social, and the implications for practice of the Disability Discrimination Act 1995. This chapter does not attempt to provide the reader with a definitive guide to all the complex issues this subject generates, as this in itself would diminish the message that there is no homogenous group within the community of disabled young people.

Medical and Social Models of Disability

The prevalent attitude towards disabled people has been one of segregation, and dependence on charity and the welfare state. Disability has been pathologised and the individual has been viewed as 'the problem', based on the view that the body is seen as defective and being in need of a 'cure'. This is the central theme of the medical model of disability and one which is imposed upon people with disabilities. It also asserts that the individual needs to change and become more 'normal' in order to fit into society.

Alternatively, the tendency is to hide people with disabilities in institutions of care. A young person surrounded by this belief is never seen as an individual with a variety of needs. Often the only needs that are addressed are related to 'treating' their disability. They are defined in terms of their diagnosis and are denied access to influence the decisions made about their lives. In youth work this

has often led to service providers assessing whether a young person is 'able' enough to join their project or whether they're emotional, physical or behavioural needs etc. can be catered for. The focus, therefore, becomes the young person's 'ability' to 'fit in' with the existing provision rather than the focus being on the provision itself and what needs to change to make it more inclusive.

As part of numerous civil rights movements disabled people have campaigned for the right to self-determination and to non-discrimination, resulting in the development of the social model of disability.

This model of disability shifts the emphasis from the individual into a wider socio-political framework whereby societal structures and individual attitudes are now seen as the barrier to inclusion, in contrast to the medical model which imposes external norms and standards of acceptability. Practitioners and governmental policy are attempting to demolish these barriers in order to create a more inclusive society. Within this model, the disabled person ceases to be seen as 'suffering' from an 'affliction' and attention is drawn to discriminatory societal barriers and how they can be constructively addressed. This model also allows the individual to be seen in a wider context than their disability and promotes a holistic approach. This, in turn, allows for an acknowledgement that issues of multi-oppression not only exist but also should be addressed. For youth work to be inclusive the social model of disability must be embraced.

Legislation

After extensive campaigning from civil rights activists the British Government introduced the Disability Discrimination Act (DDA) in 1995 and established the Disability Rights Commission (DRC) in 2000. The DRC has a duty to ensure that the DDA (1995) and all other legislation relating to the prevention of discrimination against disabled people are enforced. The DRC also offers information and advice to disabled people, to anyone who provides a service to the public and to employers. The provisions of the DDA (1995) gives disabled people new rights in the areas of employment, getting goods and services and buying or renting land or property. In this chapter it is the provision of services that will provide the focus.

Figure 1: The application and impact of both models can be seen diagramatically below:

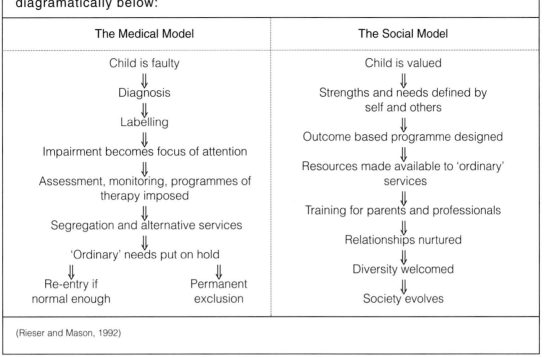

The Medical Model	The Social Model
Child is faulty ⇓ Diagnosis ⇓ Labelling ⇓ Impairment becomes focus of attention ⇓ Assessment, monitoring, programmes of therapy imposed ⇓ Segregation and alternative services ⇓ 'Ordinary' needs put on hold ⇓ ⇓ Re-entry if Permanent normal enough exclusion	Child is valued ⇓ Strengths and needs defined by self and others ⇓ Outcome based programme designed ⇓ Resources made available to 'ordinary' services ⇓ Training for parents and professionals ⇓ Relationships nurtured ⇓ Diversity welcomed ⇓ Society evolves

(Rieser and Mason, 1992)

The Disability Discrimination Act 1995 offers the following definition of disability:

A physical or mental impairment which has a substantial and long-term adverse effect on a person's ability to carry out normal day to day activities.

If you are a provider of goods, facilities or services you have duties under the DDA, which makes it unlawful to discriminate against members of the public on the grounds of disability. These duties came into force from 2 December 1996 on a phased basis. It is therefore unlawful to discriminate against disabled people by:

- Refusing to provide a service without justification.
- Providing a service to a lesser standard without justification.
- Providing a service on worse terms without justification.
- Failing to make reasonable adjustments to the way services are provided for disabled people.

In addition, from the year 2004:

- Failing to make reasonable adjustments to

the physical features of service premises, to overcome physical barriers to access is unlawful.

Under the Act discrimination also occurs when anyone knowingly aids someone to discriminate against a disabled person, or victimises anyone who tries to make use of rights under the Act.

It should be noted that health and safety legislation takes precedence over the DDA, and it would only be for such concerns that a disabled young person can be treated less favourably. For example, a young person with a back injury wants to 'work out' by using the weights in the gym. The youth worker believes that the young people would be at risk of injuring themselves. However, the young person informs the worker that there is no risk because, for example, their doctor has advised that exercising will not strain their back, the worker must be ready to change their mind (Minister for Disabled People, 1996)

Whilst this chapter does not attempt to comprehensively cover all legislation in this area it is important that workers are aware of the implications for legislation contained within The Human Rights Act 1998 (HRA). The HRA, already in force in Scotland and Wales, came into force in England and Northern Ireland on 2nd October 2000.

The aim of the HRA, and of the European Convention, upon which the HRA is based, is to protect the human rights of individuals against the abuse of power by the State, meaning any public authority, and in many cases to give compensation when rights are breached.

The HRA is expected to impact on the way in which the DDA is interpreted in the courts. The DDA requires service providers to make reasonable adjustments to their policies, practices and procedures. In deciding what is 'reasonable' for the youth service in, for example, providing its publications in alternative formats, the court may need to take into account that a disabled young person, under the HRA, has a right to freedom of information.

Planning and Delivery

The key message is that inclusive youth work must be seen as good youth work practice. You do not need specialist skills. Inclusive youth work is primarily about attitude. The key thing to remember is that the youth project may have some parameters for who can use the facility e.g. a specific age range, gender, ethnic origin, sexual orientation etc., but it should never exclude young people on the basis of 'ability'. As youth workers we have a responsibility to ensure our projects are welcoming and inclusive. However, due to lack of thought and the need for more careful planning, provision can more often than not, become inaccessible for young people with disabilities.

In order to ensure youth provisions are inclusive we must plan for diversity. When designing a youth project the first question that needs to be asked is who is likely to be attending before deciding what the programme of activities will be. Think about how diversity can be provided within the programme delivery and make the curriculum flexible enough to enable young people to engage at a variety different levels. Evaluating a programme of activities that has the flexibility to enable participants to engage at a variety of different levels can seem daunting. However, just as the activity itself is flexible so must be the process of evaluation. It is essential that all young people can be included in the evaluation process.

One way of trying to establish this principle is to encourage young people themselves to be involved

in the design and delivery of the service. There is no need to second guess others needs; the young people themselves are your experts.

It is important that all policies and procedures are written within a framework of inclusiveness. Particular care must be taken in the area of health and safety. For example, think about how you ensure that all young people will be evacuated safely from a building in the event of a fire. A policy on how young people are expected to behave in the project is also important. Project staff should consistently reinforce what is acceptable and what is not. Young people should be clear as to what the sanctions will be if they behave outside of the agreed policy. If a young person is presenting challenging behaviour staff should try and understand the behaviour from the young person's perspective and not just respond to it as a behaviour that is disrupting their activity. Often 'difficult' behaviour is borne out of frustration. It maybe that the young person is finding it difficult to express themselves or is having difficulty in understanding the activity or what is expected of them. Useful strategies could include assigning a key worker to the young person who will be able to build a closer relationship with them and offer them a high level of pastoral care, provide the young person with the opportunity to opt out of sessions and most importantly liaise with parents or guardians and other agencies who maybe able to offer strategies. However, ethical issues concerning the rights of young people to socialise without reference to parents or carers need to be considered.

When joining the project a two way sharing of information needs to take place with all young people. Users need to be aware of the policies and procedures you work within and the young people should have the opportunity to declare any needs they have. Simple questions can be used, such as asking what the young person likes or dislikes doing, things they may find difficult to do, what things they may need help with etc. If a young person is unable to tell you these things themselves then you should invite someone to advocate on their behalf.

Due to the high level of segregation in society, many non-disabled young people will not have had the opportunity to socialise and share provision with disabled young people. The youth provision may provide their first opportunity, and although they may hold prejudicial views it is important to remember that our role as youth workers is to educate, dispel the myths and create an environment where attitudes and beliefs can be aired, discussed and challenged in a positive and educative way, in the same way that we should challenge any other discriminatory behaviour.

One of the tools that can promote an environment of respect and inclusion is our use of language. In all areas of discrimination challenging people's use of language has often been one of the first ways of encouraging people to question their views. For example, the difference between using the phrase 'wheelchair bound' and 'wheelchair user' is self-evident as is the difference between using the term 'The Disabled' rather than 'people with disabilities' or 'disabled people'. It is essential that you do not allow words that are related to disability to be used in a negative way or as insults; always challenge it and also be aware of your own use of language. Having positive images of disabled people displayed in the project is a simple but very effective way of challenging stereotypes.

The use of language evolves constantly, so what is considered to be acceptable language now will inevitably change in the future. There is sometimes a fear of not getting it right' so it's easier not to try. Clearly this argument is not acceptable with regard to sexist or racist language and neither is it acceptable in the context of disability. Youth workers have a responsibility to keep up to date with the political context within which they are working, especially if they are to fully embrace the social model.

Frequently the lack of resources is offered as a reason for not being able to provide inclusive provision. Whilst of course there are financial constraints in making physical adjustments to buildings, there are many other things that can be put in place to make the environment more accessible, for example, simply painting doorframes in a distinctive colour to distinguish them from the doors themselves, or ensuring the publicity material is available in different formats i.e. large print will assist people with partial vision. There may be no budget for a major refurbishment, but there is likely to be access to funding for activities. When costing activities the need to be inclusive must be taken into account, for example, the development of the use of Information Technology within youth work must encompass within it the costs and requirements for appropriate software to meet different users needs. Similarly if you are organising a trip the cost of hiring accessible transport needs to be taken into account. Too often activities are costed without considering

the variety of needs participants may have and making activities inclusive is seen as an on cost. This is an attitude that needs to change. The cost of inclusive youth work should be incorporated in all budget areas at the outset of project development plans and funding applications. Opportunities for partnership with the voluntary sector will often allow for funding applications to be successful.

If planning a project trip, the following practice and resource implications will need to be considered:

- The potential for a reconnaissance visit needs to be explored. If this is not possible, detailed telephone enquiries need to be made. This should cover whether the site is appropriately accessible and whether site staff have an inclusive attitude.
- The need to book accessible transport.
- Ensuring that there is an appropriate ratio of staff to young people.
- Checking that all dietary and medical requirements can be catered for.
- Checking that the proposed programme can cater for a variety of different needs and levels of engagement.
- If the visit includes input from site staff, are they equipped to meet the needs of the young people, e.g. does the venue provide signers?
- Checking that the evacuation procedures are safe and appropriate for your user group.
- Checking that all other elements of the risk assessment have been undertaken.

Inter-agency collaboration is essential in providing and maintaining an inclusive environment; it will help enhance workers learning by sharing knowledge and ideas and may be a source to provide an additional resources.

Inter-agency and parent or guardian input is also important in providing the necessary consistency to support individual development. For example, if a young person is using a picture board to assist communication in their school and home environment, they should have the opportunity to extend this practice in their youth provision.

Confidentiality is another area that needs to be considered. A common experience for disabled young people is that information about themselves is given out without their permission being sought first. Information sharing should be negotiated with the young person or where appropriate, with the parent or guardian.

Key Questions

1.   Who is going to be involved in the project before deciding on a programme of activities?
2.   Are staff welcoming and willing to understand the different needs of all the users?
3.   Do you have a range of resources and materials that are appropriate of a variety of
4.   Are there appropriate structures in place to enable young people to get involved in the decision making process?
5.   Have you designed an appropriate induction to your project so participants are clear about the policies and ideology within which you work?

Disability awareness training for staff must be included in all staff development opportunities. Whilst it is important to offer specific input on issues relating to disability and legal responsibilities, the principles of inclusive practice should be embedded throughout the training curriculum.

Conclusion

Disability awareness should inform all aspects of youth work and should not be dependent upon whether there is a disabled young person using the project. In youth work the responsibility to end discrimination against disabled people lies with service providers by modelling inclusive and respectful environments.

References

Department of Health (1995). *Disability Discrimination Act.* London: HMSO.

Minister for Disabled People (1996). *Disability on the Agenda.* London: HMSO.

Reiser, R., and Mason, M. (1992). *Disability Equality in the Classroom, A Human Rights Issue.* London: Disability Equality in Education.

Rieser, R., and Mason, M. (1992). *Altogether Better: From 'Special Needs' to Equality in Education.* London: Hobsons Publishing.

Further Reading

Barton, L. (Ed.) (1996). *Disability and Society: Emerging Issues and Insights.* London: Longman Sociology Series.

Manchester City Council Education Dept. (1997). *Guidelines for Working with Disabled Young People* (first draft) Manchester: Manchester Youth Service.

Morris, J. (1998). *Pride Against Prejudice, Transforming Attitudes to Disability.* London: Women's Press.

Oliver, M. (1994). *The Politics of Disablement.* Hampshire and London: Macmillan Press.

Smith, N. (1999). Are you Inclusive? In *Youth Work,* September. Leicester: NAYC.

Video Resources

HAPA (1995). *A Place to Play: Making Play Services Accessible to Children with Disabilities and Special Needs.*

Contacts

Disability Rights Commission Helpline, Tel: 08457 622 644, Textphone 08457 622 644

Disability Resource Team, Tel: 01920 466005

British Council for Organisations of Disabled People, Tel: 01332 295551, e-mail: bcopd@bcdopd.demon.co.uk

Council for Disabled Children, Tel: 020 7843 6000, www.ncb.org.uk

Links to useful information on the net: www.disabiltynet.co.uk

2

Black Young People
Mark Webb

Key Points

1. It is essential to locate 'targeted work with young black people' within a critical framework that acknowledges how institutional racism may have an impact on the way in which services are resourced, designed and evaluated.

2. An open critical examination of race, representation and identities should be included in all services provided for Black young people. Therefore, culturally specific work will complement existing services and not replace any inadequacies within them.

3. Although Black young people may experience racism they are entitled to have services that equip them to deal with all forms of discrimination. Service should be innovative and visionary and should maximise their potential. Such services may be invisible, seen as unachievable, or even unfair within white dominant institutional cultures.

4. Experiences of racism, or being 'Black' does not necessarily provide analysis that will inform a 'holistic inclusive vision' or problem solving in any agency, and why should it? There is a need for critical dialogue amongst Black practitioners to work towards inclusive processes that acknowledge race, racism and shifting identities in terms of the needs of all Black young people.

5. Work with Black young people should include a critical examination of the location of all workers involved based on knowledge, skills and experiences. Black workers should not be assumed, set up or used as experts for all Black young people.

Introduction

Youth workers, social workers, teachers...even my parents only saw parts of who I am, and they didn't know everything about me. I didn't want them to know everything about me, but they all felt they knew what was best for me.

This quote from a British born Moroccan young man in care reflects on the involvement of professionals and family in his life. Although this is an individual example, it reveals how intervention in a young person's life can be based on a partial understanding of their needs. The complex dynamics of 'race' and racism and the political, professional and personal perspectives of Black young people and those who intervene in their lives, are integral to informing what constitutes 'appropriate' youth work intervention.

I use the terms 'Black' and 'White' and acknowledge their limitations, as they do not begin to capture the rich ethnic and political diversity of youth and community work and young people.

However, I agree with Patricia Williams (see Further Reading) when she states 'the simple matter of the colour of one's skin so profoundly affects the way one is treated, so radically shapes what one is to think and feel about this society, that the decision to generalise from such a division is valid.

The quote at the beginning also illustrates the disjunction between the individual perspectives of Black young people and the individuals situated in professional services. It could be argued that Black young people are getting on with their lives. Irrespective of this fact, professionals spend an inordinate amount of time talking about them, politicians categorise them in terms of the social exclusion agenda assessing who is 'Included' or 'Excluded.' These perspectives fail to acknowledge that Black young people are the living embodiment of 'diversity' and they represent a fascinating multiplicity of identities in contemporary British society. If they manage to negotiate the miasma of racism in every day life, what is the problem? Why should they be delineated into a target group? Immediately there are two issues at stake.

Firstly, there is the danger that the process of targeting actually intensifies the marginalisation and 'othering' of Black young people. Secondly, there is evidence to suggest that intervention from professionals is unnecessary as many young people are progressively absorbing ways of negotiating their changing and shifting identities and addressing issues of discrimination.

If one looks at the picture from afar, the idea of British society as a multi-cultural and multi-racial haven appears to be a reality, but closer inspection of this image reveals a society in which the experience of inequalities and discrimination against Black young people are rife. The bringing to the foreground of the social inclusion agenda by the government functions as an acknowledgement that Black young people are effectively disenfranchised from active participation as British citizens. It could be argued that a passport to full participatory citizenship in Britain must include full participation in social, personal, professional, educational, economic and political spheres. According to the government's Social Exclusion Unit a large number of Black young people are short-changed in nearly all areas of public and professional life. In order to develop a viable and sustainable strategy for the inclusion of Black young people, it is essential to develop a praxis that reflects a holistic sense of their social reality, whilst refusing to collude with inferior pathways for them within British society.

Post-war Black immigration has been characterised by the ability to survive and deal with the challenges of everyday racism that is integral to Black experience in Britain. Black young people quite rightly have refused to acclimatise to cultural and institutional racist practice that has attempted to limit their potential. However the success and mobility of a few individuals can give the impression of Social Inclusion and equality of access for all Black young people. Individual successes and role models should be celebrated but they should not distract from our understanding of the social reality and marginalisation of the majority of Black young in contemporary British society.

The function of this chapter is to examine the development of work with Black young people in the post-war period. It attempts to capture the ways in which the needs of Black young people have been assessed. The experiences of Black young

people have been characterised by both binary and opposition politics. On the one hand, within the discourses of a right wing and essentially racist politics Black young people have been pathologised and considered to be 'problematic' in British society. On the other hand, within the discourses of a largely sympathetic white liberal practice, their location has been perceived as encompassing a wide range of diverse positions that need to be recognised and valued and this has functioned in conjunction with a well-intentioned drive towards social inclusion.

An analytical model has been provided to assist in the critical location of the process of identifying preventative, empowering, visionary, and sustainable work with Black young people as a targeted group situated within the context of institutional and cultural racism and diverse, changing Black identities in contemporary Britain. Key points and questions for practitioners will be highlighted focusing on key concepts in the delivery of services.

Assessing the Needs of Black Young People

> *We believe that as young black people, we are at a disadvantage in life. We encounter inequality in education, employment, in the recognition of our health needs, in our representation in the media: we suffer over immigration issues, we are denied our separate and distinct cultural needs in our living environments and in the facilities that are needed for recreation; we suffer injustice...*
>
> (Black Youth Forum, 1999)

This statement taken from the Black Youth Charter captures how nearly a thousand Black young people across the UK clearly acknowledge the erosion of their rights in many aspects of their lives. The historical developments of how services for Black young people within British society have been shaped needs to be critically examined, mapping the political phases that have attempted to address the question of race equality. There have been a series of political developments that focused the attempts to articulate the processes involved in racist practice, the categories and aspects of discrimination including class, gender, disability and sexuality (Anthias, 1992; Brah, 1996; Modood et al.,

1994; Ellis, 1997) and the forms that discrimination takes (Dominelli, 1988; Sivandanan, 1982; Thompson, 1996 and 2000; Fanon, 1986). Gilroy (1992) argues persuasively in his seminal text that Blackness and Britishness are still perceived as mutually exclusive identities.

The complex processes of racism and race equality politics have been thoroughly mapped out through the colour blind, multi-cultural, integration, equal opportunities, the (anti-isms), anti-discriminatory notions of social inclusion/ exclusion. Essentialist notions of inclusive political categories of Blackness have been widely contested. The term 'Black' has traditionally been seen to represent Black, heterosexual, middle class men, and clearly this delineation of Blackness has excluded the vast majority of Black people. In recent years with the advent of Black feminism (Hooks, 1982, 1984 and 1994) and Queer theory (Abelove et al., 1993) the categorisation of Blackness has been challenged and expanded to include issues from a wider range of peoples. This has enabled multiple forms of discrimination to be exposed and evidenced.

These public and intellectual debates have influenced the ways in which the needs of Black young people have been interrogated and understood within areas of social policy. After the inner city riots in the 1980s in St Pauls, Toxteth, Brixton and Tottenham, the needs of Black young people became central to race and social policy debates. Currently, the discussion of Black young people's needs are articulated between the findings of the *Macpherson Report* (1999) and the development of the government's Social Exclusion agenda. Historically, the paradigm for understanding Black young people's needs has been consistently associated with the problems emerging from a 'white dominant institutionally racist culture' and the need to absorb assertive, racially diverse communities that have made and continue to make demands to dismantle racist structures. Generations of Black young people's needs, despite the enactment of 'good faith', have been often lost in wider political agendas.

This brief description of policy approaches is indicative of the manner in which social policy approaches to the needs of Black young people have been reactive to situations rather than proactive or preventative. Reactive policies have consistently failed to recognise the depth and

complexity of the identities of Black young people and have displayed a failure to get to grips with the entirety of Black young people's cultural, social and political experiences. Youth work with Black young people has tended to emphasise the 'difference' of Black young people to White young people. Difference in this context acts as a culturally loaded sign, whereby difference also signifies inferiority. The reactive process reinforces existing stereotypes of Black people in British society in the sense that Black young people are considered to be lazy, aggressive, having a tendency to criminal activity, and are intellectually inferior to their white counterparts, and this process ultimately excludes them from debates that affect young people generally. This in turn has resulted in the need for the social exclusion policy, which provides an opportunity for youth workers and youth work intervention to play an important role in the development of innovative and politically astute approaches to preventative and inclusive services for Black young people.

It is common knowledge that an unacceptable number of Black young people, mainly African Caribbean young men, are underachieving educationally and are more likely to be excluded from school than their peers. Black young people are over-represented within the criminal justice system, and mental health institutions. These combined life experiences for many Black young people reveal a more sinister experience of their objectification in a post-colonial and marginal context. Frantz Fanon (1986) suggested that racism results in the externalisation of the Black subject as the 'other'. This process of 'othering' is instrumental in 'Classifying him, imprisoning him, primitivising him'. Concomitantly, Black young people also begin to internalise the notion that they are inferior.

The exclusion in British society, based on race (black), age (young), needs (problem) has resulted overtly or covertly in the pathologisation of Black young people. They are considered to be 'problematic', 'good', 'bad' or 'other'. The multiplicity of services offered to them has reflected these constructions of Black young people on macro and micro levels politically.

It is essential to have detailed empirical data about patterns of social exclusion. Although recent breakthroughs in the analysis of patterns of social exclusion have been very useful, it does not negate the fact that these findings that have finally been socially and politically verified have circulated as common knowledge in the Black community. This suggests that being able to name the problem is not the issue, but rather finding sustainable answers to the problem has proven thus far, to be elusive. Additionally there are regional variations of the type of services offered based on the number of Black young people actually undertaking services.

In the meantime, we face the danger of failing a generation of Black young people who are excluded, pathologised and dehumanised. Liberal approaches that bring to the fore notions of increased tolerance or revolve around ideas of 'social divisions', consistently fail to take into account the impact of racism on an individual's development. These approaches have a tendency to equalise difference, failing to adequately locate the very real differences between gender oppression, class oppression and oppression on the basis of sexuality or disability. Human beings are not all oppressed equally; there are real material and political factors that govern the different natures of oppression. A refusal to recognise this fact, simply reconfirms the dominant ideological structures at play in oppression and in some ways simply inverts them. This cannot and does not function as an adequate critique to form the basis of significant social policy. An understanding of 'race' and racism should be viewed as a valuable, empowering analytical tool which does not compete with other oppressions but contributes to a holistic understanding of the complex nature of oppression.

Historical experiences of overcoming oppression should influence any new pathways created for young Black people. We have much to learn from Frederick Douglass an American abolitionist, orator, and writer who highlighted the necessity not only to understand the nature of oppression, but also to understand that reform processes for 'total social inclusion' will be always be difficult. He argued powerfully in relationship to African American slavery:

> *The conflict has been exciting, agitating, all-absorbing, and for the time being putting all other tumults to silence. It must do this or it does nothing. If there is no struggle, there is no progress.*

The design of services for Black young people has often departmentalised many of them into problematised behaviours, issues and people. For example; the Black young offender, the Black young drug taker, the Black non-attender, have become widely prevalent stereotypes. The current government acknowledges in the work around the Social Exclusion Unit, both that they failed and equally had not adopted preventative approaches to dealing with excluded young people:

> *In the past, governments have had policies and tried to deal with each of these [policies'] problems individually, but with little success at tackling the links between them, or preventing them from arising in the first place.*

This inability to examine different areas of policy and simultaneously cater for the diversity of Black young people's needs has resulted in Black young people's needs being lost in a social policy minefield, which can be represented in cyclical form.

Figure 1 illustrates the cycle that youth service providers can find themselves in if the dominant ideological constructions of young Black people's needs are not addressed at the design stage. The effects of this cyclical process are the reinforcement of problematising beliefs and marginalisation, and, many would argue, the dehumanisation of Black young people. The institutional problem has been the inability to offer a visionary, preventative service that is empowering to its users and sustainable in real political terms. Consequently, the inability of the institution to provide an adequate service is translated into the notion of the 'problematic' individual service user. Inadequate structural processes thus become personalised. These principles apply to all aspects of exclusion experienced by Black youth service users.

Phase 1 of the cycle highlights the manner in which the inability to offer a sustainable service model results in the offering of a 'different' service. Phase 2 illustrates the manner in which diversity, race, class, gender and sexuality can be negotiated or accommodated but this takes place outside of the mainstream model. Phase 3 focuses on the resource issue and the way in which resources are allocated for the 'different' service and are perceived as 'special.' Therefore, any development of this service is deemed as requiring 'additional' and 'special' resourcing. Phase 4 details the reaction of the service users to the inadequacies in the original service offered. Phase 5 is characterised by a

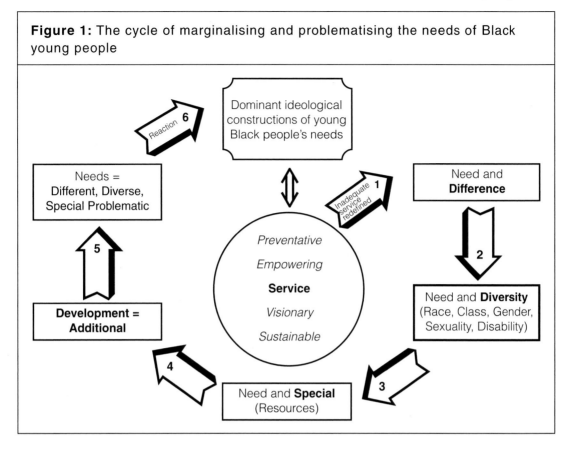

Figure 1: The cycle of marginalising and problematising the needs of Black young people

reaction *against* the service users whose needs are then perceived as not only being 'different and special', but more importantly, 'problematic.' This then informs and reinforces the dominant ideological constructions of what Black young people need, thus returning both youth workers and young people to the original phase in the cycle.

The key significant factor of this cyclical process is that Black young people are made to feel different, special, problematic, and 'other' in many services offered for them.

Black Young People and Diversity

The introduction of the concept of Diversity (Roosevelt, 1996) has complemented the desire to humanise and respect the multitude of identities and issues integral to discussion of inequalities and discrimination. The concept has chameleon qualities in its usefulness when examining the question of race equality. 'Diversity' is presented as the universal inclusive term that encompasses the totality of identities, the utopia of equalising narratives, yet it can act as a smoke screen which detracts from the significance of evidenced institutional racism. Diversity is an extremely positive concept but its development needs to be handled with caution as it can fragment subtly what has taken generations to articulate in relation to institutional racism. Specifically designed work for Black young people has been problematically located as dealing with a single issue: the race issue, which implies race and diversity are too complex to combine and locate strategically for Black service users or providers. This is both patronising and displays an ignorance of the multiple of locations Black young people occupy and negotiate every day of their lives.

Black Young People and Institutional Racism

The miasma in which covert, unintentional racism has existed has been explored historically and has remained a phenomenon that everybody knows exists but of which no one can define the impact, particularly within institutions. *The Macpherson Report* (1999) is one of the most significant contributions for exposing both 'institutional racism' and 'unwitting racism'. By 'institutional Racism' I mean collective failure of an organisation to provide an appropriate and professional service to people because of their colour, culture or ethnic origin. It can be seen or detected in processes, attitudes and behaviour which amount to discrimination through unwitting prejudice, ignorance, thoughtlessness and racial stereotyping. By 'unwitting racism' I mean the racism which arises because of the lack of understanding, ignorance or mistaken beliefs, or from well-intentioned but patronising words or actions. It can arise from unfamiliarity with behaviour or cultural traditions of people or families from minority ethnic communities. It can arise from racist stereotyping of Black as potential criminals or trouble makers. These have serious implications for any work designed for Black young people as a targeted group. The evidenced national acknowledgement of the processes of institutional racism has placed all human service providers under inspection. This focus reaffirms the social and institutional reality in which discussions about forms and categories of discrimination take place. Here we must avoid an 'institutionalised racist exclusive framework' in which the concept of social inclusion is one that negates the importance of race and class, sexuality, disability.

The clarity of institutional and unwitting racism provides an excellent platform from which to critically and constructively develop the conceptual tools of 'diversity' and 'social inclusion' as workable, practical realities to provide a better more appropriate range of service for Black young people.

Targeting Groups: Not Labelling Individuals

In order to capture a holistic assessment of Black young peoples' needs and provide services that reflect these, the desire to identify all key issues affecting and influencing their lives is necessary. There also needs to be the willingness to assess to what extent dominant ideological constructions of Black young people influence the service offered. This applies also to services provided by Black

organisations, in order for targeting to be preventative, empowering, visionary and sustainable. The principles of youth and community work need to be empowering, educative and participative to ensure equality drawing on a range of informal and formal youth work educational working methods (NYA, 1997). Youth and community work services need to make central the task of accommodating all Black young people examining their identities, their diversity and multiplicity of oppressions, together with negotiating the impact of racism in their lives.

Identifying needs based on self-definition by Black young people and an objective political analysis of their situation does not necessarily mean that Black young people are being labelled. Instead, this dual approach acts as a rationale for the provision of specific and appropriate services. For example, to describe a young Black working class woman in care, who is facing racism within the care system, is not to label her. Similarly, to describe a young, Nigerian, middle class, educationally gifted, man who experiences institutional racism through not being pushed academically is not to label him. These examples highlight the realities of the lives of Black young people, which need to be better reflected in professional settings and the services provided to them. In this sense then, there is a conceptual difference between 'labelling' as an act of negative judging and 'targeting' as positive action by which more appropriate services can be delivered to Black young people. Many institutions struggle to respond to the demands made of them especially when these are articulated by a small minority of people such as Black service users, Black families, Black youth and community work practitioners, Black researchers and Black academics. However, these demands require fuller consideration by service providers as they also represent the voices of the Black community albeit sometimes from a different perspective.

Holistic Youth Work with Black Young People

Mission statements and statements of purpose should reflect an agency's desire to provide services that attempt to holistically identify the needs of Black young people. The values captured the aims of the New Black Organisation, the Bibini Centre in

Manchester, UK. This is an independent non-profit making organisation which delivers a range of services specifically for young Black people in care, and provides some excellent principles to work with. The organisation stands for:

- Self determination.
- Valuing cultural diversity and difference.
- Challenging racism.
- Building on the strengths of Black people.
- Keeping links not breaking them.
- Young people's rights.
- Challenging discrimination of Black disabled people.
- Supporting Black young lesbian and gay men.

These are described as aims and aspirations that can be made integral to any service designed and provided for Black young people. Let us now look more closely at what 'holistic' practice actually involves when working with Black young people. Firstly, the dynamics of young people's lives must inform what are seen as 'needs'; and secondly what is deemed appropriate to the programme of work or methods of working adopted to meet them. It is important therefore to acknowledge:

> *The totality of young people's lives involves identifying the perspectives which would be likely to inform their experiences, needs and attitudes as individuals, members of families, members of communities, members of society...*
>
> (Webb, Kenny and Cockburn, 1995)

Targeting work involves therefore respecting the totality of Black young people and the multiplicity of locations in which identities exist. Work with a group of young Asian women could involve a number of dynamics of individuality; a young Asian woman can be member of an Asian family, a member of a young Asian women's group, and a member of a mosque. Race is not the only connecting factor of specific work. As stated by Brah:

> *Cultures are never static. While the cultures of different groups in society will differ considerably, it is also the case that, in so far as at a particular point in history all groups are subjected to certain common socio-political and economic forces, they will share some aspects of one another's cultures.*
>
> (Brah, 1996)

Figure 2 illustrates a model that attempts to capture the complexities that have been discussed throughout this chapter, when designing and delivering work that is targeted at Black young people. This figure visually represents the way in which targeting work can be located. This process acknowledges the way in which services can emphasise difference and exclusion and be reactive to the exclusion of Black youth. Equally, the image shows how services can be designed in such a way as to acknowledge diversity, being inclusive whilst being visionary. The positive upper half of the target focuses on inclusiveness, preventative practice, recognition of diversity and vision. Inclusiveness should not be politically correct or dictated by stereotypes of Black young people. Inclusiveness acknowledges potential and questions of power and powerlessness within the paradigms of a predominantly racist culture.

The aspects of identity and belonging together with needs can provide a good framework from which to capture individual dynamics and work towards a holistic approach to specific services and work with young Black people. The Bibini Centre's holistic approach to meeting the multiplicity of needs of Black young people is combined with the key principles of youth and community work to illustrate a useful framework for designing services targeted at Black young people.

Any work with young Black people uses the aspects of identities from Figure 2 to complement their specific type of service. This holistic framing of the work means a focus on the potential of young people, helping them to deal with the problems they face together with drawing on strengths, qualities and positives in their lives. This will work towards diversity and not difference, inclusion and not exclusion. The principles and values of youth and community work should indicate:

- Respect for human rights, the individual's right to self-determination.
- Respect for different cultures and religions.
- Equality and commitment to anti-discriminatory practices.
- Empowerment and participation.

(NYA, 1997)

These approaches should be made pivotal in any service offered. These elements of the work with Black young people are essential and explore preventative approaches to the issues, individuals and groups. The dangers of designing and reacting to the limited constructions of Black young people as potentially criminal, dangerous or problematic service users have been outlined above, and is regressive.

The identification of what constitutes a good appropriate service for Black young people requires mechanisms for the measuring of effectiveness quality standards and performance indicators in youth work. The importance of quality standards has been critically examined (Wilcox, 1990; Wylie, 1999) and is essential when developing and promoting the concept and reality of youth services. Young black people deserve an integrity in design of both work that embraces the desire to capture the richness of the multiplicity of identities within British culture, and placing this within a global context.

Preventative practice should not focus solely on damage limitation, it is concerned with preventing misinformed choices or actions that might result in negative outcomes for Black young people. Diversity recognises from the outset that Black young people inhabit a number of locations simultaneously spanning gender, class, sexuality, and disability, not to mention differential racial and cultural heritages. A visionary practice should be able to project perspectives based on the challenges of a changing society. Holistic approaches capture the reality of Black young people's lives in all of their dimensions, recognising their political location, the impact of family relationships and individual, family, community, societal and political ones. Good practice should also have specific measurable outcomes linked to all of the above where Black young service users and Black service providers have been integral to the design and evaluation of the model in practice.

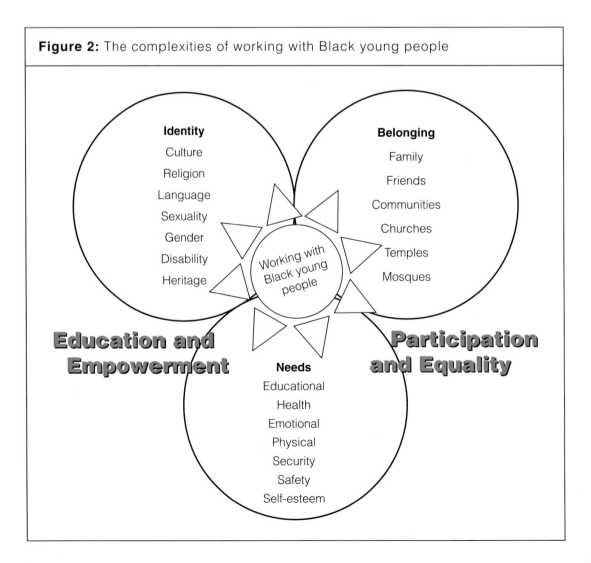

Figure 2: The complexities of working with Black young people

Identity
Culture
Religion
Language
Sexuality
Gender
Disability
Heritage

Belonging
Family
Friends
Communities
Churches
Temples
Mosques

Working with Black young people

Education and Empowerment

Participation and Equality

Needs
Educational
Health
Emotional
Physical
Security
Safety
Self-esteem

Figure 3: Holistic service design model targeting work with Black young people

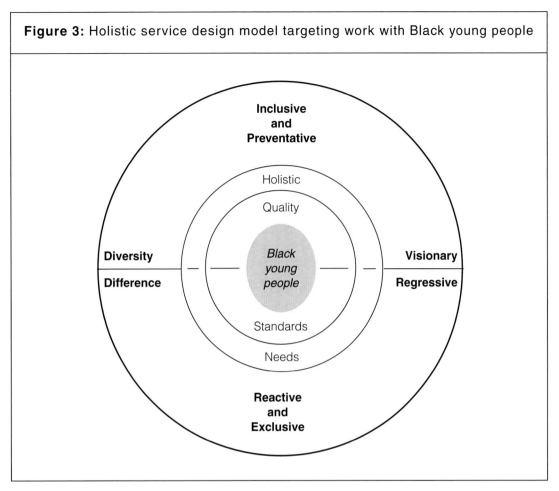

Key Questions

1. What processes exist to alter the impact of a dominant white organisational culture on the design of the service provided for Black young people?

2. How are questions of 'race' and 'representation' considered when examining the effectiveness of youth work intervention with Black young people?

3. What performance standards are used to examine the quality of services based on offering:
   - holistic understanding of needs
   - diversity of Black young people's experiences
   - visionary outcomes for Black young service users
   - preventative outcomes for Black young service users?

4. Consider how and when the debate in relation to labelling, stereotyping and highlighting racism merges with targeting services for Black young people.

5. How will the quality standards established for monitoring and evaluating the service provided for Black young people and communities be owned by them?

Conclusion

A principle underpinning this chapter is that all Black young people have the right to good quality, sustainable, visionary, and empowering services that maximise their potential. This should be a nationally recognised principle, so that regardless of where a Black young person lives they are offered a consistent standard of service. Young Black people deserve political integrity in the design of the services that are offered to them. Services should embrace the desire to capture the richness of the multiplicity of identities whilst dealing with the reality of racism in all its forms within British culture. There should be no regional, rural or urban deviations from this aim. The Black Youth Charter not only constructively reveals how the holistic impact of racism denies Black young peoples' rights and opportunities, but perhaps exposes the silences as to total potential damage of a generation of young people. Targeted work for Black young people has to be about preventing damage and maximising the potential of individuals where racism is made integral, exposed and something that must be overcome by all. Fanon's vivid phrase reminds us of straying from path:

> ...individuals without an anchor, without horizon, colourless, stateless, rootless: a race of angels.

(Fanon, 1963)

References

Abelove, H., Alina, B.M. (1993). *The Lesbian and Gay Studies Reader*. London: Routledge.

Aluffi-Penti, A., and Lorenz, W. (Eds.) (1996). *Anti-Racist Work with Young People: European Experiences and Approaches*. Lyme Regis: Russell House Publishing.

Anthias, F. (1992). The Problem of Ethnic and Race Categories and the Anti-racist Struggle. In *Social Policy Review*, 4: pp. 220–241.

Baumann, G. (1996). *Contesting Culture*. Cambridge University Press.

Black Youth Forum (1999). *Black Youth Charter*. NBYF.

Brah, A. (1996). *Cartographies of Diaspora: Contesting Identities*. London: Routledge.

Braham, P., Rattansi, and Skellington (Eds.) (1992). *Racism and Anti-Racism*. Sage.

CRE (1995). *Young and Equal: A Standard of Service working with Young People*. Commission for Racial Equality.

Dominelli, L. (1988). *Anti-Racist Social Work*. London: Macmillan.

Ellis, A. (1997). *Dealing with Differences: Taking Action on Class, Race, Gender and Disability*. Thousand Oaks, CA: Corwin Press.

Fanon, F. (1963). *The Wretched of the Earth*. London: Paladin.

Fanon, F. (1986). *Black Skins, White Masks*. London: Pluto Press.

Gilroy, P. (1992). *There ain't no Black in the Union Jack*. London: Routledge.

Hall, S. (1997). The Work of Representation. In Hall, S. (Ed.). *Representations and Signifying Practices*. London: Sage/The Open University.

Hooks, B. (1982). *Ain't I a Woman, Black Women and Feminism*. London: Pluto Press.

Hooks, B. (1984). *Feminist Theory: From Margin to Center*. Boston, MA: South End Press.

Hooks, B. (1994). *Outlaw Culture: Resisting Representations*. London: Routledge.

Macpherson, Sir W. (1999). *The Stephen Lawrence Inquiry: Report of the Enquiry*. London: HMSO.

Modood, T., Beishan, S., and Virdee, S. (1994). *Changing Ethnic Identities*. Policy Studies Institute.

NYA (1997). *Statement of Purpose*. National Youth Agency.

Roosevelt, R.T. Jr (1996). *Redefining Diversity*. Amacon.

Sivanandan, A. (1982). *A Different Hunger*. London: Pluto Press.

Thompson, N. (1996). *Anti-discriminatory Practice*. London: Macmillan.

Thompson, N. (2000). *Promoting Equality*. London: Macmillan

Webb, M., Kenny, S., and Cockburn, T. (1995). *Moss Side Initiative Youth Audit: Stage One*. Manchester Metropolitan University, 24.

Webb, M. (1995). Calling Me Racist? The Experience of Developing Black Perspectives in Youth and Community Work Course in Higher Education. In *Youth and Policy*, Issue 49.

Wilcox, B. (1990). Performance Indicators: The Search for the Holy Grail of Quality. In Fitz-Gibbon, C.T. (Ed.). *Performance Indicators*. Clevedon: Multilingual Matters.

Wylie, T. (1999). *Towards A Performance Measures and Indicators for Youth Work Services: A Discussion Paper*. Youth Policy, update issue; 5: pp. 1–2

Further Reading

Admas, Bell, and Griffin, T. (Eds.) (1997). *Teaching for Diversity and Social Justice*. Routledge.

Hooks, B. (1994). *Outlaw Culture: Resisting Representations*. Routledge.

Mirza, H.S. (1997). *Black British Feminism*. Routledge.

Sullivan, M. (1996). *Racism, Ethnicity and Social Policy*. Prentice Hall.

Williams, P.J. (1993). *The Alchemy of Race and Rights*. Virago.

Woodward, K. (1997). *Identity and Difference*. Sage.

Journals

Youth and Policy (1995). Black Perspectives Edition, Issue 49.

3

Working with Lesbian, Gay and Bisexual Young People

Lucy Ashby

Key Points

1. Coming out is usually a gradual and never-ending process.

2. The decision of whether to come out in any situation is entirely personal and can have negative and positive consequences.

3. All youth workers should be aware of the particular issues facing young gay people in school, in the family and at work.

4. Many young gay people are particularly vulnerable to mental health problems, which may be manifested in depression, low self-esteem, self-harm and drug or alcohol misuse.

5. When working with a young gay person the most important thing is to put them in touch with other young people who feel the same.

Introduction

Young gay people are potentially a highly vulnerable group within our communities. When they are still trying to come to terms with their sexuality many of them suffer from anxiety and depression and have no idea how to access support services. Their position is exacerbated by the fact that their parents or the rest of their family may not support them. It is also true that generally schools are failing to create environments where young lesbians and gay men are safe and free from verbal or physical abuse. There are many reasons for this unsatisfactory situation and there is also a positive way forward. If young gay people are to develop into healthy and productive adults who take part in our community along with everyone else then we must provide safe spaces in which they can explore their feelings, talk about issues which are important to them and build their self-esteem.

In Practice

There are four main areas where young gay people need support and where there is disturbing evidence that many of them are not receiving it.

1. The family

While many young people are accepted by their families when they come out, many are not. One

study found that 50 per cent of lesbian and gay youth were rejected by their families when they came out (Remafedi et al., 1991). As a result of such conflict, which may include violence, many young people are forced to leave home. There are some agencies which work with young gay homeless people specifically, either by settling them in housing co-operatives with other gay people or by placing them with older gay people in a kind of fostering arrangement.

Another difficulty for many young gay people is that even if they are able to be 'out' to their parents, the family may not feel able to equip them with the appropriate coping strategies for gay adult life. Even if they are welcoming they may know very little about gay lifestyles and may hold some unhelpful misconceptions.

2. The school

Schools often have a very homophobic subculture and young people who come out at school and even those who do not conform to straight sexual stereotypes suffer verbal and physical taunts. In 1999 a study by the gay rights group *Stonewall* found that of 1000 people 77 per cent had suffered homophobic bullying. The problem is exacerbated by the fact that although teachers are often aware that homophobic bullying is taking place they do not know how to deal with it. They are certainly not helped by current legislation (Section 28, Local Government Act 1989), which makes even the most supportive teachers think twice before being openly supportive of a young gay pupil. Young gay people tell us that they would have liked to be able to talk about sexuality in their sex education classes or during personal and social education.

The effect of social isolation and bullying can be profound. A 1993 study of 416 lesbians and gays aged 15–26 showed that 19 per cent had tried to take their own lives (Shaffer, 1993). Other common ways in which young people's pain is manifested is in incidents of self-harm or in the abuse of drugs or alcohol. Some young people find the atmosphere at school so unbearable that they drop out altogether although there are no specific inclusion programmes in the UK to ensure that young gay people are able to continue in education in a safe environment.

3. The work place

Once a young person leaves education and begins work they may feel that their sexuality makes them feel compromised. Since there is no current legislation to protect lesbians and gay men from discrimination in the work place and there are no plans to introduce protective legislation, some young people may choose not to come out at work at all.

This may be a very sensible decision in many cases but it can also be a very stressful way to be forced to behave at work. It is perhaps difficult for a heterosexual person to imagine the difficulties faced by a gay colleague as most people are so used to being able to talk openly about their partner, family or where they went at the weekend. This kind of conversation is commonplace in every workplace and a gay person who is afraid of being harassed or discriminated against may feel particularly isolated at these times.

Some organisations have comprehensive equal opportunities policies, which state that they will not discriminate on the basis of sexuality just as they have a commitment not to discriminate on the basis of race or gender. This kind of small print on application forms will be very important to gay people applying for jobs as they may feel that an organisation which shows an awareness of minority issues could be a safe place for them to work and be themselves.

4. Coming out

Before any young gay person can come out to family, friends or colleagues they must first come out to themselves. This may sound like a strange concept to anybody who is not gay but almost every gay person can remember the moment when they first made sense of their feelings and thought 'maybe I'm gay'. Perhaps they have been attracted to people of the same sex for many years before making the connection or maybe they have only recently begun to question their sexuality as a result of a crush on a friend or a pop star. This doesn't mean that everyone who questions their sexuality in this way is actually gay; some will explore same sex relationships (or the idea of them) and then decide that they are in fact straight.

Some people describe coming out to themselves as exciting while others find it terrifying. Most people have mixed feelings. Many people may not know anyone else who is gay. They may have heard their families or friends make homophobic comments or they may have made comments like these themselves. They may have seen unfavourable representations of gay people on the television or they may just be unable to relate to the very narrow, stereotypical images of lesbians and gay men in the media. One young man says, 'I knew I fancied men but I was into sports and I was one of the lads so I never thought I could be gay'. A young lesbian says, 'all the lesbians I've ever seen have short hair and tattoos. I have long hair and look feminine.' Two important points can be drawn from these comments. The first is that it is important to challenge stereotypes and to present a whole picture of lesbian and gay lifestyles. The second point is that many of us, even gay people, have some internalised homophobia and so view the characteristics of the 'typically' gay man or woman such as a very camp gay man or a very butch woman as negative. Also there are few opportunities for young people to see happy, successful gay adults living a normal everyday life in healthy relationships. Bearing this in mind it is not surprising that many young people deny their feelings for a long time before seeking support.

The interesting thing about coming out to others is that it is a never-ending process! It is also a very personal issue. Some gay people feel strongly that they need to be out to everyone that they meet whether they are a close friend or a casual acquaintance. Other gay people are very selective about who they choose to come out to. Just like straight people some gay people are very private and some are less so. For most people the first time they come out is a nerve-wracking experience. One young person says 'it was awful, I just couldn't get the words out and then once I had it felt like hours before I knew whether my friend was going to reject me or not'.

It is useful in a youth group setting to explore people's experiences of coming out on a regular basis. This is not only helpful for people who are new to the group, but also for regular visitors who may have needed to come out again because they have started a new job or school or have met some friends. It is useful to discuss the positive as well as the negative effects of coming out. Young people at a youth group were asked to think about the way that coming out had made them feel. Amongst the positive responses were comments that people felt more relaxed and calmer and that they were relieved not to have to hide their true feelings anymore. They also said that they felt proud of themselves for doing something that took a lot of courage and that they felt excited to become a part of the gay community. Negative effects included sadness at being rejected by some friends, having to put up with some name calling and feeling worried that the news would be treated like gossip to be spread around the school or community. Exploring both the negative and positive effects helped us to consider some ideas for handling either outcome.

When supporting a young person who is trying to decide whether to come out it is helpful to remain positive but it is unhelpful and untruthful to tell them that coming out is always the right thing to do. It is an unfortunate fact of life that while some people are accepting of their gay friends and family others are not. Some parents say, 'if any son or daughter of mine was gay I'd throw them out'. Luckily in many cases when actually faced with this scenario lots of parents find that they feel differently and want to support their child. In other cases parents can react negatively or even violently and the young person may indeed find himself or herself thrown out of their home. It is important to explore these possible outcomes with the young person to ensure that they know where they can go for help if the reaction is hostile. Some young people may decide

to delay coming out until they have left home and some may choose not to come out to their families at all. Other young people can help by sharing experiences and offering support afterwards but only the individual can decide whether he or she is ready to take that risk.

Below are some ideas for ways in which youth workers can approach and explore the issue of coming out with young people:

Role-play. One young person plays himself or herself practising coming out to another young person who could play the part of a parent, friend or colleague. The youth workers could add to this activity by giving each young person a description of their character and the way in which their character may react. This can help to prepare a young person for a variety of outcomes and also help them to work through experiences of coming out, which may have been unpleasant.

Comic strip. Young people try to fill in the words on a comic strip showing a young man or woman trying to come out to their family or friends.

Writing a 'guide to coming out'. The young people offer their own ideas and experiences to make a leaflet to give to new young people joining the group. This type of activity is great for building self-esteem and confidence and also makes the group feel as though they are supporting others just as they were supported when they first came to the group.

Make posters describing the positive things about being lesbian and gay. Display the posters at the project.

Gay Youth Groups

It is necessary to examine the issues, which affect young gay people when deciding what needs to be provided for them in the context of a youth service. Certainly these young people need a safe space where they can meet other young gay people. This is particularly important for young people as very much of the 'gay scene' takes place in pubs and clubs which young people may be too young to get in to. Even if the young person is old enough to go into a gay pub it may be a daunting experience for them as a first experience of gay life. It is not always easy in any pub or club to find people to talk to on a purely friendly basis and it is often difficult to make yourself heard above the music! In a youth group setting a young person should have the opportunity to talk quietly on a one to one basis with a trained youth worker who will be familiar with some of the issues they are facing and will be able to guarantee confidentiality. They will also be able to make some friends and to be a part of group discussions.

Gay Youth Workers?

Should those working with young gay people necessarily be gay themselves? Clearly another gay person is likely to have many experiences in common with the young people in the group. They may also serve as a rare and welcome role model for young people concerned about their future in a homophobic society. Some young people who were consulted about the appointment of a new female project worker for their group were emphatic that she should be a lesbian.

Besides the reasons already mentioned they felt that the group would not feel 'safe' if it were to be run by straight people and that this would mean that they were no longer coming to a place where gay people were very much in the majority. The latter point is helpful in showing us just what a gay youth group can achieve that a general youth group cannot. Gay people in general spend most of their lives feeling compromised in one or another situation and are often unable to 'be themselves' in at least one if not most areas of their lives. The youth group can provide that safe space where young people can freely express their thoughts and explore their ideas with other like-minded young people without fear. Since they know that they will be in the majority at the group they can make light-hearted conversation about their sexuality without feeling that they are making a momentous statement and that they will be the 'token gay person' in any setting.

The Venue

The venue where the youth group is held should be given careful consideration. Ideally the venue needs to be in a place whose entrance is both discreet, easy to find and wheelchair accessible. Many first time visitors may feel extremely self conscious about entering a 'gay building' and so although it is important that the interior of the building displays positive gay images the outside needs to be neutral enough to attract potential service users and detract any negative attention of bigoted passers by.

Unfortunately many gay people have experienced verbal or physical abuse when entering or leaving gay pubs or clubs and some people have been known to frequent these areas specifically to attack gay people. In larger cities where there are many gay-run businesses situated together (such as the gay villages of Manchester or London) this can provide some protection. In smaller places though, and particularly in rural areas, it may be wise to hold the youth group within an existing youth centre on a certain night or perhaps to have a room booked specifically for the group. If a young person is especially worried about coming to the group for the first time they could be met by a youth worker in another central location before the group begins.

The venue needs to be secure with a lockable door so that each person may be let in as they arrive. This precaution may seem a little over cautious but it is important that the group and the youth workers feel safe and have some method of excluding people who may attempt to enter the group purely to cause trouble. The environment inside the venue needs to be comfortable and welcoming and should have posters and photos, which present a positive image of gay lifestyle. The images need to take into account other minority groups by depicting black and Asian gay people as well as those with disabilities. If the venue is shared with another group this may cause a problem and care may need to be taken to prepare the room each time so those gay visitors feel welcome. The structure of the sessions may take a variety of forms but it is essential that there is some place where visitors can talk privately on a one to one basis with a youth worker. This can occasionally cause problems where a youth group is understaffed. Ideally there should be two or three youth workers present so that there is always someone to greet new visitors and stay in the main group room.

Confidentiality and other Ground Rules

When young people are talking amongst themselves or one to one with a youth worker it is important that they all understand the confidentiality policy of the group. This is particularly important in a gay group as many people who visit may be hiding their sexuality and attendance at the group from family, friends or colleagues. Many youth workers tell visitors that they will not acknowledge them outside the group unless they are approached first. This prevents the young person from having to explain to an inquisitive friend or relative that they know this person from attending a gay youth group. It is sensible to encourage similar sensitivity amongst group members. They may of course make many friends within the group and have no problem acknowledging them outside, but they need to be aware that for others the situation is not so simple. Sometimes young people may express very personal thoughts and feelings as part of a discussion or of their own volition. They need to know that when they do so their contributions will be treated sensitively by the youth workers and the rest of the group and it is worth reminding people of this before an activity begins. It is also useful to display the ground rules of the group around the room and to review them regularly as part of an activity. This not only helps members get to know the rules, but they feel that they have had a part in forming them, so are more likely to understand and respect them and encourage others to do the same.

First Time Visitors

Once the young person has gathered the courage to contact the group and come along it is essential that their experience is a positive one if they are to return. Many people think about coming out for many years before they act on their feelings and a youth group may be their first port of call. Project workers need to be fully aware of the significance of this first contact. In order to make the first visit less overwhelming it is a good idea to offer half an hour at the beginning of each session purely as a space for new visitors. This will give them time to come into the room before the rest of the group arrive, chat to a youth worker about their situation and find out more about the group and the particular programme for the evening. Other group members need to be made aware of this rule and encouraged to respect it. Many gay groups have telephone lines as well as or instead of drop in spaces. These can prove invaluable for a person who would like to find out more about the group before they come or who may need to call and talk to someone privately several times before they decide whether the group is right for them. Sometimes advertising the address of a gay group can attract the wrong kind of attention so giving a telephone number to call first helps to put off all but those who are genuinely seeking support.

The Structure of the Sessions

Some youth groups run in a very informal way providing a safe, comfortable space for young people to meet, have a coffee and chat with friends, and others are more curriculum based. If you are lucky enough to have either several sessions a week or several rooms at your disposal it is possible to offer a combination of the two. However, if the session is structured, it is important for visitors to have some informal time to catch up with friends, share experiences and meet any new visitors, after all this is one of the main reasons that young people give for attending gay youth groups. Once the group is settled it may be appropriate to introduce an activity or discussion. New visitors may not feel comfortable joining in with a large group discussion or activity and should not be forced to do so. They may prefer to sit and listen or they may wish to leave and come back at another time. Alternatively if there are several new visitors at one session they may wish to have a separate discussion with a youth worker in a different space. There are many interesting issues, which may be addressed in the form of games, discussions, role-plays or even visits to other venues. The following are examples of some that have been successful:

- Coming out: the pros and cons.
- Do gay people make good parents?
- Do people choose to be gay?
- What do gay men and lesbians have in common?
- Should straight people go into gay pubs?
- Do gay people have the same approach to relationships as straight people?
- Is the gay scene welcoming to everyone?

● Do gay activists help or harm our cause?

These suggested titles could be approached as a simple discussion or they could be made more interesting by splitting the young people into smaller groups and asking each group to formulate arguments from differing points of view. Alternatively each group member could be given a character description and asked to debate as if they were that person. After the discussion it is interesting to talk about the motivation of the different characters. In a group discussion about gay rights one young person played the character of an older man in his 70s from a traditional background who thinks that all gay people should be imprisoned. Even though the character was extremely homophobic the young people were able to give some thoughtful answers including the fact that the man probably hadn't met any openly gay people and that for most of his lifetime it was illegal for men to have gay sexual relationships. The kind of insight gained from this activity can help to make young gay people feel less hurt or threatened by homophobic behaviour.

Safer Sex Workshops

Most young gay people receive no guidance about safer sex from sex education classes at school and so it is important to find opportunities to explore it within the youth group. Some youth groups cater for young people from early teens to early twenties and it can be a challenge to approach the topic of safer sex in a way that is helpful to those of all levels of knowledge and experience. We must also be sensitive to the fact that some people are victims of sexual abuse and may find it extremely difficult to discuss sex in a large group or even at all. The whole group needs to be made aware of the topic for the evening and given some idea of the way in which it will be approached so that they have an opportunity to opt out. It is often helpful to approach the topic in an imaginative way and some humour can help to lessen feelings of awkwardness and embarrassment. One fun idea is to make a 'pass the parcel' containing condoms, lubricant, dental dams and femidoms and as the lucky group member unwraps the parcel and reveals the contents begin a discussion on how it is used and how it can help us to practice safer sex. You may also include other items such as an empty beer can or a party popper to represent alcohol and

drugs and to promote a discussion on the way that these can affect our decisions about safer sex. This type of activity works particularly well in a group where the members know one another and are prepared to make their own contributions. The youth workers must ensure that the main areas are covered and should also be aware of any group members who seem uncomfortable or upset by the discussion.

Building Links with the Community

One worthwhile use of a session is for the group to host members of other groups or from organisations within the community. The young people may give suggestions for topics that they would like to learn more about such as aromatherapy, astrology, making music or film making and experts in these fields may be invited to the group to share their knowledge. Alternatively it may be more sensible for the group to try out activities such as watersports or pottery in different locations. Many local authorities have facilities like this available to youth groups.

Visits may take a slightly different form if the group try to build links with other organisations such as the police or the local health authority. A police officer could visit the group and listen to the young people as they share their experiences of being gay in the community. Equally the officer could ensure that the young people are well informed about their rights and responsibilities and can take the opportunity to share what they are doing to make life easier and safer for gay people and other minority groups. In the same way a visit from the local health authority can bring about a very valuable two-way discussion about the needs of young gay people and how they are or are not being met. It can give young people a real boost to feel that through sharing their opinions they really can help to form policy that will directly affect them. This kind of acknowledgement from statutory agencies gives much needed validation to young people who will hopefully see that their views are respected and sometimes acted upon.

Any visitor to the group should of course be made aware of the group's policy on confidentiality and group members should be warned if a visitor is expected or if a trip is planned so that they may take steps to protect their own privacy.

Some Issues to Think About

How can we work with young gay people in a mixed setting?

Many of the ideas mentioned here could of course be used within the context of any youth group to raise awareness of gay issues. Some youth workers may feel that young people's needs are better served in an inclusive youth group with strong equal opportunities policies and equally some gay people may prefer to attend such a group. Youth workers who work with any particular client group will want to be well informed in this area and will hopefully seek to make their own group welcoming to young people from all backgrounds. For example, there is no reason to assume that every young person who attends a youth group for people with hearing problems is straight.

How can we indicate to a young person that we are not homophobic?

Even in a mixed group it is possible to communicate implicitly and explicitly an atmosphere of tolerance and a celebration of diversity. We can do this by decorating our space with posters depicting young people from all walks of life. We can also help by using non gender specific language such as asking a young person 'do you have a partner?' rather than 'girlfriend' or 'boyfriend'. It is also important to tackle homophobic comments with the same vigour as we would racist comments not only to indicate that they are unacceptable but also to use the opportunity to raise discussion of issues around sexuality. Organising an activity where young people discuss characters from soap operas or from pop groups can provide opportunities to talk about gay characters or celebrities. It is interesting to ask the young people themselves whether they think their group is welcoming to people from all kinds of backgrounds including gay people or people with disabilities.

Young people at a gay youth group unanimously said that they would not attend a mixed youth group because they did not trust that it would be accepting and because they would not feel safe enough to come out. They had mostly experienced a more traditional kind of youth group, which is not particularly closely supervised and more based around sports or a weekly disco. In these settings perhaps there is little opportunity for young people to get together in order to share thoughts and feelings. However when the young people were offered the opportunity to participate in a watersports programme at a council run facility they enthusiastically agreed once they had been told that the instructors had specifically invited them and knew they were gay. They were also insistent that their gay youth worker should accompany them.

Is it possible to work alongside parents and carers while still protecting the privacy of young gay people?

This is a very complex issue and one, which arises frequently for youth workers in this field. Occasionally we may be approached by a parent or carer who is concerned about their child who they think may be, or who they know is gay. In this situation it is easy to feel that we are working alongside parents and carers in providing support for their child. Frequently the young person does not feel ready to come out to parents or carers and so attends a gay youth group without telling them. Obviously many young straight people also visit groups or places without telling their parents but it is easy to see how some parents would be less than pleased that a gay youth group exists let alone that their child is a member of one. It is necessary to think of honest yet discreet ways of describing the group if we need to make contact with parents or carers. If planning a trip to a Gay Pride event and needing consent forms to be signed ensure that this is done in a sensitive manner. By describing the group and the destination in general rather than specific terms, you will be offering the young person additional sensitivity.

If young people feel that their parents may have some difficulty in coping with their sexuality then it may be appropriate to offer to talk to the parent or carer. Some youth workers may be prepared to help a young person to come out their parents by facilitating the conversation themselves. In this case full consideration should be given to the time and place for the conversation, and safety procedures should be agreed upon in advance in case the reaction is unpleasant. Another positive way to work alongside parents is to offer an

---

Key Questions

1. When working in a mixed environment, is it welcoming in appearance and atmosphere to young gay people?

2. Are equal opportunities, including gay issues, being actively promoted within the general youth group curriculum?

3. If helping a young person to come out have they been encouraged to explore a variety of consequences and been given strategies to cope with each?

4. How can youth workers work alongside parents, teachers, and employers to support young gay people?

5. Are enough opportunities provided for young gay people to get together in a safe, supportive, alcohol free environment?

---

evening where they may come along to meet others in their situation. It may be reassuring for them to hear about the experiences of others.

What coping strategies do young gay people use to cope with life in a homophobic society?

When we consider the pressures placed on gay people of all ages in our society it is inevitable that many will sometimes find it difficult to cope. These anxieties can be assuaged with support from the family and the peer group and perhaps a youth group, but since many young people do not have these advantages, some may seek other forms of comfort. It is very common to find that young gay people have suffered from mental health problems such as depression and some may self injure or attempt suicide. Other issues very likely to affect young lesbians and gay men are misuse of alcohol and drugs. They may learn that using drugs or alcohol can appear to lessen their feelings of not belonging or it may be that they end up spending a lot of time in pubs and clubs because that is the only place for them to meet a partner or indeed platonic gay friends. Youth groups can help by providing an alternative, safe meeting place for young people. Youth workers can also help by taking members who are old enough to be out on the gay scene. Most people gay or straight feel slightly uncomfortable about going into a pub on their own, but with a group of friends we usually feel more confident.

Conclusion

Whether you are seeking to set up a gay youth group or improve your practise as a youth worker in general, it is helpful to know that the young gay people I have worked with all agreed that the worst part of being young and gay was the sense of isolation and what they wanted most was an opportunity to meet other young gay people. Gay youth groups can be enormously successful in building confidence and in providing young people with perhaps the only opportunities they may have to meet other gay people and build a circle of friends who may support them for years to come.

Further Reading

DeCrescenzo, T. (1994). *Helping Gay and Lesbian Youth.* New York: Harington Park Press.

Epstein, D. (1994). *Challenging Lesbian and Gay Inequalities in Education.* Buckingham: Open University Press.

Remafedi, G., Farrow, J.A., and Deisher, R.W. (1991). Risk Factors in Attempted Suicide by Gay and Bisexual Youth. In *Paediatrics*, 87(6): pp. 869–875.

Shaffer, D. (1993). Suicide Risks and the Public Health. In *American Journal of Public Health*, 83(2): pp. 171–172.

4 Work With Boys and Young Men

Baljeet Singh Gill

Key Points

1. You do not need to be an expert or have masses of resources before you can begin thinking about developing effective work with young men.

2. Effective work can be done in any and every youth work setting, but be aware of the limitations imposed by some. Even in detached work settings, being on the young men's 'turf' does not mean that you cannot challenge them and embrace youth work principles.

3. A quick comment to show that you don't necessarily agree with their sexist, racist or homophobic attitudes may not make you their best mate, but it won't make you their enemy either.

4. If you really do practice youth work principles then you should be questioning and challenging yourself first with a view to educating and raising awareness, as opposed to being bound by tradition, or specific and rigid moral standards.

5. When developing work with young men do not suddenly abandon the principles and models of effective youth and community work, namely, participation, anti-discriminatory work, educational values and so on.

Introduction

Anyone walking into the majority of youth centres up and down the country today will still be faced with a scene which, in essence, has changed little since the 1960s, despite the dramatic changes that have occurred in the words and theory behind the present day Youth and Community Services. Most of the provision that is offered in youth centres today is still aimed at young men and tends to be dominated by physical activities.

Young men displaying their machismo in smoke-filled rooms, filled to the brim on a disco night but almost empty on other nights: this is how a typical youth centre is often caricatured. Bustling with activities, in many people's minds, youth centres represent places where young white men or often, young Black men, colonise such spaces by their physical as well as their verbal being, hitting each other, using abusive language and gesticulating. This way of male bonding may be good for some but it is a very exclusive ritual. The discos may have faded in many youth and community services but through physical activities such as pool, football and table tennis, machismo still rules, ok!

Despite the wide array of equal opportunities policy initiatives and the anti-sexist and anti-racist training that workers have had, very little seems to have changed. The question that still remains is, why is it still taking so long for men to explore their experiences of masculinity? (Seidler, 1994). Very little, if any, work has been done with young men by the youth and community services in the way which reflects the core principles that the service stands for. If workers challenge any of the attitudes or behaviours exhibited, then it's usually in the same macho style that is being used by the young men themselves. The work at the moment has more to do with the enforcement of power and control than creating an understanding of masculinity and anti-sexism.

The picture is not totally gloomy though and in recent years there have been many new and innovative initiatives in the youth and community service on issues such as disability, Black young people, arts and theatre, detached work, sexism, young women, homelessness, substance use and so on. The challenge facing developmental work with young men is to reflect such innovation and creativity and build a bridge with the learning that has emerged from working on these other issues.

In the current context then, work with boys and young men will refer to the type of youth work that encompasses exploring substantial issues about masculinity and anti-sexist work as opposed to purely activity orientated youth centres for young men. Also, at this stage, let me state quite categorically that to carry out such work, no additional resources are required. What is essential is to analyse how current provision is offered, what it consists of, what its impact on the lives of young men is and how existing practices need to change:

> *...I have recognised that without insisting on monitoring and assessment and subsequent action I merely colluded with white men in power...*
>
> (Gill, 1994)

Historical Development

In the 18th and 19th centuries there were wars, revolutions and famines that affected America, Britain, Ireland, France, Germany, Norway, Sweden, Denmark, Belgium, Holland and even Switzerland. State intervention in formal education in this country grew out of a two pronged concern for the education and welfare of the illiterate masses as well as a genuine fear of those masses overthrowing the establishment. For those in power, the congregation of large groups of working class young men in the emerging urban areas created feelings ranging from fear to concern, particularly as levels of awareness of class oppression increased and became more organised. Many people found this unacceptable with crime and homelessness on the increase and young men fighting on the streets, blatantly defying authority and questioning the status quo (*The Times*, 1860s and 1870s). Lord Shaftesbury, the 19th century philanthropist, stated that:

> *The middle classes know that the safety of their lives and property depends on having around them a peaceful, happy and moral population.*

Similarly, W.E. Forster, Vice President of the Committee of the Privy Council on education, also recognised this and recommended to the Privy Council that by providing compulsory state education the constitution, the state and the economy would benefit tremendously (Forster, 1868). Almost a century earlier, in 1798, Rev R.T.

Malthus in his infamous *Essay on Population* had expressed the fear of revolution due to the growth of the working class population and the potential inability of the ruling classes to control this trend (Malthus, 1798)

Just as educational reforms were rooted in a concern about the potential threats posed by the masses, so too do the origins of the Youth and Community Service lie in misgivings about the working classes. Concerns were particularly expressed about young men (and women although for different reasons) migrating to the emerging industrial heartlands of Britain and having spare time on their hands.

Manchester, founder of the Ardwick Lads Club, and William Smith, founder of the Boys Brigade, both felt and wrote about the need to gentle the masses by promoting habits of obedience, reverence, discipline, self respect and all that tends towards true Christian manliness and were quite open about wanting to improve working class men and women:

> *...Abhorrence of brutal sports, cheap entertainments, drinking and gambling, all of which were seen to be 'ungodly' and seeing leisure time as...that dangerous time for working boys...*
>
> (Smith, 1988)

These quotations of Greenwood (1869) by Smith, clearly sums up the moral attitudes prevalent at that time.

Thus, the roots of the youth and community services and indeed work with young men, are double-edged. There were the pioneering, philanthropic and voluntary initiatives of individuals who were concerned about the welfare of young men on the one side; and on the other, the activities of those who sought to bring them under some sort of control. This dichotomy exists to this day where workers are torn between providing social education to all young men and responding to pressure from politicians, managers and communities to police them.

Arguably also, the Christian zeal which informed much of the earlier work and the urgency to impose middle class values on working class communities, still persists today, albeit under a different guise. If one considers the fact that the majority of the young men who use statutory youth and community services are 'working class' but that the service continues to be based on middle class values and predominantly managed by middle class people, it does raise a fundamental question about the underlying agenda of such work.

Anti-Discriminatory Practices and Work with Young Men

The youth and community service is seen by some as the vanguard of progressive thinking and practice. The depth, range and variety of its policy statements, its intentions and its style of delivery would lead you to believe that this is true. There is however just one snag, and that happens to be that there are parameters beyond which you venture at your own peril.

You have only to put up posters that heterosexist men find offensive before censorship within the youth and community service becomes blatant, and has become worse now that 'they' are able to hide behind 'Section 28'. This legislation should make no difference to the way in which educators should be interacting, they should not be there to indoctrinate but to question, challenge, confront and provoke.

In reality, Section 28 has imposed very few restrictions for professional youth work practice. However, heterosexist men have used the legislation to implement their own homophobic attitudes in practice. What does all this have to do with working with young men? Work with young men is not done in isolation and has to be seen as part of an overall picture. The traditional ways of working with young people, especially men, are usually said to be a thing of the past. It is said that current trends are being absorbed and practice is moving with the times. Hence, alternative ways of working with young men are acknowledged as good practice, but anyone waiting for a miraculous change shouldn't hold their breath.

How can young people be educated effectively when so many workers choose to ignore how the state uses it's considerable resources to perpetuate prejudicial attitudes and discriminatory behaviours? 'Section 28' was a prime example of this and raises a fundamental question about the role of key organisations such as the youth and community services in the perpetuation or challenging of such policy initiatives (Gill, 1989).

If we choose not to intervene, then the situation for young men especially young gay men is likely to remain unchanged. However, it is possible to make a difference if the choice is made to engage, and evidence shows that through effective intervention, it is possible to reduce levels of homophobic anger (Sears and Williams, 1997).

Racism also features quite extensively in current statutory youth and community service as mainly white middle class workers try to impose their values on Black young men and their communities. Despite the riots, lynchings, rapes, mutilations and murders of Black people that had occurred on these 'fair shores' since the time of Queen Elizabeth I (Fryer, 1984), no official acknowledgement of the existence of racism has been made. Even after the rebellions by the Black communities (mainly young men) in the early 1980s, the *Scarman Report* only accepted individual culpability. It was not until 1999 that the *Macpherson Report* told the nation what other writers had previously suggested (Chauhan, 1989); namely that racism was enshrined in the institutions of Britain. This included the youth and community service which was exemplified by a total lack of Black perspectives in its service delivery and the perpetuation of services operating on outdated and contested notions of assimilation and multiculturalism.

The question of whether the youth service is an informal agent of social control or an educative service is raised again with *Bridging the Gap* and *ConneXions* (1999) the latest documents designed to respond to those who have 'fallen by the wayside' and are not deemed to be doing anything useful because they are not in education, training or employment. Whether this is truly a response to those who have very little, or is yet another means to control a group of young people by targeting them specifically, remains to be seen.

Overall though, white male managers in the youth and community services (for it is they who still tend to dominate most services in this country) need to examine their managerial practices and question the degree to which these reflect the ethos of the service. This is especially so when the challenge comes to tackle inequality and develop anti-oppressive practices. Having worked with young men for over twenty years in youth work as well as in Intermediate Treatment, I have observed that, whilst innovation and professional initiative is welcomed when working with clients, the same creativity is not encouraged and is seen to be threatening when working around issues of oppression.

Principles of Practice

In order for effective alternative forms of work with young men, men working in the service have to give up a lot of the power and control that they have. They need to change and internalise the notion that oppression is unjust and has to be challenged (Gill, 1985). Until then, real change will remain an illusion and the young men receiving the service will recognise the hypocrisy in the words and actions of those who deliver it.

The youth and community service, its employees and volunteers currently work to the core principles of education, participation, equality and empowerment nationally agreed at the second Ministerial Conference of 1990. Consequently, why are youth workers not open about their educational brief, but still lure young people in with pool, football, etc.? Why do young men not have complete control over their own provision and why are workers not answerable to them instead of to people even older? How can workers possibly empower young people when they retain so much control over them? And why do white men, especially at the decision-making levels, still mainly dominate the service?

Many workers are happier instructing young men from a position of power because they seem unable to accept them as equals and as people who ought to be treated with respect. This is particularly true in outdoor education and expedition work where workers and organisations often exercise their power and control through assumed superior knowledge of rules and regulations. This is then justified and legitimised on the grounds of safety as if young people have no sense of responsibility, care or ability to learn.

Only recently I worked for a national organisation which was still treating young men as inept imbeciles who had to be told rather than be asked. The same organisation made many of these young people suffer by making them wash up in cold water when the temperature was below zero even though hot water was available. It bordered more on sado-masochistic tendencies than on social education!

Workers also seem to act in a patronising manner with young people and direct their anger

and energy into leisure activities. One could draw parallels from the great genius Steve Biko who criticised liberals in apartheid South Africa of being more dangerous to the Black cause than the Afrikaners, because the liberals channelled the energy, direction and strategies of the Black people into what was acceptable to them to liberals:

> *The liberals must realise that they themselves are oppressed if they are true liberals and therefore they must fight for their own freedom and not that of the nebulous 'they' with whom they can hardly claim identification.*
>
> (Biko, 1978)

Unfortunately this depoliticisation is exactly what many youth workers do with young people. They must be consistent in their opposition to all forms of oppression and encourage freedom, whether it is in their professional work with young people or with adults, or if in their personal lives. Unless that genuine sincerity is there then workers will be seen to be false, and worse still, the message will be seen to be hollow.

Applying Principles to Practice

Most people today know that men have been socialised into seeing women as sex objects, and women and children as property to be controlled by men; consequently this knowledge and experience can be used to challenge the covert as well as the overt sexism that exists (Stoltenberg, 1989).

It is in this context that the kinds of attitudes and behaviours which can eventually lead to the oppression, abuse and rape of women and children, and to the ostracisation of men from their own inner feelings, can be challenged.

Although issue based work with young men can and should take place in all contexts, the ideal settings are residentials and projects where there are no distractions. Such residentials enable a more effective curriculum to be delivered, the focus of which should be the exploration of relationships. Some of the reasons for the success of these courses are due to:

1. Young men knowing exactly what they are doing, how they are going to do it, when they are doing it and, most importantly, why.

2. Young men and the workers making agreements and contracts with each other to which they are all bound.

3. Both parties knowing the ground rules which have been formulated through active and equal participation. This includes issues from, the time people go to bed (or not), to changing part of the course if it seems irrelevant or boring.

4. The workers adopting a consistency of approach, attitudes and behaviours where all forms of oppressive attitudes and statements are challenged and discussed from the beginning, including assumptions such as everyone is heterosexual, including the workers.

5. Being aware that unlike working with young women, if the size of a male group exceeds five or six, individuals will 'hide' and not participate. This occurs when focusing on those that are participating; others may try to distract the issue to other areas with which they are far more comfortable, especially if the topic of discussion is homosexuality, or men having positive feelings for other men.

This basic framework creates the sort of atmosphere and environment where we can look at all aspects of relationships, beginning with exploring young men's self-esteem and self confidence through to exploring different aspects of relationships (Gill, 1991).

A typical curriculum programme for such work with young men could look as follows:

1. Introducing yourself and the things you like.

2. What you like about yourself, exploring self-esteem and confidence.

3. Your relationships with other important, or relevant, or irrelevant people (mums, dads, friends, teachers, relations, pets and so on).

4. Looking at sexual relationships, especially at the myths surrounding homosexuality and heterosexuality (Greenberg, 1988).

5. Looking at gender and masculinity e.g.:
   - What are men supposed to be like?
   - What are men really like?
   - How would men like to be?
   - Being consistently positive!

Such a structure enables young men to carry out more creative and open explorations about themselves and others around them. It will help them examine what it means to be male and whether the expectations that all males should display particular qualities applies to them and those around them. The qualities might be being:

- self-sufficient
- independent
- strong
- aggressive
- brave
- emotionally insensitive
- competitive
- angry
- cruel
- mean
- suspicious
- jealous
- possessive
- ruthless
- confrontational
- athletic
- dominating
- intimidating
- exploiting
- to always be right
- (perhaps most importantly) to be heterosexual!

It will also enable young men to examine how they do not always fit into such categories and look at those who display other qualities, who want or need to rely on others, are seen to be weak, submissive, recognise their own emotional needs and want to respond to the needs of others. Or those who are gentle, kind, generous, peaceful, trusting, happy, wrong; or those who wish to treat others as equals and those who are gay? (Lancashire County Council, 1993)

Fundamentally, through such an educative process, young men will be enabled to look at the reality of how masculinity is defined: how many of us know men who fall into either of the above categories, as if emotions and behaviours could be categorised into such separate compartments? Because of the pressure on young men to be something other than who they truly are and live up to an idealised image, they need to understand the consequences on their own lives. It is possible that their own relationships will suffer as well as their self-confidence and self-esteem.

By approaching work with young men in this way, you are not imposing a barrier on your relationship with them. If workers challenge young men aggressively or inappropriately, what tends to happen is that it's much more difficult to build relationships with them because you are seen to be 'jumping down their throats', even if you are gently questioning. Once you begin to question, the process does not stop because there is just so much more to question:

- their whole life-styles, what makes you say that?

- why do you think that?

- would you let your partner do the things that you do or say, and still feel good about them?

- do you share the domestic jobs? how do you feel about it?

Many workers try to steer a group away from the storming stage, perhaps due to their own insecurities about conflict, yet this is the stage where a properly handled group of young men can really develop. Similarly, dealing with conflict in a positive manner can be very meaningful in enabling young men to understand and develop relationships. Young men will often then end up sharing views, thoughts and expressions which they may never have done with anyone else before.

For instance, on one such course when discussing maleness and homosexuality, all the young men admitted that they had all cried but never told anyone before. They also recognised that love and sex wasn't necessarily the same thing, and just because you acknowledged that you loved another man didn't automatically mean that you were gay. One young man 'the cock of the school' shared how he had sometimes wondered who he would have a relationship with if he were gay.

As this example illustrates, another positive aspect of doing, working and adopting an anti-sexist approach is that a great deal of trust is created in a relatively short space of time. Young men will tell you about the sexist manner and behaviour of other male youth workers, which is all very well until you take it up with the line manager and the system begins to obstruct the process of either educating or disciplining the worker.

In exploring such views, behaviours and emotions the whole curriculum is geared around positive feedback where people are encouraged to share and be open—workers as well as young people. There is constant challenging and exploring of issues but in a non-judgmental and supportive way. It also offers an important opportunity to explore issues of multiple masculinities and inclusive anti-oppressive practices so that, for example, Black and gay perspectives are explicitly built into the learning process (Connell, 1996).

Doing effective anti-sexist work or work around maleness and masculinity is more manageable on a course because better conditions for such work can be created. When I have tried to do similar work on a sessional basis in a youth centre it has been much more difficult particularly because of the lack of ideal conditions. For effective youth and community work to take place, practitioners need to be aware of the limitations of the setting, the purpose of the work and participants' expectations (Vinter, 1979).

In most centres there are too many distractions: the disco, table tennis, video, TV, football, pool and so on. Almost everything is activity based and often, the youth and community service is very 'hush hush' about its social education approach, even to politicians and young people. Although we say that activities are merely a means to an end, it certainly isn't the case for the majority who see activities as an end in themselves.

Competitions may create teamwork but there's an awful lot of competition to get into a team and to then beat your opponents! Thus sports and other activities almost become self-perpetuating. Workers need to constantly challenge the notion of competitiveness or create a climate where non-competitive and co-operative games are cherished and valued. Otherwise, questions will emerge about reinforcing male values and existing masculine traits under the guise of working with young men, or about activities as a means to an end. We could learn from other communities such as the Inuits (Canadian Eskimos) who thrive at, enjoy and celebrate a strong tradition of sports but in a way that is co-operative, develops team work and tests the skills of individual participants in a non competitive environment. Team development training in the youth and community services already builds on such principles within staff, why can these not also be applied to work with young men?

Conclusion

Effective work with young men involves them taking personal risks and workers taking professional ones such as the potential of being ostracised by our peers or not getting promotion. If men took a few more risks in the pursuit of such work, then at least we would be trying to put into

Key Questions

1. Do you want to intellectualise or work on issues around masculinity in a more wholesome and substantial manner?
2. Are you prepared to take the time to find out about the young men who you want to work with—their backgrounds, the communities from which they come, their expectations and so on?
3. How confident do you feel about challenging oppressive behaviour and views?
4. In order to do this work effectively and to achieve something, there needs to be a complete openness and honesty, at least within yourself, around the issue of sexism and sexuality; are you ready and prepared for this?
5. How can I question and challenge myself?

practice a philosophy of anti-oppressive values and beliefs. In turn, this should enhance you as a person and the quality of the relationships that you have with other people including young men.

Workers may be afraid to challenge oppressive behaviour for fear of offending or because they want to collude with the sexism and other men. Or, they may use the perceived religious and cultural traditions of a community as an excuse for not challenging oppressive behaviour. Men, as we know, will use anything they can to justify their oppressive attitudes and behaviours whether they are workers or the young men with whom we work (Gill, 1991b).

Developing effective work with young men offers a fresh look at something, a different approach and a different experience of belief systems. When young men question themselves and through this, question you as the worker, by having to explain and justify your position and beliefs, as a learner yourself it will provide an incredible opportunity for further self-examination and change.

Only the great Malcolm X could have phrased it so appropriately:

Liberate our minds by any means necessary.

(Malcolm X, 1970)

Further Reading and References

Biko, S. (1978). *I Write What I Like.* Penguin.

Chauhan, V. (1989). *Beyond Steelbands 'n' Samosas: Black Young People in the Youth Service.* Leicester: NYB.

Connell, R.W. (1996). *Masculinities.* Polity.

Forster, W.E. (1868). *Privy Council Papers.* HMSO.

Fryer, P. (1984). *Staying Power.* Pluto Press.

Gill, B.S.C.T.D. (1985). *Men, Power and Control* Unpublished paper.

Gill, B.S.C.T.D., and Rushton, L. (1989). *Challenging Racism for White Workers.* GMCWTG.

Gill, B.S.C.T.D., (1991). *Anti-sexist Work with Boys and Young Men* (update).

Gill, B.S.C.T.D. (1996). *Black Young Men and Sexism: Working with Men.* Unpublished.

Greenberg, D.F. (1988). *The Construction of Homosexuality.* University of Chicago Press.

Lancashire County Council (1993). *Curriculum Group Report on Working with Young Men.*

Malcolm X (1970). *By Any Means Necessary.* Pathfinder.

Malthus, R.T. (1798). *Essay On Population.*

Sears, B., and Williams, B. (1997). *Overcoming Heterosexism and Homophobia.* Columbia.

Seidler, V.J. (1994). *Unreasonable Men.* Routledge.

Smith, M. (1988). *Developing Youth Work.* OUP.

Stoltenberg, J. (1989). *Refusing to be a Man.* Fontana.

Vinter, H., (1979). *The Essentials of Social Group Work Practice.* publisher.

Names, addresses and telephone numbers of relevant agencies

Commission for Racial Equality, Elliott House 10–12 Allington Street, London SW1E 5EH; Tel: 0207 828 7022

National Youth Agency, 17–23 Albion Street, Leicester LE1 6GD; Tel: 0116 285 3760

Terence Higgins Trust, 52–54 Gray's Inn Road, London WC1X 8JU; Tel: 0207 831 0330

The B-Team, 302 Commercial Way, London SE15 1QN; Tel: 0207 732 9409

The Naz Project, Palingswick House, 241 King Street, London W6 9LP; Tel: 0207 41 1879

Youth Clubs UK, Kirby House, 20–24 Kirby Street, London EC1N 8TS; Tel: 0207 242 4045

5 Work With Girls and Young Women

Jo Steward

Key Points

1. Maintaining flexibility through service provision and accessibility engages young women; initial contact with vulnerable young women needs to be supportive.

2. Building confidential, trusting and honest relationships enhances the quality of work undertaken.

3. Voluntary participation by young women in services will engender their commitment: young women must set their own agendas and determine the pace of any work undertaken.

4. Working consistently in partnerships with families and vulnerable young women and other agencies can enhance the intervention but requires careful negotiation to build effective relationships.

5. Workers should challenge their own ability to discriminate and judge young people.

Introduction

This chapter will identify the history and origins of work with girls and young women within single-sex environments, and the relentless struggle for this area of work to be incorporated into the mainstream of service delivery to young people. The current context and New Labour's focus upon those at risk of exclusion creates new opportunities to develop effective services for young people generally, but young women are still rarely profiled within such policy directions. Finally, I will record the successful development of a particular project working with a targeted group of young women which attempted to incorporate the principles of best practice drawn historically from the work with girls and young women's movement, whilst responding directly to local research identifying this particular group as vulnerable.

The History of Work with Girls and Young Women

Work with girls and young women is not new. It has taken place in both mixed and separate settings, voluntary and statutory sector projects since the early days of what one would now recognise as the youth service. The National Organisations of Girls Clubs was established in 1911, although girls' clubs had existed since 1861, concerning themselves with the welfare needs of predominantly poor young women. As Maude Stanley, an early pioneer stated:

> Our work with many girls is to help them find out their own powers and to raise them more in their own estimation, for if a girl is stupid the fact of being thought so will put out even the small spark of intelligence that remains in her.
>
> (Stanley, 1890: p. 72)

Although set up and run by the middle classes working as volunteers with the 'less fortunate', informed by a humanitarian sense of duty, there also needs to be a recognition of the role of those many women who worked within such environments to create change within the Suffragette movement and for example the Women's Social and Political Union (Carpenter and Young, 1986).

Since 1945, statutory and voluntary youth services have offered a generic service to engage all young people during their leisure time. In 1960, *The Albemarle Report* commented that:

> Fewer girls than boys are members of youth organisations and much thought will need to be given to ways of attracting them, and studies made of their particular needs.

However, the domination of boys and young men in such settings meant that the needs of girls and young women were continually secondary to such endeavours (Sawbridge and Spence, 1991). As Batsleer (1996) noted, such failure opened up the opportunities for feminist and woman-centred practice from the 1970s onwards.

Further emphasis upon the duty of services to respond to the needs of girls and young women was highlighted in *Experience and Participation, the Report of the Review Group of the Youth Service in England* (DES, 1982). However, the report went further by identifying the need to challenge the broader attitudes blocking such service development:

> ...the operating styles that we have noted in the youth service, participation, advice and counselling, community involvement and so on, all provide scope for a concerted effort to promote reflections of the status of girls and young women and as to the validity of current social attitudes. Ingrained attitudes can be challenged and unconscious assumptions brought to the surface. In short, the Youth Service should be committed to the eradication of sexist attitudes.

Work with girls and young women during this period was not based upon activities, nor was it problem-centred or focused on crisis:

> The work is about young women: who they are, and how they live their lives. It starts from where young women 'are at' and offers them opportunities for choice and development of their potential. The work is important, therefore, not only because of the opportunities it offers young women, but because of the challenge it presents for all youth work and all youth workers.
> (Carpenter and Young, 1986)

Additionally this period also saw the development of a range of services responding to the needs of young women from ethnic minority communities. Although marginal in terms of resource allocation and profile, such work raised the awareness of racism and the struggle of particular communities to enjoy the same access as their white counterparts.

The report of the National Advisory Council for the Youth Service (NACYS) in 1989 on *Youth Work with Girls and Young Women* quoted the HM Inspectorate Report:

> ...the attendance pattern recorded during this survey showed that, nationally, boys outnumbered girls in a ratio of 3:1; this reflects a rejection by girls and young women of the present service to which, in theory they have equal access. Moreover, where they did attend, they were less likely to be involved in activities. In practice much current youth work is largely recreational and for boys.'
> (HMI)

The NACYS report (1989) went on to identify key recommendations to ensure the appropriateness of provision for girls and young women across the voluntary and statutory sectors. However, the marginalisation of young women's needs continued and as a consequence of the Conservative re-structuring of local education authorities, appropriate provision for girls and young women was further eroded during this period. Inevitably the development of Black women's perspectives informing the work also suffered as a result of the cuts endured by services.

New Labour, New Girls Work?

Young women today have increased opportunities and freedoms; however this brings with it increased pressures and responsibilities. They can rely less on support mechanisms within the family and local community. Yet modern concepts of 'girl power' and 'ladette' culture mask the underlying need of young women who still suffer from low self-esteem and poor self-image. The media and society in general continue to place expectations on young women that generate stress and are often contradictory.

Characteristically young women who are stereotypically perceived as being vulnerable are often those who are associated with some form of risk taking behaviour. Most often vulnerability is associated with a combination of complex difficulties, which leads to exclusion from mainstream services, such as education. It is frequently the combination of issues rather than isolated concerns which seem to lead to some level of vulnerability. Vulnerability in young people suggests that accessibility to services can be problematic, especially if they are seen as difficult to engage, or lack the motivation to commit themselves.

The need for work with young women has therefore not diminished as the pressures have continue to increase, and specific issues such as teenage pregnancy and exclusion from education remain in the limelight.

New Labour's focus upon young people has placed the needs of particular groups back upon the policy agenda. Whilst it may be too soon to identify the implications for girls and young women's work, the priorities with regard to services for those deemed to be at risk is well established. (Social Exclusion Unit, *Report on Teenage Pregnancy*, 1999). As youth services re-focus their work to meet these needs, the opportunities for numerous developments in this area of work become more evident, although it is apparent that such initiatives will undoubtedly be designed for those young women in need due to a particular issue that may be blocking their transition and integration to the economic mainstream. This may of course mask the other issues young women are contending with in their day to day lives, for example abuse and violence, drug use, eating disorders and self harm to name just a few.

A Service for Young Women

The particular project that I worked with was established in 1986 as the direct result of a piece of research into the escalation of young women entering the 'care system'. The research was commissioned by a local authority and highlighted the fact that whilst young men were more likely to receive custodial sentences for offending, young women were more likely to receive care orders, for being 'beyond parental control' or 'in moral danger' (Children and Young Persons Act 1969).

This research and thinking formed the basis for a project whose main aim was to divert young women from the care system, young women who were deemed vulnerable in the sense that they had been labelled as having difficult behaviour and were beyond the control of their carers. Typically the profile of young women at whom the service was aimed were defined as having chaotic or unstable lifestyles. They might have stayed out late at night without carer's consent or knowledge and mixed with peers who were either much older than themselves or who were deemed inappropriate and likely to lead them astray, by carers and the local authority.

The age range was 13–17 years and the target groups were young women on care orders, young women in the care system and young women at risk of being received into care. The framework devised to work with this group was based on one-to-one work using a preventative philosophy. This incorporated a strong sense of befriending young women and working alongside them emphasising their positive attributes.

Each young woman whom the project worked with was allocated a key worker who remained her primary contact through her time with the service. This system was found to be extremely helpful for the young woman since it represented a continuity that may have been lacking in other aspects of her life.

The services offered were based on voluntary participation by the young women, hence there developed a real commitment to ensuring the accessibility of service provision. It was recognised early on in the development of this particular project that the work should be empowering for the young women who received a service (even though vulnerable young women are sometimes chaotic in their use of services and difficult to engage). The one-to-one work aimed to help young women take responsibility for the decisions they made, without passing judgements on those choices.

Changes in Child Care Legislation

Working with vulnerable young women within this context and with this type of service provision has been effected by changes in legislation. The criteria and remit of this project took on the language of the Childrens Act 1989. Most significant was Section 17 defining children as 'in need' as well as the new emphasis on working in partnerships with families to prevent family breakdown. This was an important change as legislation now supported the philosophy of early intervention as an effective way of preventing crisis. In terms of working with vulnerable young women legislation encouraged development of services for those who were 'in need' before circumstances led to the more invasive arena of protection.

In this context there became less need for care orders for adolescents and an increase in voluntary accommodations underpinned by partnerships between families or carers and local authorities. The new criteria for working with young women within this setting was based on 'vulnerability' where the young women were being 'looked after' by the local authority or at risk of being 'looked after'. Family breakdown remained the most significant concern but the new criteria allowed services to be developed to work with young women much earlier, before situations reached crisis point.

The Departments of Health's own research highlighted that a shift in resources towards voluntary sector provision for work with families requiring support would be advisable (Department of Health, 1995). This message supported my experience of working with vulnerable young women in a voluntary setting, which allows sufficient freedom to explore creative and flexible approaches in an organic way. One of the most significant areas for constant re-evaluation in terms of service delivery was accessibility for these young women. Even though the Children Act 1989 supported early intervention, actually providing services that vulnerable young women might find useful or interesting remained an on-going challenge.

Delivering Services Specifically for Young Women

Referrals to this voluntary sector setting came from a variety of sources including social services, education welfare, health, schools and other voluntary sector services for young people. Therefore because the first contact was with a referrer it was essential that the actual first contact between the service and a young woman was as positive as possible. Feedback from users of this service suggested that first impressions made a difference in terms of whether they would take up a service at the project.

Firstly the young women were given the choice of how they wished to be contacted, either by letter or phone, as this often depended on an individual's circumstances. They were then offered an informal visit to explain the project work and to discuss with them what the project could offer.

Young women could decide at this point if they wanted to take up the offer of a service, or they could take the opportunity to think it over. It was important to let young women know they did have a choice and that all participation in services were on a voluntary basis.

Within this setting a gender specific staff team delivered services, based on the premise that young women are more likely to feel comfortable discussing sensitive issues with another woman than a man. This premise started in the 1980s when the project was set up and there was particular concern for working with survivors of sexual abuse.

It was felt to be important to provide a safe space for vulnerable young women and this was justified by feedback from service users who reported feeling relaxed and comfortable. Service users also commented on the project having a special feeling, as it was the only space where most young women were in a single-sex environment. However having worked in other environments with vulnerable young women, it is important not to make assumptions about the needs of young people, but that young women should be given a choice wherever possible about who they feel is appropriate to work with them.

Confidentiality is always important when working with vulnerable young women as is ensuring that policies and statements are thoroughly understood. Experience suggests that it is only at times when the boundaries of confidentiality are questioned that it becomes clear that the subject needs to remain on working agendas. Vulnerable young women often need the security and safety of confidentiality, knowing that issues will not be shared with others unless there are risks of significant harm. Young women also need to be consulted about the sharing of information at multi-agency forums and work needs to be incorporated about the implication of working in partnerships (if this is necessary).

This project also operated an open file policy in which young women could access their files and read any recordings their worker may have made following a session. Frequently young women would want to see the first couple of recordings. It was felt that this encouraged openness and honesty and helped to establish trust over a period of time.

An Approach Centred on the Young Person

The recognition that young women are young people first and foremost has been crucial in delivering services which young women feel comfortable using and which have proved effective. This means that from referral to the end of a piece of work the process should be centred on making the service accessible, supportive and useful. It is important for young women to be involved as much as possible in the service, and that they should be consulted about any sharing of information, and plans for work and assessment.

To try and ensure service user take up it is important to make any literature about the service or the accompanying forms as simple as possible and to give young people choices. Experience has suggested that to make a service accessible to vulnerable young women early contact has to be supportive and encouraging. Some success can be gained by using reply slips and self-addressed envelopes to encourage a response and facilitate communication. Any service with vulnerable young people needs to recognise that accessing a service can be frightening and requires a certain level of self-confidence. Therefore vulnerable young women need to be given choices and generally supported to access a service according to their individual needs.

In maintaining a service centred on the young person it is vital to examine how the services, policies and procedures could support the personal development of young women. A service should physically incorporate positive images of young women, including positive images of young women from various ethnic backgrounds, and young lesbian and bisexual women. Providing refreshments and comfortable furnishings enables some vulnerable young women to access a service (it also can provide a nurturing environment). It is also useful for a young women's service to provide a range of readily available information on other services that young women may want to access, family planning, childcare services etc.

One–to–One Work

An individual worker and young women can work together on identified issues using a process of assessment and regular reviews. One-to-one work aims to develop an honest and trusting relationship between a worker and a young woman. There is no systematic and prescribed manner of working. In recognition that each young woman's needs may be different the model of working requires an eclectic and flexible approach.

This framework for one-to-one work consists of a period of assessment to allow for the relationship to develop and for basic information to be shared. Work on identifying issues or problems then follows, allowing young women freedom to explore their own agenda and make decisions on prioritising the work. Although the referrer will produce a certain amount of information it is an important step to ask young women to set their agenda and own the

work, thus creating opportunity for the young woman to feel empowered, in control and, most importantly, listened to.

The worker and service user can constantly review work together. This allows workers and young women to share progress and achievement and to incorporate celebration following difficult pieces of work. This is particularly important in reinforcing feelings of self worth. This framework also increases awareness around issues of dependency and attachment, which many vulnerable young women experience.

Similarly endings for vulnerable young women are usually very important especially if there has been a pattern of loss or separation. Again the validity of the relationship between workers and young women can be celebrated as an acknowledgement of the work achieved. One idea can be to stagger the last sessions so that the ending can be at a suitable pace for each young woman.

A variety of work tools can be used with young women to capture their imagination and encourage motivation. For example these can include art materials, worksheets, musical instruments, video recorders, puppets or computers. Working on issues in a creative way enables some young women to experience a sense of safety whilst also creating opportunities for providing positive feedback. For some young women verbalising will be the most appropriate form of communication but for others it can take them time and encouragement to feel able to use some of the tools.

Group Work

Specific-themed short-term groups can be identified in order to reflect the needs of young women in the local community. Moving-on groups for young women can be useful following a period of one-to-one work, especially if service users need help in transferring new skills to peer relationships. A group can be based on activities that require young women to work in small groups or pairs, therefore providing opportunities for individuals to make new relationships and use their skills in groups. An important element of peer support can be introduced which may continue when young women leave a service, enabling them to move on. This model recognises the need for good support networks for young women as a continuum, not just whilst using a specific service.

Other types of groups with vulnerable young women are equally important. General personal development groups with a strong focus on improving feelings of self-worth based on a rolling programme can be successful.

Advocacy

Advocacy involves the representation and support for young women attending meetings or statutory procedures such as reviews and case conferences. Workers involved in advocacy need to ensure that young women are clear about the worker's role. At times workers will be asked to give professional opinions which have to be distinguished from advocating the young woman's wishes and feelings. This is an important point and all thoughts and feelings should be explored with a young woman before any meetings.

Family Support Work

This may involve either informal occasional contact or more formal structured sessions depending on need. It is increasingly recognised that the family environment does have a role to play in the well-being of a young woman and that her contact with a service can be maximised if some work is undertaken with the family or carers. This support however can produce dilemmas, as some young women do not feel that it is appropriate for their one-to-one worker to support other members of her family. The feelings of vulnerable young women should be thoroughly explored as it may be possible to co-work with other colleagues or agencies so that families or carers and young women feel supported and get a service. It is this honest approach to the work with young women that enables these issues to be resolved without

necessarily disengaging the young women from the service.

Future Development of Service Provision

A commitment to evaluating service provision for vulnerable young women is essential for ensuring good quality services are developed according to their needs. Service user consultation is vital in gaining direct feedback on existing services, whilst enabling young women to directly influence future development. Consultation should not just be limited to new services but to evaluating present ones and improving the standard for all service users. Providing a regular consultation forum can help access young women's views whilst developing their own skills.

Partnerships across agencies and disciplines mean that services for vulnerable young women can develop in many new exciting areas. For example mentoring services and peer education can meet the needs of some young women, whilst others will require perhaps more therapeutic intervention offered through a range of theoretical perspectives.

Working with vulnerable young women should look at different methods of working, guided by young women, who more frequently request one day workshops or shorter term practical services rather than lengthy long term therapy. This also ensures that services reach a wider range of young women due to the variety on offer, and goes further towards accessibility for those who find other services difficult to use. For the most vulnerable young women services need to be providing outreach or satellite services where the service users congregate. Accessibility will continue to be problematic for this group and support needs to be part of the plan to enable young people to use services.

Key Questions

1. Are young women's needs at the centre of all service provision?
2. Is the service accessible to young women as young people?
3. Do you have a range of information available on other services relevant to young women?
4. Are the appropriate partners involved in the delivery of a 'joined up' service?
5. Does the service recognise and build on the strengths of young women?

References

Batsleer, J. (1996). *Working with Girls and Young Women in Community Settings.* Hampshire: Arena.

Carpenter, V., and Young, K. (1986). *Coming in from the Margins: Youth Work with Girls and Young Women.* Leicester: National Association of Youth Clubs.

Department of Education and Science (1982). *Experience and Participation, Report of the Review Group of the Youth Service in England.* London: HMSO.

Department of Education and Science (1989). *NACYS: Youth Work with Girls and Young Women.* Wales: HMSO.

Department of Health (1991). *Working Together under the Children Act 1989, A Guide to Arrangements for Inter-agency Co-operation for the Protection of Children from Abuse.* London: HMSO.

Department of Health (1995). *Child Protection: Messages From Research.* London: HMSO.

HMSO (1960). *The Albemarle Report.* London: HMSO.

Sawbridge, M., and Spence, J. (1991). *The Dominance of the Male Agenda in Community and Youth Work.* University of Durham.

Social Exclusion Unit (1999). *Report on Teenage Pregnancy.* London: HMSO.

Stanley, M. (1890). *Clubs for Working Girls.* London: Macmillan.

Further Reading

Coleman, J. (1980). *Nature of Adolescence.* London: Methuen.

Davies, M. (1998). *The Essential Social Worker.* Aldershot: Assignee.

Owe, D. (1987). *An Introduction to Social Work Theory.* Aldershot: Gower.

Payne, M. (1991). *Modern Social Work Theory.* Basingstoke: Macmillan.

Youth Work and Regeneration
Sajid Butt

Key Points

1. The facilitated participation of young people and their communities in regeneration work is paramount.

2. Youth and community workers need to ensure that they secure places on policy tables and on partnership bodies as equal partners.

3. Community organisations, statutory providers and other adult led bodies need to look more critically at how they can increase the participation by young people.

4. Regeneration is not just about economic development but also about social and political change, active citizenship and community development.

5. Local regeneration strategies need to be inclusive of young people from different backgrounds and to work on anti-discriminatory principles.

Introduction

The term 'regeneration' is very much in currency today although there is no precise definition of what it is. In definitional terms there are, however, understandings about what constitutes effective regeneration in terms of community development processes and outcomes that would be beneficial to local people and agencies. Youth workers, government, community development workers and other practitioners involved in the field of regeneration generally point to the following as its overarching features:

1. Physical regeneration of the land, buildings, the neighbourhood, key landmarks and so on.

2. Social regeneration which includes the development and consolidation of people's skills and capacities as well as responding to social needs such as health.

3. Economic regeneration which includes changes in the infrastructure of local communities and the development of greater political understanding about, and the empowerment of local communities.

These three distinct types of regeneration are complementary; for example, to develop disused land or renovate old buildings requires a pool of skilled labour and business activity to deliver the final product. Due mostly to the decimation of England's manufacturing base but also to political concerns about socially excluded communities, an array of mainstream regeneration programmes and schemes have been introduced over the years to transform areas suffering from urban decline into areas of thriving economic activity and social interaction. However, regeneration initiatives tend to primarily target neighbourhoods of economic decline rather than specific socially or economically excluded groups within them.

Good community and youth work practice tells us that where there is a need to regenerate a neighbourhood, all stakeholders in that particular area, especially local communities, should be consulted and engaged in the planning, design and delivery of the eventual regeneration programme. This would seek to ensure that there is shared ownership between local communities and delivery agencies and that the outcomes are appropriate and relevant.

Yet guidance from central government has done little over the years to influence the eventual delivery of regeneration programmes, which has been well documented. For example, Black and ethnic minority communities are often explicitly identified beneficiaries within regeneration bids, yet in reality they do not directly benefit from them in the long term. Additionally, a lack of co-ordinated information at a local level about such programmes has also limited a proper analysis of the true impact of regeneration programmes upon its intended beneficiaries.

This chapter will explore some of these issues and seek to give a broader overview of economic regeneration. In particular, it will look at ways in which youth work and community development approaches can add value to the design and delivery of local regeneration policies and programmes.

Historical Developments

During the late 1960s, the *Urban Programme* was introduced by the then Labour Government to improve the socio-economic fabric in deprived areas, particularly council estates and areas where Black and ethnic minority communities were concentrated. However, despite the link between the origins of the *Urban Programme* and concerns about racial conflict and discrimination, there was no explicit targeting of Black and ethnic minority groups within such policy initiatives (Beazley and Loftman, 1998).

The Inner Cities White Paper (1977) sought to co-ordinate regeneration policy in areas with acute socio-economic disadvantages. However, the policy directives of the then incoming Conservative government in 1979 shifted regeneration away from its social emphasis to one that was largely of environmental development, mainly through the encouragement of private rather than state investment. The rationale here was to secure the well being of inner cities and their communities through the establishment of an economic infrastructure of new housing and retail developments that would secure the long-term prosperity of local economies. Communities were deemed to be the eventual beneficiaries of these developments rather than a direct target recipient of regeneration 'aid'. The general approach to regeneration during the Thatcherite era served to pathologise communities especially the Black communities after the street rebellions of the early 1980s. Rather than directly benefiting from regeneration activities such as the 'Inner Cities Task Force' initiative, Black communities in many parts of the country continued to be socially excluded and all that they witnessed were superficial and tokenistic changes in and around their neighbourhoods.

The early 1990s saw another shift in regeneration policy, as it became apparent that the heavy emphasis on physical development was excluding local communities and local authorities

from regeneration programmes. The introduction of *City Challenge* as an area-based initiative principally gave local authorities the lead role in formulating bids and partnerships and for local communities to be fully involved in the process. Whilst *City Challenge* had its merits, there were still a variety of social and physical regeneration programmes which prevented any meaningful change occurring due to the complexity of different programmes and the bureaucracy involved in administering them all at the local level.

The introduction of the *Single Regeneration Budget* (SRB) arose through the merger of 20 separate programmes in England and from five different government departments, with the aim of providing a flexible mechanism for economic regeneration that could meet local needs as well as complementing principal government programmes. However, the introduction of SRB also absorbed Section 11 funding (Local Government Act 1966), a fund specifically targeted at the then incoming Commonwealth immigrants. This funding was mainly aimed at facilitating the integration of these immigrants into British society and focused on their educational needs. The administration and application of this was much criticised by the Black communities because the money was often abused by local authorities to supplement their own coffers, with very little direct benefit to the intended beneficiaries. Despite the criticism about Section 11 funding, its absorption within SRB symbolically stated to the Black and ethnic minority communities that there would not be dedicated funds to respond to some of their more specific needs and that they would now have to compete with other groups for the SRB pot.

Furthermore, the dominance of local authorities and Training and Enterprise Councils (TECs) in the first few rounds of the SRB confirmed the exclusion of communities and young people from any meaningful involvement in regeneration processes. The arrival of 'New Labour' with its political commitment to strike a real balance between the different and often competing regeneration objectives, heralded the makings of a 'joined-up' approach to ensure there was local co-ordination and proper impact assessment.

This new approach put partnership working at its centre. The bidding guidance in recent rounds, SRB 5 and SRB 6, points to the critical role of community involvement, even to the extent that applications would stand a better chance of securing project funding if there was a good case of such engagement by the community. In addition, as well as the involvement of young people, the engagement by Black and minority ethnic communities are seen to be central. Within the new guidance, in the first year of its delivery plan ('Year Zero'), local SRB partnerships can use some of the funds to establish more inclusive management structures and undertake extensive community consultations to shape the implementation of regeneration programmes.

This approach has been reinforced by other recent initiatives that seek to ensure transparency and true ownership in regeneration programmes. The aims of the *New Commitment to Regeneration*, developed by the Local Government Association, for instance, are to create a framework for all partners to pool their resources around an agreed long-term plan for the regeneration of their area.

Young People and Social Exclusion

The Social Exclusion Unit (SEU) report, *Bringing Britain Together: A National Strategy for Neighbourhood Renewal* (1999) sets out the first steps towards a national strategy for tackling the problems associated with poor neighbourhoods. Its first major outcome was the establishment of *New Deal for Communities* (NDC) initiative, a 10-year programme to regenerate Britain's poorest neighbourhoods in a true 'bottom-up' approach. 'Bottom-up' is a term used to describe the process through which the ideas and vision of local communities are used to inform and drive a particular (regeneration) programme. The NDC has four key areas:

- tackling worklessness
- improving health
- tackling crime
- raising educational attainment

Again, each partnership has to demonstrate that it **is** working in partnership, that all stakeholders are consulted and that their needs are translated into detailed action plans. For the first time also, central government has produced specific race equality guidance for regeneration to assist NDC partnerships in shaping their delivery plan (DETR, 2000).

The SEU report marked a political commitment to close the gaps between the poorest neighbourhoods and the rest of the country. In addition to setting up the NDC initiative, the report also recommended the establishment of 18 Policy Action Teams (PATs) to examine the underlying causes of social exclusion and economic disadvantage in poor neighbourhoods and make recommendations for future action. The remit for one of the PATs, *Young People*, was to report on the key costs of youth disaffection and the most effective interventions for preventing it. The respective roles of the different agencies and how the design of services could take greater account of the perspectives of young people was also to be examined.

Much of the SEU's work focused on individual dimensions of the issues that affect young people and their communities such as exclusion from school, truancy, teenage pregnancy, youth homelessness and unemployment of 16 to 18 year olds. However, this report highlighted two repeating themes:

1. The complex disadvantage faced by certain groups of young people such as those who grow up in care or who do badly at school.
2. The inadequate response young people receive from an uncoordinated set of services.

The PAT report tried to examine the reasons for this. For example, young Black people face a number of these problems disproportionately, not least because they live in poverty and disadvantaged neighbourhoods, but also because of the additional effects of racism. If a more comprehensive approach to youth inclusion was to be implemented, three main shortcomings needed to be addressed: gaps in individual services, allocation of resources and fragmentation of policy thinking and service delivery. The report concluded that government should:

- Set overarching youth inclusion objectives for its policies and ensure that they are reflected in departmental policies.
- Establish a Youth Unit to support ministers in carrying forward strategy and as a common resource for all departments.
- Make clear that it wishes to see effective co-ordination of information and policies about young people at local level and devise a strategy with targets to improve access to

services and facilities for young people in deprived neighbourhoods.

- Ensure all departments and agencies whose work has an impact on young people have a policy of consulting and involving them in policy development and service delivery that affects them.

The conclusions from all the 18 PATs have been used to develop a *National Strategy for Neighbourhood Renewal.* The strategy is underpinned by a set of four drivers, one of which is Leadership and Joint Working where it recommends 'better co-ordination of policies and services for young people', (Social Exclusion Unit, 2000).

Towards Social Inclusion

One of the earlier SEU reports, *Bridging the Gap: New Opportunities for 16–18 year olds not in Education, Employment or Training* (Social Exclusion Unit, 1999), identified the problems affecting the current mechanisms for supporting young people and especially those who are:

- from disadvantaged backgrounds
- disaffected
- suffering the effects of multiple problems

Similarly, the DfEE White Paper *Learning to Succeed* (1999) identified learning as the single most important investment government could make in a young person, with high quality education provision as a starting point. Both reports recognised that such an investment could only be effective if it were integrated with measures that address other aspects of young people's lives.

Central to this would be the creation of a *ConneXions* service, dubbed a 'Youth Support Service' designed to end the fragmentation of services to young people through the creation of a network of personal advisers. These personal advisers would be involved in providing information, advice and guidance to individual young people, and tracking their progress, so that no young person could 'go missing' and end up outside of education, work and training.

However, the government also recognised that involving young people is critical to the development of the service. There are successful ways of involving even the hardest to reach young people, through outreach work, work in clubs, street work and through community radio. In addition, a pool of mentors will be drawn from local communities to provide role models and encouragement to young people. Peer mentors, particularly young people who have themselves experienced difficulties, will be encouraged to act as role models to help young people deal with similar challenges.

The Involvement of Young People in Regeneration

The common method used to target young people in regeneration has been through linkages to existing training and job opportunities. What has been limited are regeneration projects that look to increase the 'quality of life' for young people (housing, health etc.) or that tap into their needs and issues that affect their everyday life, such as their relationship with the police or peer pressure and role models.

For the future it is important to ensure that young people have every chance of succeeding in life through appropriate support and resources being made available to nurture their self-respect and realise their full potential. However, the future is only in the hands of the few who, for example, excel at school or have strong family support. There is a rise in the numbers of young people who are excluded from mainstream socio-economic activity, which is why the focus on young people and their current and future contribution to society is of pivotal importance to the government.

Given the fact that there is a political commitment to invest in the future of young people, how can we ensure that economic regeneration takes account of the needs of young people and organisations working with and for young people?

A report produced by the DETR for dissemination to SRB partnerships, *Youth and Regeneration: Good Practice Guide* (DETR, 1997), identified two broad approaches that regeneration partnerships should adopt when examining the issue of youth involvement in regeneration strategies:

- *Combating multiple disadvantages* through assisting young people who are disaffected, in trouble or at risk. Here, regeneration programmes would aim to reduce marked socio-economic disadvantages through ensuring provision meets the needs of those who are most vulnerable.
- *Participation and empowerment* in activities which encourage young people to participate

in regeneration and community life generally, building capacity and combating potential disaffection through the process of active involvement.

The DETR report goes further to identify good practice for youth inclusion in the design and delivery of regeneration projects. For example, youth participation should be embedded within regeneration strategies and young people should have representation on relevant groups. As before, whenever a programme or activity is likely to have an impact on young people, regeneration partnerships should seek to consult and involve young people. In addition, monitoring should be built into regeneration projects to assess the impact it is having on its young constituents.

The involvement of young people in regeneration programmes as advisers and representatives on strategic bodies needs to be supported by training, mentoring and the financing of their expenses to enable them to contribute fully to the decision-making process. There may well be existing groups with young people taking the lead, which could be incorporated into the main decision-making body, so as to create an environment where young people as a whole would feel comfortable in making a contribution.

The way to maximise regeneration programmes, therefore, is to ensure there is sufficient provision to meet the needs of young people through recognising the range of problems that they face. Hence, regeneration programmes with a youth focus should be integrated into regeneration strategies and other services (Fitzpatrick et al., 1998). This requires their involvement from the start to nurture their self-development and bring about sustainability of a particular regeneration project. Common methods of involvement (Fitzpatrick et al., 1998) include:

- Consultation exercises such as youth surveys and focus group discussions.
- Joint management initiatives such as the involvement of young people in the management of specific projects.
- Projects mainly managed by young people where they have the delegated powers over specific projects and budgets.

Such participatory initiatives can bring about increased self-confidence and skills for young people and can have a positive impact in the way regeneration practitioners and policy makers perceive young people, in particular their capacity to contribute to decision-making processes. As part of such a process, it is important to remember that there is a diversity of need in local communities and populations of young people and an effective regeneration strategy has to incorporate these different but equally valid perspectives.

Young Black people continue to experience significantly different outcomes in the training and jobs market. Several important factors can be identified to explain this including racism, poor career advice and access to high quality training. On many predominantly Black housing estates, there are virtually no opportunities for economic advancement. Residents are discriminated against often because of their postal address whilst others may lack the basic skills necessary to break into the job market.

However, because of institutionalised racism, many young Black people have simply not been encouraged or motivated to achieve in education or work and have not had validating experiences from role models from a range of different occupational sectors. A number of factors impact on youth development work in Black communities, for example, the high exclusion rates of African-Caribbean schoolchildren. Also, violence permeates many aspects of young Black peoples' lives: they are more likely to be the victims of violent crimes than their white counterparts.

The government's *New Start* project aims to re-engage 14–17 year olds that are currently not in learning or are at risk of leaving learning prematurely. A good practice guide, *A New Start for Minority Ethnic Young People* (Department for Education and Employment, 1999) has been produced for institutions and agencies that are setting up initiatives to tackle disaffection and disengagement amongst young Black people.

The guide has outlined five key principles of promoting racial equality in youth work, which could also be used as good practice in regeneration programmes:

1. *Baselining the population*: knowing the make-up of the local minority ethnic population is important, as is finding out the differences between all ethnic groups in achievement and exclusion.

2. *Ethnic monitoring*: necessary to measure the progress in minority ethnic youth participation, achievement and long-term outcomes from all learning routes.

3. *Knowledge and understanding*: essential to know how institutional racism and lack of cultural awareness can impact on a young person's achievement.

4. *Language and communication*: effective communication is not only about English language and interpretation facilities being readily available for speakers of other languages, but also about consultation with young minority ethnic people and their parents to find out their views.

5. *Multi-agency working*: partnerships and projects that develop effective networking and collaborative work with all sections of the local community are usually better able to develop a shared understanding of the problem, and an ability to work towards eliminating barriers which result from discrimination and disadvantage.

Good practice case study

In Bradford, young people are playing a central part in improving the area where they live. The Manningham and Girlington area of the city received SRB funding to regenerate the area and will support the Manningham and Girlington Youth Partnership, where local young people aged 16 to 25 share in the management of the SRB programme. Young people have been actively engaged in the management of funding into the area. For example, young people have four representatives on the Key Fund decision-making panel, which assesses SRB and ESF bids and resource allocation.

The Youth Partnership is responsible for informing local young people about the programme and encouraging them to get involved, and for developing projects and initiatives to benefit other young people. Members are trained in management skills and helped to gain the background knowledge they need through an on-going development programme.

Young people's influence has grown steadily since they helped draft the original bid, to the extent that they now have the leading role in allocating grants of up to £25,000 through the project's community development fund.

The Youth Partnership now has its own accommodation, and is starting to secure better facilities for local young people. The aim of the partnership is to develop a lasting initiative that will ensure a voice for young people in the long-term regeneration of the area and its communities. A critical success factor has been that the Girlington Community Centre now acts as a focal point for youth activity and a sound foundation from which to develop the assets of the organisation. It will soon become a legally constituted organisation, borne out of the partnership, which will act as a stimulus for young people's personal and career development. This will involve accredited training programmes (based on in-depth needs analysis) and the acquisition of key skills such as marketing, fundraising, and advocacy.

Young people have gained much confidence since being involved in this work and are now taking steps to further develop the whole initiative.

Making a Difference: What Can You Do?

This chapter has intended to show what prominence youth issues have within regeneration programmes. A recent study (Fitzpatrick et al., 1998) makes a number of recommendations at different levels, including:

- *Regeneration practitioners and decision-makers* need to maximise the impact of youth-focused initiatives by ensuring good links to mainstream youth programmes. They should clarify the purpose of developing youth involvement and ensure that participation projects are scheduled early in initiatives or, if possible, before they begin. Effective youth participation requires a dedicated worker, appropriate resources and that adult decision makers are prepared to listen to young people.

- *Youth workers or dedicated support staff* may need to learn about both regeneration and

---

Key Questions

1. How much do you really know about the local community and neighbourhood in which your organisation is based?
2. How much do you know about the range of organisations and agencies that operate in the local area?
3. How much do you know and are involved in the development and delivery of regeneration policy initiatives that affect the local area?
4. To what extent does your agency carry out community development work and other forms of strategic developmental work in the neighbourhood?
5. How effective have you been in increasing the involvement of young people in regeneration activities in your area?

---

community participation in order to link youth participation into wider community and regeneration processes, and to help them to develop more accountable structures for youth involvement. They should recognise that youth forums are not the only answer to participation and that a range of mechanisms will be more effective.

- *Community organisations* need to prioritise the needs of young people as young people and not only as 'future citizens'. They should try and build structures which link generations and consider how their attitudes, procedures and language can inhibit youth participation.

- *Young people* need to learn from other young people how to get organised and to think how their language and behaviour might build barriers between them and adults.

Conclusion

Social exclusion has had a profound impact on the lives of young people, particularly those living in deprived areas. Neighbourhood deprivation arose mainly through the decline in the UK's manufacturing industries but was exacerbated by governmental failure to ensure effective and sustainable regeneration programmes. Regeneration policy over the last twenty years has created a culture within delivery agencies, which fails to target communities (including young people) as the most important beneficiaries of any regeneration programme. Recent policy measures and recommendations (for example, the Social Exclusion Unit reports) aim to counter this trend.

Despite the best intentions of regeneration programmes and the resultant partnerships, the benefits

for young people and their involvement has been limited. Sustainable regeneration is now the new term being used to draw in all aspects of regeneration which will have lasting effect for its intended beneficiaries. What regeneration practitioners, youth organisations and workers should realise is that any regeneration programme will have a huge impact on the opportunities that young people now and in the future can benefit from. Hence, the real outcome will be the extent to which these initiatives serve the needs of young people and whether young people, youth workers and organisations are engaged in and benefiting from this process, from 'conceptualisation to commercialisation'.

References

Beazley, M., and Loftman, P. (1998). *Race and Regeneration: A Review of the Single Regeneration Budget Challenge Fund.* Local Government Information Unit.

DETR (1997). *Youth and Regeneration: Good Practice Guide.* Produced on behalf of the DETR by Roger Tym and Partners with GFA consulting and the University of the West of England.

DETR (2000). *New Deal for Communities: Race Equality Guidance.* HMSO.

DfEE (1999). *A New Start for Minority Ethnic Young People.* HMSO.

DfEE (1999). *Learning to Succeed.* HMSO.

Fitzpatrick, S., Hastings, A., and Kintrea, K. (1998). *Including Young People in Urban Regeneration: A Lot to Learn?* The Policy Press in association with the Joseph Rowntree Foundation.

Social Exclusion Unit (1999). *Bridging the Gap: New Opportunities for 16–18 Year-olds Not in Education, Employment or Training.* The Stationery Office Ltd.

Social Exclusion Unit (1999). *Bringing Britain Together: A National Strategy for Neighbourhood Renewal.* The Stationery Office Ltd.

Social Exclusion Unit (2000). *National Strategy for Neighbourhood Renewal: A Framework for Consultation.* The Stationery Office Ltd.

7 Youth Work with Young People in Rural Areas

Janet Watson

Key Points

1. Involve young people at all stages of identifying their needs, planning and decision making. Do not sacrifice the fun element by trying to satisfy adult agendas.
2. Harness local community support and partnerships for potential funding, volunteers and other resources from the start.
3. Be flexible and imaginative in seeking out and making use of all available resources.
4. Raise the profile of youth work and young people by regularly publicising your project and its activities.
5. Take care not to take on too much by yourself, tackle too many issues, cover too wide an area and burn yourself out.

Introduction

Young people are an important part of every community. They have much to contribute to the life of rural areas. Their imagination, creativity and energy can make a valuable contribution to creating vibrant, balanced, forward looking rural communities. Yet all too often the contribution that young people can make to rural communities is overlooked. Their needs are often ignored. Young people everywhere face major challenges in making the transition to adulthood in a modern society: finding work; finding a place to live; finding their place in society.

(Rural Development Commission, 1998)

Generally young people living in rural areas have the same basic needs as those living in urban situations. They may enjoy some of the benefits popularly associated with living in the countryside such as pleasant scenery, open spaces, close knit communities and strong family bonds: but not all of these maybe the reality. Their choices and life opportunities can be restricted because they are not concentrated in large numbers, and their needs can go unnoticed. Policy makers tend to direct resources to providing services that reduce social exclusion, youth unemployment and crime where the numbers are greatest and where the impact will be most visible.

Rural youth work responds to the particular needs of young people who are denied the variability of access to services and provision. Its purpose is to counter some of the effects of rural deprivation, which can restrict social, educational, economic and broad life chances. Fabes and Knowles (1991) state that working with young people in rural areas is not just 'youth work' in a different setting, but involves distinctive approaches, including a commitment to work with all young people living in a locality whilst accurately attempting to raise and address the issues that affect them.

History

Historically youth and community services have concentrated youth work development mainly in urban areas where the problems and tensions for young people have been clearly visible. The result has been that considerable resources have been located there. In more recent times, inner city problems have focused political attention again on the provision in urban areas.

The *Salter Davies Report* (1964), the result of an *Albermarle Report* recommendation, was the first government report on youth work in rural areas. There was very little change over the next twenty-five years. The *Thompson Report* (1982) referred to work with young people in rural areas and the first major project was the National Association of Youth Clubs (NAYC) *Rural Youth Work Education Project* which gave the work a higher profile through its publications between 1983 and 1984. The National Advisory Council for Youth Service (NACYS) Sub-Committee (1988) Appendix 3 compiled detailed models of rural settings and styles which led to many Youth Services devising rural policies and rural work developed as a specialist area of practice. From the 1980s De Montfort University (then Leicester Polytechnic), ran a 'rural' option in the initial training for youth and community courses and later in the post-graduate diploma qualification.

The main support organisation for rural youth workers, now known as the National Forum for the Development of Rural Youth Work, began the first National Symposium in Rural Youth Work in 1986 which was heavily over-subscribed. An ad hoc steering group of six people involved in rural youth work, who were concerned at the isolation and lack of support for rural youth workers, initiated a biannual newsletter, training meetings twice a year in different parts of the country and further conferences and workshops. The membership of rural volunteers, principal youth officers, voluntary organisations and others working predominantly in rural areas continues to grow.

Most of these developments have been due to the persistence of individuals in certain localities and for the most part, work undertaken has been specific and not generally taken up on a wider basis. Change has mainly been achieved by reshaping limited resources designated for rural youth work rather than through a more equitable distribution of overall resources. External funding sources for supporting new developments have been limited and short term.

Traditionally, rural youth work has been reliant on voluntary workers who have not had training to meet their real needs and paid staff who are few and far between. These workers and volunteers have workloads that are unrealistic in terms of distance to be covered, time and transport costs. The situation remains very much the same today (Watson, 1987).

Social Context

The context of rural life is important to rural youth work. The quest for identifying 'What is rural', has been the subject of considerable research and debate and as Les Roberts, Chief Executive of ACRE pointed out at the 1999 Conference (Scott and Russell, 1999) more time has been given to this than the finding of solutions to the problems. Rural deprivation is at last being acknowledged with new social indicators emerging in the form of 'sparsity factors'.

There is no single definition of 'what is rural'. The Department of the Environment and the Rural Development Commission (RDC) define a rural settlement as having a population of less than 10,000. Ten million or one-fifth of the population live and work in rural England but rural settlements vary greatly. Phillips and Skinner (1994) define five types of rural locations:

1. remote rural areas
2. villages
3. market towns
4. collapsed industrial areas
5. coastal areas and hinterland

Some rural settlements are wealthy and expanding with access to shops, reasonable transport and other local amenities. Others are deprived and declining with few, if any, resources, long journeys to access basic services and reliance on personal transport. Some are affected by seasonal contrasts, with facilities and opportunities available during the summer tourist season and limited opportunities for young people for the rest of the year. Many areas have two extremes with marked pockets of poverty and deprivation, which are hidden and often denied within relatively well-heeled areas.

The *NACRO Report* (1997) points out that many causes of deprivation are the same in rural and urban areas but rural areas have specific features, including greater isolation, which makes the problem less obvious. These include:

- difficulty of access including poor public transport
- lack of local suitable housing
- lower wages
- limited local services and employment opportunities
- the gradual closure of village shops, post offices, pubs
- isolation from family networks, especially for newcomers.

These are experienced particularly acutely by young people, and form the backdrop against which some young people can drift into drug taking and crime:

If you are on your own in the village there's nothing to do except hang around...and it's

*boring, boring, boring...just hanging around.
Boring.*   (NAYC, 1984)

Needs Analysis: Young People and Rural Life

The National Youth Agency (NYA) publication, *Nothing Ever Happens Around Here* (Phillips and Skinner, 1994), examines in depth the experience of young people living in rural areas and gives examples of a range of youth work responses to those needs. The main issues are identified as isolation, identity and access.

Isolation

- The likelihood of few other young people living nearby of the same age, gender and social class or with similar interests.
- Dependence on adults for relationships and to maintain contact with chosen friends.
- Adult actions, attitudes and beliefs that make young people feel unwelcome and unwanted.
- Lack of places to meet their friends where they are out of public gaze.

Identity

- Attachment to familiar surroundings but a desire to be somewhere different or better.
- If locally born, a sense of territorial threat from incomers; if an incomer, a sense of loss over previous surroundings and friendships.
- Having to accept or encounter traditional expectations of gender roles and behaviour.
- Harassment and prejudicial behaviour towards travellers, young people and others with visible differences or different sexual orientation.
- Long lasting labelling of individuals or their families experiencing unemployment or involved in criminal activities.

Access

- Reliance on school buses or someone else providing a lift.
- Limited choice of education, training opportunities and work often involving lengthy travel: increased likelihood of stereotypical choices.

- Local work opportunities restricted, with a likelihood of low pay and seasonal variation.
- Few opportunities for play or to take up sports, arts or music seriously.
- Little access to leisure activities.
- Little access to affordable housing and few choices over medical care.
- Little or no access to specialist advice and support.

Methods of Delivery: Responding to Needs

Fabes and Knowles (1997) give many examples of developments and initiatives that occurred in rural youth work in the late 1980s and these are detailed in a plethora of individual youth and community service publications, policy reviews and other evaluation reports produced since then. Recent developments and initiatives have been marked by a distinction between the general youth work provision and a few high profile rural projects, which have received large amounts of external funding.

Two factors are important for the success of rural youth work; the response of young people and the availability of voluntary workers and well-trained staff within small communities. The *NAYC Report* (1994) points out that rural young people are much more likely to attend or become a member of a youth organisation than their urban counterparts: probably four or five times as likely due to the lack of other amenities and things to do.

It is often difficult to recruit voluntary workers from small communities willing to work with the 14+ age group in their immediate locality. Their 'respectability' can be questioned if they explore controversial issues with young people. Village communities can blame youth workers for all the youth misdemeanours occurring in the village and put enormous public pressure on them to try and sort out all the problems. Voluntary support is difficult to find on a regular and long-term basis.

The *NYA Training Pack* (Hand, 1994) summarises eight main ways in which youth work is delivered in rural areas:

- **Mobile projects:** Youth projects using purpose-built and converted double and single buses, mini-buses and vans, some activity based, some curriculum based and some providing an information and advice service.

- **Local activities:** Young people getting together with each other and with interested adults take part in joint activities and pursue common interests, such as sports, drama, art etc.
- **Area activities:** Where adults or older peers transport young people to youth centres or other specialist buildings for specific purposes, activities and events.
- **One night a week groups:** Clubs or groups run by volunteers or sessionally paid workers, often in village halls. They may or may not be supported by district worker, church, county association or uniformed organisation.
- **Rural Teams:** Teams of part-time youth workers and volunteers, co-ordinated by a full-time member of staff. The workers relate to a geographical patch, support existing provision and offer particular activities and training opportunities for both adults and young people.
- **District or Patch Development work:** Peripatetic workers operating from a central location with responsibility for developmental work within a given geographical area. This type of work is often a targeted response to the needs of particular groups of young people. It often takes place where young people are, on their own terms, and works towards involving them in a group or project.
- **Detached work:** Youth workers employed to engage in work with young people on their own territory and on their own terms. Workers operate as 'brokers', enabling individual young people to widen their interests and introducing them to specialist activities and services.
- **Distance initiatives:** Using radio, telephone and computer services to link isolated young people: for example, phone-ins, answering machines and free phone numbers, computer networking.

Current rural project initiatives, both small and large scale, set up as issue based work are well documented in recent publications (see References and Further Reading at the end of this chapter). Good network contacts can also be made through the National Forum for the Development of Rural Youth Work which has a wide membership of rural youth workers and specialist rural projects.

Using the methods of delivery described above, particular issues explored within different settings have been:

- **Mentoring and social contract work:** telephone networks and key village contacts.
- **Mobile youth information and advice services:** mobile computers, careers advice.
- **Transport issues:** 'Wheels to Work' projects: travel grants, moped loans.
- **Housing and homelessness:** rural foyers, surveys and videos on homelessness experiences.
- **Rural schools and school bus contact work.**
- **Health projects:** peripatetic health information workers.
- **Mobile information.**
- **Education initiatives.**
- **Gender based issues:** young women's groups.
- **Gay/lesbian support networks:** peripatetic telephone and support.
- **Disability:** integration projects, exchanges.
- **Rural racism:** arts and media projects, peer education.
- **Junior youth and shadow parish and town councils.**
- **Other forums and consultations:** environment projects.
- **Work with travellers:** bus, caravan projects.
- **Library mobile projects and literacy projects.**

Principles of Good Practice

General principles of all good youth work practice apply to those working with young people in rural areas. The benefits of effective youth service provision are acknowledged by many agencies concerned with young people. *The NACRO Report* (1997) states that:

Youth work aims to enable young people to make informed decisions about their lives, provide access to activities and learning, help them to develop skills and extend knowledge and experience. Although little of this very valuable work necessarily intends, or is designed, to reduce crime, it can simply by virtue of its own existence, make a significant impact on youth crime by contributing towards diverting young people away from behaviour or situations which place them at risk of offending.

Fabes has listed the key principles of good practices:

- **Educative:** Workers will negotiate with young people what they might be challenged by and what they hope they might learn.
- **Participative:** Young people are active partners and are engaged in critical dialogue on everyday issues that affect them on problems such as access, isolation, acceptance for training courses or work.
- **Empowering:** Young people can take the lead in junior shadow or youth parish councils or a variety of consultative bodies that give them decision making opportunities.
- **Equal opportunities:** The challenging of abilist, sexist or racist comments and attitudes. Acknowledging that rural racism exists even when the numbers of Black and minority ethnic communities are low.
- **Voluntary involvement:** Young people decide to engage freely in youth service activities; this is not forced on them to meet adult agendas.
- **Relationship based:** Trust and acceptance of adults and a basis of support and stimulation which encourages young people to widen their horizons and explore beyond their given circumstances.

The RDC (1998) reviews twelve case-studies of well-funded, high profile projects that fulfil these principles but also recommends where possible:

- the need for strategic approaches to ensure that all issues affecting young people are addressed and not considered in isolation
- building local support bases
- partnerships approaches and networks
- more widespread adoption of previously tried and tested methods to meet the needs of young people.

Resource Implications

The provision for young people in rural areas has its particular problems too, and these are exacerbated by too little recognition of this fact in either general or specific funding. The changing pattern of agriculture and its associated industries has led to rural depopulation, which has in turn resulted in loss of communal facilities. It is obviously more difficult to maintain the community life of the village, including that of its young people, if the traditional meeting places such as village schools, churches, shops and pubs have closed. Young people will move away, increasing the isolation of those left; and homes will be sold to retired people, or as second homes to owners who may well bring new life to a village but not for the younger age group.

(The Thompson Report, 1982)

Resources for rural youth work have usually been very limited. The *Bedfordshire Rural Youth Work Consortium's report* (1997) pointed out that rural resourcing has often been the result of piecemeal provision by an individual with personal charisma working in isolation with weak support. From necessity, rural youth workers have to be particularly skilled at seeking out and making the most of local premises and equipment. Voluntary groups have found it difficult to meet the cost of keeping up premises and maintaining equipment.

The *NACYS Report* (1988) summed up many of the problems concerning shared use of buildings: typically village halls with problems of storing equipment, sharing time with other users e.g. badminton clubs, and conflict about young people's behaviour within the building and following departure. The report recognised that the absence of purpose-built accommodation could open up valuable opportunities for creative activities but that this had to be balanced with the provision of good quality facilities that most young people are now familiar with, such as sophisticated audio visual and computer equipment.

The *NYA Training Pack* (1994) advises rural youth workers to make good use of five main local contacts to resource their work:

1. press, radio, television
2. parish council
3. district council
4. voluntary organisations
5. local authority youth service

High profile projects require considerable resources to initiate and fulfil all the requirements

---

Key Questions

1. Should the project have a limited timespan to see through the needs of a particular group or be of longer-term duration?

2. Could I do more to involve other groups of young people in the local community including more isolated individuals?

3. How can I win the support of the community and get more adult involvement?

4. Have I explored all the agencies operating in the area for possible partnership approaches to projects with young people and asked for advice from experienced rural practitioners?

5. What is the best method of delivering the service needed to this particular group of young people?

---

necessary. Major funders of rural projects may include the Groundwork Trust, Millennium Volunteers, the Single Regeneration Budget, *Rural Challenge*, the Health Authority, the National Lottery, the European Social Fund, and the Countryside Agency. There are also many national and local trusts, foundations and companies who support particular work with young people.

Rural projects have found it notoriously difficult to attract funding, particularly in the more isolated rural areas. Local Authority rural team projects which support voluntary groups may not be eligible to apply for the majority of grants because they are only open to voluntary organisations. It can be difficult to try and form the local associations of voluntary groups who can jointly submit these projects. Smaller voluntary organisations may not be eligible because they are not registered charities. They may not be in a position to develop the partnerships now a necessity for attracting sponsorship, or have the professional back up and expertise needed not only to fill in the detailed forms but also to ensure that they are seen as 'experienced' in handling larger banking accounts that funding would provide. Many projects often require a long time scale, which may be way beyond the immediate needs of a particular group of young people for whom the response is originally being made.

Conclusion

Working with young people in rural areas can be both challenging and frustrating but its rewards are enormous. Young people are very responsive to youth work initiatives because they have access to so few facilities and opportunities for self-development:

When the police ask us if we have anything better to do we sit and think and think: No we haven't.

(NACRO, 1997)

The challenge for the millennium is to ensure that young people living in rural areas, particularly where the rural economy is under threat and services declining, receive their fair share of resources to enable them to participate on an equal basis with their urban counterparts in having access to the services they need for their development. The challenge for government is to ensure that its policies are equally rural friendly and that they do not debar rural young people from participating. The ultimate challenge is for youth workers and others to work with young people to help them gain the experience and skills that will enable them to find new solutions to accessing employment, training, housing and social opportunities all of which may ultimately help to keep many rural areas flourishing in the future.

References

Bedfordshire Rural Youth Work Consortium (1997). *Provision for Youth: Rural Bedfordshire: Experiences, Concerns and Responses.* Bedfordshire Youth Association.

Davies, B. (1999). *A History of the Youth Service in England. Vol. 2. 1979–1999.* Youth Work Press.

Fabes, R., and Knowles, C. (1991). *Working with Young People in Rural Areas.* Leicester Polytechnic.

Hand, J. (Ed.) (1994). *Youth Work in Rural Areas: An NYA Training Pack.* NYA.

HMSO (1982). *Experience and Participation* (The Thompson Report). HMSO.

National Advisory Council for the Youth Service (1988). *Youth Work in Rural Areas.* DES/Welsh Office.

NACRO (1997). *Hanging Around the Bus Stop: Youth Crime and Young Offenders in Rural Areas.* NACRO.

NAYC (1984). *Delivering Rural Youth Work.* NAYC.

Phillips, D., and Skinner, A. (1994). *Nothing Ever Happens Around Here.* National Youth Agency.

Rural Development Commission (1998). *Young People in Rural Areas: Making Things Happen.* RDC.

Scott, D., and Russell L. (1999). *Uphill Struggles: A Report on the Conference on the Evaluation of the Peak District Rural Deprivation Forum.*

Watson, J. (1987). The Reality of Rural Youth Work. In *Young People Now,* July.

Contacts

Janet Watson, National Forum for the Development of Rural Youth Work; Tel: 01335 300668; E-mail: janetwatson@waitrose.com

National Youth Agency, 17–23 Albion Street, Leicester LE1 6GD; Tel: 0116 2853700.

Ray Fabes, De Montfort University, Faculty of Health and Community Studies, Rural Issues, Scraptoft Campus, Scraptoft, Leicester LE7 9SU; Tel: 0116 2551551.

Further Reading

Rogers, A. (1999). *Project Portfolio: A Collection of Reports and Case Studies from Somerset Rural Youth Project.*

Streich, L. (1999). *Alternatives to the Bus Shelter: Imaginative Ways to Make it Happen for Young People in Rural Areas.* The Countryside Agency.

8

School Based Youth Work

Parminder Kuar Puar and Leona White

Key Points

1. School based youth work can be extremely frustrating, challenging and a tiring form of delivering youth work, but without a doubt it is a unique opportunity to work with a vast number of young people, delivering many different styles of positive and educative youth work.

2. It may be impossible to work autonomously within a school based setting even though there may be only one full-time youth tutor. Communication and relationship building is imperative, not only with young people but also with the adult members of the school, in order to maintain and develop a vibrant youth work programme.

3. That all adult members within the school setting do not always understand youth work, is often a harsh reality. The youth tutor and their team of part-time youth workers must be clear about why they are there and what they are striving to achieve.

4. Youth work is ultimately about social education within a school context, youth tutors are in a perfect position to contribute both formally and informally.

5. Youth tutors within schools are an asset, particularly in relation to the relationships they are able to form and build with young people in both formal and informal settings.

Introduction

The policy of basing youth work on school sites offers a range of potential benefits to young people, schools and youth workers...Co-operation on the same site between the youth service, schools and colleges was advocated in the McNair Report (1944) and since then has been recommended in every major report on the youth service. Some LEAs within their community education policies locate youth work on school sites because they believe that their institutions should respond to the needs of all age groups in the local community. Others do so in order to optimise the use of the building and the equipment. (HMI report, 1989–90)

This chapter is concerned with school based youth work, from the ideologies to the practicalities of working within a school based setting, viewed primarily from a youth tutor's perspective, though at times, aspects of the chapter reflect our personal experiences and working situations. We are two youth tutors based in secondary schools one of which is a school for girls and young women. Although one of the schools has a designated space for youth work, youth work at both schools still requires regular negotiations about space in order to maintain and develop the youth provision.

Historical Development

School based youth work has evolved over a number of years, from an initial starting point that:

...In an age of limited resources, the erection of separate schools and youth service buildings used for a few hours each day, each week is indefensible, so that a merging and over lapping of their functions has become essential. Now that we have become so community conscious, the educational campus, incorporating provision for school, youth work and many other educational services is clearly the ideal means of serving a neighbourhood or geographical area. Educational, professional, economical and social conditions, therefore all point to a merging of youth work and the schools.

(Youth Service Information Centre, Davis, 1969)

The reasoning behind favouring a school based youth service seems incontestable, especially as now in the new millennium the emphasis is heavily placed on raising educational standards. However, it is important to recognise that the school setting may not always be the most appropriate place to carry out informal education with young people.

Youth work is principally concerned with the social, personal and political education of young people, priority being given to those who are between 14 and 21. It aims to help young people identify and develop their own capacities, recognise and accept their responsibilities and evaluate the contexts in which they live. Young people's spontaneous or continuing interests are used as a means of achieving these goals, but this does require a great deal of careful planning and preparation by youth workers.

The role of the youth tutor in a school based setting is to provide activities, projects and groups that encourage social, personal and political education informally. This is likely to be far more effective if it takes place in a context where it is understood and valued.

Youth Work in Leicester City

In Leicester City, youth work is now in the newly adopted 'Lifelong Learning and Community Development' approach and located in the Education Department. Since local government re-organisation in 1997, youth work in Leicester City has continued to work to the Leicestershire Youth Work Curriculum Statement.

The Leicestershire Youth Work Curriculum Statement provides a framework for youth workers as educators to engage with young people on realities of their daily lives. It recognises the need and creates opportunities for workers to make a positive contribution towards the social, personal and political development of young people through learning. It also acknowledges the existence of young people and their issues. It recognises young peoples' lives within a multi-cultural society in which there are many forms of structural inequalities and discrimination.

We chose to work in schools because of our commitment to the philosophy of integrated youth and community education. Youth work in schools provides an excellent opportunity to work with a large number of young people utilising various styles of youth work i.e. drop in lunch provision, single gender work, work with Black (Asian, African

and African Caribbean) young people, sports etc. It seemed that the world was our 'oyster', a large captive audience on your doorstep, to which we could sell our 'wares', so to speak.

We believe that youth work can be developed, by ensuring that the informal curriculum of youth work supports the formal curriculum of education and vice versa. It is important to value how the different styles of youth work make their contribution towards discouraging bullying, racism, and exclusions etc. The value of the life long learning process is engaging with young people as a whole person whose needs may vary depending on their membership of a family, community, culture, race and youth culture.

Youth Work Settings

Youth work on school sites takes place in three main settings. These may be categorised as:

1. Purpose built, or adapted youth work areas

On school campuses these are more often than not preferred, as they offer young people and youth workers an opportunity for autonomy. The young people and the youth workers have a space which is recognised as theirs, where information and posters can be displayed, furniture and equipment can be installed and so creating a more young people friendly atmosphere and a sense of ownership which is extremely important. It also allows the worker freedom to develop one-off pieces of work. Such a setting also requires less need to negotiate space for the work; instead the tables are turned where school staff negotiate the use of your space.

2. Allocated accommodation for youth work

In schools without purpose built or adapted areas for youth work, designated accommodation is allocated such as classrooms, a sports hall, or community room, in an effort to support the youth work programme. In these situations it is imperative that the youth tutor has a good working relationship with the principal, community vice principal, premises staff team and all those who share or are responsible for the allocated space. In the absence of established effective systems of communication, youth work will suffer and be marginalised.

For youth tutors working within this type of setting a lot of time is spent negotiating space and equipment. At times, it can be extremely frustrating, as often it seems that work by everyone else is deemed to be more important than yours. An example of this is when the school has large functions such as parents evenings and open evenings that take precedence and then encroaches on the adult programme space, which in turn causes problems for the youth work programme.

3. *Shared school accommodation*

School accommodation such as classrooms, or sports hall may be allocated for youth activities at given times. The use of classrooms for youth activities is often quite difficult as young people may see it as a return to the classroom situation, which may not always be or have been a positive experience. As a result sessions often begin by moving furniture around in order to create a different type of space or environment. It is however extremely important to return the furniture to their original places, in order to keep the premises officers and teaching staff happy! Keeping people happy can be a very big element of the youth tutors' role.

Whichever types of setting the youth programme operates from they all have varying positive and negative attributes. The credibility of youth work differs greatly from school to school, which has a direct impact on how effectively spaces are negotiated. If the principal views youth work as a 'waste of time' then you are less likely to receive an equitable allocation of time and space within the school. It is highly unlikely that the youth tutor and the principal will interpret youth work similarly regardless of the support given. The principal may require the youth club to be a reasonably orderly activity, where young people can go and 'let off steam'. The youth tutor on the other hand, is often striving towards offering a space which encourages young people to share and take responsibility, make decisions with minimum rules and operate a more participative style of working. This may not always bring about that orderly activity situation required by the principal.

Furthermore, it is interesting to explore the types of youth work that may be valued by the principal and the school in general. For example a performing arts group, which devises pieces and performs on a yearly basis both at school and at National Youth Arts Festival is viewed as an excellent piece of youth work by the school, and because it has tangible outputs: the school can see it, evaluate it and often read about it in the media.

However, the small group of young people that have been meeting for the last three years, undertaking small projects and pieces of work, remaining together and developing solid relationships with their peers and the youth tutor, are invisible in comparison which begs the question as to whether this provision is viewed as equally excellent as the performing arts and to what extent is it valued by the school. The reality is that often those responsible for managing youth work and the youth tutor have very different agendas; the managers favour activities which look good with solid visible outputs as they add prestige to the school. Whilst it is nice to have quantifiable results, the youth tutor is less concerned with that but places more emphasis, importance and value on sharing the journey with young people.

For youth workers, their strength is in their commitment to foster participation of and enable and empower young people. In order to ensure that they fulfil their commitment, they too have codes of conduct or ground rules which are negotiated by youth workers and young people. We prescribe to the view that the conduct in the provision should be based on mutual respect as this provides a fundamental premise from which to move forward.

There may be some variations in what is deemed as acceptable behaviour, e.g. smoking during lunchtimes around the designated youth space would be unacceptable and in breach of school policy on smoking. Whereas, during activities outside of formal hours, smoking may not be so unacceptable. Negotiating such variations offers opportunities which not only challenge young people to arrive at decisions which they would be responsible for collectively, but also give rise to possibilities for examining the rules of formal education, the reasons behind them and their impact on informal education during and out of school hours.

It can help to encourage a sense of ownership to the designated space for youth work so that young people may be able to express themselves more freely, and create an environment in the designated youth space which allows for listening to music (loudly), making use of mobile phones, taking part in an organised programme of activities, even taking responsibility for certain areas of the programme and generally being able to chill out with friends and have access to youth workers and youth work resources.

Case study

On a Wednesday evening I have three different types of youth groups running simultaneously, attracting approximately 60 young people. The groups meet in various classrooms and lounges. These youth groups run alongside an extremely large adult education programme, 32 different classes with at least 230 adult students. Although, for the majority of the time, this situation runs fairly amicably, there are down sides. As the youth tutor, I feel that much of the time is spent 'policing the joint,' in order to ensure that the young people are behaving appropriately, both in their sessions and when moving around the school. If a school has a large adult education programme, with a lot of 'fee paying students', the last thing they want to be faced with is young people, being young people, in the corridor.

Often, what the youth tutor would deem harmless behaviour, is interpreted by other adults, as young people being rude, aggressive and unruly. In this situation the tutor is not only the person who is trying to encourage the young people to think about their behaviour and how it is viewed by adults within that particular environment, but also the peacemaker when things go wrong. I often spend my evenings apologising to adult students, regarding noise levels, young people playing football in the corridor, which, if the young people had their own space, would not be a problem. Although sometimes it feels like a chore, I do recognise the importance of integration in relation to young people and adults, as both hold very set ideas and views about each other, which are all too often negative. I think it is extremely important for adults to see young people undertaking positive and educative activities on a regular basis and using the same spaces as they do responsibly, i.e. the coffee bar. These types of dynamics would not occur so easily if the adult students and young people did not share the space.

Role, Diversity and Marginality of the Youth Tutor

Youth tutors need to wear many hats.

This is a comment often heard, but which does not even begin to sum up the intrinsic diversity of the role.

For youth tutors, there are three major strands to their role:

1. Developing working links within the college and surrounding areas.
2. Development and maintenance of youth work, including face to face work with young people and communities.
3. Developing and supporting part-time and voluntary youth workers.

Alongside these principal areas of work, come a series of other job related tasks. These can vary from typing consent letters, undertaking risk assessments, buying table tennis balls, getting publicity for youth groups, shopping for the snack bar, counting endless amounts of loose change from subs or snack bar, to buying £400 worth of shopping for a residential trip.

In most situations youth tutors are required to be educators, teachers, administrators, counsellors, facilitators, trainers, providers, supervisors, caretakers, fund-raisers, mini-bus drivers and of course youth workers! Not only is there an expectation to undertake all of these roles, also attached is the expectation to be effective in at least three different settings; the school, the youth provision and to some extent the community. The expectation for a youth tutor to be everything to everyone is unrealistic and can make fulfilling the role somewhat difficult and even frustrating.

Although youth tutors are based in schools and despite carrying out a multitude of roles, quite often they are not seen to be 'professional' members of staff. This is quite ironic considering that the majority of youth tutors are highly qualified, up to Degree or Masters levels. This erroneous perception is compounded by the fact that staff meetings, heads of year meetings, senior management team meetings, governors' meetings, etc. only reflect the perceived priority of the statutory educational requirements. There is thus very little emphasis on youth work often leading to the further marginalisation of youth tutors.

Whilst some senior managers and teachers say that they value the contribution of informal and social education, the vast majority fail to recognise the true educational value of youth work. As a result this does not only make the youth tutor feel invisible, it accords youth work with low status which then lowers the morale of workers. The youth tutors' skills and youth work style can make an extremely positive contribution to the formal curriculum in areas such as PSE (personal and social education). However the best practice takes place where there is an initial understanding and acceptance by youth tutors and teachers of the differing attitudes and methods of working. It is important that youth tutors are involved with the overall development of the programme and not just expected to deliver curriculum areas which teachers find difficult to do or to manage pupils which the school finds difficult to cope with. In the formal setting of the classroom there should be an understanding by teachers that often, youth tutors have very different relationships with the young people that are present and this should be recognised and valued.

As line managers of the youth tutor, the principal and the community vice principal need to support and promote youth work as a credible practice. Without the commitment and high priority to youth work, the work of the youth tutor will be a continuous struggle and marginalised within the school. It would be very easy for youth tutors to fall into the trap of continually explaining their role to teaching staff in order to gain acceptance and be part of the status quo but we do not prescribe to this way of working. We share the view that although it is important to promote the work youth

tutors are not there to legitimise the work to staff who often think that youth work is about 'hanging out with the kids.' An integrated youth and community education provision is the philosophy of all school based youth work but what has that really come to mean in terms of the economic, educational, social and political aspects? And in any case, who is integrating with whom?

Delivery and Evaluation

Youth work provision in school is as different as the people that manage it. Although in principle, youth workers deliver services shaped by a youth work curriculum statement, there is no uniformity in service provision. Also, despite the framework there are no clear signals from the service managers as to what **must** be provided. Thus, the actual provision depends largely on and reflects the specific skills and interpretation of the worker. In the absence of more direct central line management of workers' provision has tended to stagnate and often does not really reflect the needs of a multi-cultural society where there are structural inequalities and discrimination.

As part of an educational establishment, the focus of youth work in schools may tend to lean more towards social education. School based youth work must be able to demonstrate the educational nature of the social education process which requires planning, reviewing and evaluating work with young people. Such a process usually involves work in small groups, which are targeted specifically. School based youth work, requires youth workers to accept as their contribution, that working within a school based service requires a commitment to the development and support of the school curriculum. Youth workers need to understand the nature of the teacher/student relationships and its relationship to the principles of youth work.

Youth workers need to be aware of the distinct differences of mutual respect and trust, which contribute to the relationships that exist between teacher/student and youth worker/young person and the nature and circumstances under which they are developed. Whilst in their effort to support young people it is important that they remain mindful of the fact that they are not setting young people up. It is all too easy to be influenced by either one's own experiences or even today's reality of education. Young people need to be equipped with the tools, which enable them to make informed choices about the realities of their own experiences in education. Throughout their school life young people may experience many different types of relationships with adults, the majority being with teachers.

The teacher/student relationship is based on respect and authority along with other attributes, which are not debatable. As a result, there is very little mutual dialogue between the teacher/student as to defining the kind of relationship that they may have. On the other hand, youth workers are in a unique position to contribute towards those many different types of relationships, with adults whilst at school, which are based on mutual respect and trust. We are not totally free from authority, we recognise that we hold positions of power in our relationships with young people, but are able to offer opportunities to have positive and meaningful relationships with adults.

Our youth provisions operate as voluntary associations and the young people participate in the provision on a voluntary basis. We feel that this is a significant element, which contributes to the uniqueness of youth work. Our youth provision, as any other provision offering a service, is required to provide to all staff clear guidelines with reference to policies, structures and systems, which aim to support the organisation of youth work. On the whole, we are expected to adhere to all school policies, but arrange our own structures and systems of operation.

The provision is heavily reliant on the enthusiastic and committed endeavours of part-time and volunteer youth workers, many of whom work on a sessional basis usually for only two and a half hours per week during term times. Recently there seems to be an increasing demand (rightly so) from service managers that youth work is monitored, reviewed and evaluated on a regular basis, especially in light of the variations in local authority expenditure on the youth service. As a result, the focus is once again on the ability to deliver services of high quality in an efficient and effective manner. So as local youth services stake their claim to resources they are expected to demonstrate the benefits of social education.

Most youth tutors already struggle to monitor the work due to pressure on their time in fulfilling the intrinsic diversity of their role. Within their limited contractual hours, many part-time youth workers are also expected to plan, deliver, review and evaluate their work with young people. This has resulted in increasing demands on the part-time worker whose main attraction to the work may have been the principles and purposes involved in the face to face element of the work with young people. The rest may be deemed to be the responsibility of the youth tutor.

Many part-time youth workers undertake youth work in addition to their main job. So, whilst they are extremely committed to the work, they are often unable to become involved in the debates about any current national agendas and its impact on the work.

Integrating Youth and Community Work Principles

There are also opportunities in school-based settings to contribute to areas of the curriculum where youth work knowledge and skills can make a particularly valuable contribution, e.g. school student councils. These can be developed utilising youth work processes.

In 1989 Lord Elton chaired the Committee of Enquiry into Discipline in Schools. During the Enquiry the committee also recognised the gap in the education process in regard to the role that students can play within their own school community:

> *We consider the main advantage of school councils is that pupils are able to discuss school policies openly and make positive suggestions. This encourages a sense of collective responsibility.*
>
> (School Councils, starter pack supplement, 1989)

However, on the whole, student councils have been misused. Co-ordinators of the student councils have generally tended to concentrate on the challenges and problems that every day school life brings, i.e. improving standards of behaviour, fund raising, improving the image of the school. Whilst these are important, it is equally important to listen to and deal with issues of specific concern to students in their daily school life, i.e. the impact of a behaviour policy, bullying, racism etc.

Youth workers involvement with the student councils can ensure that the process is educative, participative, empowering and promotes equality of opportunity. The student council offers young people an excellent opportunity to air their views, discuss issues and to participate in some of the decision-making processes of the school. Teaching staff should aim to ensure that the process of electing student representatives is an enjoyable and an empowering learning experience for young people involved. Whilst ensuring this process, it is equally important that the teaching staff and all others with responsibility for the student council share this common purpose. Conflicts in the purpose can cause difficulties for adults, who are unable to adjust their relationship with young people from their being simply a student to their becoming a young person who is actively involved in the life of the school community. As a result, young people often find themselves being patronised, which negates the young person's experience as an active member of the school community.

Positive contributions are also made by youth workers when working with young people who have been excluded or are at risk of being excluded from school. Although the school and the youth workers are committed to the learning needs of young people, the way in which these commitments manifest themselves may vary. The school's primary concern would be to deal with the perceived difficulty and to remove the young person from the establishment, whereas youth workers would aim to establish strategies and mechanisms to ensure that the young person remains within the school system. Almost immediately there is a situation which gives rise to conflict, especially when the school may consider their responsibility at an end when arriving at the decision to exclude. Although youth workers make no formal links with the schools on the issues associated with exclusions from school, we recognise that despite some of the challenges this area of work may bring in schools, many youth workers are active in their commitment to support those young people who are either excluded or find themselves at risk of exclusion.

Resource and Funding Implications

Let us return to some of the main features which helped to determine why school based youth work was deemed to be an ideal way forward for the delivery of youth work. One is the ideology that on a school campus there is a captive audience of young people aged 11–18 years. The large number of young people is hopefully representative of the community and obviously this is an extremely good starting point from which to begin work. There is now in schools a greater move towards social education and an understanding that young people should be 'partners in their own education.' From this premise school based youth work looks undeniably attractive.

The availability of the school campus itself was a major reason for placing youth work in schools, where youth work's limited funding and shortage of resources contrasts with the:

> *Great deal of capital and plant available on the school's campus...*
>
> (Youth Service Information Centre, Haywood, 1969)

It made sense to utilise schools for youth work, instead of having a number of free standing youth work provisions, which would have to be resourced. Schools have an abundance of space, equipment, purpose built areas such as sports halls, computer suites, cooking areas etc., which even the most resourced free-standing centre provision is unlikely to have. Funders might argue: what more could you possibly want?

The reality of youth work within a school is not so simple. Yes, youth work is often placed in schools, which are highly equipped and very well resourced but how often does our service really get to fully utilise the resources? Almost immediately you become the 'poor relation'; how important is your work viewed within the school and does your work take priority over a mainstream school activity or even a fee-paying group? Who gets priority on usage of the sports hall or the drama studio? Often, the end result is that we are in a well-resourced building to which we have limited access, which then limits the range of youth work provision that we can offer. Once again, communication and a good working relationship with all those who share or are responsible for the space is essential in order to ensure that you are able to gain adequate access.

Moving away from looking at the school building as a resource and focusing on what else the school setting has to offer to youth work, things begin to look a little brighter. The school holds a repository of information on young people, their circumstances and their communities, and this in itself is a very powerful tool of support and resource to youth tutors. Although, we have stated previously that our perceived role by school staff within the school can sometimes be a hindrance, the sheer volume of staff that a school requires, with all the skills and knowledge that they have individually is a great resource to be utilised.

Often youth work is based within schools without sufficient funding to run the youth work programme. Most schools have one full time youth tutor, which realistically is the largest resource in relation to youth work. Although the local authority gives the school money to provide adult education, which includes youth work, the bulk of the money is paid to schools for overhead costs such as heating, lighting, caretaking and in some cases, administration. Each school is allocated a part-time youth worker's budget in the form of salary hours, which is all too often inadequate. As a result very little 'hard' cash remains to develop the work.

As with the rest of the youth and community services, school based youth work is becoming increasingly reliant on external funders such as the Lotteries Board, the Prince's Trust, Crimebeat and so on. Unless you are in a school which is fairly affluent and considers youth work a priority, there is very little choice but to look outside for funding to support new initiatives and projects. In the past, local authorities were able to support new initiatives and projects but with persistent and regular financial cutbacks each year, it is no longer possible to rely on this as the sole means of funding such work.

The new millennium has brought with it an abundance of new initiatives and funding bodies all working for and on behalf of young people, in line with the national agendas which are ultimately about raising educational standards and the skill levels of young people, for example, the *ConneXions* Service. Without a doubt there are more opportunities for obtaining money to undertake projects within schools, but whose agenda do you have to work to? Many funders have set criteria which have to be met in order to qualify for their awards, so that it is possible to meet criteria but not really address the needs or the wants of the young people you are working with.

The request for collaborative work between different agencies is also on the increase and in some cases an expectation, if there is to be any chance of qualifying for funds. This may place youth tutors in a compromising position, as all too often with different agencies comes a clash of ethos, working styles etc. However, this is not to say that we should not collaborate with other agencies but funding should not be the driving force for collaborative work. The new national agendas, initiatives or strategies are not really that new, they are issues that have been under the spotlight for a number of years, and merely use different terminology. In an ideal world, where youth work was funded adequately, and valued and viewed as a professional area of work, many of the current debates on the position of young people would be significantly different.

Conclusion

School based youth work is particularly effective when the following is accepted:

1. Where youth work is understood and valued within the school context, especially in relation to line managers, senior management and the governing body, and youth work issues are discussed at the highest level.

2. Where school based youth work is supported by the local authority, in relation to youth work policies, the curriculum and relevant training needs.

3. Where the youth work policy is linked with the overall school development plan.

4. Where the youth tutor is able to demonstrate the educational nature of the social education process i.e. evidence of planning anticipated outcomes and evaluation mechanisms.

5. Where there is an enthusiastic and committed team of part-time youth workers whose status is clearly important and valued by all members of school.

6. Where there is a clear commitment to youth work by the school, which is reflected in its approach to the education of young people.

7. Where youth tutors accept that working within a school based building requires a positive commitment to this context.

8. Where the youth tutor's role contributes to areas of the curriculum, and where the youth worker's knowledge and skills make a particularly valuable contribution.

Key Questions

1. Why choose school-based youth work?
2. How does the work of a youth tutor based in a school differ to that of a youth worker in a free standing centre?
3. How will you work within an environment which often has little understanding of your methods and styles of working?
4. How do you develop partnerships and collaborative working with colleagues in a formal educational setting?

As two youth tutors we have attempted to give the reader an insight into our working lives, the ups and downs, frustrations and challenges of working within a formal educational setting, where the prime objective is that of educating young people formally, preferably to academic level.

Whilst writing this chapter we were painfully aware that at times there were lots of negatives. It is important to stress that although there are many difficulties when working within this type of environment, the positives i.e. types of work which can be developed, the relationships formed and developed with young people far outweigh the negatives. As youth tutors we are in a unique position and in a sense have the best of both worlds because we are able to place ourselves in a position where we can build relationships and undertake youth work in both the formal and the informal setting.

Young people have the opportunity to work and converse with us both during the school day and straight through into the evening. As a youth tutor we are a non-threatening adult who young people can confide in, have a laugh with and gain support in relation to their lives and aspirations. We often have the added bonus of watching young people develop into young adults, in both settings. Youth work is ultimately about working with young people and even in complex situations such as a school setting, the work can still be undertaken positively and consequently be extremely rewarding to all those involved.

References

Dunlop, S. (1985). Youth Tutor Role: A Way Forward? In *Youth and Policy*, 12.

HMI (1989–1990). *A Survey of School-based Youth and Community Work*. The Department of Education and Science.

Leicestershire County Council (1991). *School Based Youth Work*. Working party report. Leicestershire: Local Authority Collection.

Leicestershire County Council (1998) *Leicestershire Youth Work Curriculum Statement*.

Priority Area Development (1991). *Growing up With Pupil Councils*. Priority Area Development.

School Councils (1989). *Developing Pupil Potential*. Starter pack supplement. School Councils UK.

Youth Service Information Centre (1969). *Debate: A Collection of Professional Papers on the Future of Youth and Community Work in the 1970s*. Youth Service Information Centre.

Further Reading

Burley, D. (1999). First Contact. In *Young People Now*, 122.

Carley, T. (1994). *School-based Youth Work in Hampshire*. Hampshire County Youth Service.

Hand, J. (1995). *Raising Standards in Schools: The Youth Work Contribution*. Youth Work Press.

Somerset Youth Service (1999). *Guidelines For Establishing Schools Outreach Work*. Local Authority Collection.

West Sussex Youth Service (1998). *Practise and Partnership Report*. A National School-based Youth Work Conference, Lodge Hill Residential Centre, West Sussex, 7th–9th October 1997.

9

Community Safety: Involving Young People

Joan Bailey

Key Points

1. A large proportion of juvenile crime is committed by a small number of juveniles.

2. Young people are more likely to be victims of crime than perpetrators.

3. Consultation with young people is crucial in an effective intervention as it enables a strong sense of ownership if their views are considered equally alongside those views expressed by adults and professional groups.

4. The enthusiasm of young people who participate should be utilised at all levels and creative methods should be employed.

5. Practice suggests that consultation with young people, if considered seriously, can impact effectively upon the local community safety strategy.

Young People, Crime and Victimisation

In 1996 the Audit Commission report *Misspent Youth* estimated that seven million offences are committed each year by young people under the age of 18. The youth justice system was costing the country over £1 billion per year, and the victims, £2–3 million. In 1997, over one third of all known offenders were aged under 21 and one quarter of all juvenile crimes were committed by just four per cent of offenders, (NCH Action for Children, 1999). In relation to gender, the same report, states that the number of young offenders aged 10 to 17 who had committed indictable offences and been found guilty or cautioned constituted 120,100. This was made up of 95,700 young men and 24,400 young women. In relation to ethnicity:

White and black 14–25 year olds were equally likely to have committed an offence (44% and 43% respectively). South Asians had significantly lower rates, with 30% of Indians, 28% of Pakistanis and only 13 per cent of Bangladeshis.

(NCH Action for Children, 1999)

With statistics like these, often profiled in the media, along with the vivid images portrayed on our television screens and newspapers we may be left thinking that young people spend their time involved in anti-social behaviour. The truth however is that young people are more likely than

adults to be victims, rather than perpetrators of crime. It is important to recognise that 'young people do not only commit crime disproportionately, they suffer from it disproportionately' (Home Office, 1997).

The British Crime Survey (Edwards, 1998) found that young people were more likely to be victims of personal crime than adults. Young men aged 16 to 29 have the highest risk of being murdered, mugged or attacked. In 1997, 21 per cent of young people aged 16 to 24 had been a victim of a violent crime compared with five per cent of the general population. In relation to burglary the survey found that in homes where the head of household was 16 to 24, burglary had been experienced by 15% of the households, compared to the national 6% for all households.

During the period 1988 to 1992, young people aged 16 to 25 were offenders in 53 per cent of offences against Asians and 36% of offences against African Caribbeans. Young people from ethnic minorities not only experience high levels of discrimination, they are also fairly heavily represented amongst the perpetrators of racially motivated attacks. In other areas of discrimination more than 61% of young people under 18 who are gay or lesbian have been harassed, 48% of these experiencing a violent attack.

In addition to the myth that crime is, the virtually exclusive preserve of the young, there is also a belief that young people do not want to get involved in community safety. This is not necessarily true as many young people have shown through current local and national work that they would like to be consulted and can make a significant and constructive contribution to the development of community safety if given the chance.

What is Community Safety?

In 1991 the Home Office Standing Conference on Crime Prevention published *Safer Communities: The Local Delivery of Crime Prevention Through the Partnership Approach*, better known as *The Morgan Report* after its Chairman James Morgan. The key message of the report was to encourage a partnership approach to addressing crime.

The term 'crime prevention' is often narrowly interpreted and this reinforces the view that this is solely the responsibility of the police. On the other hand, the term 'community safety' is open to wider interpretation and could encourage greater participation from all sections of the community in the fight against crime (Home Office, 1991).

The report called for a range of community safety initiatives that would promote social measures which addressed the 'causes of crime', reduced the opportunities for crime to be committed, tackled specific crime problems and helped victims of crime, and reduced the fear of crime.

The report advocated the creation of multi-agency community safety partnerships, run jointly by the police and the local authority, which would consult with, and involve, all sections of the community. The major focus of the report was the involvement of young people in crime and the ways in which adult professionals and community representatives might address the issues of youth crime. The priority given to the consultation of young people themselves appeared, on the whole, to be low.

In response to *Morgan*, in 1993 Prudential Insurance and *Crime Concern*, a new voluntary organisation supported by the Home Office, forged a partnership to support the establishment of Youth Action Groups in secondary schools and youth organisations across the UK. These groups were set up to address a diverse range of crime issues within the young people's local communities. In these groups, young people work with a variety of community safety partners, which may include the police, local authority departments, teachers, governors, parents, youth agencies, neighbourhood watch and crime prevention panels. It is evident that consultation with young people is key to the success of this work.

Luton had already established itself nationally as a town recognised for its good practice in the identification, planning and implementation of community safety initiatives. Established in 1989 by the local authority, with the police and local businesses, Luton has one of the longest running independent multi-agency, crime prevention programmes in the UK. In the autumn of 1996 a *Prudential Youth Action Scheme* was set up in Luton, under the auspices of The Safer Luton Partnership, a branch of Crime Concern. The project aims were to recruit young people from Luton's high schools and train them to deliver drug education in their schools as part of a programme to address substance misuse. The work focused on equipping young people with information about drugs, addressing attitudes and enabling them to acquire skills to deal with difficult situations. By developing effective educational strategies for addressing the issue of drugs it was hoped that problematic drug use and the incidence of drug related crime amongst the young would be reduced.

The rationale for the *Youth Action Scheme* was based on local research and a local crime audit. On the basis of this data, an all-adult, steering committee set the direction of the project, while day-to-day management was undertaken by an all-adult steering group. Young people, while willing to volunteer for the project recognised that it had a pre-planned programme with prescribed aims. The omission of young people in the planning of this programme was partly due to the funding criteria and partly due to the expectations of those managing the project that services would be provided for, rather than in partnership with, young people.

Once the work began it became clear that the young people involved had little idea about community safety or local strategies, and least of all how the work they were involved in might reduce crime. It was through the involvement of the youth action co-ordinator that young people began to understand the issues around community safety. Helen Edwards says:

> *If we are to sell crime prevention to people we have to make clear what it is, in a language they understand, in the context of their concerns about crime and in ways which are interesting and grab people's attention.* (1998)

Although young people in Luton were already involved in a range of initiatives related in one way or another to community safety, it was the consultation process required by the Crime and Disorder Act 1998 in the development of local community safety strategies which created a major opportunity for their voices to be heard.

The Crime and Disorder Act 1998 placed statutory responsibilities on local authorities and the police to work together with others to:

- audit local crime and disorder problems, consulting widely on the issues
- analyse the findings
- publish a report on the findings and seek views on this
- draw up and implement a strategy for dealing with the problems identified

Guidance was given on drawing up the strategies, which were to be in place, by April 1999. The Home Office stressed the importance of meeting and involving young people as 'part of the solution' to crime rather than always seeing them as the problem. The government recognised the value of youth action groups and stated in the guidance that they expected to see youth action groups featured in all local strategies being drawn up across the country to reduce crime and disorder.

In practice, the legislation meant the setting up of new structures, which included a partnership group to oversee the strategy, a forum for people to feed in their views and the establishment of task groups for neighbourhoods and issues. Consultation was highlighted throughout the Home Office guidance notes. This involved seeking the views of people both during the audit and after. The strategy needed to reflect the views of the people who lived and worked in the area in furtherance of the goals of 'openness, accountability and more effective local action to combat crime and fear of crime'. Luton took on the challenge and young people from youth action groups across the town were encouraged and supported to engage in the process in order to influence the agenda. As a result, not only were their concerns highlighted in the report of the consultation exercises and the research, they were also written into Luton's three-year community safety strategy.

Why Consult Young People?

Whilst the Home Office recognised the value of youth action groups across the country and the involvement of young people in addressing community safety it is important to review the reasons for consulting with young people. Though some of these may seem obvious it is worth considering the facts.

Young people make up a significant proportion of the community and it is important that their voices are heard in the same way that other sections of the community are heard. However, young people need to be involved in a meaningful and un-patronising way. Young people have energy, enthusiasm, creativity and commitment that can be channelled into positive causes.

Experience of many community forums and neighbourhood discussion groups highlight the issue of young people, crime and drugs as a priority concern for residents. By involving young people in these discussions their views can be heard and taken seriously. Young people will often know far more about local crime problems than the adults at these meetings. Responses to the crime at a local level need to draw on the wealth of information that young people can supply that comes from their street level or grassroots knowledge as victims, witnesses and perpetrators.

Young people have a stake in the future of their community. They are unlikely to recognise this however, if they are not involved in determining the response to issues like vandalism, bullying, theft and drugs. These are the issues which emerged from the public consultation in Luton.

Young people have access to, and an influence upon, their peers, teachers, parents and some other adults. This influence should be harnessed in order to get crime prevention messages across. Additionally, young people need to be given access to the local professionals and politicians who influence the community safety agenda at local and national level.

The Consultation Process

The consultation process that was undertaken in Luton with young people was carried out primarily through the *Youth Action Project*. At the time, there were 18 youth action groups set up throughout the town. Eight of these were in Luton's High Schools, seven in youth clubs and three in community-based projects working with 'at-risk' young people. This existing network was used to ensure as much diversity as possible in regard to ethnicity, age and geographical location. The co-ordinator targeted particular gender groups to ensure a balance in males and females, and made visits to those places where there were young people with disabilities.

The *Youth Action Project* in Luton had already gained credibility with professional agencies and organisations, along with voluntary groups. Drawing upon this local credibility, the co-ordinator gained the support of schools and youth organisations to carry out consultations with the young people.

An analysis of the Luton data revealed that young people were most concerned about alcohol and solvent abuse, along with safe leisure and play areas. This differed from older people who were more concerned about 'nuisance youth' and 'anti-social behaviour'. The over-50s raised concerns about violent crime and burglary while the under-20s were concerned about issues such as bullying, racial incidents and domestic violence. When asked how they thought these problems might be dealt with, young people tended to favour educational and diversionary measures. This differed from the older respondents who tended to favour strict law enforcement as a means of dealing with these crimes (Agbewu-Lokko and Marlow, 1999).

The lessons learnt from the consultation process in regard to young people have laid the foundations for their future involvement in the town's community safety strategy. There has been recognition that in order to involve young people in community safety they need to be involved right from the beginning in the initial consultations. Young people must lie at the core of this process with value laid on their ability to identify the issues of concern to them, their vision for addressing the issue and the provision of support to facilitate this process.

In Luton this was addressed in a variety of ways. In the first instance, young people were brought together to comment on the draft of the community safety strategy. Following presentations of the findings and the key objectives, workshops were established for young people to feed back their comments. These were recorded and incorporated prior to the final document being circulated. The borough council made a commitment to the young people by establishing structures and resources for town-wide youth forums. These aimed to ensure that young people had a place to voice their opinions, heard about the progress of the strategy and had access to the relevant professionals.

Support was provided for young people to attend committee meetings, to prepare presentations for elected members on the issues of concern to them and to offer their solutions. Once the local strategy had been drawn up, young people were actively encouraged to join task groups to address specific elements of the strategy.

After the benefits of participation for the young people and the community at a national level, the *Youth Action Scheme* has monitored the impact of participation by young people in community safety strategies. In Canterbury and Thanet an independent evaluation found a 50% reduction in the number of assaults, particularly bullying, in schools where youth action groups had participated in the development of anti-bullying strategies. Those schools which had not taken part in any similar projects showed either no change in the number of reported incidents or a slight increase. Also in Kent, a number of youth action groups operated cycle theft projects. In those areas the police recorded an 80% reduction in the number of cycle thefts. Clearly, young people can play a part in the reduction of crime and fear of crime.

Seeing young people involved in community-based initiatives that address issues of concern to those living and working in the area helps to break down adult stereotypes. The view of young people as perpetrators, being always part of the problem rather than part of the solution, is challenged through the positive impact that young people make and the positive image it promotes.

As these programmes have developed, schools and youth clubs have begun to build the community safety work of the young people into their programmes of work. For schools this can mean integrating it into the curriculum, particularly in Personal, Social and Health Education, (PSHE). Youth action groups in schools throughout the UK have been endorsed by OFSTED Inspectors. Young people can improve school safety and strengthen community links through the projects they become involved in. Moreover, tackling issues like bullying, substance misuse and truancy in partnership with staff, governors and parents can help to build a more positive school ethos.

In Luton, youth action projects were being delivered by young people in schools, youth and community organisations as well as by young people who were living in homeless hostels, excluded from school, or on the street. Reactive work with young people from minority ethnic youth organisations, that initially set out to address increased heroin use in particular communities in Luton, has been successful in involving young people as problem-solvers. The difficulties experienced at the outset where vulnerable communities, comprising a high proportion of young people from minority ethnic groups, had felt that they were being labelled, have been managed better through consultation with the young people. Two youth organisations in particular helped to change the view in their communities that a focus upon drug use by certain young people in their community did not mean that their communities were being identified as particularly problematic. Rather, they emphasised that, potentially, everyone could have a role to play in devising an appropriate solution.

Young people from the Mitalee Youth Association wrote, rehearsed and performed a series of drug information plays to their community, in both English and Bengali, to raise awareness about drugs and their effects. The play was acted by young people from the Bengali community in front of their peers, parents and relatives, along with others from professional organisations. This was followed up with information booklets in a number of different languages. The young people presented a picture of substance misuse at a global level and then focused on drug misuse amongst young people in their home country. With the support of the Commonwealth Youth Exchange Council the young people raised additional funds to visit Bangladesh and meet with young people there, to share experiences and concerns about drug use, education and treatment. The lessons learned on this exchange visit helped the development of work at a local level in both countries.

The Pakistan/Kashmir Youth Forum played a major part in raising the issue of drugs in their community and providing a range of educational activities to address these. Young people became involved in a peer-led drug education project and presented drug education workshops utilising a broad range of media. One particular piece of drama written by the young people gained the group first prize in the Gill Blowers Memorial Awards, an award for young people involved in the development of community safety.

The Future

Whilst Youth Action is recognised nationally, the success of local work lies in the consultations with young people and the commitment of staff to support them in raising the issues, identifying strategies to address these issues and facilitating a process that empowers young people to tackle crime and community safety. Young people are the driving force behind these groups. The adult's role is to support them to put their ideas into practice.

In Luton and elsewhere, many young people now feel far more confident to define the nature of their projects. As a result, these have developed from peer-led drugs education programmes in classrooms or youth clubs to a diverse range of activities. In two of the school-based projects, young people have moved to establish peer support services within their school to enable young people to gain the support of their peers in addressing their concerns and fears on a range of issues. Now, town-wide events are run throughout the year in an attempt to raise awareness about substance misuse. Young people have come together to share experiences of their work with other schools and youth-based organisations. Some groups have extended their work from a local level to a national level, while others have become involved in international projects. Young people have played a significant part in the community safety partnership in Luton. Their imagination for seeking out new ideas and resources for delivering community based initiatives appears to be endless.

In 2000 the Youth Justice Board has introduced Youth Inclusion Programmes (YIPs) throughout the country. These programmes focus on young people aged 13 to 16 in an identified area who are offending or 'at-risk' of offending. Luton's YIP has been running since April 2000 and as with all YIP's, consultation with young people has been an integral part of setting it up. The consultation that took place in Luton involved young people who raised a number of issues about their own offending, and that of their friends and peers, and made recommendations for reducing offending in their neighbourhoods. While this piece of work was carried out in only one area of Luton, it is probably the most 'in-depth' consultation with young offenders undertaken so far and it will certainly influence future work in community safety. The target area for the work of the Luton Youth Inclusion Programme is an area with a high concentration of young people, many of whom are from minority ethnic groups. This work will therefore need to be carried out sensitively if it is

---

Key Questions

1. How do practitioners consult and how should they ensure that young people are part of the process that moves from consultation, to action and evaluation?

2. How do we ensure that the young people consulted are representative and that the issues raised are a true reflection of the concerns of the majority?

3. What types of young people have community safety concerns, and what are their 'agendas'?

4. How can practitioners raise the profile of young people's contribution in order to redress the public perception that young people and crime go hand in hand?

5. Should practitioners be advocating for resources to work with those who are victims of crime rather than as the delivery agents of funding aimed at those committing crime?

---

not to reproduce concerns amongst community members that they are being 'labelled'.

It has taken a long time for young people to be granted a voice in the decision-making process. The openness of professionals and practitioners, not only to listen to young people but also to hear what is being said by them and to alter their plans accordingly, has been crucially important to the development of community safety in Luton. The other side of this has been the willingness of young people to put to one side the negative stereotyping which is all too common in the sphere of crime and justice, to enter a partnership with adults, and to take on a sense of ownership of their shared activity. As Khan has observed:

> *Ownership, which is often seen as the key to successful policy implementation, is most likely to be gained in circumstances where people had the opportunity to discuss and alter the policy at an early stage in the policy process.*
>
> (Khan, 1998)

The young people involved in community safety work throughout the town of Luton may tell us that all is not right yet, but they will all agree that they feel ownership of their projects. Even if we haven't got everything right we have proved that we listen, we hear and we act. Now that we have started to involve them in the process, it is essential that we maintain this involvement if we are to practice the true meaning of empowerment.

References

Agbewu-Lokko, D., and Marlow, A. (1999). *An Analysis of Community Safety Priorities Emerging from a Process of Consultation within Borough of Luton.* University of Luton.

Audit Commission (1996). *Misspent Youth.* London: The Audit Commission.

Edwards, H. (1998). Planning for Safer Communities. In Marlow, A., and Pitts, J. (Eds.). *Planning Safer Communities.* Lyme Regis: Russell House Publishing.

Home Office (1991). *Safer Communities: The Local Delivery of Crime Prevention Through the Partnership Approach.* (The Morgan Report). London: Home Office.

Home Office (1997). *No More Excuses: A New Approach to Tackling Youth Crime in England and Wales.* Cm. 3809.

Home Office (1998). *Guidance on Statutory Crime and Disorder Partnerships.* London: Home Office.

Khan, U. (1998). Putting the Community into Community Safety. In Marlow, A., and Pitts, J. (Eds.). *Planning Safer Communities.* Lyme Regis: Russell House Publishing.

NCH Action for Children (1999). *Factfile 2000: Facts and Figures on Issues Facing Britain's Children.* NCH Action for Children.

Further Reading

Bright, J. (1997). *Turning the Tide.* Crime, Community and Prevention. Demos.

Farrington, D. (1996). *Understanding and Preventing Youth Crime.* York: Joseph Rowntree Foundation.

10

Reclaiming the Evaluation Agenda
Gersh Subhra

Key Points

1. Evaluation has to take into account the context of practice. De-contextualisation of practice can result in taking a blinkered approach that ignores the dynamics of funding, legislation, policies and the tensions of inequality within British society.

2. Community work often generates more questions than answers and highlights needs rather than meeting or resolving them. This may not be what funders want to hear but highlighting of further needs should be seen to be an acceptable outcome of evaluation.

3. A core part of community work is adversarial and often a challenge to institutions, policy makers, employers and funders and this often limits the openness with which information is presented.

4. The evaluation agenda can be reclaimed if there is a persistent assertion of the centrality of qualitative data, life experiences and values in community work.

5. Evaluation takes time! If funders or employers want evaluation material then resources need to be made available to generate this.

Introduction

In recent years the evaluation material required from practitioners operating in community work and related sectors has been directed not by those carrying out this work but by external stakeholders such as funders. This has led to a change in the type, amount, scale and emphasis of evaluation material being generated. Everitt and Hardiker (1996) identify the origins of this to be the increasing influence of 'New Public Management', which is shaped by elements of scientific management. This technocratic approach is seen to offer an 'objective' and value free approach to evaluation and supposedly provides funders and managers with data to make sufficient judgements about efficiency, effectiveness and value for money.

In this chapter, it will be argued that these requirements ought to emerge from a shared agenda if practitioners are to 're-claim' the evaluation agenda. This also means that practitioners need to assert and demonstrate the impact and value of the work that they are doing and not just leave it to funders and managers, who often only make their own case. This chapter aims to provide workers in community work and related sectors with a strategic framework for evaluation which involves generating evaluation materials that correlate more closely to:

- the value base, philosophy and methods of working in these sectors
- the ability and capacity of the agency to undertake evaluation
- the level of funding provided for the work
- the nature of the work being funded
- the informal educational purpose of this work

Such a framework offers a more flexible and appropriate strategy for individuals and organisations to begin the process of re-claiming the evaluation agenda for the community work sector.

Historical Developments

Evaluation as an activity, has been influenced and utilised by many disciplines with much borrowing of ideas between them. It is now confusingly, yet fascinatingly, multi-faceted, resulting in a number of contrasting perceptions about evaluation as an activity:

- That is normally undertaken by 'outsiders' ('external stakeholders'), checking up and assessing other people's work practices.

- That is 'neutral' and 'objective' attempting to demonstrate value for money constrained only by practitioners hanging onto process-oriented practices embedded in an anti-discriminatory value base.
- That overemphasises quantitative and mechanistic performance indicators, inputs, outputs and outcomes.
- That searches for accountability rather than allowing processes to develop organically by workers and communities as part of their good practice.
- That is largely summative, 'objective' and takes place once a project is complete, contrasting with formative evaluations which consider developments as they occur and feed into the decisions and practices of agencies (Dale, 1998).
- Whereby its conceptual underpinning is informed by a medical (treatment) model rather than a social (empowering) model (Everitt and Hardiker, 1996).

Thus, many practitioners currently view evaluation as '...one of the increasing array of strategies of managerialism and control of policy, practice and professionalism, in and across social welfare organisations...legitimising managerial and top-down decisions' (Weiss, 1986).

In order to change evaluation from being a tool of control to one that will contribute to the development of good practice, the evaluation agenda has to be reclaimed by community work and other related fields. This should not be interpreted as a plea for reducing accountability to funders or employers, or lessening the priority of evaluation as an activity. On the contrary, it is an argument which aims to encourage the increased production of evaluation data, that more accurately reflects the real impact of community work and also encourages a higher profile for evaluation within organisations by integrating it even more closely into routine activities such as supervision and planning.

House (1986) examines the origins of evaluation by comparing the delivery of social programmes by social services and the voluntary sector, to the metaphors of industrial production. In this analysis he points to the transfer of ideas and ideologies from the commercial sector to produce a mechanistic and quantitative series of concepts.

These include many that are currently in wide use, such as inputs, and outputs, and operational indicators of success, such as cost efficiency and unit costs.

The dominance of scientific objectivity or in sociological terms, formal rationality and positivism have supplemented this influence. This underpinning logic emphasises the importance of tried and tested, objective procedures that result in predictable measured outcomes and frameworks. This approach, it is argued by Dale (1998), reflected the training as well as the needs of scientists, economists and engineers who dominated industrial production. The fallibility of this approach is further discussed by Dale and alternatives such as 'substantive rationality' and latterly, 'life-world rationality' by Dixon and Sindell (1994) are put forward as intellectual and practical challenges. The latter two approaches essentially argue for more emphasis to be placed upon the role of values and interests of the key players within an evaluation that is much more 'naturalistic'. To exclude the subjective dynamics of communities, and interpersonal relations and aspirations is to have an incomplete analysis. Consequently this tension between science and social science goes to the heart of the tension that relates to the shaping and re-shaping of the evaluation agenda.

The historical influence of formal rationality on evaluation has been reinforced by recent developments in thinking about the welfare state and public policy. Everitt and Hardiker (1996), in examining the place of evaluation within the New Right's political economy of social welfare of the 1980s and 1990s, argue that it has been placed near the top of the agenda because of restraints on public expenditure, the need for greater accountability, inspection and quality control. This, they argue, has created a form of 'managerial evaluation' which they fear serves as a mechanism for social control by primarily meeting, the informational needs of public sector management. The repercussions of this trend for community work and related sectors, which deal principally with issues of inequality, exclusion and disadvantage, are that the full value of the work is lost in the attempts to measure it.

As Taylor (1995) says in citing a resident called Julie Fawcett from a housing estate undergoing regeneration 'working on the intangible is the most tangible thing we can do'. Taylor goes onto argue that 'evaluation needs to be built in from the start of any initiative and to be based on residents' views of what outcomes they want from the intervention in terms of both tasks and processes'.

When work being evaluated is about assisting someone who has been the victim of domestic violence by raising their self-esteem, do quantitative outputs really crystallise the processes more accurately than the qualitative impacts that occur diffusely and over an indefinite time period? As Everitt and Hardiker state:

> ...increasingly evaluation of a technical kind is being imposed on projects and on practice for reasons of policy and budgetary control...
>
> (Everitt and Hardiker, 1996)

Coombe substantiates such by stating that:

> Expert evaluators quantitatively separate, measure, and score variables to scientifically test an a priori hypothesis derived from outside the community. Although the scientific method works best for measuring only a few variables under controlled conditions and with a comparison group for interpreting results, it continues to be viewed as the 'gold standard' for producing knowledge.
>
> (Coombe , 1997)

The use of quantitative methods to evaluate, may, at times, contradict with the goals of community work which are to work primarily with individuals and groups that may be disempowered by literacy, lack of self-esteem or confidence or specific skills. To resort to detailed and technical questionnaires, which try and encapsulate a community's experience into statistics may actually add to their feeling of being marginalised:

> ...work by Black staff that attempts to change the way long established white organisations have delivered services and begins to recover this deficit, is essential groundwork but very difficult to measure. If an evaluation framework does not contain the means by which this work can be highlighted and acknowledged then clearly it has deficiencies. For Black workers such a trend has meant that much of the strategic anti-racist work they inevitably end up doing in white organisations goes unrecorded, unappreciated and unrewarded.
>
> (Subhra and Chauhan, 1999)

A historical tracking of approaches to evaluation can indeed be represented by a generational analysis and it is widely recognised that there are four broad 'generations' (Guba and Lincoln, 1989).

Wadsworth, cited in Russell (1998) critically summarises the first three generations for emphasising their technical, scientific or managerial disciplines:

> ...the 'first generation' which was preoccupied with measuring test results; 'second generation' objectives-based and outcome-oriented evaluation; and 'third generation' judgement and decision-oriented evaluation, on the grounds of their tendencies to disempower legitimate parties to the evaluation, their failure to accommodate other values, and their over-commitment to old paradigm science.   (1998)

In a review of literature in this area, Estrella and Gaventa (1998) conclude that the major criticisms of conventional evaluation approaches are that they are costly, ineffective and have failed to involve actively project beneficiaries. The activity of evaluation has become increasingly specialised and removed from the actual work of the communities. It ignores the qualitative information, which could help provide a much fuller understanding of project outcomes, processes and changes within communities. They go on to point out that evaluation practices '...remain externally oriented...attempt to produce information that is necessarily 'objective' and 'value-free' and 'quantifiable': terms that are all being challenged'.

The fourth generation of approaches to evaluation argues for a radical departure from these historical traditions and attempts to locate evaluation within the methodology and value base of the practitioners' approach such as community work. The key features of this approach as summarised by Russell, include:

- qualitative data (narratives, stories, case-studies and so on)
- a belief in multiple realities
- valuing subjective perspectives
- seeing understanding as something different from measurement
- embracing paradox and acknowledging uncertainties and ambiguities
- acknowledging that values inevitably impinge on the evaluative process

The challenge that is provided by the above analysis is that it questions the credibility of the historical approach to evaluation as being the 'right' way of assessing the value or effectiveness of community work. It is clear that such approaches have several shortcomings if they have:

- de-contextualised the work from the socio-political context
- ignored the values and dynamics between different communities
- excluded the telling of personal stories because they are subjective
- ignored how intrusive and disempowering and exclusive quantitative methods can be

Alongside this quantitative and qualitative schism is an equally contentious but related debate about who evaluation is primarily for? Russell argues that evaluation serves two purposes: firstly, accountability to external stakeholders and secondly, promoting learning and development within the organisation. Whilst it is inevitable that this debate cannot crystallise into an either/or, the question that should be raised is which of the two purposes has priority and whose needs dominate the evaluation agenda? The political and economic climate facing the sector, as described earlier, means that the need for evaluation to take place and for funders to show that they are securing accountability and value for money takes precedence over the benefit to the organisation or the clients.

Armstrong and Key (1979) present an analysis of the two competing demands for evaluation, and describe an optimistic view of evaluation as learning being in tension, with a pessimistic view of evaluation as control. They go on to describe these as two ideal types, i.e. 'the learning practitioner' and the 'controlling sponsor' and that the purpose of these concepts should be to clarify for a prospective evaluator, the political context and real purpose of the evaluation exercise to be undertaken. Their analysis then goes on to suggest that prospective evaluators should not be naïve about the above tension, that sponsors shouldn't expect too much conclusive analysis from the evaluation and that managers will be pulled in both directions!

This imbalance towards evaluation being about control, perhaps lies at the core of this whole debate and it is argued that until the benefits of evaluation activity accrue more directly to the community work sectors, this situation will not change.

The debate needs to consider how workers, projects and communities can try and demonstrate the impact, value and significance of what they achieve without compromising their need to demonstrate reasonable accountability and value for money. Recent developments in the community work and health promotion fields indicate that a move towards this reclaiming process has begun with the production of innovative frameworks and documentation on evaluation. Examples include the Achieving Better Community Development (ABCD) evaluation framework developed by Barr et al. (1996), the 'Evaluation Resource for Healthy Living Centres' by Meyrick et al. (1999) and Dale's and Rubin's (1995) work in the arena of international development. All of the above, plus the work of agencies such as the Charities Evaluation Services is symptomatic of an alternative approach to evaluation being developed, that can validate accurately the impact and contributions of community work.

A Strategy for Reclaiming the Evaluation Agenda

What follows will hopefully assist organisations and individuals to reframe evaluation into an activity that is initiated as a learning and educational process and is linked to future planning. Although the framework is presented in stages, it should be considered concurrently.

Stage one: formulate a manifesto

A manifesto which begins to locate your organisation's approach and thinking on evaluation within a policy framework can be a useful way of developing a clear consensus amongst the staff, managers, management committees and so on. The following are assertions that organisations may want to consider as part of their evaluation manifesto:

1. A recognition that subjectivity has validity and that there are different perspectives, depending on your location, relationship to the issues and the type of agency that is carrying out the work.

2. Evaluation does not have to be carried out because others impose it.

3. Evaluation ought to be integrated into the fabric of an organisation as an invaluable planning tool to help validate work, acknowledge effort, shape priorities and generate material for a variety of uses.

4. There should be a recognition that in trying to establish the 'full picture', the square peg of quantitative evaluation and its need to demonstrate value for money seldom fits into the round hole of the qualitative impacts made by community workers.

5. There needs to be a corresponding recognition that qualitative evaluation methods do not aspire to tell the whole story either.

6. Not all of what workers and agencies do can be actually measured or easily presented.

7. Evaluation can and should empower communities and community organisations and not just enable external stakeholders to make judgements about value for money.

8. Communities with whom work is undertaken need to participate in evaluation processes.

9. At the outset, the level of capacity and resourcing needed to carry out effective evaluation has to be a key part of negotiations with funders.

10. The theoretical and philosophical value base that underpins the work of your agency has also to be extended to the approaches you use in your evaluation.

Once the above manifesto is written, consideration needs to be given to how it can be incorporated into the organisation's policy structures as well as how to publicise it to the community and funders alike.

Stage two: assessing the capacity for evaluation

It is essential to carry out an assessment of the organisational capacity and resources to undertake evaluation-related activities by considering the approach, interest, capacity and skills of stakeholders such as the workers, volunteers, management committee members, managers and service users. This includes examining:

● Historically who has had the responsibility for evaluation?
(i.e. was it seen as a managerial task and primarily

located with one person or a particular level of the organisation, e.g. a management committee?)

● How can evaluation become a more democratic activity?
Can there be greater involvement of the staff team, management committee, other volunteers and community members?

● What is the predominant attitude to evaluation within the staff team and management committee?
Achieving consensus within an agency is a key strategy if the evaluation agenda is to be re-claimed and staff and other key stakeholders need to agree about the model of evaluation that they want to adopt.

● What is the level of interest amongst the staff team in this area of work?
If evaluation is essentially seen as a defensive activity that is imposed, then a strategy of training and staff development may be necessary. Part of this could be incorporated into a participative or consultative approach to drawing up the organisation's new evaluation manifesto.

● How does evaluation as an activity, integrate with the community work methods being used by the staff team?
Coombe (1997) in his description of the 'Empowerment' model of evaluation encourages involving oppressed people to identify the problems and then designing and finding the solutions. The model follows a familiar process of:

- Assessment of needs and resources.
- Mission and Objectives.
- Developing Strategies and action plans.
- Monitoring process and outcomes.
- Communicating information to relevant audiences.
- Promoting adaptation, renewal and institutionalisation.

This approach puts people at the centre of the evaluation agenda throughout and is entirely consistent with the philosophy and methodology of community work practice.

- ## What resources does the agency want to commit to evaluation?

Are evaluation costs and time being built into new funding proposals as well as into the priorities of existing staff? What part does the management committee play in monitoring and evaluation activities? Is there any utilisation of student, volunteer and/or secondment placements or indeed partnerships with universities and research assistants as examples of ways of increasing evaluation capacity?

Stage three: the integration of evaluation

It is important to assess how closely evaluation priorities and activities integrate into the various functions of an organisation's routine operations. Examples include planning, policy making, recruitment and selection, supervision and appraisal systems, equal opportunities policies and systems, staff development and training, public relations, fund-raising strategies and so on. Each of these areas offer opportunities for evaluation to feature significantly and an audit may uncover some useful ways in which the profile of evaluation could be raised.

As an example, let us consider supervision and appraisal policies. This is slightly contentious because evaluation has often been thought of as a mechanism for checking up on workers. However it is being suggested here that supervision, as a regular organisational activity should be seen as an active mechanism by which workers can actively generate, contribute and store evaluation data with their managers. The nature of this data can be anecdotal, case-studies, spin-off benefits, attitudinal changes in the individuals being worked with, impacts on deep-seated community issues etc. This sort of material is regularly discussed in supervision, is not confidential but is it called or seen as a source of evaluation data? Appraisals may involve workers providing accounts of impacts that they have made in the preceding year and could include case studies, summaries and progress reports that could easily be adapted into evaluation material.

Stage four: negotiating evaluation requirements

This is a critical part of the 're-claiming of the agenda' process and may probably take some

funders by surprise! Whilst it is recognised that many funders and other external 'stakeholders' have pre-identified evaluation requirements and pro-formas, it is worth putting this up for re-negotiation. Van Der Eyken (1993) suggests checking what the sponsor wants the evaluation information for. Is it, for instance:

- To try and calculate value for money?
- For the sponsor's public relations purposes?
- To encourage your agency to learn and develop clarity about the work being undertaken?
- Just an administrative exercise that allows the agency to demonstrate accountability to the funder?
- That they have resorted to a relatively mechanistic evaluation framework because they are unfamiliar with the type of qualitative data to ask for?

The format, approach and type of 'data' required, will naturally vary, depending on which of the above is shaping the sponsor's thinking. The key issue is whether your agency has been assertive in trying to clarify this or has passively accepted the sponsors' demands. The strategy suggested is one which involves a presentation of your manifesto and the type and quantity of data that can be collected in relation to your capacity.

An example that illustrates this need to flag up the intangible aspects of community work could be the substantial amount of time that some agencies and workers have to spend in building relationships of trust with say, young people whose life experiences have led them to mistrust authority, adults and organisations. No-one can argue that this aspect of work is not essential and a pre-requisite for further work or that it takes time, but how do you:

- Recognise and acknowledge within an evaluation framework, the complexity of skills demonstrated by the worker in engaging with a young person showing extremely challenging, perhaps aggressive behaviour?
- Measure it?
- Identify what its outcomes are?
- Remember the importance of this groundwork when, say three months later the focus is on the more tangible things that your agency is doing with that young person?

The time spent on this type of intangible work needs to be negotiated into the evaluation requirements by acknowledging its importance, the benefits of building trust and that nothing tangible may come from the work immediately. The young person may return to the project six months after the initial contact, in order to do something that is quantifiable for the purposes of an evaluation exercise.

Stage five: monitoring and data collection tools

Monitoring and data collection is inextricably linked with evaluation. The quality of the data collection critically determines the quality of the analysis presented within the eventual evaluation reports. Suggestions to consider then are:

- Whether there is a range of data collection tools or templates used?
- Have time and resources been invested into training staff and volunteers to generate evaluation data?
- What is the quality of monitoring systems, information recording and retrieval systems?
- Is there scope to establish an evaluation portfolio system, into which a wide variety of material can be located?
- What data is being lost?
- Are there systems within your agency that allow the value of this type of work to be retrospectively acknowledged? For example, are there annual reviews that give time and space to this reflection? Are there wider spin-offs, changes or benefits that have occurred within the organisation or indeed wider community as a result of a specific project?

Examples of data collection tools include:

- Diagramming: a visual means, for example, one by which illiterate farmers in 'developing' countries, could describe soil and ground changes, or the use of diaries and journals.
- Audio-visual techniques: video, story-telling, popular theatre, songs and photographs.
- Oral testimonies.
- Case studies.
- Tape recordings.
- Time-lines or chronologies of progress (Estrella and Gaventa, 1998).

A variety of tools should also be used when the results of the evaluation are to be disseminated. Edmonds (1999) in health promotion work with young people, suggests presenting the findings through:

- poster, leaflet, flyer or booklet
- a comic or photo-story
- an article, journal article or report
- a workshop or seminar
- a video or audio-tape
- a health stall in a shopping centre, street theatre or public meeting
- a web-site or by e-mail
- radio or TV

Stage six: matching evaluation activities to evolving objectives

Evaluation is commonly thought of as an analysis of how much progress has been made against the original objectives of the project. Objectives however are not static or limited in number and are usually added to, formally or informally, by the variety of stakeholders involved in funding or implementing the work. What starts out as a single objective can change into a multiplicity of objectives that may actually be competing with each other. This, in essence, represents the fluidity of community work that is constantly and cyclically involved in:

- Assessing needs of community members and groups.
- Re-negotiating how groups respond to policy changes of, say, the local authority.
- Having to re-prioritise because of changes in the composition and skills capacity of community group(s).
- Dealing with conflicts within the group that may prevent or delay the achievement of the original objectives.
- Responding to unforeseen funding opportunities.

Indeed it could be argued that a community work initiative that does not generate new objectives is perhaps being inflexible and dogmatic in its approach. It is therefore important for organisations to consider:

- How this complexity of multi-level objectives is represented within the mechanisms that your agency has for collecting data?

- Is the agency's portfolio system for collecting evaluation data, flexible enough to accommodate these changing objectives?

- Is the evaluation work being undertaken, actually reflective of the actual objectives or does it relate to out-dated ones?

Key Questions

1. How can you demonstrate the impact, value and significance of what you achieve without compromising the need to demonstrate reasonable accountability and value for money?

2. Are you clear about whom you are evaluating for?

3. Is your evaluation process democratic?

4. Are the costs of evaluation built into the project proposals at the outset?

5. How can you reclaim the evaluation agenda and sell it to your numerous stakeholders?

Conclusion

It is essential that the re-claiming of the evaluation agenda is considered at a number of levels within an organisation, including at the level of the community that it works with as well as other key stakeholders. A dialogue with funders is essential if changes in the evaluation culture are to be stimulated. There needs to be a raising in profile of the rich variety of evaluation approaches that have been written about and practised so that the field of community work has at its disposal, a range of powerful tools with which to begin re-claiming the evaluation agenda.

References

Armstrong, J., and Key, M. (1979). Evaluation, Change and Community Work. In *Community Development Journal*, 14: p. 3.

Barr, A., Hashagen, S., and Purcell, R. (1996). *Monitoring and Evaluating Community Development in Northern Ireland*. N. Ireland: Voluntary Action Unit, Dept. of Social Services.

Coombe, C.M. (1997). Using Empowerment Evaluation in Community Organising and Community-based Health Initiatives. In Minkler, M. (Ed.). *Community Organising and Community Building for Health*. New Jersey: Rutgers University Press.

Dale, R. (1998). *Evaluation Frameworks for Development Programmes and Projects*. New Delhi: Sage.

Dixon, J., and Sindell, C. (1994). Applying Logics of Change to the Evaluation of Community Development in Health Promotion. In *Health Promotion International*, 9: p. 4.

Edmonds, J. (Ed.) (1999). *Health Promotion with Young People: An Introductory Guide to Evaluation*. London: Health Education Authority.

Estrella, M., and Gaventa, J. (1998). *Who Counts Reality? Participatory Monitoring and Evaluation: A Literature Review*, IDS working paper no. 70. Brighton: IDS.

Everitt, A., and Hardiker, P. (1996). *Evaluating for Good Practice*. London: Macmillan.

Guba, E., and Lincoln, Y.S. (1989). *Fourth Generation Evaluation*. London: Sage.

House, E.R. (Ed.) (1986). *New Directions in Educational Evaluation*. London: Falmer.

Meyrick, J., and Sinkler, P. (1999). *An Evaluation Resource for Healthy Living Centres*. London: Health Education Authority.

Rubin (1995). *A Basic Guide to Evaluation for Development Workers*. Oxford: Oxfam.

Russell, J. (1998). *The Purpose of Evaluation. Different Ways of Seeing Evaluation. Self-Evaluation Involving Users in Evaluation. Performance Indicators: Use and Misuse. Using Evaluation to Explore Policy*. Discussion papers. London: Charities Evaluation Service.

Subhra, G., and Chauhan, V. (1999). *Developing Black Services*. London: Alcohol Concern.

Taylor, M. (1995). *Unleashing the Potential: Bringing Residents to the Centre of Regeneration*. York: Joseph Rowntree Foundation.

Van Der Eyken, W. (1993). *Managing Evaluation*. London: Charities Evaluation Service.

Weiss, C.H. (Ed.) (1986). The Stakeholder Approach to Evaluation: Origins and Promise. In House, E. (Ed.). *New Directions in Educational Evaluation*. London: Falmer.

Further Reading

Dixon, J. (1995). Community Stories and Indicators for Evaluating Community Development. In *Community Development Journal*, Vol. 30: No. 4.

Feuerstein, M.T. (1986). *Partners in Evaluation: Evaluating Development and Community Programmes with Participants*. London: Macmillan Education Ltd.

Reader's Guide

This section of *The Russell House Companion* identifies the core methodologies employed by practitioners in the field and the uniqueness in their application in numerous settings. It also documents some of the tools available to practitioners in their delivery of social education to further enhance the personal development of those young people with whom they engage.

Group Work

The essence of good youth work practice, Janet Adams asserts, is that the role of the group worker is often the least recognised and most misunderstood. Built upon the basis of voluntary relationships with young people, she describes the key skills required in the delivery of effective group work alongside an acknowledgement of the recognition of motives and hidden agendas that may exist. The chapter is underpinned by a theoretical framework and strategies for dealing with conflict within the group setting.

Mentoring

Drawing upon his recent experience of evaluating mentoring schemes, David Porteous identifies the different models of mentoring schemes and the varied nature of their intention and delivery style. Including direct quotes from young people in receipt of such interventions, he highlights the crucial importance of appropriate support for volunteer mentors. The tensions that exist with regard to the 'professionalisation' of the process and the questioning of the effectiveness of such initiatives in the lives of disaffected young people are critically explored.

Detached Youth Work

Revisiting the history of the development of street-based initiatives with more marginalised groups of young people, Sacha Kaufman offers a four stage model in the development of such work; research; contact; intervention and closing. Now highlighted

as a key strategy within the *ConneXions* Service, the importance of transparent and accountable practice together with the need for appropriate resourcing is well highlighted. The place of detached work as a complementary method to other youth work interventions is clear.

Peer Education

Peer education is not new, but this form of practice has enjoyed a rapid growth in the last decade. Annmarie Turnball explores the clarity of the purpose and target group of such initiatives; who constitutes a 'peer'? Methods of delivery are varied, and the intentions of the learning process, cognitive or affective, must be established. The systems of selection, support and training of peer educators and evaluative frameworks are critical to their success. The potential contribution in the area of equality and exploitation are also discussed.

Advice and Information Work with Young People

Differentiating between these two roles, Cindy Writing identifies a model of good practice for youth workers moving into Personal Advisor roles within the *ConneXions* Service. How to provide information and advice is balanced within the complex issue of referral work and the identification of who is most appropriately placed to deliver such services. Guidance about the monitoring of advice and information services is also offered.

Youth Exchange

The opportunity for learning through the experience of youth exchange activity is well established. However, alongside offering a process to ensure the effective delivery of such experiences, Caroline Tippen offers a critical analysis of the dangers of exploiting exchange partners or making prejudicial assumptions based upon misinformation. From the identification of a need through to the evaluation of the event, Caroline offers the benefit of her experience in an accessible style whilst highlighting the need for on-going flexibility from all involved.

Mobile Work

Early evangelists used mobile vehicles for informal education purposes as far back as the late 1700's. Practical advice is given here by Kathy Edmonds about the determination of the project's intentions, vehicle choice, costs of maintenance and health and safety considerations. The scope for the delivery of social education through mobile provision, particularly with those young people, whose access to other services may be restricted, is identified.

Global Youth Work is Good Youth Work

The role of development education in both identifying and tackling global inequalities provides the basis of Bisi William's chapter. The political shift in acknowledging the global interdependence of us all becomes apparent. Strategies for how practitioners can make the global 'local' and relevant to young people's lives call for the incorporation of the issue into all good youth work practice.

Environmental Youth Work

Against the backcloth of the intentions of Agenda 21 (1992) to involve young people in decision making and planning about their environments, Tracie Trimmer documents her experience of integrating environmental concerns into the youth work curriculum. Through a seven-stage model, based upon the concept of 'safety auditing', the reader is offered a structured model of good practice.

Investing in Children: Using a Children's Rights Approach to Achieve Change

Translating the UN Convention on the Rights of the Child into the delivery of services to young people in Durham, Liam Cairns offers the reader an insight into the obstacles, and identifies strategies to overcome them. He documents the progress of the innovative *Investing in Children Initiative* and its universal ethos in promoting children's rights across the board for public services.

Using Information Technology in Youth Work

As access to the internet continues to impact upon all our lives, Paul Oxborough shares his experience of incorporating this new technology into his youth and community work practice. The dilemmas and tensions that this work generates are explored alongside ideas for practice, and useful website addresses.

11

Group Work

Janet Adams

Key Points

1. Start where young people are: not where you think they should be.
2. Trust that young people will make the right choices for themselves.
3. Think about *what* you are doing and *why* you are doing it.
4. Don't be afraid to guess at what's happening in the group: it's all you *can* do.
5. But don't act on guesses without checking them out as far as is possible.

Introduction

Youth work is about relationships. Its success can be measured through an analysis of the number and quality of voluntary relationships which have been developed between adults and young people within any given area of work, project or period of time. This chapter will examine the most common method used by youth workers for developing those relationships, namely, group work.

Groups provide opportunities for change as a result of both individual and collective action and the effects on members of belonging to certain groups can, in the words of Butler and Wintram (1993) '...transcend the confines of the group itself'. This is the ultimate outcome for the youth worker: to be proactive in the facilitation of positive change which the young person owns and takes with them, independently of the worker, the project or the service. The opportunities to focus on the underpinning values of youth work within a social group are endless. It is the responsibility of the group worker to capitalise on these opportunities for informal education, participation, empowerment and the promotion of equality of opportunity via the medium of social group work.

Human beings live in groups. We are social animals who develop our sense of self through our involvement (or lack of involvement) with other people in group settings throughout our lives (Sprott, 1967). But what does 'group work' actually mean? How is 'working' with a group different from just 'being' with a group? The skills involved are immediately clear or obvious and are not generally understood. How is an adult, sitting with a group of young people engaged in chatting on no particular topic considered to be undertaking group work?

Youth workers adopt other roles, in order to do their job, which are more familiar and better understood than that of 'group worker'. For example, when 'youth worker' becomes 'counsellor' both parties know why each is there and what is expected of them in their respective roles. Those roles have widely understood and accepted names 'counsellor' and 'client'. In a teaching setting (however informal), the expectations of the role of teacher are widely understood. This is not the case when 'youth worker' becomes 'group worker'. The name of the role and the associated skills are comparatively unfamiliar and yet I would assert that working with **groups** of young people is the **essence** of youth work and that other roles adopted by youth workers such as teacher and counsellor are duplicated elsewhere in young peoples lives—not so with group work. This relative unfamiliarity is not surprising when you consider that an understanding of how groups function and their use in education and training has become established only in the latter part of the 20th century and in particular since the 1960s (Reynolds, 1994).

Accepting this assertion leaves the paradox that the most significant role a youth worker can adopt, is the least well recognised or understood. However, the behavioural role of a group worker is expected by those who use youth service provision: even if it isn't commonly given the name of 'group worker'. Napier and Gershenfeld (1993), talk of behavioural roles being adopted at regular times by individuals within groups as creating 'role expectations': it is these 'expectations' that relate to the skills of group work for the youth worker.

Informal Education and Building Relationships

Group work in a youth work setting is the core of informal (or social) education and provides the basis for the building of voluntary relationships between adults and young people. Over 40 years ago, Kuenstler (1954) drew links between informal education and social group work when he referred to groups working '...consciously towards a given end'. Youth work uses informal settings for educational purposes and provides non-directive support as part of the relationship between adult and young person, (Dwivedi, 1993). It is the voluntary nature of these relationships which is so unique. Young people use youth service provision, in whichever form it is offered, because they **want** to. Adults working in such a setting usually offer a programme of activities, a specific project, a sporting event, a trip away: all of which provide the vehicle through which the youth worker builds a relationship with the young people participating in the programme. In one sense this activity can be considered an irrelevance: simply a means to an end, an opportunity or focus through which the youth worker can make contact with young people. But this is to take the youth workers perspective: not that of the young person.

So right from the beginning agendas are different; whilst the young person believes they are simply building a carnival float the youth worker is busy 'building' adults. This is not the only difference. Whilst youth workers need to be a part of the group they must also recognise and own their position as adults. In this sense youth workers are not a part of and cannot be a part of the groups with which they work; their role and function are different. They are 'outside' the group because they are not young people and yet they need to be an integral part of the group in order to do their work. This is an inherent tension, which can only be addressed by ensuring that the interventions made by the worker are welcomed and wanted by the group.

Leighton (1972) stresses the need for such co-operation if the outcomes of the work are to have real value. In social educational terms, real growth will only occur when group members feel they are a part of the decision making process and share in the responsibility of the group progress. The progression of individual self-determination and group self-determination are considered by Leighton (1972) as an inherent problem. However, recognising one's own needs (individual self-determination) and the corporate needs of others (group self-determination) can be described as part of the natural process of adolescence. The skill is in striking the balance so that one can learn to make a useful contribution to the group process, which at the same time develops one's own personality and self-image and meets one's own personal needs. It is this balance that the group worker in a youth work setting is aiming for and in order to strike that appropriate balance the worker may need to adjust their interventions accordingly.

Adopting a facilitative style, taking a back seat and allowing the group to find its own level and work at its own speed may work well with some groups, particularly those which have a history and a maturity about the way in which they communicate with each other, (Heron, 1999). However, when young people gather together there may be those who wish to stake their claim on a place in the pecking order by virtue of their physical strength, (Dwivedi, 1993), and in order to do so adopt a bullying approach to others. In such circumstances it may be necessary for the group worker to take a pro-active and possibly even protective stance, although they will need to make clear choices about whether the bulk of their attention is focused on the victims or the persecutors and also about the type of attention given. An over-protective attitude to the victims may only serve to increase an individual's isolation and a too heavy approach towards the perpetrators may confirm the 'might is right' theory, (Olweus, 1994).

It's important that group workers recognise their own limitations and accurately evaluate situations in order to make appropriate interventions. For example, it can be crucial to recognise the process of transition between 'groups' and 'gangs' which may not be as obvious as one imagines. Social group work is not an alternative to policing or a euphemism for crown control. Use and abuse of power or influence by individuals or groups can be subtle and covert, or 'in your face' (literally) and whilst Besag (1994) suggests there are few obvious, effective, solutions or easy answers, the notion that prevention is better than cure is promoted by Smith and Sharp (1994) who advocate that the most powerful method for prevention involves a group based approach which encompasses the bullies, the bullied and the bystander. Effective group work not only enables the building of relationships with individuals in each of these forums: more importantly it recognises that these forums exist.

Working with a group of young people in an informal environment where your agenda differs from that of the young people, requires knowledge of and an ability to recognise the different stages of group development. The way in which groups end their life can vary between a gradual closing or fading away which group members hardly notice until it's complete, and a deliberate, clearly defined and timed ending. Preston-Shoot (1993) is reluctant to talk about evaluating a group process at its 'end' because most groups within an informal education setting do not 'end' in a clear and distinct manner: the overt task (if there is one) may be completed, but the process continues. The skill of the group worker is in recognising the different stages of group development as they occur, in particular the point at which the group task is completed because this is clearly identifiable and workers can capitalise on this stage of the group's life by recognising successful task completion and appropriately rewarding group members. In 1965 Tuckman theorised four different phases of group development; 'forming, storming, norming and performing' but it was not until twelve years later that the complexities of the ending process were further recognised by Tuckman and Jenson (1977) with the addition of a fifth phase called 'adjourning or mourning'. Where there is a clearly defined 'end' to a group's life, or part of that life, then it's important for the group worker to recognise and exploit that stage for the good of the group and the support of individuals.

Group structures will change as group tasks change, roles and norms will adjust accordingly with the groups changing goals (Johnson and Johnson, 1991), and this is the very core of the work which defines the group worker's role. Whilst this may be a definition of the work, there is no foolproof blue print to producing the perfect group, rather a common sense check list of things to consider **before** starting work and as a tool to enable formative evaluation **during** a piece of work. This chapter continues with the promotion of five key points for consideration at these times.

We often guess at young people's beliefs, attitudes and values based on our own and other's stereotypes and experiences, and as a result we make assumptions and subsequently misjudge the position of opinion of young people. This process is disempowering and runs contrary to the underpinning values of youth and community work. So, how do you **know** where young people 'are'? Quite simply, the answer is to listen. Listening to a group involves all of one's senses, not just the obvious one of hearing. Sight is particularly important in making an assessment of the way in which the group is functioning. Body language is a window to unconscious feeling and often seen through facial expressions which are a potent indicator of a person's mental and emotional state (Heron, 1999). 'Listening' to a group involves making a mental assessment of how individuals are responding to what the worker is doing, simultaneously with their actions. Similarly, when the group is working independently you need to have an awareness and recognition of the mood and energy of the group without having direct involvement in the group's activities. You are more likely to make appropriate and helpful interventions if you spend time making an assessment of where they are 'at' by listening to the group's verbal and non verbal behaviour (Knapp and Hall, 1997).

Group work is about facilitation and enabling, both of which are democratic processes designed to help young people make decisions and consider the consequences of those decisions, for themselves. It doesn't mean leaving young people to get on with it, nor does it mean directing their movements: it's about providing them with opportunities to build their confidence and take risks within a safe environment, this is participation at its best. For example, the pressure from peers can sometimes lead young people to collude with a group decision when in truth they disagree. Many forms of collusion occur in group life and part of the group worker's task is to sensitise members to their own and others' collusive behaviour. This enables group members to have a greater control over their part in the group's existence (Douglas, 1991). Young people (just like adults) don't always get it right, they very often get it wrong, but that's fertile ground for social education and personal development: group work is about **providing** those sorts of opportunities not **preventing** them!

It's not unusual to just 'do' things in a particular way because you have always done them in that way or because that's the way you are familiar with seeing them done. This is not likely to be a problem in relation to the repetition of general tasks or administrative procedures, but how often does repetitive familiarity apply to your responses to young people? When time is short and multiple demands are made on you, it's not surprising that one selects an automatic response which is likely to be 'fired' at whomever gets in the way. The clue here is the word 'select', that is, we have a choice. Sometimes our choices may seem pretty limited, depending on the stress and pressure around at the time but youth work is about building up a tool kit of responses which enlarge the choices we make. We are our biggest resource and our primary function is to make relationships with young people, which are positive and enabling: we cannot afford to waste opportunities.

Group Dynamics and Interventions

Collins and Guetzkow (1964) undertook a number of experiments, which emphasised the close relationship between individual psychology and group psychology. The practical implications of their research indicated that even though it took longer, some decisions were better taken collectively rather than by individuals. This is fertile ground for the group worker to make suitable interventions in three specific areas; the task in hand, the group itself and individuals that make up the group. It is important to consider **what** you are doing and **why** you are doing it in relation to each of these areas. Is the task being achieved: how important is it to the group? Does the group work well together: is there a positive atmosphere? How are individuals placed within the group: does everyone have a role that they seem to be OK about? These questions are not exhaustive, they are merely an example of the sort of thought process an effective group worker needs to adopt before and during interaction with a group of young people.

Alongside these thought processes is the necessity to 'tune in' to a young person's wavelength, or the need to 'start where young people are'. This requires the worker to observe and have an understanding of the group dynamics. In fact what they're doing is 'guessing' at what people are feeling and motivation for taking certain

actions but these guesses aren't made blindly, they are informed by the group dynamics, a strange phenomenon described by Houston thus:

> *Dynamics simply means forces that cause movement. Different people in the group do this or that, and their behaviour affects what others do, and so on. I like spelling that out, as I sometimes hear people use the phrase 'Group Dynamics' as if it means something quite mysterious, and nothing to do with people.*
>
> (1993)

Group dynamics make up the 'group process' which can be defined as everything that happens in the group **apart** from the overt task. For example, if the overt task is building a carnival float, the process is not about what the theme **is**, (that's the content), but **how** the theme is decided upon.

You can never be a hundred per cent sure of why an individual took a certain action without asking them. So whilst it is essential that you make informed guesses, it is also essential that you check them out. The simplest and easiest way of doing this is to ask. This needs to be at a suitable time, either with the individual or the group, depending on what it is you're checking out. It is important to investigate your assumptions as often as possible so that you can decide on the most appropriate intervention and be as sure as you can be that you are treating individuals fairly. Don't worry if the response you get implies that you were barking up the wrong tree, it's not always possible to get it right, in fact it's quite usual to get it wrong. An assessment of one situation may be accurate for one setting but inaccurate for another. When talking of social workers selecting approaches to their client's problems, Ruddock (1969), describes an increase in confusion alongside an increase in the consideration of possible alternatives. Checking things out with young people can cut a path through this sort of confusion.

It's important to allow time to consider inputs and outcomes and to reflect on intended processes prior to starting work with a group. The following five key questions are intended to serve as an aid to that consideration and reflection.

Be sure that you are clear, open and honest about why you are investing time and energy into a particular venture or project. It is important to remember that the process is as critical, some would argue more so, than the task. The danger is

Key Questions

1. What is the purpose of this specific piece of group work?
2. What are my motives—do I have a hidden agenda?
3. Are my goals the same as those of the young people?
4. Are the group's goals realistic?
5. What's the most appropriate style of working with this specific group?

that the overt task will become more important than young people's involvement. When a task is going well it may be easy to forget that our primary focus is that of building relationships, after all a tangible task like building a carnival float can be seen and admired: it can win a prize and be recognised as successful by everyone. Not so with building relationships. The process is slow, full of pitfalls, hard to measure and success is not always apparent to all concerned. There are no set regulations about human behaviour that will guarantee success in the way that they might for the building of a carnival float. Homans makes this point quite strongly:

> But one truth must first be made clear beyond possibility of misunderstanding. There are no rules for human behaviour that apply in every situation without limit or change. Humanity yearns for certainty; it has looked for such rules for thousands of years but has not found them. For every principle it has discovered, it has also discovered a conflict of principles.
>
> (1968)

Simply because human relationships are so complex it is easy to see why it may be tempting to forget that they are the main focus of our work in favour of what might appear to be an easier and more measurable option.

How often do you spend time reflecting on your motives for working with young people? What is the driving force behind your work? Sometimes employers or local councillors put on pressure to work with young people whom others have identified as the causes of a problem e.g. young people hanging round the escalator in a shopping precinct. This is not to suggest that there is anything wrong with working with a group as a result of such a request but rather that it be recognised as providing an additional motive for

yourself. You may not have chosen it but you are nevertheless adopting it, even if your rationale is that of keeping your employers happy. It is important that you recognise your motives and possible hidden agendas. The latter usually represent what people **really** want, rather than what they **say** they want (Napier and Gershenfeld, 1993), and whilst there's nothing untoward about having a hidden agenda, be as sure as you can that you're not hiding it from yourself.

Bion (1974) asserts that all groups, however casual, meet to 'do' something. Youth workers are usually only too keen to facilitate the desired goals of a group, especially if it's something tangible and realistic, but who decides what's realistic? What is your response if, in your judgement, the chosen goal of a group of young people is unattainable but they are keen and motivated and start working together with energy and commitment. Will you be the damp squib who asks the questions which deflate the group's ego, but makes them face the harsh realities of the world; or will you praise their commitment and enthusiasm knowing that they are setting themselves up for failure and disappointment? In their research into the aspirations of adolescent boys, Sherif and Sherif (1964) found that high motivation to achieve often accompanied a low probability of achievement in certain groups of boys.

Imagine a group of young people about to go on a camping trip to France. They have worked together for the past year, fund raising, getting equipment together, organising rotas and lists and now it's the night before departure and all that the young people can talk about is how cheap the booze is going to be in France and how many French boys or girls they are going to 'get off' with. The youth worker has hopes of introducing them to a different culture, food, language, and customs, intent on broadening their horizons, and the young people show immense delight when they discover that MacDonald's is available in France.

This is a fairly trite example, but the meaning should be clear. Don't assume that young people participate in the events for the reasons that you expect, or even for the reasons they give, their motivation may be different from the obvious or from what they say. The question is, does if matter if they are different? The opportunities for being with the group, and building relationships through shared experiences during an exciting venture are all part and parcel of the trip, they are the 'process' bits, not the 'content' and it is the process that group workers are interested in. The example also shows how as a group matures it develops its own agenda independent of (and despite!) the influence of the youth worker and in doing so, develops its ability to make decisions and think for itself in the same way as children learn independence as they mature (Foulkes and Anthony, 1971).

Maturity, independence, making informed decisions are all desired outcomes for the group worker and can be best achieved by using different ways of working. It's important to consider using different styles or approaches when working with groups and equally important to remember that you always have a choice. You do not have to work in a specific way because you always have done. Cartwright and Zander (1968) describe three well known styles of leadership: 'laissez-faire' giving complete freedom for group or individual decisions, with a minimum of leader involvement; 'democratic' ensuring all policies are a matter of group discussion and decision, encouraged and assisted by the leader; and 'authoritarian' where all decisions and policies are determined by the leader.

In the main, it is reasonable to assume that group workers in a youth work setting will quite naturally veer towards a democratic style, but don't be too quick to write off the other two as never being appropriate. The important point is to know and understand the differences so that you can **choose** how you work with a group of young people, rather than finding yourself working in a particular way simply because you know no other. You will also have a preferred style of working: one which you slip into most easily and feel most comfortable with. Beware of persuading yourself that this is the right way to be at all times: you are limiting you choices. Push yourself to adopt different styles in different settings.

Conclusion

This chapter began with a focus on the importance of relationships between adults and young people being the core and very essence of youth work. Intrinsic to these relationships is a strict and unbending commitment to fairness in the treatment of all human beings and a belief in the right of young people to self determine their lives through supported participation in social groups.

In social group work it cannot be assumed that fairness and equality mean the same thing. It may indeed be unfair to treat people equally. The universal history of the treatment of women and minority groups is so imbalanced (Butler and Wintram, 1993), as to justify the allocation of long overdue resources in the support of women, minority groups and the training of group workers to facilitate the education and subsequent empowerment of such groups. Group workers need to do more than simply react to incidents of unfairness, they need to proactively seek out and challenge discriminatory practice. Unfortunately, one does not have to look too far. Social groups, such as those which have been focused on in this chapter will be fertile ground for examples of discriminatory behaviour in all its forms simply because social groups are a microcosm of the wider society to which they belong. Social group work does much more than build carnival floats: it aims to build empowered young people able to take charge of their lives.

References

Besag, V.E. (1994). *Bullies and Victims in Schools*. Buckingham: Open University Press.

Bion, W.R. (1974). *Experiences in Groups and Other Papers*. London: Tavistock.

Butler, S., and Wintram, C. (1993). *Feminist Groupwork*. London: Sage.

Cartwright, D., and Zander, A. (1968). *Group Dynamics, Research and Theory*. London: Tavistock.

Collins, B.E., and Guetzkow, H. (1964). *Group Processes*. London: Penguin Books.

Dwivedi, K.N. (1993). *Group Work with Children and Adolescents*. London: Jessica Kingsley.

Foulkes, S.H., and Anthony, E.J. (1971). *Group Psychotherapy, the Psychoanalytic Approach*. London: Penguin Books.

Heron, J. (1999). *The Complete Facilitators Handbook*. London: Kogan Page.

Homans, G.C. (1968). *The Human Group*.

Houston, G. (1993). *The Red Book of Groups and How to Lead Them Better*.

Johnson, D.W., and Johnson, F.P. (1991). *Joining Together, Group Theory and Group Skills*. New Jersey: Prentice-Hall.

Knapp, M.L,. and Hall, J.A. (1997). *Non-Verbal Communication in Human Interaction*. USA: Harcourt Brace College.

Kuenstler, P. (1954). *Social Group Work*. London: Faber and Faber.

Leighton, J.P. (1972). *The Principles and Practice of Youth and Community Work*. London: Chester House.

Napier, R.W., and Gershenfeld, M.K. (1993). *Groups, Theory and Experience*. Boston: Houghton Mifflin.

Olweus, D. (1994). *Bullying at School What We Know and What We Can Do*. Oxford: Blackwell.

Preston-Shoot, M. (1993). *Effective Groupwork*. London: Macmillan.

Reynolds, M. (1994). *Groupwork in Education and Training*. London: Kogan Page.

Ruddock, R. (1969). *Roles and Relationships*. London: Routledge and Kegan Paul.

Sanders, G. (1996). *The Pictorial Guide to Group Work Activities*. ISBN 0 9517302 1 5.

Sherif, M., and Sherif, C.W. (1964). *Reference Groups: Exploration into Conformity and Deviation of Adolescents*. New York: Harper and Row.

Smith, P.K., and Sharp, S. (1994). *School Bullying: Insights and Perspectives*. London: Routledge Kegan Paul.

Sprott, W.J.H. (1967). *Human Groups*. London: Cox and Wyman.

Tuckman, B. (1965). Developmental Sequence in Small Groups. In *Psychological Bulletin*, LX111(6).

Tuckman, B., and Jenson, M.A.C. (1977). Stages of Small Group Development. In *Group and Organisational Studies*, 2: p.4.

Further Reading

The following six books have been selected for further reading on the basis of their practical application to everyday settings, their employment of inclusive language and their ease of use.

Butler, S., and Wintram, C. (1993). *Feminist Groupwork*. London: Sage.

Heron, J. (1999). *The Complete Facilitators Handbook*. London: Kogan Page.

Johnson, D.W., and Johnson, F.P. (1991). *Joining Together, Group Theory and Group Skills*. New Jersey: Prentice-Hall.

Kemp, T., and Taylor, A. (1993). *The Groupwork Pack*. Essex: Longman Group.

Napier, R.W., and Gershenfeld, M.K. (1993). *Groups, Theory and Experience*. Boston: Houghton Mifflin.

Sanders, G. (1996). *The Pictorial Guide to Group Work Activities*. ISBN 0 9517302 1 5.

12

Mentoring

David Porteous

Key Points

1. We need to be clear about the goals of mentoring and who sets them, particularly in a situation when the young person's needs and wants are at odds with those of the sponsoring agency.

2. The evidence suggests that 'emancipatory' rather than 'correctional' mentoring will be the more effective.

3. The mentoring co-ordinator and the matching process are key to the success or otherwise of mentoring projects.

4. Change may be slow and gradual and a young person's predicament may 'improve' in one area only to deteriorate in another. Sometimes the mentor will have to settle for making things less worse.

5. Evaluation needs to capture the complex nature of the mentoring task and the lives of the young people being mentored.

Introduction

As little as five years ago, a chapter about mentoring would have been unlikely to appear in this book. Whilst there is a century-long tradition of mentoring in the United States it is only in recent years that it has become established in Britain. The Dalston Youth Project, Crime Concern's flagship for mentoring and probably the most well known scheme of its kind, was formed in 1994. The US-based Big Brothers/Big Sisters programme, though founded in 1904, was only imported into this country in 1997. Although in businesses and schools, mentoring has been around some twenty years, as a broad-based form of youth work, it is a new phenomenon.

And a popular one. In 1999 for instance, the Youth Justice Board for England and Wales awarded £2 million of funding for projects with a mentoring component in London alone. Competing with drug and alcohol services, restorative justice programmes, parental support initiatives, cognitive behavioural interventions and arrest referral schemes, these projects accounted for around a quarter of those supported in the capital from the Board's development fund. Mentoring has also been incorporated in central government initiatives to combat under-achievement and disadvantage in education and employment and to enhance prospects for residential care leavers. The *New Deal*

for unemployed 18–24 year olds, the *New Start* for 14–17 year olds, *Excellence in Cities*, *The Learning Gateway* and *Quality Protects* all involve some form of mentoring.

A Flexible Friend

In essence, mentoring involves the pairing of older 'role models' with young people so that the former can befriend, advise and support the latter towards an agreed set of objectives. In practice, it comes in different shapes and sizes. Box A summarises four kinds of scheme by way of example but this is by no means an exhaustive list.

A recent study undertaken on behalf of the National Mentoring Network (Skinner and Fleming, 1999a) identifies seven types of scheme but acknowledges that even within these categories there is considerable variation. Schemes differ, for example according to:

1. the model of mentoring offered:
   - adult to young person
   - older to younger peer
   - group mentoring
2. the circumstances, needs and aspirations of potential mentees:
   - care leavers
   - school students
   - offenders

Box A

Types of Mentoring Schemes

Mentoring Plus

The Dalston Youth Project provides the model for this type of scheme in which mentoring is one component of a wider programme which also includes residential courses and support with education and careers. Matching takes place following the first residential which includes outward bound activities, action planning, games, videos etc. The Education and Careers component includes a college taster course, a pre-employment training programme, job shadowing and ongoing educational activities and careers advice. Mentors and clients are encouraged to meet on a weekly basis for approximately two hours. Meetings may involve trips out or simply chatting in a café; essentially the role of the mentor is to encourage and support the young person to realise the goals they have set themselves within the context of the broader programme.

Full Time Volunteer Mentoring

CSV On-Line aims to reduce youth crime through the development of mentoring relationships between full time volunteers and young people who have been excluded from school or who have offended. The mentoring relationship may last for anything between six weeks and a year according to the young person's needs. The mentors work with the young people on a one to one basis for up to 40 hours per week in a variety of ways including accompanying them to appointments as a condition of a court order, taking them ice-skating and helping them with school work. Because they are full time, mentors will sometimes work with more than one person at a time.

Positive Action Mentoring

Positive Action Mentoring centres on the potential of mentors as role models. Targeted at young people from ethnic minorities and in some cases young women, the focus is on helping them to achieve their potential in education and careers by matching them with mentors with the same ethnic identity or gender who have 'succeeded' in their chosen field. There is no set model for this kind of scheme, for example mentors may work on a one to one basis or with groups, although they are usually based in schools and organised by local community groups. Whilst many other mentoring projects adopt a positive action framework in matching young people with mentors, these schemes have an explicit anti-racist and anti-sexist rationale.

Mentoring with Younger Children

The evaluators of the CHANCE project, which matches volunteer mentors with 5–11 year olds in primary schools, observe that 'children of this age are…probably more open to adult influence than adolescents' (St James Roberts and Samlal Singh, 1999). The mentors spend two to four hours a week in primary schools with vulnerable children with the emphasis on building a trustful and affectionate relationship, developing confidence and social skills and supporting learning. Friends United Network also work with children as young as five years old, who are from single parent families and who are matched with an older adult 'friend' who takes them out once a week. The mentor's commitment is for a minimum of two years although relationships often last a lot longer.

- youth club members
- minority groups

3. the mentors:
   - local employers and their staff
   - volunteers from overseas
   - former mentees

4. the organisational context:
   - schools
   - youth offending teams
   - churches
   - careers offices
   - prisons

Box B

Young People's Descriptions of Mentors

'She spends money on me. She's like a Mum.'

'I can talk to her, with other adults I can't talk about some things but I can with her.'

'I know she won't judge me and that's important, other adults do.'

'I'm getting better at my school-work, especially using the computer, that's because my mentor and I often go the Internet Café, where I learn to use the computers. It's also been good, because I want to be an Air Hostess and we've been able to look up on the computer what I need to do at school.'

'She makes things better, shows me the way to find the answer. I've learnt to control my feelings; not to get into a tantrum. She teaches me to count to ten.'

'Someone who will actually listen to what you have to say, someone in the job you'd like to go for 'cause they can give you a lot of advice and that. Me mum and dad felt it was really good, it got me motivated in a way that they couldn't.'

'We can phone him at any time: he is very accessible. If we have a problem we can phone him late at night or early in the morning, he is there for us.'

---

5. the framework in which it is delivered:
   - as part of a wider 'mentoring plus' project
   - as a 'stand-alone' mentoring scheme.

For those working with young people, as for young people themselves, mentoring is a flexible friend.

The multi-faceted nature of mentoring can be seen in a different way in mentees' comments about what they like about their mentors. The quotations in Box B, drawn from various research studies (Porteous, 1998; Skinner and Fleming, 1999a; St James Roberts and Samlal Singh, 1999), describe a range of possible roles: parent, confidant, friend, teacher, counsellor, role model, expert, even emergency hot-line number.

The Theory of Mentoring

The European Mentoring Centre (EMC) describes mentoring as 'a means of achieving *development and personal growth*' (EMC, 2000, emphasis in original). Implicit here is the notion that everyone can benefit from having a mentor and within the context of the workplace, the EMC notes that from being an activity aimed primarily at 'high flyers', mentoring has been used as a human resource tool throughout organisations: 'it is now increasingly common for chief executives, in all sectors, to have personal mentors'.

Within the field of youth work, the recent interest in mentoring is linked to a commonly held perception

that some young people more than others need a mentor. What mentors have in common, says one project leaflet, is 'their commitment to uncovering the rich seams of ability and energy which these young people possess, *but which have lain smothered for so long under the dust of self doubt and compounded failure*' (Beginning Employment and Training (BEAT) Project Information Leaflet, 1997, emphasis added). Or as the Dalston Youth Project expresses it:

> *Mentoring offers at-risk young people...a positive, non judgmental and supportive role model. For the first time in their lives, these young people will have the undivided attention of an adult, trained to listen to them and take their concerns, problems, hopes and accomplishments seriously.*
>
> (Dalston Youth Project Information Leaflet, 1997)

Here the theory is that by channelling their previously untapped energies in a positive direction, mentors can help a particular group of young people, those 'at-risk'. It is this conception which dominates current practice: the 'Quality Framework' recently published by the National Mentoring Network (Skinner and Fleming, 1999b) is not for mentoring with young people in general but the 'socially excluded'. The government initiatives referred to above all see mentors as helping disadvantaged groups—children in care, young offenders, the unemployed and those excluded from education.

Setting up a Mentoring Scheme: Good Practice

Central to all mentoring schemes is the project co-ordinator and this is the role most likely to be performed by professional youth workers. Their core tasks and responsibilities will include:

- Developing and maintaining project systems and records and liaising with management and steering groups.
- Establishing links with partner organisations and managing the referral process.
- Recruiting, training and providing ongoing support to mentors.
- Assessing clients' needs and organising the matching process.
- Liaison with families and carers and with other professionals with whom clients are working.
- Supporting and monitoring mentor–mentee relationships and managing the end of relationships.

Those with experience emphasise that the project co-ordinator's own mentoring role, vis-à-vis volunteers, is very demanding and critical to the success of schemes (Benioff, 1998; Porteous, 1997). Whereas the mentors will typically have one mentee, the project co-ordinator may have between ten and twenty. As well as providing individual supervision, co-ordinators run support group meetings, organise ongoing training and offer a first point of contact should difficulties arise. It is worth noting that most volunteers will have relatively little experience or knowledge of working with young people and rely heavily on project co-ordinators and on each other for practical advice and emotional support.

A flurry of handbooks and guidance on setting up mentoring projects has been produced over the last three years, some of which are listed at the end of this chapter. In the broadest terms, the implementation of a mentoring project involves three phases:

1. Establishing the structure and organisation of the scheme

Setting up partnership arrangements, recruitment of staff, definition of aims, objectives and activities, developing office space etc., defining procedures and designing forms for assessment, referral, monitoring etc.

2. Recruitment, selection and training of mentors and mentees

Involving on the one hand advertisement, open days, interviews, screening including police checks and initial training and on the other developing links with referral agencies, securing parental consent, undertaking needs assessments, running introductory sessions etc.

3. Matching, ongoing training, support and related activities

The matching process may involve residential weekends and the initial meeting between mentor and mentee will be facilitated by the project co-ordinator. The mentoring relationship will often take place in the context of a wider programme of activities for mentees, involving education and any training, structured leisure time, health awareness and prevention etc.

A fuller outline of this process together with good practice guidelines is given in Box C. This summarises the 'thirty core principles' identified in the National Mentoring Network's Quality Framework. Drawing on a study of 46 mentoring projects, the guidelines are structured so as to inform the mentoring process from start to finish. It is noteworthy that several of these principles—clarity of aims and objectives, the careful targeting of clients, inter-agency collaboration, a needs-led approach, attendance to health and safety issues, the importance of training and of evaluation—could be equally well applied to youth work or indeed to public services in general.

Box C

Thirty Core Principles for Mentoring Projects

1. Projects should make a clear commitment to a high quality service.
2. Projects should have a clear rationale and specific expectations of what it will deliver.
3. There should be clear criteria for the referral of clients.
4. Selection and screening criteria for clients should be clear and explicit.

5. Projects should secure the commitment and involvement of staff in other agencies.
6. Sufficient staff should be employed such that the ongoing support of young people and mentors is separate from overall management.
7. Participation for clients should be voluntary.
8. There should be clear criteria for the recruitment of mentors.
9. There should be equal opportunities in recruitment.
10. There should be an induction programme for clients.
11. Mentors should be subject to an effective screening process and a probationary period.
12. Pre-programme training for mentors is essential.
13. There should be shared agreement between young people and mentors concerning their commitment and responsibilities.
14. There should be shared understanding between young people and mentors about acceptable boundaries.
15. Parents and carers should be involved where possible and desirable.
16. The length of the mentoring programme should be determined by the young people's needs.
17. The matching process must involve a face to face meeting between the young person, the mentor and the worker making the match. It should reflect the mentor's qualities, the young person's needs, be participative if possible and allow for choice.
18. Action plans should be agreed at the outset of the mentoring relationship.
19. The length and location of meetings between young people and mentors should be negotiable and flexible according to need.
20. The costs incurred by mentors and young people should be reimbursed by projects up to an agreed level.
21. Written records of meetings should be kept and ideally shared and agreed by the young person and their mentor.
22. The welfare of young people should be continually monitored and they should have access to a specialist worker. Clear guidelines are required about contact between mentors and young people in between sessions
23. There should be ongoing support and supervision for mentors.
24. There should be clear procedures and training on child protection matters.
25. There should be clear policies and procedures on health and safety.
26. Young people and mentors should contribute to project design and running.
27. Clear guidance should be given to both parties on ending the mentoring relationship.
28. Outcomes should be measured against action plans and take in different perspectives.
29. Evaluation is essential.
30. Successful graduates of mentoring schemes should be enabled to share their insights and skills.

(Adapted from Skinner and Fleming, 1999b)

Within this overall framework of good practice, there remain a number of potential tensions, which need to be resolved at a practice level. The first concerns the referral, selection and screening out of young people and applies to projects targeted at those who are 'socially excluded' or 'at risk'. To quote from the Youth Justice Board Guidance Notes (1999), 'Some young people will not want or need a mentor, others may have multiple problems so deeply entrenched that a volunteer mentor proves ineffective'. The problem for practitioners is that they have to balance the need to identify people who have sufficient problems to justify intervention with the fact that a significant number of this carefully targeted client group may be inappropriate candidates for the scheme. The other side of the coin is that some young people who could benefit from mentoring may miss out because they are not sufficiently deprived. One way out of this dilemma is to target under-achievement rather than problematic behaviour but this itself is difficult—we are all under-achievers in some ways.

A second tension concerns the extent to which the mentoring process should be 'professionalised'. Although, as the comments in Box B highlight, mentors may perform roles akin to that of parents, teachers and counsellors, a central tenet of mentoring is that they are *not* any of these things. Indeed one of the ironies of mentoring as a method of youth work is that it calls upon paid workers to 'leave it to the amateurs'—because, the theory goes, volunteers are untainted by the authority or status which can serve as a barrier to trust and friendship between young people and adults in professional contexts. At the same time, good practice guidelines inject a significant degree of professionalism into the mentoring process, through their insistence upon clarity of goals, rigorous procedures for the recruitment and training of mentors, action planning, record keeping and so on. I do not want to suggest that these are unimportant or unnecessary, on the contrary, but simply that there may be some dissonance between the friendship dimension in mentoring on the one hand and on the other the pressures on projects to be structured and rule governed.

For mentors there can be some tension between their friendship with young people and their responsibilities to the wider project and its partners. For example in relationships that 'work', young people may well divulge information about themselves which they do not wish to be passed on. If this information suggests that the young person may be at risk of significant harm, however, mentors may well be obliged to report it to the appropriate authority, which in turn risks upsetting their relationship with their mentee. A slightly different problem is where the mentor identifies with and takes on their client's frustration with other adults, be they parents or professionals, to the point where they are in conflict with the very organisations and people who have enlisted their help. Training on issues of confidentiality, child protection, setting boundaries, and contacts with other agencies are identified in practice guidelines as essential, because it is recognised that these dilemmas will arise, are unavoidable and have to be managed on a case by case basis.

At a more general level, John Pitts has identified a tension between 'emancipatory' mentoring, 'born of a critique of an inequitable social order', and 'correctional' mentoring which 'finds the origins of such 'social exclusion' within the person being mentored (2000). This refers to the way in which mentoring has, at least at the level of policy, been transformed from a developmental tool for disadvantaged and marginalised young people into a device for correcting 'those shortcomings in the 'client' which prevent them from entering the social, economic or moral mainstream'. Importantly, evaluative studies (see below) provide reasons to believe that the emancipatory model is the more effective.

Inter-agency Working

It is the norm for mentoring projects to operate in a partnership framework. The DIVERT Trust's

mentoring handbook, for example, cites three key partners in one of the schemes it sponsors:

1. The Westminster Youth Service line managed the project.
2. The DIVERT Trust raised funds for the project and offered good practice guidance, mentor support, training and advice.
3. The schools provided the accommodation and the young people.

In addition to those agencies with a direct stake in the project, other organisations may be involved in various ways and at different stages. For example, local community groups and businesses offer one source for the recruitment of mentors; a range of voluntary and statutory service providers will have clients whom they could refer to the project; outward bound centres offer residential facilities; professionals in different fields can provide mentor training; and university researchers might be invited to conduct an evaluation. Good practice suggests that steering or advisory groups assembled from the managers of participating agencies provide a means of ensuring their commitment and resources as well as offering a source of guidance should conflicts of interest arise.

Resources

The cost of mentoring projects varies widely according to the nature of the scheme. However, there is a consensus that at least one full time project co-ordinator is required, often with additional administrative support. As indicated above, inter-agency working allows for some project costs to be absorbed in the normal budgets of partner agencies. However, it is not clear at this time how the large number of new projects which have recently received funding for new projects will be resourced in the future. The economics, in every sense, of mentoring will come into sharper focus when statutory youth services are forced to finance core functions from within their own budgets rather than government grants.

Evaluation

Monitoring and evaluation are now routinely included in Good Practice guidelines with funding bodies making it a condition that procedures and resources are in place for this purpose. The key question is how to measure the effectiveness of mentoring. In my own work for example, I have found cases where the mentor's input has been helpful and yet the mentee's situation has remained relatively unchanged or even deteriorated because of extenuating circumstances.

Although mentoring has been presented in the media and by politicians as a solution to a whole manner of ills, mentors are more circumspect:

> It's little steps towards it, it's gradual and more of a long term process. For example you can take pleasure from the fact that the young person no longer drops litter in the street, because you repeatedly told them not to. The young person is generally disaffected by the time they get on the scheme, so it could take months or even years, but it's little steps. (quoted in Porteous, 1998)

In evaluating the 'little steps', researchers usually seek to obtain the perspectives of different parties to the mentoring process through the use of questionnaires and interviews. It is also important to verify the length and the intensity of contact between mentor and mentee by examining mentor diaries and other project records. As important as the methods chosen, however, is the spirit in which evaluation is conducted. In an environment where (relatively short term) funding is contingent on the realisation of measurable outputs and outcomes, the pressure on projects and researchers (who may not be asked back!) to report and highlight successes, and overlook failings, needs to be resisted.

Conclusion

Without honest and *realistic* (Pawson and Tilley, 1997) evaluation, the danger is that, in the longer term, we might be setting up mentoring to fail. For example, whilst mentoring projects targeted at youngsters assessed as 'at risk' are currently those most likely to receive government funding, there is little to suggest that mentoring is most effective with this group. Indeed, evaluative studies (Porteous, 1998; Crimmens and Storr, 1998) have suggested that the 'at riskiness' of young people is negatively correlated with the success of the mentoring relationship—the more problematic the young person's circumstances, the less likely the relationship is to work. The theory that mentoring can enhance personal development is born out by the evidence. The promise that it can make a significant impact upon problematic behaviour is more suspect. Such findings raise important questions about to whom mentoring should be targeted, about the causes of disaffection amongst more difficult client groups and about what other methods, policies etc. might be deployed to meet their needs.

Key Questions

1. What is role-modelling? What is a role model? Is the mentor's job to make the young person more like them or more like themselves?
2. What do I do if what the young person wants is at odds with the project goals?

References

BEAT (1996/7). *Beginning Employment and Training.* Project Information. BEAT.

Crimmens, D., and Storr, F. (1998). *The Hull Compact Mentoring Programme: An Evaluation.* Humberside Education Business Partnership and Hull Compact Ltd.

Dalston Youth Project (1996/97). *Project Information.* Dalston Youth Project.

Pawson, and Tilley (1997). *Realistic Evaluation.* London: Sage.

Pitts, J. (2000). Review of Mentoring Research. In *Research Matters*, April–October 2000.

Porteous, D. (1997). *Befriender Mentoring in Camden: A Feasibility Study.* University of Luton.

Porteous, D. (1998). *Evaluation of the CSV On Line Mentoring Scheme.* London: Community Service Volunteers.

Skinner, A., and Fleming, J. (1999a). *Mentoring Socially Excluded Young People.* Manchester: National Mentoring Network.

Skinner, A., and Fleming, J. (1999b). *Quality Framework for Mentoring with Socially Excluded Young People.* Manchester: National Mentoring Network.

St James Roberts, I., and Samlal Singh, C. (1999). *Using Mentors to Change Problem Behaviour in Primary School Children.*

Research, Development and Statistics Directorate Research Findings No. 95. London: Home Office.

Youth Justice Board (1999). *Mentoring Guidance Notes.* London: Youth Justice Board.

Useful web-sites:

National Mentoring Network: www.nmn.org.uk
European Mentoring Network: www.mentoringcentre.org

Further Reading

For guidelines on setting up new projects:

Benioff, S. (1997). *A Second Chance.* Swindon: Crime Concern.

DIVERT Trust (undated). *DIVERT Mentoring Handbook.* London: The DIVERT Trust.

For a review and summary of best practice in mentoring:

Skinner, A., and Fleming, J. (1999a). *Mentoring Socially Excluded Young People.* Manchester: National Mentoring Network.

Evaluative Studies:

Royce, D. (1998). Mentoring high risk minority youth: evaluation of the Brothers Project. In *Adolescence*, 33(129): pp. 145–158

13

Detached Youth Work

Sacha Kaufman

Key Points

1. Reconnaissance—familiarise yourself with the area, resources, and other professionals.

2. Identify aims, objectives and time limits, to keep your work focused. Make recordings and evaluation reports creative.

3. Be prepared to negotiate, acknowledge young people's involvement and share practice.

4. Establish an effective working relationship with young people, colleagues and managers, address boundaries and expectations. Be open about the reasons for your presence.

5. The youth worker is required to work as part of a team and in partnership with relevant agencies; however partnership work requires careful planning to be successful.

Introduction

This chapter is primarily about a 'purist' style of detached work. Many confuse detached work with outreach work, although many of the principles are similar. Detached work operates without a centre on the streets where young people 'are at' geographically and developmentally. Centre-based or project workers often undertake outreach work in their communities or in young people's homes as a method of contacting young people 'at risk' i.e. those homebound, with different abilities, or for cultural reasons such as Asian young women, Lesbian and Gay young people.

Detached youth work however, is a method of delivering informal or social education. The approach adopted is that of working with young people 'where they are at', in a physical sense e.g. on housing estates, in parks, on the streets. It is sometimes perceived as superior, cheaper or more effective, whereas it should be seen as complementary to other provisions. It is concerned with the needs that are presented to, or perceived by youth workers and has its basis in building supportive relationships, trust and a clear understanding of confidentiality.

Rural detached work also differs from urban work in terms of issues such as:

- poverty
- isolation
- lack of transport
- access to public and commercial provision
- employment and education opportunities
- restrictions on knowledge or information

Additional references on the rural dimension to youth work can be found in the bibliography.

History

Detached youth work in Britain was first written about by Mary Morse in *The Unattached* (1965) and then in Goetschius' and Tash's *Working with Unattached Youth* (1967). Obviously, much practice was informed by the earlier sociological research undertaken on youth subcultures and in particular street gangs in the States (Thrasher, 1963; Whyte, 1943; Maguire et al., 1997). As Pearson (1983) indicates, youth on the streets have always attracted a disproportionate amount of attention, in particular for their deviant behaviour, dating back as far as the early 1600s when organised gangs dominated the streets of London and other major cities.

From the turn of the century workers were targeting young people 'at risk' to encourage them away from crime or immorality and into employment and the army. Despite this trend, surprisingly little analysis of such youthful motivation has been undertaken in Britain (Maguire, 1997). Parker's (1974) was the first study undertaken into the reality of 'joy-riding' in an inner city area, and a greater understanding of the violence amongst female gangs was identified by Campbell's *The Girls in the Gang* (1984). Such studies have provided policy makers and practitioners with the opportunity to examine the services they deliver on the street to groups of young people. However, much work is still developed as a reactive response to local issues and national policy priorities.

Keele University research into the youth service in 1974, found that 43 out of 86 local authorities were undertaking detached work. During the financial difficulties of the youth service during the 1980s, detached work became more mainstreamed, (possibly seen as a cheap alternative), and by 1998, all but one local education authorities were using detached work (Davies, 1999).

Detached youth work is once again widely recognised as a method of contact with those not willing or able to take up centre-based provision and for tackling social problems in deprived areas. For some it is seen as a cheap alternative to youth club or centres and as an effective way to combat crime and unemployment. By the mid 1990s, it was considered a useful method to work with disruptive and disadvantaged youths; most of the detached work in London focused on drug misuse, crime prevention, racial harassment and sexual health, often linked to key government strategies of the time, e.g. 10 Year Drugs Strategy, Crime and Disorder Act 1998. The national Youth Service Audit 1998, acknowledged detached youth work as reaching and engaging older young people and the 'disaffected'. The present government has acknowledged detached work as an effective mechanism of contacting young people, by recommending that they be placed in the new *ConneXions Strategy* as key deliverers of the new Youth Support Service (DfEE, 2000).

The detached youth workers conference was an annual event at Keele University from the 1960s. This event, whilst historically and professionally useful for some, became the focus of much discord during the 1980s and led to the establishment of other more suitable arenas for professional debate. The *Black Detached Workers Statement* was developed and published in 1990 (NYA). From the early 1990s, the conference organisation shifted, and the National Federation of Detached Youth Workers was established.

As young people choose to congregate on the streets, estates, open spaces, parks etc. youth workers have identified the need for different methods of delivering social education. In some

areas other agencies have also understood the value of this way of working and contributed resources. With estimates of 3 in 10 young people using the youth service, detached youth workers are viewed as one of the only key professional groups able to contact and develop relationships with the unattached and over-16s.

Following the introduction of the Crime and Disorder Act 1998, Home Office Minister of State, Alun Michael, produced a paper on how detached youth workers would be affected and could contribute to its delivery (Michael, 1998). Throughout its history detached youth work has battled to develop universal guidelines and policies and a coherent method of ensuring quality and consistency. Pressure from numerous sources creates new detached work initiatives and projects, whilst individual managers and workers continue to grapple with their aims and strategies to develop their teams and their work with young people.

Planning and Delivery

Working with young people on their 'territory' requires careful negotiation since it is the young peoples' space into which the worker is entering. The work starts with a non-judgmental approach to establish contact and build up relationships. In order for positive, trusting relationships to develop the youth workers need to continually negotiate with the young people.

Equal opportunities should feature throughout delivery across all areas including recruitment and selection, access to training and curriculum planning. Care should be taken that staff are appropriate for groups with whom they are expected to engage in terms of ethnicity, sexuality, ability, gender, culture, as well as being sensitively deployed. Statements on all publicity should reflect your intentions, and policies should be in place and include strategies for challenging inappropriate attitudes and behaviours as well as awareness raising.

The relative autonomy of detached work demands that it be planned and structured in a conscious and deliberate manner. Detached youth workers operate in unconfined spaces without any claim to authority over the people they meet. Therefore the need for clear aims and guidelines, together with an organised approach is fundamental to the work, as is the need for explicit professional boundaries. There are four key stages to carrying through detached youth work:

1. Reconnaissance, mapping, research

This stage provides the opportunity for workers to build up a picture of their area without making contact with young people. This time should be used to get to know the area: visit local facilities, both commercial and community, i.e. shops, laundrettes, cafes, pubs, arcades, sports centres, youth clubs. Identify key agencies and individuals in the area, i.e. police, housing, community centres, libraries, caretakers, park keepers, youth provision, schools, health centres, drug projects. In addition, make contact with and introduce yourself to key individuals to get their views and opinions, and other information, and to explain what you are doing. Walk around the area and check out alleyways, dead ends, underground car parks, walkways, open spaces, 'cut throughs', stairwells, garages, play areas and structures, football pitches.

This research should occur at different times of the week, initially during the daylight in order to begin the process of risk assessment. Then at night, noting where visibility is good and bad. Observation skills are vital: identify and read graffiti, note where debris is clustered, e.g. cigarette ends, cans, food wrappers, and drug paraphernalia etc. Take note of where phone boxes are. Take note of any groups seen, their gender, age, ethnicity, disability, sexuality, study and/or employment status. How many are doing what? where? when? Good records need to be kept about what is seen but sensitivity about when and where workers make notes is needed. Suggested headings for a reconnaissance recording form would include:

- Staff
- Conditions
- Date
- Place
- Time
- Observations
- Comments
- General impression or recommendations

If contact does occur or there is pressure from others to start work, no commitments should be made until a reconnaissance report has been completed, which should include areas or groups to be prioritised. This process can take several months and requires an open mind.

A reconnaissance report should attempt to include the following:

- History and background: why was the area identified in the first place?
- Area: buildings, roads, estates, and shopping areas.
- Observations: what? when?
- What others said: Police/youth club/shopkeeper/residents/caretaker etc.
- Recommendations: places/times/groups/ issues/inter-agency support required.
- Intended outcomes and timescale.

Once a project has been running for a while further reconnaissance may be needed. If new members of staff are recruited some reconnaissance should form part of their induction.

2. Making contact

Just by being around an area people would have already noticed youth workers. Also, you are recommended to drop into local youth clubs, community centres, open tenants meetings and any other places that members of the community are likely to frequent. Actually initiating the befriending process can occur in a number of ways, though sometimes an opportunity will occur naturally: an incident on the streets; a member of the community may invite you to speak to young people; young people may approach you on the streets.

On the other hand none of the above may occur and you will have to be proactive and make 'cold contact'. You could walk up and just say 'We are detached youth workers, you've probably seen us about and so we just wanted to introduce ourselves...' or make it more casual: eye contact; smiling; nodding; saying 'hi'. Alternatively some people prefer to use a 'tool' such as a project card to introduce themselves, others may use some information about something they believe the young people may be interested in e.g. a skateboard park, an event such as a local rave, sports sessions or an employment and training fair.

Another tool could be a questionnaire about young people's views or needs. There might be a national event with resources that you could give to young people i.e. National Youth Work Week,

National Condom Week, No Smoking Day, International Women's Week, Black History Month. Raising the project's profile can also aid the process of making contact: 'you may have seen our poster in the chip shop or newsagents?' and lots of other methods and strategies can be developed and tested.

Sometimes workers can receive a frosty reception and encounter wariness until a level of trust can be built up. Workers should be open about who they are and their reasons for being there. This will usually lead to discussions about the work and negotiations around future contact. Regular times and places that workers can be met can be key to developing relationships.

During the initial contact phase, limitations and boundaries are negotiated and tested, this is an ongoing process and as detached youth workers cannot refer to their policies the same way centre-based workers can point out the rules displayed on the wall of the youth club, the skills of negotiation, explanation and discussion around issues are explored. It is important that workers are not tempted to 'buy' the trust of young people by offering resources immediately. This does not usually lead to honest relationships and although young people may expect or ask for 'trips out' a speedy response can prove disastrous if an initial relationship between youth workers and young people is not present. However a trip out can further develop relationships and allow workers and young people to find out about each other as well as provide a focus for contacts.

If work occurs off the streets, a process of negotiation about ground rules for appropriate behaviour and language etc. needs to occur, due to the authority of detached workers shifting to 'in loco parentis', when workers take responsibility for the young people in their care, in a minibus or at a centre or project.

3. Intervention

Once a trusting, working relationship is established with young people, intervention can occur which involves offering a particular course of action to young people with whom the worker is negotiating. This could be decided upon through detached youth workers reflecting on the recordings and analysis of sessions, using varied methods to enable the group to explore their needs, and assessing the willingness of the young people to proceed. Areas

young people may identify that they need support with, may include:

- health education
- drug advice
- alternative ways to spend their leisure time
- having their views and opinions heard within their community
- developing a better relationship with neighbours, older people, police and others in authority etc.

A variety of tools may be used to deliver these:

- conversation
- discussion and debate
- materials and games, some of which may need modification for street sessions
- visits to exhibitions, places of interest or beauty, theatres, cinemas, clubs, projects etc.
- articles from newspapers and magazines
- residential experience
- using a building space, equipment or other resources for drama, video, group work etc.

All provide ample opportunity for the delivery of social education.

The stages and nature of intervention can be as varied as the young people with whom you work, developing programmes is an opportunity for creativity and can offer a number of outcomes for a variety of stakeholders. Ideally the programme should come from young people but inevitably there will be opportunities for targeting specific issues. Funders and managers may also have other agendas and priorities that may inform the practice. Sometimes the job of detached youth worker is to meet everyone's needs, without compromising the young people they are working with to develop trusting relationships. Honesty, diplomacy and negotiation skills are the keys to successful work.

Another useful structure is to set aims and outcomes for workers and young people. Always build in an evaluation and review for all throughout the process as well as at the end of the project. Evaluate with young people, workers and stakeholders. Think about whom the information is required by; refer to aims met, additional outcomes, recommendations and follow-up. The overall aim is to encourage the personal development of the members of the group through youth work interventions. Outcomes may include raised self-esteem and confidence, participants working better as a group, increased organisational and communication skills, greater ability to be assertive, problem solve or develop a plan of action.

4. Closing

Towards the end of intervention, programmes will finish, workers will move on to work with other or emerging groups, priorities will change and young people will move on and not need the relationship with workers. Contact does not usually end completely but the intensity and frequency will decline. If detached workers are still in the same area they may still see young people and catch up with them but not for a specific piece of work. The key to this stage is how closing occurs, usually a final meeting or clear evaluation will ensure the process closes formally but often relationships drift. The exit plan from a group or area needs to be planned and negotiated so all involved are clear. One-to-one follow-up may be necessary and contact numbers may be exchanged. Other relevant opportunities could evolve and specific pieces of one-to-one work or referrals may continue.

Key elements of this phase are communication and celebration. The way the evaluation occurs requires a level of broad thinking; not all young people communicate comfortably through writing. Some suggestions are:

- using video cameras
- through 'good–––OK–––bad' ratings
- interviews
- art or drawing
- comment sheets
- value lines
- picking words from a selection
- scoring numerically
- questionnaires
- individual goals
- assessment of achievements development
- outside consultants
- members of the community

Recognition of young people's development and growth as well as positive feedback are essential components of an evaluation process.

Detached youth workers need to be accountable and as their work is not always visible, ways to raise awareness and promote the work always need to be sought. These could include invites to:

- street sessions
- minibus and walking tours
- young people's events
- open days for your project
- celebrating achievements and explaining methods of work

A Complementary Style?

Detached youth work is not in opposition to other youth work practices and processes. It complements and is of equal value to other styles of work with young people. The youth work skills of enabling, empowering, group work, listening, advocacy and challenging are also generic to other youth work settings. As detached youth workers meet and work with young people on 'their ground' the skills of contacting, negotiating and recording will be all the more important. Having to explain who workers are and what they do become daily conversation pieces, so clarity of purpose is also more essential. In terms of equality, accessing those who are not in contact with services forms the basis of the work, although specific targeted work with young women and men and those of minority ethnic origins or different ability may also be useful. As mentioned previously, equal opportunities are at the heart of the work and should be reflected throughout the project and its staff.

Networking with other agencies and developing interagency protocols in terms of information sharing, professionalism and confidentiality are vital to successful and sustainable work. A two way flow of ideas and advocacy strategies will enable others to offer and organise effective and flexible services to meet young people's developing needs.

Detached youth workers operate on the streets in pairs, and this team work is both the main resource of the project and the key to successful intervention and rapport developed with young people. There are expectations to back each other up both physically and verbally, be consistent in approach and in what is said. Getting to know your co-worker in terms of personal disclosure, safety, boundaries, and even discussing scenarios and situations that may occur is all part of the process of developing a working relationship which will ensure a positive encounter with young people. There needs to be a development in the understanding of each other's skills and abilities as well as styles of intervention. To aid this process there should be mechanisms in place to promote communications and reflective practice by monitoring and recording the work on sessional recording sheets. There are other issues such as power and equality, changing dynamics and testing professional and personal boundaries that need to be talked through in order to familiarise and build up trust between co-workers. I believe this co-working relationship is fairly unique and is a real strength for this style of work.

Health and Safety

As the work occurs on the streets, it is of paramount importance that managers and workers pay attention to personal safety. A systematic approach, clear agreement and regular reviews on the street will ensure that isolation and other risks are managed effectively. Here are some guidelines, which could be used as a starting point and discussed with the team:

1. *Before you start*

- Make sure local community police officers and police stations are aware of your work.
- Make contact with any places that are open when you are about and make sure you know key members of the community whom you could contact in an emergency.
- Ensure enough research into the area to know which are isolated and risky places.

2. *On the street*

- Always work in pairs, in sight of each other.
- Carry some ID that is recognised by Police and Housing Department and familiar to locals and young people (these could be photocopied and put into police stations, schools or youth centres).
- Have clear start and finish times.
- Choose well-lit areas to meet young people after dark.
- Carry a mobile phone or know where public phones are e.g. pubs or garages.
- Carry the phone numbers of line managers and solicitors or other lawyers and their emergency numbers.
- Know what the purpose of your session is, and have a plan.
- Meet up and leave from a place away from young people.
- Wear suitable clothes.

- Keep personal items hidden or leave them at home e.g. valuables, money.
- If appropriate, clock in and out with another person.
- In some circumstances it may be best advised for workers to be withdrawn from an area for a period of time, due to conflict or attack.
- Promote safe sex, healthy eating, harm reduction etc.; if your workplace has a tobacco policy find out how this translates to a street session. Do not hand out cigarettes or papers to young people.
- In work with drugs: it is not always possible to constructively work with young people who are using drugs or alcohol and workers should make their own judgements about withdrawing when necessary.
- In work with violence: you may decide that you can intervene before a fight starts because you know the young people involved. Think about what your role is and how best you can help the situation: pick up the pieces; call the police or ambulance; talk with the perpetrators, victims, bystanders, observers; or withdraw and raise it another time.

The weather is changeable and sometimes freezing and wet. In terms of sustaining work through the winter months, plan ahead and arrange specific projects or indoor venues. Winter is a good time to undertake team building, staff development, appraisals linked to the unit plan, evaluation, report writing or visits to agencies.

Be aware of the laws, which may affect your work, e.g.:

- aiding and abetting
- undertaking the function of 'appropriate adult'
- public order offences
- the powers of arrest, search and detention
- the provisions of the Crime and Disorder Act 1998
- the provision of the Children Act 1989
- Section 28 of the Local Government Act 1989.

In addition, familiarise yourself with the sex education guidelines as interpreted and implemented by your employer. Do not take legal advice from anyone other than a legal advisor. The work of detached youth workers varies greatly; some authorities have very clear and comprehensive policies. Whilst it is essential to have them as back-up, I would also emphasise the value of drawing up your own guidelines, engaging in the process of discussing them amongst the team and leaving regular opportunities for review.

Resource Implications

As mentioned before some see detached youth work as a cheap alternative to centre-based provision. To an extent this can be true but should not be at the expense of delivering quality youth work in a variety of settings. Some argue that centre-based work is with, on average 20 per cent of young people so detached workers should get 80 per cent of the budget! Here are some suggestions for the basics:

- An office base and meeting room for planning, meetings, recordings and evaluating.
- A phone line.
- Locked filing cabinets.
- Resources store: leaflets, board games, sports and art equipment, storage.
- Mobile phones for safety and accountability.
- Torches, umbrellas, personal alarms.
- Outdoor clothes for promoting an identity and for practicalities.
- Bag for resources.
- Project cards and stationary.
- Computer to compile database, reports, letters and correspondence.
- Minibus to travel to and from areas, as well as to meetings inside premises with young people and for trips out, activities, residentials etc.
- Petty cash.
- Travel expenses.
- Expenses for refreshments or to pay for coffee in a café etc.
- Ongoing training for staff needs, policy updates, team building.
- Money to develop social education, curriculum activities, and programmes of developmental group work.

Management Issues

In terms of managing detached work, books like Mountain's *Management of Detached Youth Work* (1986) and Arnold et al's, *Management of Detached Youth Work* (1981) are recommended for further reading. They are mainly concerned with the manager

being away from the face-to-face sessions and highlight issues of lack of contact, understanding and communication. Encourage the worker to explore what they do and how they handle situations. Consider what could be improved? Who staff are working with? How to develop through the four stages, offer structure and focus and read recordings.

My experience has been of co-working with workers that I manage and so the issues are different. Sometimes an effective way of managing and enabling new workers to be supported and educated is through reflecting on joint experiences, observing how others deal with situations and offering feedback, as well as providing opportunities for workers to develop new skills or assay different experiences. With the relationship between manager and co-worker there are also tensions around the areas of power, inequality and accountability and managers may find themselves having more knowledge about staff than they usually would. Managers taking obvious authority when out on the street can lead to the young people looking to them as retaining all the power and ability to determine the work, thereby leaving their co-worker de-skilled, feeling dis-empowered and de-motivated. Being too close to get a sense of perspective, blocking the process of reflection and analysis, or of challenging, can be seen as a personal attack and can make co-working difficult. It can sometimes prove a difficult tension, especially when inducting new staff.

Supervision is one place where this can be addressed (or in team meetings) where the co-worker and manager relationship should be discussed openly and ongoingly. Clarity about roles and responsibilities is essential as is the creation of opportunities for co-workers to develop their own work initiatives, aims and targets.

If workers are clear about their role of accountability, education and support, and enter into a two-way communication about the direction and development of the work, a successful and useful relationship can be developed. There may also be times when staff cannot work through certain situations and will require additional input. The help of non-managerial supervision, a consultant, management committee member or other professional with an understanding of detached youth work, i.e. similar project, conference (regional/national), or training, can provide invaluable support and new insights.

For positive and effective detached work, interagency relationships are essential as well as presenting

---

Key Questions

1. Is detached work necessary and realistic in this instance/area?
2. What is the overall aim or mission statement of the detached project? Does your practice reflect the key principles of youth work?
3. Are workers suited to detached work and co-work? Is the safety of workers prioritised?
4. Are the mechanisms in place to manage, monitor, evaluate, review and get support and training and development?
5. How will you ensure your written evidence of work will reflect the involvement and interests of young people?

---

opportunities for joint initiatives and funding opportunities. Detached youth workers are sometimes in the unique position of being the only agency in contact with various groups who may be known to others but not engaged by them. This places the workers in the best position to address various issues and concerns. Funding related to crime, safety, health, employment, education etc. could, with imagination, be re-deployed to detached workers. Sometimes the challenge is to be clear about the purpose of the project and its aims and not to compromise values for the sake of monetary incentives. From experience, interagency work can be most rewarding but also most problematic. Again clarity of purpose and professionalism coupled with an ability to pre-empt difficulties and record all meetings and agreements will help in developing positive relationships.

The challenge of detached work is to bring structures to support work with young people in an alternative, informal environment.

References

Arnold, A. et al. (1981). *Management of Detached Youth Work; The How and Why?* Leicester.

Brent, J., and Brent, M. (1992). *Outreach Work.* Unpublished. Hounslow Youth and Community Service, London Borough of Hounslow.

Campbell, A. (1984). *The Girls in the Gang.* Oxford: Blackwell.

Davies, B. (1999). *From Thatcherism to New Labour.* Leicester: Youth Work Press.

DfEE (1998). *Youth Service Audit.* Youth Work Unit. London: Department for Education.

DfEE (2000). *ConneXions Strategy.* London: Department for Education.

Goetschius, G.W., and Tash, M.J. (1967). *Working with Unattached Youth: Problem, Approach and Method.* London: Routledge.

Hertfordshire County Council (1993). *Youth Workers and the Law.* Unpublished.

Home Office (1998). *Crime and Disorder Act.* London: Home Office.

Maguire, M., Morgan, R., and Reiner, R. (1997). *The Oxford Handbook of Criminology.* New York: Oxford University Press.

Michael, A. (1998). *Briefing for Youth Workers on Action to Cut Crime and Disorder.* London: Home Office.

Morse, M. (1965). *The Unattached.* Middlesex: Penguin.

Mountain, A. (1986). *Management of Detached Youth Work in Youth and Social Work.* Leicester: NYB.

Mountain, A. (1989). *Starting out in Detached Work and Helping Others Manage It.* Leicester: NAYC.

Parker, H. (1974). *View From the Boys: A Sociology of Downtown Adolescence.* Newton Abbott: David and Charles.

Pearson, G. (1983). *Hooligan: A History of Respectable Fears.* Hampshire: Macmillan.

Thrasher, F. (1963). *The Gang.* Chicago: Chicago University Press.

Turner, Gold, Kaufman, and Lilley (1996). *Camden Detached Project: Policies and Guidelines for Detached Youth Workers.* Unpublished.

Whyte, W.F. (1943). *Street Corner Society.* Chicago: Chicago University Press.

Further Reading

Dadzie, S. (1997). *Blood, Sweat and Tears.* Leicester: Youth Work Press.

DES/Welsh Office (1984). Detached Youth Work with Young Women. In *Working with Girls Newsletter.* Leicester: NYB.

National Advisory Council for the Youth Service (1988). *Youth Work in Rural Areas.* National Advisory Council for the Youth Service.

Night Shift Enterprises (1997). *Starting Out in Detached Work.* Gwent: Night Shift Publications.

NYA (1990). *Black Detached Youth Workers Statement.* Leicester: NYA.

Phillips, D., and Skinner, A. (1994). *Nothing Ever Happens around Here: Developing Work with Young People in Rural Areas.* Leicester: National Youth Agency Publications.

Streich, L. (1999). *Alternatives to the Bus Shelter.* Leicester: National Youth Agency and Countryside Agency.

White, P. (1991). *Working With Rural Youth: Windows on Practice.* Leicester: Youth Work Press.

14

Peer Education
Annmarie Turnball

Key Points

1. There is already a substantial literature available on peer education in formal and informal educational settings, which workers need to read and familiarise themselves with before embarking on peer education initiatives.
2. There is scepticism about the relative effectiveness of peer education as a method of working with young people and criticism that it can exploit young people—as a youth and community worker you need to be aware of your motives for engaging in such work.
3. Selecting, training and retaining credible and committed peer tutors is time-consuming and demanding and this time needs to be built in at the planning stage.
4. Clear boundaries around roles and responsibilities need to be specified for everyone involved.
5. The impact and outcomes of peer education initiatives can be very difficult to evaluate.

Introduction and Historical Development

Young people learn from their peers all the time. Through listening to and watching each other they explore ideas to increase their knowledge of the world and to develop their own social and life skills. Talking with peers can be a way of gaining information and also of getting support, having a laugh, establishing a standpoint or trying to gain status. Sometimes learning from peers can have negative outcomes, such as responding to peer pressure to become involved in destructive activities, but young people can influence each other in many positive ways and this power can be harnessed by workers using peer education.

Peer education is the attempt to structure the natural learning among peers more systematically. It has been a late arrival to the vocabulary of youth and community workers outside the formal framework of education. In formal education its origins lie in the eighteenth century models of Bell and Lancaster (Adamson, 1964) that they developed to support learning in the newly developing school system. Since World War Two a rich and distinct youth culture has grown up, as the worlds of childhood and adolescence in many areas of the world have been increasingly differentiated from the adult world. This has happened through things such as changes in

legislation and the resulting occupational and social segregation and by the development of distinct cultural activities and consumer markets for young people. In this context peer education has enjoyed a growing popularity as a method of work both in schools and in other forums for learning about living as an adolescent or young adult in complex and swiftly changing societies.

Young people's worlds are not homogeneous and they live in many worlds simultaneously. Analyses of their conversations often highlight their parochialism: content and style can vary between the sexes and from group to group (Walker, 1997). There is both a wider society of their peers—their age group world-wide—and a series of quite specific sub-cultural groups that they inhabit, through necessity or choice, and that may be only vaguely understood by the adults from whom, traditionally, they are supposed to learn. Many of those adults find it difficult to communicate appropriately on issues from which, by virtue of their status as adults and not young people, they are inevitably distanced. Mutual trust, understanding and respect may be more easily established among our peers.

There are many areas of knowledge and skills that are not necessarily formally taught in schools, but are nevertheless important in contributing to any young person's development. These can be broadly termed personal health and safety issues and wider issues of social justice. Relevant topics include:

- legal rights
- dealing with employment, unemployment and homelessness
- understanding drugs
- masculinity and femininity
- sexual health and personal relationships
- eating disorders
- citizenship
- environmental and technological issues
- dealing with racism, sexism, heterosexism and violence.

Young people may talk about these issues together, but are not necessarily well informed. For example, one study found that important topics like homosexuality, STDs and body changes were rarely discussed (Walker, 1997).

Peer education has many synonyms and near-synonyms: peer-assisted learning, peer tutoring, peer learning, peer training, peer counselling, peer support, proctoring, co-tutoring. All denote schemes where we learn from each other and from some kind of teaching, but the 'professional' teacher is absent. Whatever the actual aims, content or methods of the work, and these can vary enormously, what peer education always attempts is to contrive a learning situation based upon the controlled relationship between peers. Something more than the accidental learning from human observation and intercourse is intended. Having specific intentions about the educational objectives to be achieved are central to the process, as are the monitoring and evaluation of the progress of the peer relationship.

The last decade has seen a growing interest in the potential of peer education amongst all those working with young people. Partly perhaps, because of the growing use of peer education in health education programmes, there has been an awareness of its possibilities in other informal education settings. Another powerful antecedent is drama work in schools and the work of theatre in education companies. Both have used peer to peer communication since the 1970s. From the early 1990s articles, project listings and letters in youth and community work publications increasingly reported a wide range of peer education projects. By 1994 even a Youth Work Week conference in Birmingham was celebrating peer health education

work. More recently the celebratory emphasis has been joined by a more analytical approach to the work. In 1996 the National Youth Agency supported a conference on *Peer-led Approaches to Education*, with the aim of critically examining such work and defining what constitutes good practice. What is apparent from all this activity is that many different models are being developed for peer education in informal education.

Whatever the reason, peer education has become respectable. For example John Huskin's elaboration of the rationale and methods for developing young people's social skills displays a 'peer education role' at the pinnacle of a seven stage curriculum development model. Developed from work by Gloucestershire Youth and Community Service this progressive model of youth worker involvement with young people culminates in a stage where 'young people take full responsibility and control their actions—independence achieved' where young people lead their peers, initiating, planning and running activities (Huskins, 1996).

Delivery and Evaluation

The focus

When considering using peer education, first establish what you want to do and achieve. Is it to increase knowledge? Increase communication skills? Change behaviour? Change attitudes? Or all of these? Specific and realistic goals are crucial here. It is common for projects to flounder early because the initial thinking is unclear. One project that planned to focus on mental health issues with boys and young men found they needed to change the focus to explore feelings. 'We needed to go back one stage. Young men's lack of opportunity to engage with issues of communication needed to be addressed before any possibility of peer education work could be considered' (Davidson, 1998).

Targeting

When you know what you want the project to do, the next thing to get clear is what you mean by 'peers'. Surprisingly this can be a difficult issue. One dictionary describes a peer as 'A person...who is equal in ability, standing, age, rank or value' and a peer group as 'a group of people of the same age, status, interests, etc'. The question of who precisely we regard as our peers has important consequences for the planning and delivery of peer education schemes. If age is your criteria, do the learners and tutors have to be exactly the same age, or will there be a range? If you are looking for similarities of status or interests how are you going to attract your chosen grouping? Will you work with both sexes together or separately? Next consider whom the peer education project is for. Is its focus the peer learners, the peer tutors or yourself as the peer educator? Can it be all three?

Planning and design

Peer education projects frequently fail because of planning and design weaknesses (Walker and Avis, 1999). The many different models of peer education can be differentiated on two main dimensions:

learning content and learning methods. Whatever the topic, the content emphasis may range from the predominantly cognitive to predominately affective, with any combination in between. What is it believed that young people could learn best through the process of peer education? All indications are that the key issues are a combination of cognitive and affective learning in the broad area of communication and interpersonal skills. But also learning around many specific knowledge areas is possible. The methods of delivery can range from one-to-one conversation, advice, tutoring or counselling, through group training using games, role-plays, discussion, and practical tasks in workshops, to dramatic performances. The simple matrix below can help to clarify the purpose and scope of projects, whatever the content or delivery techniques.

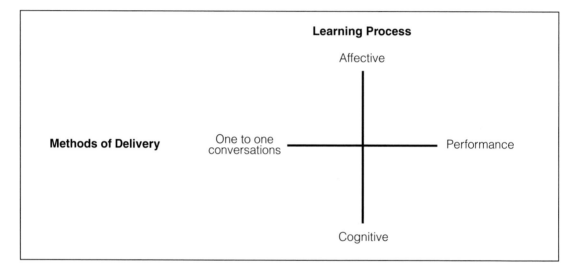

Some detailed examples illustrate the scope here. The Woodcraft Folk Peer Education Project recruited and trained ten peer workers, aged between sixteen and twenty, to participate in running a peer-led advice and information centre at an International Summer Camp. The project highlighted a number of content and method issues. First, there was an emphasis on both cognitive and affective learning. In order to advise others the peer educators were involved in learning about a wide range of issues where young people are potentially at risk: abuse, drug-use, eating disorders, self-harm and other mental health problems. The centre staff worked with over five hundred young people, individually and in-groups. 'From the start, the young people

were clear that they were not counsellors, but understood that counselling skills around reflective listening needed to be practised and developed' (Carr, 1996). These skills were used alongside a range of other methods to deliver the programme.

In contrast to this multi-content, multi-method project, Tunbridge Wells Voluntary Service Unit (VSU), Youth in Action, ran a more content-limited, method-limited project. Its aims were to increase knowledge on a specific subject, youth homelessness in South East England, and to raise funds for further work in that field. 'VSU decided to use a peer education approach, recruiting a group of students with whom we would work to produce a presentation on youth homelessness, which they would perform to other young people at schools, youth groups and various other venues' (Dolling, 1995).

For individuals, the learning from projects can be a complex mix. One peer tutor, trained to work on a Black Sexual Health Project in Leicester, noted: 'I learned about sexual health issues on the course, but it also gave me an opportunity to be in a safe space with other people who shared the same cultural background' (Hingorani, 1999).

Selecting appropriate peer tutors is vital. While every young person can communicate a message to her or his peers, not everyone will have the desire or the skills to do so. One project set up to tackle school bullying used the following criteria in selecting its peer trainers:

- Enthusiastic about trying out new experiences.
- Interested in learning and helping others to learn.
- Capable of receiving and giving constructive criticism.
- Respectful of other people, particularly those in the age group targeted by the project.
- Willing to participate even if their friends are not selected.
- Able to maintain an interest over a sustained period of time.

(Lewisham Young Women's Resource Project, 1999)

Some young people, who may be regarded by adult workers as having a negative influence on their peers, can make very good peer tutors when their energies are directed to a project to which they are committed. Whatever the peer education project is, its success is likely to hinge on the credibility of the tutors. As Shiner and Newburn have pointed out, this credibility can have three dimensions: *person-based*, for example, the tutors' sex or ethnic origin; *experience-based*, that is the learners' belief that they have experienced the learning issue, for example bereavement or drug misuse; and *message-based* arising from what the tutor is saying and how they say it (Shiner and Newburn, 1996). You may aim for credibility on all three counts, but there is no research evidence that this will necessarily make the project more effective.

Training

The next step is the training of the tutors. At the outset it is vital to set clear boundaries. Tutoring involves many skills which, though the professional worker might have forgotten, can be initially difficult to learn. Young people's capabilities need to be built up gradually. What they can assimilate, and then be expected to pass on to their peers effectively, must be carefully boundaried. They are not simply a replacement for the professional worker and the respective responsibilities of all involved will need to be constantly reiterated. To help this and whatever the nature of the project, include a contract for all involved and timetable individual supervision sessions for the peer tutors. Theirs will be a challenging new role and the issues and dilemmas they may face include:

- Not wanting to appear to be 'know-alls'.
- Fear of not knowing enough facts.
- Fear of offending people.
- Relating their role to their ideas of friendship.
- Being drawn into areas beyond their competence.
- Difficulties in making peer education happen (away from the structured setting of workshops and performances).

The initial training may need to include:

- factual information on the subject area
- an exploration of the tutors' personal attitudes
- consideration of how people learn
- communication and observation skills
- action plans
- monitoring methods

Beyond this it is impossible to be prescriptive. The training of the tutors might be in so many different areas and the project might be delivered in such differing ways that it would be better to look elsewhere in this book or to the further reading for guidance. There are some excellent practical workbooks providing detailed checklists to guide you through every stage of a project from the legal and policy contexts, through funding, planning and evaluating a project.

Evaluation

Evaluation needs early attention. Here peer education is dogged with difficulties. 'Numerous papers which provide...subjective qualitative reports of tutoring interventions testify to the success of schemes in improving the attitude, behaviour and self-esteem of tutors. These reports, however, are not supported by more quantitive, psychometric studies' (Goodlad and Hirst, 1990).

Yet evaluation is crucial to the success of peer education and must be an integral part of any project. From the outset all participants experience an enormous number of new learning opportunities. Self-evaluation is an integral aspect of any learning and by developing the participants' capacity to reflect on the strengths and weaknesses of what is going on in every phase of the work, useful pointers will emerge both for its on-going development and in providing evidence on the outcomes for all involved. However, evaluation can serve so many purposes for the different people involved that each project needs to clarify at the outset what it is that should and could be evaluated. While some projects culminate in a *product* aimed at the learners, for example, an advice service or a performance, the *process* is likely to have proved more valuable for the learning of tutors and educators than the product.

Evaluation models for learning activities are legion and it would be useful to examine existing models used in similar projects and adapt those judged to be useful, feasible (i.e. can it be done!) ethical and technically sound.

Theoretical Underpinning

Peer education has no single theoretical underpinning. It draws its strength as a method from the broad acceptance of the importance of the peer group during adolescence, particularly its use as a source of psychological and emotional support. From this perspective the theoretical claim is simply that it helps the successful psychological and social development of young people if they are encouraged to work together to learn. There are also many specific theoretical claims for the efficacy of schemes. These emphasise its superiority to 'chalk and talk' education and have usually been formulated by comparing peer education projects with the alternative formal education methods of learning about something.

As three groups are involved in the process of peer education, the 'learners', the 'tutors', and the supervising and managing professional 'educators', its theoretical underpinnings are complicated. Claims can differ for each of the groups. And of course some claims are only applicable to specific

techniques of peer education. One-to-one tuition for example claims different outcomes from peer-led whole group tuition. The advantages may be different for each group. This is an important consideration and the potentially uneven nature of the rewards of peer education is a constant concern. This is not, in itself, a negative aspect, but it does need consideration.

Theoretical claims for the usefulness of peer education can be grouped into four broad areas. The first and second sets of claims focus on two broad areas of learning for the individual: the development of cognitive and of affective capabilities. Thirdly, pedagogical advantages for peer education are claimed. Fourthly, peer education has possible economic, political and professional advantages as a method for the educator.

Cognitive claims

Both tutors and learners may benefit here. For the tutor a range of cognitive processes can be developed including perceiving, differentiating, selecting, storing, simplifying, inferring, applying, combining, justifying, clarifying and responding. The meta-cognitive skills of planning, monitoring and evaluation may all be enhanced in the course of learning by teaching. Tutors might also gain an enhanced understanding of knowledge in use, as they will have had to struggle to make their subject matter intelligible to the learners. In one sex education project the peer tutors reported 'feeling better informed and better able to talk about sex than their untrained peers' (Walker, 1997).

For the learner the process can constitute an 'apprenticeship in thinking' where a meaningful context for the learning, the use of verbalisation and questioning and of challenge can all lead to an enhanced learning experience. Some discussions of peer education have also suggested that there will be a better application of knowledge and skills in new situations than with other methods and more ownership of the whole learning process. In some projects relationships with the tutors may also give companionship that will develop the learner's wider understanding of both intellectual and social worlds.

Affective claims

Here benefits seem to be mainly for the tutors. Affective gains are linked to the development of self-concept in adolescence. There is often a strong emphasis on social role theories in the claims made for the tutor's learning. Experience of the responsible adult-like role of 'the tutor' is believed to provide motivational and attitudinal gains. The learning by teaching that the tutor experiences might include strengthened commitment, co-operation, empathy, self-confidence, and self-esteem. This is the explicit focus of the Prince's Trust's *M Power Millennium Awards* where £2.7 million will be given to up to 25,000 young people for projects they run with a clear community benefit. 'We're looking to encourage new projects that are peer led. The aim is to bring out young people's sense of initiative' (Beebee, 1999).

A vital claim for the learner here is that there will be enhanced communication in learning as a result of the perceived similarity in culture and background between learner and tutor. This was a central focus in the peer-led anti-racism workshops of a Devon-based project tackling rural racism (Rolt, 1999).

Pedagogic claims

The learners might benefit from more active and participative learning, with lowered anxiety. Peer education also has the potential for providing opportunities for more teaching and more individualised instruction than in traditional teaching methods.

Economic, professional and political claims

Here all three groups, educators, tutors and learners may benefit. Over the years economic claims have increasingly been made for peer education. Crudely they can be summarised as the assertion that it saves money and other resources by multiplying the effect of educators via the use of peer tutors and, additionally, frees the supervising and managing educators for more demanding work.

There may be a diverse range of potential professional benefits for the peer educator: a good tutor to learner ratio, and less discipline problems, a pleasant working environment with peer tutors working co-operatively as colleagues of the educator, and delegation of routine work to the tutors, have all been claimed. The challenge involved

in reducing complex subject areas to activities which non-professional tutors can deliver and an increased opportunity to focus on the assessment of learning rather than its delivery may be areas where workers can expand their professional skills.

The political claims for peer education centre round two distinct issues, the political education of children and young people, and the wider politics of successful educational management. The delegating of learning to learners, of empowering learners, of more democratic learning and of reduced learner dissatisfaction have all been suggested as reasons why peer education is an important tool for political education. These claims are especially interesting given the current political situation of informal education and particularly the political aspirations of much work with young people. A recent project in Redditch, *Young Mums Educating*, aimed to counter the prejudices against single mothers (Beebee, 1999).

How the Key Principles of Youth and Community Work are Integrated in the Practice

If peer education's specific relationship to social science theory can be difficult to pinpoint, its relationship to the value base of youth and community work anchors it firmly as a valuable working method. The purposes and practice of peer education link it directly to the key principles of education, empowerment and participation (Banks, 1996). Its relationship to issues of equality is more complex. In some ways the whole idea of peer education is based on inequity. While it uses the notion of peers to signify some kind of equivalence between people, its practice is constructed by differentiating three quite disparate groups; learners, tutors and educators. It is not surprising then that it has the potential to undermine the very principal that, in its bid to enhance learning, it claims to promote, equality. Some critics have claimed that it is inevitably exploitative: a way of delivering education on the cheap, using unpaid volunteers (the peer tutors). This is an important ethical issue for peer educators to examine. It may be a valid criticism of poor projects, but if properly resourced, planned, evaluated and delivered no project need be exploitative.

Another concern relates to issues of equality. This is the degree to which we should emphasise the occupational skills the 'tutors' develop. In some projects the emphasis on training and dramatic skills and polished performance is to the forefront. Debates about the purpose of performance in learning have existed since the 1960s in relation to drama teaching. There may be a tendency in peer education work to applaud (figuratively) the work of the more verbal and out-going young people, to equate this with self-confidence and measure success in facilitating learning in terms of such performances. Here, because of the emphasis in some projects on methods that veer away from one-to one or small group work and towards the use of training and performance techniques with larger groups, the question of what is actually being learned in the way of 'communication skills' or knowledge needs to be addressed squarely.

Resource Implications

A great strength of peer education is its applicability to inter-agency work with young people. As a method it is transferable to any setting where young people gather. It can take place in churches, hospitals, family and residential centres, health promotion units, theatre companies, supermarkets, factories, youth organisations, leisure centres, playing fields, nightclubs, schools: anywhere. It is also a method that can be used globally as in the child-to-child projects, that involve children in the spreading of health practices within local communities, demonstrate (Bonati and Hawes, 1992).

If used properly, peer education is unlikely to be a cheap method. The importance of training the tutors and thus the considerable emphasis on them in terms of time and resources can skew the focus of a scheme. They become both the recipients of the bulk of the learning involved in the scheme, and the primary focus of evaluations of its effectiveness. The outcomes for the other two sets of participants may receive less consideration.

A second concern is linked closely to some of the economic, political and professional claims outlined above. There is a danger that peer education may be more exploitative than educative. It could be argued that the ultimate aim of some projects has been to use unpaid volunteers for 'real' work and to save or even make money (Jeffs and Smith, 1999).

Key Questions

1. Why is peer education and not some other method the way to work on the issue?
2. What are the anticipated learning outcomes for the three groups of participants?
3. How will the process of learning be managed and assessed?
4. Where will the peer education project need to take place?
5. When and for how long will you and other participants need to be involved in the project?

Acknowledgements

My thanks to Sharon Long and the workers at Lewisham Young Women's Resource Project.

References

Adamson, J.W. (1964). *English Education 1789–1902*. CUP.

Banks, S. (1996). Youth Work, Informal Education and Professionalism. In *Youth and Policy*, 54: pp. 13–25.

Beebee, S. (1999). The Power People. In *Young People Now*, 122: pp. 34–35.

Beebee, S. (1999). Young Mums Educate. In *Young People Now*, 125: p. 24.

Bonati, G., and Hawes, H. (Eds.) (1992). *Child-to-Child: A Resource Book*. Child-to-Child Trust.

Carr, S. (1996). Peer Education the Woodcraft Way. In *Young People Now*, 81: p. 17.

Davidson, N. (1999). Behind the Bravado. In *Young People Now*, 122: pp. 34–35.

Dolling, J. (1995). Peer Tutoring in Action. In *Youth Action*, 56: p. 11.

Goodlad, S., and Hirst, B. (Eds.) (1990). *Explorations in Peer Tutoring*. Blackwell.

Hingorani, M. (1999). Talking About Sex. In *Shabaab*, 26: pp. 16–17.

Huskins, J. (1996). *Quality Work With Young People*. Youth Clubs UK.

Jeffs, T., and Smith, M. (1999). Tainted Money. Ethical dilemmas in the Funding of Youth and Community Work. In Banks, S. (Ed.), *The Ethics of Youth Work*. Routledge.

Lewisham Young Women's Resource Project (1999). *How To Set Up a Peer Training Project to Tackle Bullying in Your School*. Lewisham Young Women's Resource Project.

Rolt, S. (1999). Taking on Rural Racism. In *UK Youth*, pp. 8–10.

Shiner, M., and Newburn, T. (1996). *Young People, Drugs and Peer Education: An Evaluation of the Youth Awareness Programme (YAP)*. Home Office.

Walker, B. (1997). 'You Learn From Your Mates, Don't You?' Young People's Conversations about Sex as a Basis for Informal Peer Education. In *Youth and Policy*, 57: pp. 44–54.

Walker, B., Walker S., and Avbis, M. (1999). Common Reasons Why Peer Education Fails. In *Journal of Adolescence*, 22(4): pp. 573–577.

Further Reading

Bonati, Grazyna, and Hawes, H. (Eds.) (1992). *Child-to-child: A Resource Book*. Child-to-child Trust.

British Youth Council (1998). *Youth Agenda: Peer Education*. British Youth Council.

Brodalla, A., and Mulligan, J. (1999). *The Peer Aid Book. Approaches to Setting Up and Running Young People's Peer Education Projects*. CSV.

Harvey, M. (1995). *A Framework for Peer Learning*. Youth Clubs UK.

Topping, K., and Ehly, S. (Eds.) (1998). *Peer-assisted Learning*. Lawrence Erlbaum Associates.

15

Advice and Information Work With Young People

Cindy Writing

Key Points

1. Enable the client to fully explore their information needs by actively listening to their request.

2. Offer accurate and relevant information in response to the client's request, including any local knowledge that may influence a decision, but don't offer a personal opinion.

3. Present options and encourage the client to explore associated costs and benefits, but don't base these on your or others' experiences.

4. Offer potential courses of action that the client might follow, but don't assume you know the solution to the client's request or predicament.

5. Allow the client to make any decisions or choices, seeking the help and support of others when needed.

Introduction

Advising, informing, counselling, teaching, befriending, guiding, mentoring, supporting...there are a bewildering number of labels and definitions for the different ways we work with young people. If the young person is benefiting from the work we are doing with them does it really matter what method of work we are using?

The subtle differences between advising, informing, guiding and counselling young people may initially seem trivial but are important to grasp if we are to offer our client group an effective, up-to-date service that holds empowerment of the young person receiving the service at its core. The youth workers awareness of the method of work they are using and the service they are delivering is important in ensuring that our clients are offered a service relevant to both their short and long term needs.

Constant change in the issues facing young people and the implications of their actions or non-actions mean that the need to offer young people information in a way that it will be received and understood is greater than ever.

The proposed *ConneXions Service* (DfEE, 2000) outlines the development of the personal advisor role and the emphasis on information and advice within this role. Key Theme 4 of the ConneXions Strategy highlights the importance of the availability of 'Outreach, information, advice,

support and guidance'. Involvement with the delivery of such services creates new challenges for youth services and the work of staff within them.

Historically, the development of advice and information services for young people has been linked to the development of counselling and other one-to-one support services via generic advisory and counselling services aimed specifically at young people and specialist agencies dealing with issues such as housing, benefits etc. The DHSS research report *Advisory and Counselling Services for Young People* (Tyler, 1978), acknowledged that counselling and advice services often overlapped, especially where a less clinical approach to counselling was taken:

> *Counselling in this context is seen as only a part of a range of help offering access to information and the opportunity to develop skills which will enable young people, particularly those who have been disadvantaged, to take responsibility for their own lives.* (Tyler, 1978)

Young people approaching youth workers and agency staff for help are often unsure what type of help they want and what is available to them. As Mabey and Sorenson point out in *Counselling for Young People*:

> *Workers in the field of counselling and information are aware of the difficulties of young people in knowing exactly what services*

they need. In fact they often require a combination of all three: counselling, information and advice.

(Mabey and Sorenson, 1995)

It is important that we are clear about what it is that we can offer. The use of the word counselling in relation to the delivery of information and advice services can be misleading. Counselling is a very specific relationship that should be entered into within the appropriate professional boundaries and by workers with the appropriate training and supervision. Counselling skills however, can and should be used to great effect in information and particularly advice work:

...nowadays, teachers, youth workers and social workers learn effective ways of working one-to-one with client groups and will acquire the skills of active listening as part of their training. Many workers attend counselling courses or in-service training where such skills can be learned or further developed. These skills are then used informally to improve communication and facilitate the delivery of the service involved. Formal counselling is the contracted relationship between counsellor and client where the two parties meet at an agreed time and place for the sole purpose of the counselling interview. (Mabey and Sorenson, 1995)

In short, advising and informing is **not** counselling, but the delivery of these services will benefit from the use of counselling skills.

The National Association of Young Peoples Counselling and Advisory Services (NAYPCAS), founded in 1975 and now reorganised and renamed Youth Access, has been instrumental in developing counselling, information and advice services for young people and has historic links with generic youth work agencies and the National Youth Bureau, now known as National Youth Agency. Youth Access has more recently been involved in developing quality standards relating to the delivery of services. The standards include definitions of information and advice, these are useful in separating out the roles of advisor, informer and counsellor and will be examined further in the chapter.

Youth workers can offer advice and information to young people in tandem with many other services and in a variety of different settings. The implications of the *ConneXions Service* and a general trend towards

more one-to-one work with young people, particularly young people at risk of becoming marginalised, mean a likelihood of more youth workers becoming involved in information and advice work. Information and advice work has been and remains a vital service. It is important that it is properly planned, maintained and offered in a way that will be of benefit to the young people that access it.

Providing Information to Young People

The Youth Access Quality Standards definition of information work is a useful starting point in planning information provision or assessing your current practice:

The provision of systems and processes which make comprehensive, up-to-date and accessible information available to young people. There is no assessment or recommendation about the information's appropriateness, and decisions, choices and action are left with the young person. Information work can include signposting to other services or providing young people with resources to discover their own answers to their question and needs.

(Youth Access, 1998)

So, in providing information to young people, we are looking to do **just** that: provide the information. If we have not got the information we can suggest that the young person concerned tries another source or they can be offered the means to find the information for themselves.

With any information work a good place to start is in developing or reassessing an overall aim and specific objectives in relation to the provision of information to young people. There are a number of questions to consider in developing these aims and objectives.

1. On what areas should you aim to provide information?

When deciding what areas of information to cover in service provision there are a number of things to consider. A good starting point is to gain feedback from young people and from other organisations working with young people on current information needs. It is important to ensure that any feedback is representative and that it covers all groups of young people to be worked with. Check out what information is already being provided and assess whether it is appropriate to duplicate any. It may be that other information providers are not considered to be accessible to all young people.

There may be expectations from the management and funders of the programme in relation to the type of information provided. These will need to be covered in the development of the information service.

It is important to keep up-to-date with any upcoming or current national or local government changes that may affect young people and any global, national or local trends. The quicker you are able to respond to new and changing issues that affect young people, the more effective you will be in meeting their information needs. Beware of knee-jerk reactions, and check that the need for information is real and not hype. A spate of drug related incidents for example, can often result in a deluge of information on drugs that offers the receiver nothing new. This can eclipse information needs that may be more relevant but less visible, such as information on benefits, training courses or where a young person with no formal identification document (i.e. birth certificate, medical card etc.) can get some.

The implications of the ConneXions Strategy may increase the need for specific information to be supplied as a compulsory element of the package of information and advice offered.

2. Are you in a position to provide this information?

It is important to have a clear idea of what you are able to achieve within the resources available.

This begins with assessing your ability to obtain the relevant information required on the areas you are covering and ensuring its accuracy. It is important that you are able to maintain the information and keep it up-to-date (often a time consuming, ongoing and laborious task), as well as being able to consistently deliver it.

Consider issues of gender, race, sexuality and differing ability in relation to those delivering the service and those receiving it. Does the staff team represent the client group you are aiming to serve?

Rather than create a new service it may be more appropriate to support existing agencies and organisations in providing the information. This may be both more effective in making the best use of

resources. It may also be beneficial to the potential users. Current agencies may be better placed to provide the service with your support and input. Confidentiality may also differ in other agencies and organisations, e.g. voluntary agencies can often offer greater confidentiality than statutory ones.

Finally, check out whether someone else is already providing what you are planning to. This may sound obvious, but there are often duplicated services in some areas and no service in others. It is always worth looking at alternatives in relation to information provision. If possible, link in with others who have a reputation for providing good quality, up-to-date information. If not, ensure that you have the resources to keep the information you provide up-to-date and accessible.

3. In what format should you provide the information?

Consider:

- leaflets and posters
- buying into information systems (e.g. National Youth Agency, Citizens Advice Bureaux)
- face to face
- telephone
- information technology and the Internet
- tapes and videos

Ways of providing information are developing all the time: the Internet being the most obvious new contender. There are many information sites on the net aimed at young people and this is clearly an exciting and welcome addition to the traditional sources of information.

Be aware though that, whilst the internet provides information to young people, can the informer ensure that the information is accurate and up-to-date, provides sufficient information or signposting for more detailed information and is understood by the young person accessing it? Additionally, whilst the Internet may be useful for some, remember not all young people have access to it.

4. How accessible is the information?

A leaflet with text is no good if you can't read it, a face to face service not effective if people can't get to it. Wherever possible, the information provided should be accessible to all the young people in the target area.

Consider:

- Location of the information (building based, posted out, distributed by detached work methods, displayed in public or private places etc.).
- Availability of workers in terms of times and locations.
- Availability of workers in terms of gender, race, sexual orientation, differing ability.
- Opening hours.
- Literacy and language issues.
- Whether presented to groups or individuals.
- Confidentiality boundaries and any need for privacy in delivering your service.
- Accessibility of buildings (if used).
- Images and messages being presented.
- Using local communities and networks.
- Referrals from and to your service.

Ensuring that all young people are able to access relevant, accurate, understandable information is often considered the biggest challenge in developing services. Consultation, careful planning and ongoing evaluation are key in moving toward this goal. The involvement of young people in developing information services should also be considered. Many existing advice and information agencies use young volunteers in developing and providing their services. Young people should be consulted on and involved in exploring and setting up services as well as feeding into the ongoing development of services.

In conclusion, if the phrase 'if I were you'...or...'What I suggest'...or...'what I did when I was in that situation' are on the tip of your tongue when providing information, you are not offering information alone, but your opinions and experiences, thereby 'tainting' the information. Information is just that, information, with no bias, preference or suggestion from the person offering it. It is about offering the information (or the

means to access it) and leaving the young person to use it as they choose. It is also about being comfortable leaving the young person with just this information and no suggestions, regardless of your concerns, as to how they might use the information they have been given. It offers a non-judgmental approach to the work, but may not always feel enabling for the young person on the receiving end.

Advice Work with Young People

As can be seen from the Youth Access *Quality Standards* document:

> *Advice is concerned with helping a young person to change or cope with practical issues and problems. It seeks to widen the young person's choices by providing accurate and relevant information about their rights, options and potential courses of action. The advice worker may identify and recommend ways forward, but decisions and choices are left to the young person. Any action agreed by the young person may be undertaken by, with or on behalf of the young person.*
>
> (Youth Access , 1998)

Advice work gives the worker far more scope and, if carried out effectively, it should not reduce the young person's involvement in deciding upon a course of action, but should encourage ownership and control of any decisions or actions.

Advice work relies on good quality information. Whereas information can be given without advice, advice should not be offered without good quality information. Offering advice and ensuring that the client is left in a position were they are making decisions for themselves and not 'going along with' their youth worker's suggestions can be difficult. In providing advice to young people there are a number of dos and don'ts that can help to ensure that only options are offered rather than heavy suggestion.

Case study

James is 15, he is keen to go into the army and train to be a mechanic. He is on a New Start programme and is not expected to perform well in his GCSEs (three months away). He asks his youth worker, (who is meeting with him weekly in a mentoring capacity), whether or not he should go in the army. The youth worker finds out from the local Careers Advisor what James would need to do to apply to join the army. The youth worker feeds this information back to James, she is happy that it is up to date and accurate. The youth worker suggests to James that joining the army would be something to work towards, but that he would need to really focus on his upcoming exams. James is more determined now than ever to apply to the army. He works hard over the next three months and gains two Ds and two Es in his GCSEs. His application to the army is unsuccessful: they suggest he resits his GCSEs. He blames his youth worker for his situation: he did what she told him, worked really hard, but he still did not get into the army. He is now unemployed.

The case study poses a number of questions and considerations relating to our role as advisor:

- Was the youth worker the right person to provide the information requested?
- Were any other options or information offered to James regarding his career and school choices?
- It is important to ensure that the **young person** is making a choice based on the options provided.
- Was any thorough exploration done with the young person in relation to his situation and resulting information needs?
- Whether or not James applies to the army should be his decision, reached by considering all options after exploring costs and benefits.
- More emphasis placed on James 'owning' his decisions and the resulting courses of action may have helped him deal with his initial rejection more positively.

It is important when considering how to offer advice that the benefits of the face-to-face contact are not underestimated. The use of counselling skills (particularly that of active listening) is also beneficial to the client in enabling them to work through their needs and to move towards finding a solution for themselves.

The person-centred approach, based on the work of Carl Rogers, and a model of helping developed by Gerard Egan (1986) are particularly useful and adapt well to face-to-face work with young people. In particular, the key qualities of unconditional positive regard, congruence and respect, coupled with the three-stage model of exploration, new understanding and moving on are useful frameworks to apply to advice work.

Referring On

Inevitably there are times when a worker is unable to offer the client the information or advice they need. It is worth considering how clients should be referred on to other agencies. It is helpful to the clients if you are familiar with the agencies you are

suggesting: if you can describe the place and give clients a feel for how it will be when they get there they may feel more comfortable about going. Make sure your information on the agencies is current, check opening times and locations. Make regular visits to agencies that you refer to and keep up-to-date records of essential information regarding these services. Make sure that the agency you are referring to can meet their needs and check out with the client whether or not they have been there before.

Wherever possible encourage the client to make the contact. Make available to the client the means to make the contact if possible, e.g. telephone. Explain clearly to the client why they are being referred on. It is useful to think about how you have felt in situations when you have been referred on elsewhere by an organisation: aim to make a positive referral not a negative one.

Monitoring and Evaluation

It must be said that evaluating information and advice work is, like many other areas of youth work, difficult. The same debates over qualitative and quantitative indicators exist, and the ever present 'don't know what happened to the client after we saw them, so don't really know if it was effective' is another regular statement used. Having established an aim and specific objectives for the information work you are involved in, any services delivered should be monitored and evaluated to show their effectiveness in relation to them.

There are a number of ways in which you can obtain feedback on your service(s).

Client contact monitoring is one of the most obvious ways. This would entail the recording of any contacts with users of your service. Contact monitoring may record gender, ethnicity, sexuality, any disabilities, area of residence, type of information provided, whether this was a first or subsequent contact and so on. It is particularly useful in showing the numbers using the service, checking accessibility and highlighting areas where the services are not meeting needs. You can add to your contact monitoring further categories relating to the specific needs of your service.

By monitoring the times of usage it is possible to compare service usage with availability. This may be helpful in revising opening hours for example.

It is important in the continuing development of the service to gain qualitative feedback on the types of information being used. This can be gained by feedback from a sample group of clients using interviews or questionnaires. It may be possible to follow up previous clients of the service to check whether they benefited from the service at a later date.

You may consider using 'mystery' clients to evaluate services. This is particularly effective in establishing how the service is doing in its consistency of approach.

Finally, wherever possible, gain feedback from young people who are not accessing the service. They may provide reasons why they are not themselves using it.

Consider also how selection and recruitment, training and supervision, policies, practices and procedures are monitored and evaluated, and where the responsibility for this lies.

Resource Implications

Advice and Information services are often set up and run in partnerships involving both statutory organisations and the voluntary sector. This can provide greater opportunities in terms of funding and enables a more client-focused approach to the work. Voluntary sector agencies can often respond quicker to need and offer less restriction in relation to confidentiality issues and are not perceived to be part of the 'establishment'. Voluntary agencies may also be better placed to apply for a wider range of funding for their work, e.g. National Lottery.

Many voluntary agencies however have found that the unreliability of funding from year to year has had an effect on their services. It is often the statutory bodies who provide funding on an ongoing basis either to their own information and advice services or to the work of voluntary agencies in their area.

Key Questions

1. Has the need for the service been established and has it been carefully planned in line with the identified needs?

2. Is the information and advice offered a specific service (even if it is part of a generic youth work provision)?

3. Is the information accurate, up-to-date, relevant and presented in a way that will be understood by the person receiving it and have sufficient resources been allowed to do this and to continue to develop with the needs of the service users?

4. Are you in the best position to provide the information and advice or is it more appropriate to use other agencies or refer on?

5. Have you built in sufficient monitoring and evaluation systems?

Two recent government initiatives, *Best Value* and *ConneXions*, may provide increased opportunities for partnership work to continue to develop, with the goal of providing quality services, aimed at meeting the needs of the client group at the core. As local authorities continue to be more prescriptive in ensuring services provided to users/potential users meet their needs and are of a measurable quality, so more opportunities to improve services arise.

References

DfEE (2000). *ConneXions.* London: HMSO.

Mabey, J., and Sorenson, B. (1995). *Counselling for Young People.* Buckingham: OUP.

Tyler (1978). *Advisory and Counselling Services for Young People.* DHSS Research Report No. 1. London: HMSO.

Youth Access (1998). *Quality Standards Document.* Leicester: Youth Access.

Further Reading

Egan, G. (1986). *The Skilled Helper: A Systematic Approach to Effective Helping* (3rd edn). Monterey, CA: Brooks/Cole.

HMI (1989). *Youth Counselling Services.* Stanmore: DES.

McDonald, E. (1990). *The Information Shop Specification.* Leicester: NYA.

NAYPCAS (1984). *Policy Document.* Leicester: NAYPCAS.

16

Youth Exchange
Caroline Tippen

Key Points

1. Exchange experiences, unless carefully planned can easily reinforce prejudice and racism, so ensure that yours is based upon mutual respect and a desire for learning.

2. Due to cultural differences, inappropriate expectations may be raised with regard to future relationships, and power differentials due to wealth may become apparent and thereafter control the relationship.

3. You may think that you know your group, but be prepared for unpredictable behaviours when you are away. Be aware that exchanges can be voyages of self-discovery as well as a fascinating insight into other cultures and communities.

4. Don't pack too much into the programme for either end of the exchange process, leave time to just 'chill' and enjoy your environment.

5. Maintaining the group motivation, especially after their visit and prior to the return exchange can be difficult.

Introduction

International perspectives in the youth work curriculum have been established for many years. However, 1985 gave this area of practice new impetus following the creation of the Youth Exchange Centre, providing a framework for the development and delivery of youth exchange activity (Davies, 1999).

At the same time, a more critical and political dimension was becoming incorporated into the youth work curriculum through global education, developing a greater understanding of global economic factors, the divisions between the countries in the Northern and Southern hemispheres. and the subsequent impact upon young people's lives here in Britain; see Bisi Williams's chapter on 'Global Youth Work' in this publication.

Gordon Blakely, Director of the Youth Exchange Centre UK, quoted in the journal *Youth Clubs UK* defined a youth exchange as:

...A two-way movement of a group (5–25) of young people (14–25 years old) for a minimum period of time (one–three weeks) with a programme of joint activities not dominated by tourism. (Maurice, 1986)

My own experience in this area includes several European exchanges, plus an extremely exciting UK/Indian Ocean Islands Youth Exchange Programme. My intention is to share some of the learning from my experiences in the delivery of such exchanges.

I have thoroughly enjoyed working on all my youth exchanges, and the rewards for me as a youth worker were fantastic. I was able to see great changes take place in the young people from both sides of the exchange, in terms of their social and personal development, raising of self esteem and self confidence, not to mention their increased knowledge of culture, geography, politics, and so much more.

That's the up side! This chapter would not be very helpful if I failed to say that youth exchanges are also extremely hard work, very time consuming, and often frustrating and exhausting. Thus, if you are considering embarking on one, make sure you pack the following three essentials:

1. sense of humour (always look for the funny side)
2. stamina (get plenty of sleep and eat well)
3. sustainability (grit your teeth and don't give up)

I established the first official UK/Mauritius youth exchange, and a youth exchange with nearby La

Reunion island. Madagascar and the Seychelles were also substantially researched but proved unsuitable for youth exchange at the time so were not progressed. An important point to note is that not all destinations are appropriate, so planning visits before any exchange is essential.

Getting Started

Before embarking on an exchange project, take some time to consider a few key questions:

1. What is involved in a youth exchange?

Not everyone is clear about this! A proper exchange will involve a visiting stage, and a hosting stage, with all the associated planning and preparation. In this way, young people have two separate experiences, both very different but equal in value. It is usual practice for the visiting group to pay all costs of travel to the host country, and for the hosting group to cover all costs from the time the visitors arrive. Exceptions to this do occur when one partner group is considerably poorer than the other, in which case the wealthier group will take on a bigger fundraising task in order to support their partners' travelling and hosting costs. If this is the case, take care that this does not create a power imbalance between the two partners, and that your efforts are not misinterpreted as being 'charitable', and potentially patronising (Maurice, 1986). Equally it could be that due to this power differential your partner's needs could become secondary.

2. Why is your exchange project important?

You will need to make a strong case if you want to convince others to give you the money for the exchange and support you in other ways. Write a brief one-page outline of your proposal, with bullet points showing the expected outcomes for young people. Include a breakdown of estimated costs and how you intend to cover these. This briefing note is really an advertising tool, since you want people to read it and be sold on your idea. It can be given to anyone who might be interested in supporting the exchange, as a way of stimulating their interest and encouraging their support.

3. How much time do I need to organise this exchange?

The answer is usually lots! Exchanges take time to set up, and there are many stages to go through. A good exchange should have at least one year's planning and preparation time before the actual trip takes place. Some short haul exchanges may take less time, but the important thing is to be sure that you have *enough* time. Writing an action plan for yourself with dates for the various stages will help you to assess how long you will need.

4. Will we get enough money to run this exchange?

The answer is usually yes, if you are determined that the exchange will succeed. Costs should not stop you from trying to organise an exchange. It can be scary, involving young people and telling everyone what you are planning to do, when you don't have the funds behind you. But once an exchange project has commenced, it becomes a reality and starts to gain momentum. It is up to you and the young people involved to convince others that this is a real live project worthy of their support. Extensive and creative publicity for your exchange is therefore essential, and I have included some ideas around this in the fundraising section later on.

5. How will I organise this exchange?

You will need to be organised, methodical, and adaptable. Good planning and preparation are vital to success, and the section on Exchange Process that follows is designed to help you organise an exchange from start to finish, in a methodical way. However, circumstances will be forever changing throughout your exchange project and so your plans will have to be adapted as you go along. Don't fight this, it is quite normal and to be expected.

The Youth Exchange Process

Below I have identified the nine key stages of your exchange experience:

1. Identifying a need

The first step in any exchange project is to establish whether and why there is a need for an exchange.

Whose idea is it: the workers' or the young people's? Whose agenda will it try to meet: the workers' or the young people's? Will it be done in partnership with young people? There is no point trying to organise an exchange if there is no clear reason for it as you will not attract any support. You should look at your own situation and the young people with whom you work and ask yourself and them what the particular needs are. In addition, you can use information from other agencies and youth services to help identify needs, plus any relevant articles appearing in the local or national press, and on TV.

Globalisation and the island status of Great Britain means that most people have some level of curiosity to travel and widen their horizons. It is equally important that the Youth and Community Services offer our young people the chance to widen their own horizons.

Package holidays have of course made travel much more accessible to all, but do not offer the same opportunities for discovery as do exchange projects. Also, there are still many young people in the UK who have never travelled abroad nor are likely to, given their particular circumstances.

There is often a territorial issue amongst young people in relation to where they live. For example, groups of young people from one residential estate may not want to mix with groups from another. Youth exchange projects help to break down territorial boundaries, and can also positively address racist attitudes, by enabling a rich and diverse mix of people to come together, learn about each other, and build great friendships.

2. Targeting and recruiting young people

Having identified the purpose for the exchange, the next step is to decide which young people will participate. From a conversation or incident at a project, it may be that you have already been developing the ideas with a group of young people with whom you are in regular contact, and therefore your group will be determined. However, you may also need to consider whether there are others who would benefit from such an experience? There can be many reasons to target certain young people, for example, those who:

- have low self esteem
- have particular attitudes and values which need to be challenged

- are socially excluded
- have a severe physical disability which has prevented many life experiences
- are at risk of offending
- are drifting with no purpose or ambition
- have had limited or no experience of travel

In terms of equal opportunities, you will want to ultimately have a balanced group of young people with particular regard to race, gender, and ability. It is not always easy to recruit young people as you are asking them to join a project which, as they see it, won't happen for ages. So you need to convince them of the educational as well as the fun elements of the exchange. This means not only the trip but also all the preparation and planning, group work and fundraising that will be involved. The recruitment process will not be successful if you solely promote the extensive learning outcomes and potential for personal and social development. Young people want fun, ensure that this is the message that is heard whilst ensuring that the participants are clear about the project's purpose.

If you need to recruit a new group for the purpose of the exchange, ensure that this is done fairly. Prepare an application form and project description plus a young person's role within it. Write the selection criteria, which should include key personal qualities like commitment, reliability, and being adaptable and resourceful.

Advertise the exchange in local newspapers and visit places where young people congregate, to talk to them about the project. Offer to help fill in the application form if need be. After the interview process, you will need to work with the disappointed young people who did not achieve a place on the exchange. Make a list of 'reserves', as some of the selected young people may well drop out along the way. When you have selected your group, set up regular meetings to begin the preparation and planning stage.

3. Contacting a partner organisation

Be clear about why you have chosen a particular destination; often your images of another country are misguided and you need to undertake extensive research. Some contacts come about by accident, but if you are starting from scratch, the first port of call should be the Embassy or High Commission of the country you want to partner up with. Most if not all are based in London. You could also contact the British High Commission in the partner country itself. The staff overseas are likely to have local knowledge and may well be able to put you in touch with the right person. Other places for partner contact include:

- Commonwealth Youth Exchange Council (CYEC) in London.
- Youth Exchange Centre (YEC) in London.
- Commonwealth Institute in Kensington High Street.
- The Internet.
- Libraries.
- British Council in the partner country.

Once you have established a contact, talk about your proposed exchange. With any luck they will be highly enthused and invite you to visit. Make sure that you listen to what your partner says, do not make assumptions or interpret their response into what you want to hear. You need to hear the difficulties as well as the potential opportunities. In addition it may be that the YEC can put you in touch with others who have undertaken exchange activity to your chosen destination.

4. Carrying out a planning visit

The planning visit will enable you to nurture your tentative relationship with the partner group, and to seriously consider whether the exchange should go ahead. Pack as much as you can into this trip as the more you learn about the partner group and country, the more successful your exchange will be. Upon your return, if you have any concerns about safety or quality after your planning visit, don't shy away from saying so. You may need to choose another destination. Financial support for the planning visit may come from the CYEC and YEC, and also from the following local groups in your area:

- Lions groups.
- Rotary groups.
- Women's Institutes.
- Church organisations.
- District and county councils.

5. Planning and preparation

Working with exchange participants during the planning and preparation stage can be highly pleasurable and rewarding. You will see them growing in self confidence and developing new skills, but you will also need to maintain motivation from time to time because enthusiasm will definitely lag as you travel the long and winding road to the ultimate exchanging period. This is particularly the case after your trip and whilst awaiting the return visit of your partners.

When the group first gets together teambuilding exercises should be introduced to get everyone working together effectively. Regular meetings are essential to maintain momentum and also to encourage fast forward action. A weekend residential experience will help to assess how the group will co-exist harmoniously together over a period of time (very important to know this in advance of being 12,000 miles away from the UK).

But bear in mind that you can never predict how the young people may behave when you are away. For example, during the first exchange visit to Mauritius, members of the UK group started to become very irritable and argumentative with each other. This was curious, as they had all worked so well together up until this time. In trying to find out the source of this irritable behaviour, I discovered that members of the group were bored at the base camp. Whilst the location was beside a beautiful beach, there were no 'home comforts' such as TVs, video, computer, or stereo. Thus the group was encouraged to find new ways of best occupying their time, and very soon they were organising a range of beach-based activities. These included games and sports, an it's-a-knockout tournament, treasure hunts, shell competitions, art exhibitions of collages using beach items, and making musical instruments from coconut shells and palm tree leaves. Spirits were raised and group harmony restored as the young people began to think more creatively, just as their grandparents must have done in the days before the technological revolution.

When working with young people on developing their local knowledge of the country to be visited, make sure that the information used is accurate, relevant and informative. The following objectives need to be worked towards during the planning and preparation stage:

- The creation of a dynamic working team.
- Learning about, and valuing the individual contributions of the participants to the group.
- Enabling the participants to develop new skills .

- Raising enough money so that the exchange can take place.
- Publicising the exchange so that everyone who may have an interest or contribution knows what you intend to do.

There are a number of key skills and knowledge areas which exchange participants will need to develop:

- team working
- fundraising
- positive and effective publicity
- diplomacy and tact
- reliability
- supportiveness
- adaptability
- resourcefulness
- commitment
- sustainability
- emergency first aid

As the exchange group members are all ambassadors for their country, you will need to guide them on protocols and appropriate behaviour and dress when visiting your partners. Whilst sometimes unpopular, this is a crucial part of the exchange process where young people start to learn about mutual respect, politics, diplomacy and tact. In addition, local customs as well as behaviours that may unintentionally offend will need to be explained, for example, the dress codes. Girls in mini skirts and revealing tops, and boys in cut-away frayed short shorts (or lycra cycle shorts) are not suitably attired for official visits in a predominantly Hindu or Moslem country because of the local religious beliefs.

Workshops may also need to be run so that everyone is fully aware of the importance of good diet, the benefits of physical exercise, sexual health issues, and the effects and consequences of drugs and alcohol, together with the penalties for law breaking in the country of destination.

Exchange hosts will undoubtedly want to learn about the environment that they are also due to visit. Make sure that you have prepared appropriate information and materials about their destination to take with you, and be prepared to answer questions honestly.

The preparation and planning stage is all about getting the group into shape and ready for the exchange. No doubt more ideas will emerge as a result of such regular meetings and consideration will have to be taken about how to respond to these.

6. Fundraising

First and foremost, the young people and you need to be totally committed to this exchange project. All who are involved must believe that it is a good project, that it is going to be successful and that other people are going to provide support for it. If you all convince yourselves of this, it should be much easier to convince other people. Fundraising is big business these days and everybody is doing it. You will therefore be in competition with others so try and identify the unique or unusual element to this exchange. Creativity and imagination are vital to successful fundraising.

Sponsors who supported the UK/Indian Ocean Islands Exchange programme included Air Mauritius, the Commonwealth Youth Exchange Council, the Youth Exchange Centre, Hertfordshire County Council, Kodak, plus local Lions and Rotary Clubs, shops and businesses.

In addition, during hosting phases, residential sites substantially reduced their rates to support the exchange, and transport was provided for the cost of the petrol only by a local person who was very enthusiastic about the exchange, and also happened to have his own double decker bus.

If you are asking someone to make a donation in cash or kind, there must be something in it for them. Ask yourself what would be of value or benefit to them? It may be a simple feel-good factor, or it may be useful publicity for their business.

Publicity goes hand in hand with fundraising. The more people who know about the exchange, the more likely it is that it will be a success. Invite local newspapers, TV and radio to do an interesting piece on the exchange project. Put up posters and hand out flyers in key locations. Find out what other events are happening in the community and whether you can tap into them. This is a good way to promote your project and raise funds for it at the same time. For every 50 letters you send out appealing for donations, you may receive one or two successful replies. You should also apply to CYEC and YEC, and follow up any donations made to you for your planning visit. Most libraries have a copy of the Directory of Grant Making Trusts which takes patience to read, but it often pays off.

Wherever possible try to attract donations in kind like free airline tickets. In exchange for these your group might offer to wear sweatshirts bearing the airline's name whilst in transit.

After your group has exhausted all possibilities in the big league, it's time for the fun to start! Between you, you have to raise the rest of the money needed for your exchange, or it won't happen. This is a marvellous impetus for frenzied activity. Young people's fundraising ideas might include some of these sponsored events:

- swim
- eat
- silence
- dance
- bungee jump
- abseil
- canoe
- pot hole
- mountain bike
- climb
- run
- ride
- parachute jump
- walk
- sail
- cave
- windsurf
- surfboard
- paraglide
- parascend
- water ski
- water polo
- orienteer
- residential home singalong
- fly a plane

There are the more traditional collective events:

- disco
- record a song and sell tapes
- tombola stall
- jumble sale

Do not be afraid to try out new ideas. Apart from raising lots of money, this stage of the project is also a great teambuilding exercise.

7. Finalising all arrangements

As you approach the actual exchange period, it's time to do a final checklist. Have you:

- Received signed parent/guardian consent forms for all under-18 group members and self-consent forms for over-18s?
- Received completed medical consent forms for all the group, in case you have to give consent for treatment whilst away?
- Prepared detailed lists of any special needs of group members, e.g. vegetarian, diabetic?
- Checked that everyone has a valid passport (check expiry dates)?
- Completed the risk assessment paperwork, confirmed your home based contact, and given that person a detailed list of your exchange participants and contact details?
- Insured the entire group?

- Received the travel tickets and any other relevant travel documentation?
- Ensured that everyone has had the necessary injections etc.?
- Packed a first aid kit?
- Informed the partner group of all your travel arrangements?
- Bought some official gifts for the partner group?

There will of course be many other tasks you need to complete in preparation for the exchange, and this list is intended to be a prompt for further thoughts.

8. The exchange period

The exchange period will be either a visiting or a hosting stage. In both cases there must be a planned programme of activities to ensure that the exchange time is of maximum benefit to all. Programmes can include the following:

- A 'work' element (environmental, social, community).
- Visits to places of interest (places which are famous, religious, unusual).
- High profile meetings (visits to High Commission, Embassy, government offices, TV or radio studios).
- Activity trips out (ice skating, orienteering, mountain biking, climbing, boating).
- Fun activities at exchange base (sports mini-tournaments, quizzes, fancy dress, campfire or barbecues).
- Exchange group meetings (ongoing evaluation, addressing any issues or concerns, amending the programme).

The activity programme will invariably change during the course of the exchange period due to differing needs and practical considerations. Remain flexible to both the young people and your host's requests. Whilst it will be important to explore as much as possible, also make sure that you plan for time to enjoy your surroundings and relax. This is often where great reflection and learning can take place, by just being with your partner group. Home stay experiences can often provide the most valuable learning for young people, and whilst not necessarily a recommendation for the entire trip, allows for the development of individual relationships on another level.

Personal relationships that develop can become problematic if there are different expectations from each party. Make sure that young people are aware of the boundaries that exist, and do not find themselves making promises that they are unable to keep. The interpretation of friendship by a young person here may not be the same as say, a young person in the country with whom you are exchanging. For instance, in the 1980s, a very successful exchange with Ghana took place. Both groups promised to 'keep in touch'. Within a short period of time, the British participants were receiving requests, not only from the individuals that they had met but relatives and friends also requesting substantial gifts and on some occasions requests to come and live with their British counterparts. Their expectations of generosity did not tally with those of the young people here. Eventually the young people here did not respond to the letters, undoubtedly creating a lot of confusion and hurt for the young people in Ghana (Sellar, 1990).

Another example occurred during a hosting phase in the UK. A member of the Mauritian youth group was found to be missing, causing much anxiety amongst the British leaders. The Mauritian leader revealed that the young person in question had gone into London to stay with relatives for a few days. Whilst the UK group was quite clear that the organised youth exchange programme was the reason for the visit, the Mauritian group felt that a trip to the UK was an opportunity to see long lost relatives. Had the UK group known this, a family visit might have been planned and included in the programme. However, as the UK leaders were responsible for all their visitors, they had a very worrying time waiting for the return of the young person.

At the end of the exchange period, make sure that you build in an opportunity to either thank your hosts or say farewell to departing visitors. To end on a high note, it is a good idea to hold a farewell party where all can have a good time, and where gifts are exchanged and a formal speech of thanks made by the exchange group members.

9. After the exchange

There are several tasks to complete immediately after the exchange has taken place, including:

- Write a report about the exchange, including finalising the accounts.

- Ensure the group members each write an account of their experience.
- Write thank you letters to sponsors, the partner group, and anyone else who helped you with the exchange.
- Undertake a group evaluation of the exchange.
- If you are half way through an exchange, i.e. have completed one leg, continue with your fundraising work.

Your exchange report will be required by some individuals and funding organisations, but is also a useful tool if you are about to commence the work for the second leg of the exchange. You can use this report to encourage others to support the next phase.

The purpose of the evaluation is to clarify the outcomes of the exchange, and to identify ways in which the project can be improved in the future. The exchange evaluation process can start with further group meetings where the young people can informally discuss their experiences. Key questions to put to the group include:

- What did you learn?
- What did you enjoy?
- What did you not enjoy?
- What would you have changed?

It is also important to acknowledge that whilst all the participants, including staff, will have learnt new information about the partner country, they will also have learnt a huge amount about themselves, so make sure that any evaluation process allows for such reflection.

Following the UK/Indian Ocean Islands Exchange, the young people reflected upon what the exchange had taught them about themselves.

Some of the comments received from young people included:

- Coping in difficult situations when some other people can't, e.g. having to use hole in the floor loos, eating unusual foods, coping with a range of strange insects and wildlife.
- Improving self confidence, after making speeches to partner groups or during VIP visits.
- Being a good communicator; though not necessarily speaking language, learning to use mime, hands, facial expressions, drawing, music, etc.
- Feeling that they can achieve anything if they really put their mind to it, e.g. achieving their fundraising goal).

Key Questions

1. What is the purpose of your exchange? Why are you going and whose agenda is it? Are you clear about what it is that you are hoping to achieve? Have you shared these expectations with other group members and your exchange partner?

2. What images do you have about the place that you are due to exchange with? How have these been informed? Have you developed sufficient knowledge about local cultural behaviours and how racist behaviours, attitudes and actions will cause offence?

3. Do you have sufficient knowledge and information to respond to questions about Britain and life in this country?

4. Have you undertaken a comprehensive risk assessment? Not all countries or regions may be suitable for this activity. Have you listened to what your partner has said, and are you prepared to be flexible and compromise where necessary?

5. Have you talked to other youth workers or organisations that may have been with a group to the same country?

- Being able to keep calm in a crisis, or when things went wrong.
- Doing things they didn't know they could, e.g. writing a speech, ice skating, climbing mountains.
- Working well in a team, supporting others in various situations, taking on responsibility within the group.

In addition, seek the young people's views on the accommodation, food, staff, travel, programme, and any other aspects of the project.

Finally, whether you are planning an exchange with the next village or with a country many miles away, may all your exchanges be safe, successful and enjoyable.

References

Blakely, G. (1986). *Just the Ticket, The Information And Confidence*.

Davies, B. (1999). *From Thatcherism to New Labour*. Leicester: Youth Work Press.

Maurice, N. (1986). Youth Exchanges: Valuable for Challenging our Own Values. In *Youth Clubs UK*, 40.

Sellar, A. (1990). Negative Images. In *Young People Now*, October.

Further Reading

Blakely, G., and Kingsley-Smith, S. (Eds.) (1990–93). *Planning your Youth Exchange. Training modules 1, 2 and 3*. London: Youth Exchange Centre.

British Youth Council (1999). *Youth Agenda: Youth Exchanges*. London: BYC.

Holloway, D. (1998). *Tolerance in Diversity: The Video Documentary of an Exchange Programme*. Leicester: Youth Work Press.

Jarman, H. (1992). *Help? Guidelines on International Youth Exchanges* (9th edn.). London: Youth Exchange Centre.

Youth Exchange Centre (1994). *Youth Exchanges as an Instrument for Overcoming Racism and Xenophobia*. London: YEC.

Youth Exchange Centre (1997). *Youth Exchanges: A Training Video*. London: YEC.

YEC (1992) *Youth for Europe* kit:
- Starter kit
- Cash kit
- Programme kit
- Contact kit
- Talkback kit

YEC (Quarterly Journal) *Youth Exchange News*, Youth Exchange Centre, London; website: http:www.connectyouthinternational.com

17

Mobile Work
Kathy Edmonds

Key Points

1. Identify the need for a mobile project based on a thorough area profile.

2. Involve young people at all stages of planning and decision making, and from the start, harness local community support and partnerships for potential funding, volunteers and other resources.

3. Be open minded and make use of all available resources.

4. Retain the interest and enthusiasm of young people whilst the project is being developed by regular meetings and other pieces of youth work.

5. Raise the profile of the youth work and young people by regularly publicising your mobile project: local newspaper, local radio, schools, Chamber of Trade, Community Council and other groups.

Introduction

The story of youth work and mobile provision is one of excitement and energy, of hard work and dedication. Keeping a large vehicle on the road is not always an easy task...but for those who are interested in working alongside people it can be extremely satisfying. (Shanks, 1992)

The prime aim of youth work is to further the social education of young people, to assist them to reach their full potential. It is important that young people gain access to the resources and opportunities that enable this to happen but for many young adults these possibilities are limited because of lack of transport and suitable places to meet.

Mobile projects have developed as a distinct approach to solving that problem. Mobiles supply a place where young people can be contacted where they live and offer them a suitable place to meet, as well as providing information, advice and a range of new experiences. The growth of such projects, their use in rural and urban areas and the range of vehicles in use has promoted discussion and experiment throughout the country.

Historical Development

The use of vehicles for informal educational work is thought to have started with the early evangelists working in Sunday schools in the late 1700s. The first documented evidence is a photograph of an 1890s Sunday school outing to Great Yarmouth using a horse drawn cart, part of a collection at the Norfolk Rural Life Museum and Union Farm Society at East Dereham (Fabes, 1992).

In 1908 the Scouts started taking carts to summer camp and in the 1920s, Marie Stopes set up caravans as Family Planning Clinics in rural and urban areas (Fabes, in Witt and Edmonds, 1998).

The first mobile publicity and training unit was launched in 1922 by the Girls' Friendly Society and called the *Princess Mary Caravan* (GFS, 1975, in Fabes and Popham, 1994). According to Heath-Stubbs (1926) it was a sophisticated and well-developed mobile that travelled widely throughout the country (Fabes and Popham, 1994).

All of these early mobiles aimed to widen participation and choice, often conveying important information, which would not have been accessible any other way.

In the 1940s, during the Second World War, vehicles were used by the police and the civil defence as information centres and mobile headquarters and about this time mobile libraries started. In 1962 Cliff Richards's film *Summer Holiday*, featured a double decker bus as a living space, suggesting a different use for such vehicles. The Salter-Davies report on 'the problems of youth work in rural areas' published in 1964, recommended that mobile projects be set up as peripatetic 'hop on, hop off' mobile coffee bars, with an experienced youth worker on board. Between

1963 and 1970, the first urban mobile project, a converted ambulance, was used in Great Barr, Birmingham, whilst funds were raised to rebuild a centre (DES, 1963, in Fabes and Popham, 1993).

The setting up of the National Playbus Association in 1973 to offer information, advice and training courses to those operating mobile community projects encouraged networking, initially for those working with the under 5s and their families. It gradually expanded to work with those running mobile youth work projects. NPA offers advice on all aspects of conversion, fund raising, health and safety, issue-based work and publishes a quarterly magazine called *Busfare*.

During the 1970s and early 1980s there are records of three different mobile projects. In Lancashire, an articulated pantechnicon, in Wales a Luton box van, and in Kent the Shuttle Leisure Van. All had different uses and provided some useful lessons in the variety of vehicles used and in the approaches taken (Akenhurst, 1984, in Fabes and Popham, 1993).

Mobile projects really took off in the 1980s with statutory and voluntary groups using them. They included purpose built vehicles, double deckers, single decker coaches, minibuses and even a converted furniture removal van.

By 1993, with the publication of the De Montfort University/National Youth Agency directory of 'Rural Mobiles' there were 46 mobile projects recorded as operating throughout the country. The 1998 'Celebrating Mobile Youth Work Fair' held in North Wales, was attended by 120 delegates representing 30 different projects and saw 10 converted vehicles from as far afield as Bournemouth, West Sussex, London, Essex, Birmingham, Stoke on Trent, Liverpool, the Wirral and Shropshire. The database set up following the 1998 fair has so far registered 40 mobile youth projects, and some in other parts of Europe such as in Germany and in Hungary. Membership of the National Playbus Association is 230 mobile projects of which 150 are youth projects. It is estimated that another 50 mobile youth projects are in existence but not registered.

Policy

Mobile projects are a unique way of working with young people in their communities but also act as a means of expanding horizons by visiting other communities. They can assist in combating social exclusion and in encouraging communities to develop responses to their own needs, enabling participation and empowerment.

The innovative nature of mobile projects provides the means to create a partnership between young people, the community, the youth service and other agencies. The partnership model and multi-agency approach is one that is encouraged by the government and the majority of projects are funded by more than one source which encourages self help, flexibility and diversity. These projects build on the principles of youth work derived from the Statement of Purpose from the 1992 Ministerial Conference of Education; these are: equality of opportunity, participation and empowerment (NYB, 1991).

Going Mobile

Buses demand to be seen to be recognised. They flaunt themselves.   (Shanks, 1992)

When considering setting up a mobile project, it is necessary to take into account a number of factors. These include profiling the area of work, the choice and design of vehicle, funding, equipment, staffing, maintenance, programming, and evaluation.

The first step is to assess the needs of the area you will be working in, whether an urban or rural area. Profile the area, finding out what facilities are already available, where young people meet and what their needs are. Involve young people at all stages, from choosing the type of vehicle, its design, its uses and where and how it should be used.

The profile will inform you of whether a mobile project is the best way to meet the identified needs. It will also tell you the geography of the area and whether a minibus conversion would be most suitable or a larger vehicle such as a double decker bus, a trailer or even a furniture removal van. Consider when choosing your vehicle, issues of access, driving licence requirements and suitable parking places. It is useful to visit existing projects in action and to compare the advantages and disadvantages of one vehicle over another. The choice of vehicle will be determined by its use.

The policy of your organisation will determine target areas, target groups, age range and the style of work. Some mobile projects provide information and advice, some of which is specialist, through the use of computers, videos and leaflets. *Radical*, a project based in Powys in Mid Wales, provides information, and advice on health related issues, in particular raising awareness of mental health issues for young people. The *Craven YES* (Youth Enquiry Service) caravan project in North Yorkshire visits schools and college campuses offering advice on welfare rights, employment and benefits. Some mobile projects act as mobile youth clubs providing somewhere for young people to meet with their peers, have a coffee and a chat and maybe try out new activities. Other mobile projects act as transport to take activities into an area. In Stoke on Trent a specially converted bus carries a variety of sporting equipment and floodlights, which can be set up on any housing estate. The *Octobus* project in Swindon specialises in using arts and crafts as the focus of activities. They work with a variety of groups including travellers and homeless people.

Targeting specific groups is another way of working. The Girls Breakout project in North West Leicestershire aims through the use of its bus to provide a comprehensive service to girls and young women in the area, giving them access to women youth workers, a safe environment in which to meet and opportunities to express feelings and learn how to improve relationships. Targeting can also be achieved by offering specialist workshops in art, drama, music or photography. The Tate Gallery in Liverpool has a *Mobile Art* project which takes art workshops out into the community and also has a *Young Tate* programme aimed at young people aged 14–25. Many theatre companies tour and can be used to link up with other mobile projects, to perform in the open air, on the bus, under a canopy or in a village hall. They include the *Rural Media Company, Action Transport Theatre, Red Ladder* and *Trestle*. Mobile projects can also act as transport to link up groups of young people from different estates or villages and for trips and residentials in this country and abroad. The *Hamlet Hopper* project from Shropshire took 13 young people to Northern Spain as part of a Youth Exchange using the bus as transport accommodation and for activities.

Once the purpose has been agreed, look next at finance and the choice of vehicle. Can you afford a brand new purpose-built vehicle or will you need to be flexible and buy a second-hand vehicle and convert it, perhaps using the skills of individuals in the community?

Purpose-built vehicles cost about £120,000 compared with between £2,000 and £10,000 for a second-hand vehicle, depending on the type and its condition. If you buy a second-hand vehicle you will need money to adapt and convert it. In 1989 when the Shropshire Youth Service bought their 36 foot long Dodge Commando RG16 furniture removal van, they paid £3,500 for the vehicle and £8,500 to convert it.

The importance of involving the local community and local businesses is paramount when it comes to equipping your vehicle. The *Hamlet Hopper* project (Edmonds, 1992) received a whole range of support including money, goods and services. A canning factory offered to buy a television, a video, a computer, a printer and a cassette deck. The local Women's Institute bought cooking utensils. The Borough Council gave £1,000 for Sports and Arts equipment. Two companies donated paint and scaffolding to enable the young people to put their designs on the outside of the bus. A local builder having read an article about the project in the local newspaper offered to buy CB radio equipment.

The involvement of the local community also enables projects to attract volunteers and part time staff as few projects are staffed by full time workers.

Appropriate induction training and support and supervision are essential requirements for all staff but those working on mobiles are often more isolated and need to be more self-sufficient. It is important to encourage networking and where possible cross-area work, where one mobile may meet up at an agreed spot with another, encouraging sharing of experience and practice both for staff and young people. The worker on a mobile may need to be the youth worker, driver and mechanic all rolled into one, which again may have resource implications for some vehicles which require specialist driving licences. The other hidden cost is that mobile youth work sessions may be twice as long as building-based ones because of taking the bus from its base to collect young people en route, parking up for the session and then dropping off again before returning to base. However the collecting and dropping off journeys can be part of the fun for those young people.

Regular maintenance and use of the vehicle is essential and you will need to budget for one major service a year plus several minor services every couple of months, at an average annual cost of £2,000. You will also need to consider fuel costs, secure parking, driver training and a contingency budget for replacing spare parts. With the new European seatbelt regulations some vehicles will not be suitable for carrying young people and you may need to budget for adapting the vehicle or the cost of a feeder minibus. If possible include money in the budget forecast to employ a cleaner and a handyperson.

Again look in the local community; one local company offered to service, repair and maintain the Shropshire bus free of charge. Free parking was negotiated at the high school and the school caretaker acted as an ad hoc handyperson. For more information on bus conversion, bus maintenance, health and safety, driver training, generators and important legislation, contact the National Playbus Association in Bristol.

In programming the use of the mobile and in evaluating the success of its work you should take into account:

- the aims and objectives of the organisation
- the range of work being undertaken
- the different issues that are being addressed
- the feedback from young people on how their needs were met
- the catchment area of the work
- the amount of inter-agency work
- the level of involvement of young people in running, managing and using the project
- the involvement of the community

A partnership approach can enable the delivery of a comprehensive service to young people. Multi agency co-operation is enabling the youth service to work alongside the health service, schools, adult education, social services, the careers service and the police in delivering programmes to young people.

Mobile work is highly effective and as long as the project has clear aims and objectives, is properly planned and resourced it will be providing a service to young people based on local needs, which is taken them.

Theory and Practice

Core youth work methods will underpin the practice that be undertaken on mobiles, e.g. one-to-one work, group work and community development. Theories that can help you in your practice include Carl Rogers' Person Centred Approach (Rogers, 1980), Button's Developmental Groupwork (Button, 1976) and the Community Development Approach (Twelvetrees, 1982; Thomason, 1969; Lightfoot, 1990). See also Janet Adam's chapter on group work in this publication.

Young people do not exist in isolation and the strength of the community development approach is in recognising that young people are part of a community. Working with young people should not be about the segregation of young people from

society but about collaborative working, sharing resources and skills to the benefit of young people as a group within and as part of a wider community (CEDC, 1984). This view is endorsed by June Lightfoot in *Involving Young People in their Communities*:

> *Community Development can be seen as a key element in any democracy since it stimulates and supports participation and involvement and thereby encourages effective and responsible citizenship.*   (Lightfoot, 1990)

Lightfoot believes that by employing community development as an approach, that young people are encouraged to take a constructive role in the community and the community is encouraged to view young people as constructive.

By adopting a person-centred, community development approach, which utilises groupwork, mobile projects are harnessing the human knowledge and energy within the community and enabling young people to be involved critically with their society. This builds on the view of Milson and Fairburn from their Youth and Community Work in the 70s Report:

> *...In the future young adults must be given the chance to work things through for themselves, and the opportunity to decide for themselves what must be provided and in what manner. Only then will their real needs be met.*
> (Milson and Fairburn, 1969)

Mobile youth work must not be allowed to degenerate into 'just taking young people for a ride'. That would be a waste of a resource, which can be so effective in focusing youth work.

Key Principles

> *The Youth Service operates through a process which is freely chosen by young people and which is challenging and encourages self-determination. The service strives for a relationship between youth workers and young people which is voluntary, educative and participative and based on trust, honesty and equality.*   (Shropshire County Council Youth Service, 1990)

These principles are the ones used by most youth services.

The environment in which youth work takes place is important in determining the style and delivery of provision. Young people's experience of youth work and the type of service they receive may vary because of where they live, or even whether they receive any youth service at all.

Mobile work as a method can take the service to young people where no other service exists, whether on a large housing estate or in a remote rural area, making contact with them in more informal settings and responding spontaneously to their ideas. Mobile work can help to widen equality of opportunity through providing a service to more young people where they live. This addresses issues of isolation, limited mobility, narrow horizons, stereotypes, visibility, identity, and access to information and advice (Phillips and Skinner, 1994).

The educational aim of the key principles is achieved in a variety of ways by supplying health education, information about welfare rights, by playwork and for older people providing a place to meet and discuss issues that are of concern to them. Mobile work can enhance the involvement of the community as well as facilitating work with other agencies and groups, and encourage the sharing of knowledge, skills and resources.

Participation and empowerment are achieved by involving young people in as many aspects of the planning of their mobile project as possible from the start. Involving the community through a community development approach also encourages ownership of the project at a local level.

The development of mobile projects and their use so far, demonstrates that the principles of education, equality of opportunity, participation and empowerment are being effectively incorporated into practice.

Resource Implications

Mobile projects are highly cost effective and very high profile, publicising the role and value of youth work.

There are very few single sources of funding available and it is better to adopt a partnership or multi-funding approach. The important point here is to be flexible and resourceful. Do not rule out any individual or organisation, however big or small and do not just look for money but for goods and services. Keep your project high profile even in its developmental stages, offer to talk to the local rotary club or women's institute, talk on the local radio station, write articles in the local press; if you have the vehicle, invite people to visit to see it in action. Talk to other projects, seek advice from specialist organisations such as the National Playbus Association, seek out sponsorship, apply for grants and also encourage the young people to fundraise for the project.

The project in Shropshire was funded by the Local Authority, the Parish Council, local trusts, local businesses, the Rural Development Commission and also by individual fund raising. *Radical* in Powys is funded by the Youth Service and the Health Authority. Birmingham's *One Stop Shop* received money from the Single Regeneration Budget (City Challenge) and Somerset's *Mobile* received money from the Rural Challenge Grant. Other sources include the National Lottery, the European Social Fund, the Tudor Trust, and shops such as the Co-op and B & Q. Two good resources are the *Funder Finder* available through local libraries and Nicola Eastwood's *Youth Funding Guide* (1997).

When setting up a mobile project be as innovative and imaginative as possible and do not wait to start until your plan is perfect. You can adapt and add to it as you go along, the important thing is to be mobile and to be in contact with young people, and this can be done from the beginning, on foot, on two wheels and on school buses. The crucial factor is the ability of the youth worker to develop positive relationships with young people (Williamson, 1996).

Key Questions

1. Will a mobile project supply a new service or would it be able to improve an existing service?
2. How can I involve young people and the local community in the development of the project?
3. In how many ways could I possibly use the mobile?
4. Where can I get information and advice for funding, conversion, health and safety, types of vehicle; should I visit other projects?
5. Who can I network with for a possible partnership approach to ensure the best possible service for young people?

Conclusion

Mobile projects are complex phenomena; they are attractive, welcoming and fun. They invite intimacy, encouraging conversation and discussion on a range of issues, in an atmosphere of comfort and confidentiality. They enable young people to try new activities or to just be with their peers. They offer independence, taking young people to new places, with the activity on or off the bus. Mobile projects stimulate enthusiasm, energy and independence of spirit and offer a varied workload with high job satisfaction. They can be exhausting especially when you are combined youth worker, driver and mechanic.

The adventurous use of mobiles can stimulate lifelong learning and widen participation and choice for many young people and their families and the communities within which they live.

References

Akenhurst, M. (1984). *Delivering Rural Youth Work*. National Association of Youth Clubs.

Bloxham, S. et al. (1986). *The Mobile Youth Centre*. Lancashire.

Button, L. (1976). *Developmental Groupwork with Adolescents*. Unibooks.

Cockerill, S. (1992). Equality and Empowerment, the Principles of the Youth work Curriculum. In *Youth and Policy*, 17.

Community Education Development Centre (1984). *Going Community for Secondary Schools*. The Community Education in Action Series. CEDC.

Davies, B. (1986). *Threatening Youth, Towards a National Youth Policy*. Open University Press.

DES (1963). *Is this Britain's Only Mobile Youth Club*. Department of Education and Science Newsheet.

Eastwood. N. (1997). *Youth Funding Guide*. Directory of Social Change.

Edmonds. K. (1992). *The REA Hamlet Hopper: Taking the Youth Service to Young People in Rural Shropshire*. Shropshire Youth Service.

Edmonds, K. (1997). *Young People's Perceptions of Youth Work in Rural Shropshire*. Unpublished MA dissertation. Brunel University.

Fabes, R. (1992). *Working with Wheels*. Conference Report. Leicester: National Youth Agency.

Fabes, R., and Popham, D. (1994/95). Mobile Facilities for Work With Young People in Rural Areas. In *Youth and Policy*, 47.

Frost, D., and Way, C. (1984). *Mobile Youth Unit*. Wales.

Girls Friendly Society (1975). *1875–1975 One Hundred Years of the Girls' Friendly Society*. London: GFS.

Hastie, S., and Sheridan, M. (1986). *The Shuttle Leisure Van*. Kent.

Heath-Stubbs, M. (1926). *Friendship's Highay, Being a History of the Girls' Friendly Society*. London: GFS.

Huskins, J. (1994). *Managing Youth Programmes*. Huskins.

Huskins, J. (1996). *Quality Youth Work*. NYA.

Lightfoot, J. (1990). *Involving Young People in their Communities*. CDF.

Milner and Carolin (1999). *Time to Listen to Children: Personal and Professional Communication*. Routledge.

Milson, and Fairborn (1969). *Youth and Community Work in the 70s*. HMSO.

National Youth Bureau (1991). *Towards a Core Curriculum: 'The Next Stop'*. Report of the Second Ministerial Conference. NYB.

Phillips, D., and Skinner, A. (1994). *Nothing Ever Happens Around Here. Developing Work with Young People in Rural Areas*. NYA.

Rogers, C.R. (1980). *A Way of Being*. Boston: Houghton Mifflin.

Salter Davies (1964). *The Problems of Youth Work in Rural Areas*. London: Youth Service Development Council. HMSO.

Shanks, K. (1992). *Mobile Provision for Youth*. National Playbus Association.

Shropshire County Council Youth Service (1990). *A Curriculum for Youth Work in Shropshire*.

Smith, M. (1988). *Developing Youth Work, Informal Education, Mutual Aid and Popular Practice*. Open University Press.

Thomason, G.F. (1969). *The Professional Approach to Community Work*. Sands & Co.

Twelvetrees A. (1982). *Community Work*. Macmillan.

White, P. (1991). *Windows on Practice: Working with Rural Youth*.

Williamson, H. (1996). Book review of *Quality Youth Work* (Huskins, J., see above). In *Young People Now*. NYA.

Witt, S., and Edmonds, K. (1998). *Celebrating Mobile Youth Work Fair*. Conference Report. Playbus. NEWI.

Resources

The *Celebrating Mobile Youth Work Fair Video* (1998). Interviews with members of eight different mobile projects, about the variety of vehicles and their uses in urban and rural areas. For more information contact: Kathy Edmonds on 01978 293258

Contacts

National Playbus Association
93 Whitby Road
Brislington
Bristol BS4 3QF
Tel: 0117 977 5375

National Youth Agency
17–23, Albion Street
Leicester LE1 6GD
Tel: 0116 285 3700

Wales Youth Agency
Leslie Court
Lôn-y-Llyn
Caerphilly CF83 1BQ
Tel: 02920 855 701

Further Reading

Bonnar Rosi (1987). *Going Mobile: An Introduction to the Practicalities of Working on a Mobile Community Resource*. Mobile Projects Association.

Department of the Environment (1997). *Involving Communities in Urban and Rural Regeneration: A guide for Practitioners*. DoE.

Rural Development Commission (1998). *Young People in Rural Areas: Making Things Happen*. RDC.

Sutton, J. (1998). *Buying and Converting a Vehicle*. Bristol: National Playbus Association.

18

Global Youth Work is Good Youth Work
Bisi Williams

Key Points

1. Starts from young people's experiences and encourages their personal, social and political development.

2. Works to the principles of informal education and offers opportunities that are educative, participative, empowering and designed to promote equality of opportunity.

3. Is based on an agenda that has been negotiated with young people.

4. Engages young people in a critical analysis of local and global influences on their lives and those of their communities.

5. Encourages an understanding of the world based on the historical process of globalisation.

6. Recognises that the relationships between, and within, the 'North' and the 'South' are characterised by inequalities generated through globalisation processes.

7. Promotes the values of justice and equity in personal, local and global relationships.

8. Encourages an understanding of and appreciation for diversity locally and globally.

9. Views the peoples and organisations of the North and South as equal partners for change in a shared and interdependent world.

10. Encourages action that builds alliances to bring about change.   (DEA, 2000)

Washing one's hands of the conflict between the powerful and the powerless means to side with the powerful, not to be neutral.

Paulo Freire

Introduction

In 1995 the Development Education Association (DEA) conducted a major piece of research into development education activities within youth work in the UK entitled *A World of Difference* (Bourn and McCollum, 1995). The main focus of the research was to identify ways of responding to people's global interests and concerns within the youth sector.

The research established that though young people were interested in issues involving their immediate world in the North, they were also concerned about the wider world including the countries of the South. It identified that young people need the skills, confidence and encouragement to take action on the concerns they have about the local and global inequalities that exist.

The term 'North' refers to those countries which are mainly north of the equator, are economically richer, and predominantly white. The 'South' refers to those countries mainly located south of the equator, poorer, and where the majority of inhabitants are Black. These terms also highlight the global inequalities that have arisen over the last 300 years.

The term 'development education' was used to describe the methods and outlooks concerned with tackling global inequalities and giving people the knowledge and skills to take action to secure change (ibid., 1995). Initially much development education was produced by the large Egos (non-governmental organisations) such as Christian Aid and Oxfam, and was aimed at providing information about the South to build a support base for their work. In other words, development education was often associated with the work of charities, and though it appealed to young people's sense of outrage at the injustices in the world, it often stopped short of rallying young people to act in solidarity with people in other parts of the world.

The emphasis on 'global' as opposed to 'development' education signifies a shift in consciousness and an increasing awareness of the interdependence of our world. It also recognises that within the youth service the focus is on placing the local experience within a global context. For example, young people want a game of football to be fair. They may also want fair rules to apply to the young people of Sialkot in Pakistan who miss out on school and leisure time because they work long hours making footballs.

Globalisation

It is now common to refer to the world as 'a global village' and to the fact that we are increasingly becoming global citizens. Steiner points to the way in which global citizenship has a 'visionary' element that draws on:

> ...a long tradition of thought and feeling about the ultimate unity of human experience, giving rise to a politics of desire that posits for the planet as a whole a set of conditions of peace and justice and sustainability. (Steiner, 1996)

However, there is a negative side to globalisation, and today's society can increasingly be seen as:

> a 'spiritless, familyless, communityless place... Full of people who recognise the difference between Coke and Pepsi as something worth fighting about... (Gorelick, 1998)

Globalisation refers to processes that link the lives of peoples, organisations, states and societies, across the world. The lives of ordinary citizens across the globe are increasingly influenced by activities and events happening well away from the social environments in which they carry out their day-to-day activities. The decisions and actions taken locally can increasingly affect people and communities in other parts of the world.

Both the positive and negative aspects of globalisation are characterised by the technological innovations which have accompanied its growth: air travel, the world wide web, and genetic engineering are just three examples. However, globalisation could be said to have existed in different forms for many centuries. In the fifteenth century the peoples of Africa and the Arab world were the serious players in world trade. For example it was the trade routes established by the Mali and Songhai empires in present-day West Africa, which exported goods and people to Arabia, India, China and Europe.

The unequal balance of power that has existed in the world for the last three centuries is being reinforced during the present phase of globalisation. Whilst some see globalisation as being of universal benefit to all citizens of the world, the reality is that countries in the North are the primary beneficiaries. Globalisation means that transnational corporations (TNCs) such as General Motors, Ford Motor Company, Matsui, Mitsubishi, Royal Dutch Shell—in all, about 200 of them based in the North—are expanding into the world economy, particularly the economies of the poor countries. Multilateral organisations such as the World Trade Organisation (WTO), the International Monetary Fund (IMF) and the World Bank also play a key role in the process.

Some of the main processes that have contributed to the globalisation of human activity are:

- global trade
- technological developments
- political developments
- environmental destruction, and its
- impact on humans

Government Support

The Labour government's White Paper on International Development was published in 1997 and focuses on the internationally agreed target, which is to halve the proportion of people living in extreme poverty, by 2015. The government has a stated commitment to development awareness and is keen to engage new audiences. The Department for International Development (DFID) (administered by the DEA in England, Cyfanfyd in Wales, IDEAS in Scotland and CADA in the north of Ireland) has a mini grant programme, which is intended to support this work:

> Our young people must develop the competence, confidence and contacts which will secure their place and influence in an increasingly global society. The new millennium demands that we develop international understanding, heighten awareness of Europe and the wider world, and strengthen the concept of world citizenship in our schools and colleges. (Tony Blair, November 1998, Central Bureau Annual Report)

Global youth work concerns itself with making the links between the local and the global and aims to be an integral part of youth work. Youth workers may be engaging in football training, camping, detached work, or advice work, but they are also engaging in an education process. Global youth work can inform that education process, and because globalisation makes it increasingly difficult to separate the local and the global, it is important that those who work with young people have some awareness of this. There's little doubt that in the 21st century, all of us will need to address the question of how we locate ourselves in relation to our immediate community as well as to the wider global community.

Many youth organisations in the UK have a long history of addressing global issues, in particular Black organisations. Young people in Hackney can attend a three week summer school exploring aspects of Black British history as well as African and Caribbean studies. The course brings up issues like the debt crisis, trade and the refugee situation in this and other countries and helps young people to look at their own lives as Black British young people from a different perspective. One obvious outcome is the recognition that they may be in a minority in this country but they are part of the majority world. Their summer trips include trips to the Commonwealth Institute and the slavery museum in Liverpool as well as Alton Towers and the local museum. However, development education has often been neglected within youth work, which tends to focus on issues and interests that more obviously affect young people here and now, despite the fact that many young people already have links to different parts of the world.

The following may be useful in defining global youth work. It is not an absolute definition, but it emphasises the fact that global youth work is a perspective, not an extra topic or issue, but a way of looking at global issues within existing good youth work practice. In other words it is about exploring the globalisation that exists in one's own neighbourhood: the people, cultures, religions, food, music, fashion and drugs.

Examples of Global Youth Work

Young people are growing up to be citizens of a world, which offers wonderful opportunities for some but increasing marginalisation and inequality for others. As global citizens of the future, young people can become part of the solution to many of the world's problems if they are to become involved in effective action for change.

Many young people are aware of and concerned about global issues but this knowledge does not in itself change anything. The opportunities must be given to develop relevant skills so that effective action can be taken; otherwise young people will be left feeling angry, frustrated and powerless.

To develop young people's understanding of their roles and responsibilities as active citizens in a modern democracy, it is important that they participate in the democratic process at some level. To participate, people must feel confident to join in and speak up when it matters. This may be about local issues or national issues but it may also be about international issues.

Almost any activity, issue or topic that is covered within youth work can have a global perspective. Food is an example. We all eat, we must learn something about nutrition and food preparation if we are to stay health, and increasingly we are faced with economic, moral and ethical decisions about what we buy and what we eat. The average 17-year-old will spend over £1 million in their lifetime, much of it on food. The choices we make about what we buy and what we eat, impacts on the lives of people around the world. Similarly, decisions are taken in Washington or Seattle that impact on what choices are available to us. Did you know that Pepsi Cola, Pizza Hut, Kentucky Fried Chicken and Walkers crisps are all owned by the same company: Pepsico?

Though the world produces 50 per cent more food than is needed to feed the world's population, over 800 million people go to bed hungry every night. Companies investing millions in genetically engineered crops argue that genetic engineering means higher yields, resistance to pesticides and pests and produce that stays 'fresh' longer. This means, they say, that we could end world hunger. However, two thirds of British consumers do not want to eat genetically modified food, (MORI, 1998) and young people globally are in the forefront of protesting about the way decisions are taken by supra-national organisations like the World Trade Organisation (WTO).

It is worth reminding ourselves that people do not starve because there is not enough food to go round, they starve because:

- they are too poor to buy food
- they are denied access to land to grow it
- farmers grow crops for export instead of food crops to eat
- they are displaced by civil unrest and war

If young people are concerned about food rights:

- How do we listen to them and try and ensure that their views are taken seriously?
- How do we structure activities which will help them to express and challenge different points of view and take responsibility for their actions?
- How do we open up possibilities to them but also acknowledge that there are limitations to what individuals can do?
- How do we identify change that can be made at individual, local, national and global level?

Activities that involve exchanges and visits overseas have a long history in the youth service and are valuable and may broaden young people's minds and give them insights into other people's lives. However, for young people to experience it as a learning process they must be involved in the planning and organising. Links and exchanges should not be one-sided and neither should they be first and foremost about charity. They should be based on equality and mutual learning and a genuine commitment from both sides.

Global youth work is not:

- a bolt-on extra
- a one-off activity
- an exploration of exotic and distant places
- anti-racist work with white young people
- value-free

Global youth work **is** about developing a critical awareness of inequalities and seeking young people's participation.

Global youth work is not simply about what young people learn, but about how they learn; and how people do or do not change their beliefs and behaviour as a result of such learning. An article in the *Development Education Journal* (October 1998) quotes Ann Winter:

> *To effect...any significant alterations in attitudes and values, or indeed to explicitly form them, requires the identification of both cognitive and affective objectives and the examination and exposure of beliefs and prejudices. This cannot be achieved through the mere imparting of information.* (Winter, 1995)

How Global Youth Work Fits into Youth Work

Most youth work is based on local issues and the structures that support it are set up to respond to local priorities. However, the 'core curriculum' guidelines offer opportunities for the development of global youth work, which are not always taken up by youth workers. Because process rather than outcome is stressed, there are opportunities to integrate a global perspective under the guidance it offers.

Youth workers recognise that young people do not learn by simply being told the facts. They learn by engagement, dialogue, building confidence, and swapping stories.

A group of 15-year-olds were travelling by train to a camping weekend. They began talking about literacy. One of them had seen a leaflet referring to the 125 million primary age children unable to go to school. At first the group wrestled with the concept of **125 million** individual lives (twice the population of the UK!). They then spent most of the journey discussing different sorts of education: formal education, what you would learn if you lived 'in a desert', 'in the bush', 'in the North Pole' and in what language people should be taught. The focus of the discussion was questioning the need for traditional literacy in the age of the computer. Would the Internet require people to be formally educated? Was formal education really the route to ending poverty, gender discrimination and poor health? The starting point for these young people was their own experience of education; what they had read and heard about who 'makes it' in the world of e-commerce, and the extent to which their education did or didn't work for them.

Clearly, facts would support the case for education being a primary requisite in the fight against poverty. However, those young people were engaging with a difficult issue from the perspective of their experience of the world, their aspirations for the future and their empathy with young people in the South. Good youth work is about enabling young people to explore ideas within a supportive environment. It may be that some of the ideas they expressed were racist, wrong and misguided, but they are ideas that they had heard expressed in different forms many times. With little to balance these views, it is no wonder that they are still repeated. 'Africans are poor because they have too many children', a quote taken from a member of the public during market research conducted by ActionAid. One of the key reasons why so many Africans are poor is because much of the continent's economy has been geared towards providing Europe and North America with the commodities to make their economies rich. Moreover, Africans are becoming poorer because their countries are in debt. In Tanzania every man, woman and child has a debt burden of about US$267.

Local is Global

> *When I think about young people in America or Europe, I can't see that they could have any problems, but I am sure that they do have some, even if they are just small worries like if your hair looks bad.*

(Magda Jasmin (aged 15) from Ka Toussaint in Haiti)

Many people in South Yorkshire are poor. They are poor because much of the local economy was based on steel and coal and it was decided that these could be produced elsewhere, for bigger profits. Miners and steelworkers and their sons and daughters are out of a job and so are thousands of others whose livelihoods were bound up with these industries. For many people in this area, poverty has meant not having enough money to live healthily and comfortably, and in addition it has meant becoming increasingly marginalised and excluded from society and the decision-making processes.

A Joseph Rowntree Foundation (JRF) study published in May 2000, looks at political interest and engagement amongst those aged 14 to 24. The research found that young people are less apathetic and more interested in public issues and current affairs than is commonly supposed. However, politicians, along with the word 'politics', are widely seen as boring, irrelevant and an immediate turn-off (JRF, 2000). Clarissa White, the co-author makes the point that the supposed apathy of young people is based on the assumption that they are already disinterested in a range of political issues, even though they may not see them as 'political'. In much the same way, young people often **are** interested in global issues and youth workers in global youth work, but they may use different language to describe what they do.

The so-called 'global village' has immense appeal for young people. Apart from the obvious global symbols like McDonalds and Coca-Cola, television can show live football from the other side of the planet and most places in the world are accessible to travellers. Virtually every town in the UK has an Asian restaurant and supermarkets sell food from every corner of the earth. The Internet offers young people an unparalleled opportunity to engage with other young people. Though the new technology, as any other technology, is not neutral and not truly global, it nevertheless offers additional mechanisms to build alliances and make links, though most people in the world do not have a telephone let alone a computer. This situation, seemingly global, but not really global at all, offers youth workers an opportunity to work with young people to explore different aspects of the technology: its possibilities, its limitations; the possibility that it will lead to widening the gulf between rich and poor in countries of the North as well as the South; censorship, and questions of gender, power and equality.

Evaluation

Monitoring and evaluation are essential to good practice in all aspects of youth work. The purpose of evaluation is to measure the effectiveness of the work being done and to be accountable to managers, funders and young people themselves. Evaluation is most effective if it is built in at the beginning of a piece of work. Much of global youth work involves attitudinal change which is not easy to evaluate but it is possible to structure activities which get young people to identify what they want out of a particular activity and then to assess the extent to which the outcomes match their expectations.

Acknowledgement

This article draws on the DEA's *Global Youth Work: A Practice and Training Resource Manual* which has

Key Questions

1. Does the work assert that we are all citizens of a planet, which we must find ways of sharing?
2. Does the work value difference and cultural diversity in a multicultural society?
3. Does the work make a commitment to human rights?
4. Are we seeking to create a fairer world where resources are shared and sustained for the benefit of all?
5. Are we encouraging young people to participate in decision making?
6. Are we working together and recognising that our problems are shared by many other people?
7. Do we understand how decisions made here affect the lives of people in other parts of the world?

come out of discussions among youth work practitioners and development education groups.

The DEA is a national umbrella body existing to promote the work of all those engaged in bringing about a better public understanding in the UK of global and development issues. The DEA offers information, training and support to its member organisations and a network of 46 local development education centres (DECs).

For further information about the DEA's work or for details of your local DEC see Organisations below.

References

Bourn, D., and McCollum, A. (1995). *World of Difference: Making Global Connections in Youth Work*. DEA.

Eliminating World Poverty: A Challenge for the 21st Century. DFID.

DEA (2000). *Global Youth Work: A Practice and Training Resource Manual*. London.

JRF (2000). *Young People's Boredom with Politics Should not be Confused with Apathy*. 15th May, JRF.

MORI (1998). *June 1998 MORI Poll*. MORI

Winter, A. (1995). *Is Anyone Listening? Communicating Development in Donor Countries*. Geneva: UNGLS.

Organisations

Action Aid
Hamlyn House
Macdonald Road
London N19 5PG
Tel: 0207 561 7565
bisiw@actionaid.org.uk
www.oneworld.org/actionaid

Cfanfyd
Welsh Centre for International Affairs
Temple of Peace
Cathays Park
Cardiff CF1 3AP
Tel: 01222 757067

CADA
Coalition of Aid and Development Agencies
4 Lower Crescent
Belfast BT7 1NR
Tel: 01232 241 879

CAFOD
2 Romero Close
Stockwell Road
London SW9 9TY
Tel: 0207 733 7900
www.cafod.org.uk

Christian Aid
35–41 Lower Marsh
London SE1 7RL
Tel: 0207 620 4444
www.christian-aid.org.uk

DEA
3rd Floor
29–31 Cowper Street
London EC2A 4AT
Tel: 0207 490 8108
e-mail: devedassoc@gn.apc.org

Birmingham DEA
Gillett Centre
998 Bristol Road
Selly Oak
Birmingham B29 6LE
Tel: 0121 472 3255

DEFY
(Development Education for Youth)
7 Camden Place
Dublin 2
Ireland
Tel: 00 353 1 475 1826

IDEAS
34–36 Rose Street
North Lane
Edinburgh EH2 2NP
Tel: 0131 225 7617

NYA
17–23 Albion Street
Leicester LE1 6GD
Tel: 0116 285 6789
www.nya.org.uk

Save the Children Fund
Mary Datchelor House
17 Grove Lane
Camberwell
London SE5 8RD
Tel: 0207 703 5400
www.savethechildren.org.uk

SCIAF
5 Oswald Street
Glasgow G1 4QR
Tel: 0141 221 4447
www.sciaf.org.uk

Further Reading

Changing the World: A Directory of Global Youth Work Resources (1996).Youth Work Press.

It's Not Fair: A Handbook on World Development for Youth Groups (1993). CAFOD, Christian Aid, and SCIAF.

75/25 Development in an Increasingly Unequal World (1996). Birmingham DEC.

The World in Your Pocket: A Global Youth Work Resource (1999). Action Aid.

A World of Difference—Making Global Connections in Youth Work (1995). Development Education Association.

World's Web: The Global Education Pack for Work with Young People (1997). Peter White, Save the Children.

19 Environmental Youth Work

Tracie Trimmer

Key Points

1. Environmental youth work is not just 'green' politics.
2. The audit process can be adapted for all capacities and abilities.
3. Utilise the Agenda 21 officer to involve young people in local authority initiatives.
4. Young people know when adults in authority are fobbing them off.
5. Good youth work practice is about motivating, even after disappointments: encourage young people to plan for varying responses and reactions.

Introduction

One hundred and seventy-nine government leaders signed up to Agenda 21 at the Rio de Janeiro Earth Summit in 1992. This called for them to move towards sustainable ways of living and recognised that issues such as pollution, consumption of resources, poverty, inequality and injustice were all contributing towards the destruction of the planet. Agenda 21 was one of the Earth Summit's targets for action and it encouraged local authorities to develop departments to aim to meet some of the goals set out in the summit. Agenda 21 clearly set out to involve local communities fully in planning and decision-making around their environment and believed that progress could only be made if each local area worked in its own way. Young people are highlighted in Agenda 21, as a section of society to be targeted, which is hardly surprising since they constitute such a high percentage of the population as well as, inevitably, becoming future tenants, residents and decision makers. Chapter 25 of Agenda 21 states:

> Governments should take measures to establish procedures allowing for consultation and possible participation of youth in decision-making processes with regard to the environment, involving youth at local level.
>
> (Quarrie, 1992)

Banks et al. (1992) identified that environmental issues were fourth in a list of issues important to young people between the ages of 16–19; the first three being racism, sexism and sex. Youth workers all know how difficult it can be to encourage large numbers of young people to attend a particular event if it does not seem to appeal to them. So an invitation from a local authority to attend an Agenda 21-consultation meeting is hardly going to be favoured over an episode of East Enders or a challenging game of basketball. It is a task in itself, attempting to make the topic relevant and interesting enough for young people to want to take part, never mind to continue to develop sustainable concepts and projects. Environmentally motivated youth workers might generate support for the cause, but, generally, local authorities will have found a disappointing level of real input from young people, relative to their representation in the population. Young people are already making choices about their lives and deciding when they will attend clubs, when they will attend school, when they should enter into relationships etc., and are unlikely to contribute to an adult arena when they feel their contribution will not be heard, understood, respected, or followed up. This is not to say that all such opportunities were seen in this way or had no value for those who attended, but that it is difficult to genuinely include and represent young people in such a forum.

Another train of current thought might be that being 'green' is young and trendy and that all young people are concerned about the environment, buying environmentally friendly products and supporting animal welfare, but this is possibly only true among the more advantaged youth. Those who have access to the Royal Society for Nature Conservation or the Institute for Earth

Education are likely to have interested parents with disposable income and a programme of family weekend activities. Although professional organisations such as The Woodcraft Folk, the Guides, the Duke of Edinburgh Award Scheme and the Royal Society for the Protection of Birds offer programmes and awards with environmental themes, the opportunities for most young people will be limited if they exist at all. A young person may purchase items, which are recyclable and feel they are making a huge contribution to environmental change and it may be that those who are the consumers are also those who are better informed.

Young people rarely see the environmental debate as being close to them, and recognise that only major influence can effect change. Young people do not feel empowered, even with more information about environmental problems, so there is no guarantee that they will feel either able or willing to tackle them. Awareness raising does not necessarily mean action for change, although there are ways that this can be encouraged. I recall my first experience of introducing environmental issues in a youth club as being relatively well received and resulting in the adoption of a can recycling system supported by the local authority. It felt like a major achievement to sustain the interest of the regular members from a poor and unpopular estate in central London. This had the desired effect with everyone making an effort to throw cans into the labelled receptacles and in taking the time to test whether they were aluminium or tin. All went terribly well until we realised that the cleaner was emptying the bins in the waste disposal shoot on a regular basis!

The Council for Environmental Education defines environmental youth work as a process which:

> *Should empower young people to make changes in order to achieve a better, fairer, safer, longer-lasting environment for all, and, which amongst other things, leads to positive and informed action for change.*
>
> (CEE, 1990)

This is encouraging, but if young people's living environments are to be converted, recognition must be given to the fact that both private and public spaces are planned, designed and constructed by adults. Faceless bureaucrats usually make decisions about environmental management and maybe how

an estate ought to look to the community. By encouraging and empowering young people to become more pro-active in this and become part of the decision-making process the structures which exist within society are challenged, about who decides community development issues and how they are initiated. Young people should be invited to become members of residents and tenants' associations (after all, how many residents and tenants association meetings have been spent discussing the behaviour of local young people?) and to take part in town planning meetings and processes. Locally active community members should be encouraged to advocate such input. In this way young people can have an impact upon those structures and processes that inform environmental decisions around their day-to-day lives.

Planting a tree, or clearing a pond, whilst valuable activities in themselves, do not necessarily change the environment. Does this kind of activity really tackle the concerns that young people have about where they live and play? Well, by adapting a community approach to a sense of their physical surroundings it can clearly encourage the development of self-confidence, teamwork and a sense of ownership; dimensions which exist in the social education framework. Using the environment as a vehicle for social education, participation and a broader sense of political awareness may be developed.

As with many areas of youth work, we are discovering more and more that the most effective vehicle for transferring information to and from young people is the young people themselves. The concept of peer education is not new but has recently claimed a new status. I believe that we have always encouraged young people to transfer skills and information from one to the other, and have often used peer education methods to deliver diverse programmes, but only now is this being identified as a valuable and accountable youth work style (see Annmarie Turnball, Chapter 4).

Youth workers may then be using environment as a tool for social education, but often it is assumed that this would not necessarily bring about direct environmental change. Such interventions generally create the sort of changes in individuals that are encouraged in youth work. Ultimately, the outcome of successful youth work programmes should be to produce assertive, motivated adults, equipped with the skills and experiences to become active in their communities, and effect change in their lives should the opportunity present itself. The challenge facing those who advocate the environmental youth work approach is to demonstrate firstly, how it empowers young people, and secondly what significant impact it will have on environmental change.

Young Women's Safety: An Environmental Issue

With these issues and experiences in mind, the concept of young people's safety and their local environment was considered as a relevant issue for the London Union of Youth Clubs (LUYC). The Women's Design Service (WDS) and Youth Clubs UK acted as consultants for the project which has since been developed to work in mixed as well as single gender groups (Cavannagh, 1998). Since personal safety is high on the agenda for young women, this project was particularly significant. When working with all young people it is necessary to consider the issues of safety in accessibility, transport, lighting, how a group will travel to and from a venue. Additionally, what are the risks of holding an event in a specific place, and so on, putting into context both the physical and psychological aspect of safety for those with whom we work. This may not only apply to young people but also be relevant to staff and visitors. Although this project focused on safety in the built environment, the methods and processes used could be adapted to suit a variety of environmental topics and outcomes.

It became clear early on in this project that young people's perceptions of what was or was not safe differed according to the group's make-up and surroundings. For example, one group found the route they took to and from their homes to the youth club intimidating and potentially dangerous. They travelled through a badly lit tunnel and across bridge with poor visibility. Another group of young mothers were dissatisfied with the local play facilities for their toddlers. The area was paved with jagged and uneven slabs, swings were ill maintained and the whole area was littered with unacceptable dog mess. Groups of disabled young women found public transport inaccessible and the absence of ramps and lifts at underground stations intolerable.

The project focused on safety issues for groups of young women in London, and was developed around a method of *Safety Auditing*; young

women's experiences and concerns providing a good basis for effective youth work. The audit usually develops over six or seven sessions (or stages). It is easier to look at each stage in turn.

Stage one: discussion

This forms the basis of the first session, focusing on safety (or the issue that is being addressed). Encourage the group to discuss what makes them feel safe or unsafe, or which local areas or community features cause them concern. Through this discussion the areas to be targeted in the audit will become apparent. For example, one group might highlight an unlit walkway as a cause for concern and describe how they will only venture through it in pairs or in a group. Another group might find the vandalism in a particular area disturbing or the amount of refuse dumping unhygienic or depressing. Discussing these issues and others, the group will be able to identify possible themes around which to conduct the audit. The group concerned about refuse might target patterns of litter dumping or main refuse collection areas, while those who preferred better lighting would focus on this. This part of the process encourages groups to analyse their sense of personal safety, well being and quality of life within their local work and play areas.

Use activities such as the thermometer game, where you ask members of the group what makes their blood boil, and use a giant graphic thermometer or an imaginary one. Ask participants to record the things they are most concerned about nearer the top, at the hottest or boiling point, and the things they feel less annoyed about toward the bottom and cooler part of the thermometer. You can use scrap paper for people to write the words or comments on, or for groups with language or learning difficulties you could use magazines and newspapers to cut out pictures or articles. When the group have positioned their concerns this provides a good basis for discussion.

Stage two: mapping

This is an opportunity for the group to begin to look at maps, become familiar with them and possibly make their own, and create plans or models of the area. The group might want to look at professional maps from surveyors or town planners or develop their own by using drawings, photographs, diagrams and so on. There may also be those who would like to make models of particular aspects of an estate, park or crossing, with idealised 'before' and 'after' features. This provides an opportunity for the group to be as creative as they like. It can encourage individuals to use skills they already possess or develop new ones, in say, presentations, understanding and translating maps, or simply being able to look closely at a certain area of their community. If this sounds ambitious, it need not be, as the idea here is to make or locate some frame of reference for the area you are targeting.

Maps are often thought of as highly technical and those without experience are put off by the prospect of designing their own. There are several ways of making this fun and straightforward, such as allowing each member of the group the same size of paper and a series of symbols for common things; a triangle for a tree, a rectangle for flats, a circle for a waste bin and so on; someone will have to prepare these symbols beforehand. When each person goes out into a particular part of the area it is interesting the see how the map looks when all pieces are put together. This is also fun to do as everyone has the same amount of space to map and report upon but interpret what they see for themselves either by cutting pictures from magazines or drawing or sketching and then putting the whole map together. You can also use tracing paper or transparent film to trace off professional maps or use photocopies, enlargements etc. A group who felt uncomfortable about doing anything too technical or formal, created a model of their housing estate by sticking a series of cereal boxes together; more creative types have chosen to build clay models with trees and birds; one group created a virtual estate using computer technology.

Stage three: observation

This part of the process encourages groups to look at their chosen environment feature or area and assess its affect on their feelings and perception of that space. Examples such as the badly-lit stairwell are a simple one to apply to this, as the obvious remedy might be to provide lighting. However, young people's perceptions and experiences of safety at particular times and in different places

will vary enormously. The kinds of things to look for when observing the area are the number of people around, whether they are young people, elderly, families, men or women, what the noise level is. How much litter is there, how many cars are being used, did anyone notice when you came into the area to do the project, was anyone puzzled by note-taking or photography taking place etc. It is important to note anything that occurs to you along the way, as it may be relevant later on. Depending on the amount of time you have to do this work it is useful to be able to look at the same area both at night time as well as during the day, as perceptions and experiences are likely to be different at these times. Depending also on the depth of the observation needed, it may be worthwhile observing both on weekdays and at weekends.

Stage four: recording

It is important to record the observations made by the group during the audit so that it can be analysed at a later stage. There are several ways of recording and this can be a really enjoyable part of the process. Using video equipment, you could develop a documentary style 'watchdog' or 'vox-pops' film, which might include interviews with members of the group, others you meet during the course of the session, or those involved in area management or maintenance. Once edited, a piece of video footage can be used as a tool for campaigning and lobbying or as a piece of historical evidence, as well as being something which decision-makers can see and not get away from! Photography is also a good way of recording, particularly with cameras that take instant pictures, which can be analysed and discussed almost immediately. With instant photography you are able to see straight away whether what you wanted to record was successful; with films which require developing, you do not know the quality of the photographs until they have been processed. It is also possible to carry out voice recordings to be analysed afterwards, making verbal notes of things as you go along. Once again, depending on both the time you have available and the depth of the project, you might want to carry out surveys using questionnaires or interviews with local residents, local authority representatives or councillors. There is a wealth of information to be gained using a variety of recording methods but it is essentially up to the group to decide what they want to achieve and what is manageable for them.

Stage five: analysis

The analysis of the stages so far, is important, as it leads to the selection and prioritising of the issues identified as key in the audit. This stage will enable the group to look at all of the information it has gathered and set clear and realistic aims for the future of the project. For example, if a play area was identified as a safety hazard, there are likely to be a catalogue of various issues relating to that; the play equipment itself, the flooring, the fencing around it, where litter bins are and whether they are used, how clean the sand pit is, what the general state of maintenance is and so on. It is important to prioritise the issues in order to make plans for action. If the playground is poorly painted this is disappointing, but if pieces of equipment are faulty it is more important to sort that out first. At this point then, the group could be making a prioritised list of points they want to action and possibly set themselves a timescale.

Stage six: presentation

The presentation is necessary to pass on the findings of the audit as effectively and clearly as possible, and to gain support for the group's proposals for change. Once again this depends on the scale of the project and might mean that a group present their findings to their peers in a youth club or that they invite local councillors, housing officials, local press, town planners, residents and local people to an open forum in which to share findings and gain support for positive change. It is necessary to keep the presentation as concise as possible as some of the recording made will not be of interest or necessarily relevant to those who are taking part at this stage. The presentation stage can also be an opportunity to encourage more people to come on board to support the work. For example, if appropriate and on a smaller scale in the youth project, to encourage a new system of recycling or a litter free zone or a no smoking policy. Presentations can be made as formal or informal as you like; as long as the main points are covered it rarely matters. What does matter is that the group have decided whether it will be formal or not and what impression they want need to give to the audience.

Stage seven: implementation

The implementation of the project is about gaining support from decision and policy makers to effect change or improvement in the areas which have been identified. This may involve lobbying, campaigning, contacting local government, supportive organisations, and sponsors, the police etc., the list is endless. The important issue at this stage is not to set young people up to fail. Encouraging them to approach decision-makers with the assumption that they will get the response they want, is unfair. It is an important aspect of the learning process that they are made aware of the systems and processes which exist, and of the possible disappointments that lie ahead. That is not to say there is no point to any of this, because of course there is, but to encourage young people to write a letter to an MP, for example, and have them believe that the issues will be immediately resolved is inaccurate. It should be stressed that sometimes the implementation part of the process is the most long-winded, but ultimately the most rewarding.

Key Questions

1. Who has decided the work you are about to embark on is relevant: adults or young people?
2. Are the targets the group is setting realistic?
3. Who can you call on for support, expertise and encouragement outside of the local area?
4. Has anything similar been done before and what was learnt from it?
5. How can this piece of work be made sustainable and does it need to be?

Conclusion

There is opportunity for much individual and group learning throughout this process, encouraging the development of new skills and attitudes. There is, at each stage, the potential for some excellent youth work and the personal and social development of those involved. It is also flexible enough to allow all manner of topics to be focused upon and a diverse range of young people to become involved. A local football team might look to improve their training area; a disabled group to improve their public transport opportunities and so on. Because it is adaptable, it gives youth workers the opportunity to work with young people around issues, which they identify for themselves, and to impact on the immediate, possibly larger community. The possibilities for developmental work are endless. Similar systems of monitoring and mapping could be used to address global issues and anti-racist youth work. For example, through the audit process a group may decide that they want to challenge local racism. An initial audit may highlight racist graffiti, limited minority group use of facilities, attendance at clubs and local amenities, no celebration of festivals and so on. Working through the audit process would enable an interested group to gather evidence of the issues that concern them and present findings and possible alternatives to the situation, encouraging others to examine their attitudes, values and practices.

The audit process clearly relates to the environmental change discussed earlier as well as utilising peer education methods. Many will tell you that the best educators of young people are the young people themselves and that if young people take anyone seriously it is more likely to be someone of their own age than an adult. Their peers speak the same language, have the same interests, share the same concerns and want similar things. The presentation part of the process, especially, allows young people to share with peers their findings, concerns and plans and provides the opening for others to take part, spread the word or work on their own topics.

References

Banks, S. (Ed.) (1992). *Careers and Identities*. Buckingham: Open University Press.

Council for Environmental Education (1990). *EARTHworks: Taking an Environmental Approach*. Reading: CEE.

Quarrie, J. (Ed.) (1992). *Earth Summit '92*. The United Nations Conference on Environment and Development. London: Regency Press.

Organisations

National Youth Agency
17–23 Albion Street
Leicester LE1 6GD

Youth Clubs UK
2nd Floor
Kirby House
20–24 Kirby Street
London EC1N 8TS

Council for Environmental Education
94 London Street
Reading RG1 4SJ

Further Reading

Cavannagh, S. (1998). *Making Safer Places. A Resource Book for Neighbourhood Safety Audits. Women's Participation in Environmental Planning*. London: Women's Design Service.

Investing in Children: Using a Children's Rights Approach to Achieve Change
Liam Cairns

Key Points

1. We must create ways for children and young people to participate in decisions which affect their lives—these may be different, less structured and more spontaneous than those used by adults.

2. Lack of access to a resource or service amounts to a denial of rights so access rather than simple provision must be a key focus of our work.

3. Universalism—we must ask about how the rights of all young people in an area might be realised rather than just those in the youth club or 'looked after' by a local authority. Otherwise, rights work is in danger of being shunted into a cul-de-sac.

4. We need to enter a dialogue with young people rather than just 'consulting' them.

5. Every children's right carries with it an adult responsibility and this may mean targeting adults for interventions as well as children and young people.

Introduction

The UK Government ratified the UN Convention on the Rights of the Child in December 1991. Almost ten years later, it would be difficult to find many children and young people in Britain who could describe how things had changed for them. Indeed, according to recent research (Alderson, 2000) many young people are unaware of the existence of the Convention, despite the fact that, as part of ratification, the government gave an undertaking to publicise the Convention to 'adults and children alike' (article 42).

This is not simply a question of perception, or in the language of the spin-doctors, merely a failure to get the message across, there are real and significant flaws in the way children and young people are treated:

> We continue to regard children as the property of their parents and not as individuals in their own right. How else can we explain the fact, for example, that children have no right to express a choice of school or to be given a hearing if excluded from school.
>
> (Lansdown, 1995)

It has to be said that this is not for the want of trying. Resources have gone into children's rights initiatives. For example, many local authorities have appointed designated Children's Rights Officers

over this period, and one of the conundrums is why they have not had a more widespread effect. In a similar vein, the youth service must wonder why so little progress has been made, given its commitment to:

- Treating young people with respect.
- Respecting and promoting young people's rights to make their own decisions.
- Promoting the welfare and safety of young people.
- Contributing towards the promotion of social justice for young people.

(National Youth Agency, 1999)

Part of the answer, it seems, lies in the extent to which children and young people have been able to shape the agenda themselves. I shall attempt to make a distinction between two approaches.

The first is primarily concerned to create mechanisms for children and young people to contribute to debates that adults identify as important, and to do this in ways which determined by adults as appropriate, and often modelled on adult structures. School councils, youth councils, young people's parliaments: where they work, they do provide some opportunities for some young people to participate, but these can often be subject to limitations placed upon them by adults either in terms of how they are organised:

...The role played by adults in facilitating children's meetings and organisations is ambiguous and can be manipulative and controlling.   (Ennew, 1998)

Or what they can discuss:

Some teachers told us that school councils were useless because pupils want to talk only about school uniforms and other forbidden questions
(Alderson, 2000)

The second approach tries to be open to the possibility of an alternative but equally valid agenda of issues which young people themselves identify as important. Having identified the issues, it is for the young people to determine how they will go about pursuing them. This approach has been attempted in the Investing in Children Initiative.

Investing in Children

This chapter looks at how, through the Investing in Children initiative, public services in County Durham have tried to translate the rhetoric of the UN Convention into a reality that young people would recognise. Some of the obstacles, which appear to get in the way will be examined, and also some of the strategies adopted in Durham to overcome these. Investing in Children is not being held up as a model to be adopted elsewhere, but perhaps some useful lessons could be learned from the way the project has developed, and in particular, how young people themselves have shaped this development.

Background

In 1995, the Chief Executive of Durham County Council convened a seminar of public and voluntary agencies providing services to children, young people and their families in the county. The government of the day had indicated that local authorities would have a new statutory duty to publish a Children's Services Plan (up until this point, local authorities had been advised under the Children Act 1989, but not required, to publish such a plan), and the purpose of the seminar was to explore how different agencies could collaborate in this venture.

Following the seminar, a working party was convened chaired by the Director of Social Services to establish a shared philosophy around which different agencies could unite. The most significant result of their efforts was the Investing in Children Statement of Intent.

Statement of Intent

Our *aim* is to work in partnership with children and young people to *promote their best interests and enhance their quality of life*.

We will achieve this by:
- Consulting with children, young people and their families about decisions affecting their lives and the development of services.
- Promoting partnerships between individuals and agencies to address young people's issues.
- Developing services accessible to children and young people and centred on the family, that promote dignity and independence and which do not discriminate or stigmatise.
- Ensuring that, when making decisions on policies and services, consideration is given to their potential impact on the lives of children and young people.

The *values* that underpin the Initiative's work with children and young people are consistent with the UN Convention on the Rights of the Child and the Children Act 1989.

The thinking behind this was clear, and in hindsight, extremely powerful. By making explicit what was thought to be important and why, this would be an invaluable tool to help decide on what action should be taken. Three key agencies, the county council's social services department, the education department and the health authority committed funds for a three year period to the

Initiative and in 1997 Investing in Children was created. Since then, almost every major agency in the county, including all of the district councils, the police, the environment department and the major children's voluntary organisations have signed up to the Statement of Intent. Earlier this year a further three years of funding provided by an extended group of agencies, extended the project to 2003.

How Children and Young People See the Statement of Intent

It is worth pausing for a moment to consider how young people themselves viewed the Statement of Intent. A group of young people working with the project identified the following key points:

1. Adults don't always know best

If the best services are to be designed for children and young people, adults must learn to listen to them, value their opinion, and involve them in decision-making. This is fundamental to the whole enterprise. Although this point is often accepted by agencies without question, it represents a substantial challenge in practice. For many, their professional status is tied in with the idea that they are experts in their field. Knowing what is best is often their *raison d'être* and accepting that children and young people have things to teach them is a significant hurdle to jump.

2. Adults must take care that the way services are provided does not inadvertently lock out some children and young people.

As will be shown, when given the opportunity, children and young people can provide evidence of how adults failure to listen to them can mean that services often exclude the very people who need them most.

This point was illustrated most vividly in discussion with a group of mothers and their sons and daughters in a village in the south of the county. The young people attended a comprehensive school in a town five miles away. These particular families were not particularly affluent, and as a consequence, the young people were excluded from participation in such extra-curricular activities as the school netball

team or orchestra. This was because practice for these activities happened after school and the school bus left at 3.30; if you weren't on it, you had to make your own arrangements. Effectively, participation depended upon having parents who either had cars or sufficient resources to make other arrangements for the journey home from school.

3. The approach must be based in a universal concept of children's rights.

Ask the question: Are all children and young people in County Durham being treated with respect and dignity and receiving the services to which they have a right?

A Universal Approach

This point is at the heart of Investing in Children, which has attempted to adopt an inclusive and comprehensive approach, and resisted the temptation of being drawn into narrow debates about the position of particular groups of children and young people. This is because the most powerful arguments for change are believed to lie in this universal approach.

Over the past ten years, much of the debate about children's rights has concentrated upon particular groups: most notably, children looked-after. Partly because, understandably, it was felt that the greatest need for change lay here. More practically, the majority of Children's Rights Officers were employed by social services departments, and in a climate of budgetary restraint, the emphasis was on those children and young people for whom the local authority had a statutory responsibility.

But it seemed that the effect of this was to drive children's rights into a narrow cul-de-sac, where attention was often concentrated upon children and young people's looked-after status rather than their status as children or young people, and an esoteric debate ensued which the vast majority of the population were able to ignore because it didn't affect them or their children, nephews, nieces, grandchildren etc.

This same phenomenon can be seen in the way other specific groups are treated. For example children with disabilities are often defined by their disability rather than their status as children. This process of defining young people may well be administratively convenient, but it also serves to keep groups of children apart from one another. A more powerful approach to change might be to encourage different groups of young people to consider what they have in common, and to work together to achieve common goals.

This is the approach attempted in Durham where efforts have concentrated on creating opportunities for children and young people from any background to say whatever they want to say. This has made the Initiative difficult to ignore, or to pigeonhole. Also, by concentrating on what they have in common (their status as children and young people) rather than what has previously defined them as different, some interesting and potentially powerful alliances have developed.

The Process

In 1997, the process of writing a new Children's Services Plan began. Armed with the Statement of Intent, it was accepted that the Plan should include issues raised by young people themselves. Most had a fair idea of the adult agenda: for example, concerns about the health and safety of children in relation to substance misuse or sexual behaviour, educational achievement, youth crime, etc. What was not known was whether children and young people themselves shared this agenda, or whether another set of priorities existed.

So the aim was to create opportunities for children and young people to make a contribution to the debate. A variety of methods were used, from theatre, to recruiting groups of young people themselves to act as research teams. Some of our efforts worked very well, and some less well. Not every child and young person in the County, was reached, nor every issue of importance explored. But an agenda of issues was drawn from the work, and those issues were different from those which troubled the adults.

Discrimination

Children and young people expressed their indignation at being treated differently from adults for no good reason. For example, they pointed to shops, which display signs saying, 'No children unless accompanied by an adult' or 'Only two children allowed at a time'. Shopkeepers offered the explanation that this was in response to problems with theft, but young people pointed out that not all young people steal, that adults also shoplift, and that the signs are discriminatory and unfair. Would it be acceptable, they asked, to display a sign saying 'No women unless accompanied by a man' or 'Only two black people allowed'? It is a matter of social justice.

They also challenged the differential treatment received by adults and children from public servants, why, for example, are groups of young people routinely moved on by the police when no offence is being committed?

Accessibility

Another issue which came up regularly was problems of access. Children and young people had questions about where, when and how services were provided. It often seemed to them that little or no thought had gone in to ensuring the service was accessible to them.

This was sometimes a question of attitude: young people described circumstances where it was clear that they were not welcome. It was also about organisation and location. Durham is a semi-rural county, with much of the population living in villages or small towns. Often, services are not locally available, and the limited mobility of young people can be a major obstacle in the way of accessing a service, which is only available in the town ten miles away.

Transport

Leading on from accessibility, young people described the difficulty they had in simply getting around. Comments were made about the availability of public transport, the cost, and the attitude of some transport staff.

Safety and protection

Young people described places and situations where they often felt vulnerable and in need of protection, and they asked whether their fears were taken seriously by adults. Young people noted that many schools had anti-bullying policies, but wondered why leisure centres and youth clubs, for example, didn't also have such policies. One group of children described a particular public park as a dangerous place.

Young people also raised concerns about whether their feelings of security were as important as the security of adults. A group described congregating outside the '8-till-late' shop in their village. This was a good spot, because it was well lit. However, on a regular basis the police moved them on, because adults perceived their presence as a threat. They were moved on to areas where it was dark, and where **they** felt insecure.

Dialogue not consultation

It was clear from early on that simply asking children and young people what the issues were was not enough. Many of the young people who were involved in the early work wanted to do more than offer a view: they wanted to take part, to play an active role in creating change.

The work of the Investing in Children Transport group provides the best example of this. When it became clear that transport was an issue all round the county, the different research teams were invited to get together and think about this further. Having helped to identify the problem, they were keen to help create some solutions.

The group, consisting of 16 young people aged between 14 and 16 and from a variety of backgrounds and with a variety of abilities, thought that the process should be straightforward. If all of the key decision-makers could get together, the young people could explain the issues, and through a process of dialogue, some new answers would be found.

A group of transport professionals duly assembled, from the local authority and the commercial bus companies. For a variety of reasons, however, the hoped-for dialogue never took place. In part, this was because the adults were not prepared to enter into discussions with children on the basis of there being some equality. Rather than listen, they saw the meeting as an opportunity to explain why things were as they were. The adults paraded their expertise. This had the effect of throwing the young people off balance. They found themselves unable to assert their case in the face of the apparently robust defence of the status quo presented by the adults.

The group withdrew, but rather than accept that there was no change to be had, the group determined to continue to pursue their case. Their experience had taught them that knowledge could be a source of power, so they decided to acquire

knowledge. Over the next ten months or so, the group set out to find out as much as they could about public transport. They visited other local authorities and even went to look at arrangements on the continent.

Finally, they produced their report, *Fare's Fair* in which they argued that the transport system was environmentally unsustainable because it encouraged dependence upon the private car, and socially unjust in that it favoured children from better-off families (Some areas of County Durham have the highest rates in the country of families who don't own cars). Furthermore, they produced evidence to show that children and young people in other parts of the country, and perhaps more significantly, in other parts of the region, enjoyed better opportunities for cheaper transport than children and young people in Durham.

Armed with their report, the group met again with the transport professionals. However, this time the atmosphere was completely different, and the adults present listened carefully and with respect as the young people presented their case.

As a consequence, in May 2000, 17,000 young people in Durham became eligible for a new travel card (named appropriately enough, the Investing in Children card), which allows them to travel for a reduced fare. The scheme was designed by a group consisting of local authority staff, the bus companies, *and the young people themselves*: genuine participation.

What this example demonstrates is the value of pursuing dialogue rather than a consultation process. From the experience with the Transport Group and with other young people worked with, consultation has been found to be a rather sterile and unsatisfactory process. Young people's experience has been of consultation as an event, in which the powerful (the adults) consult, and the powerless (children and young people) are consulted. Being involved in a process of dialogue is a much more satisfying experience, and the potential rewards, for everyone concerned, are much greater.

It is useful to reflect upon why the dialogue was not possible at the first meeting of the young people and the transport professionals. In part this was because the adults were not prepared for the idea that young people might have a significant contribution to make to the debate. But it was also to an extent due to the fact that the young people were blown off course so easily. At the second meeting, the young people were not just more knowledgeable, they were also much more confident.

The acquisition of confidence is one of the key results here. Arguably, the young people had a perfectly good case to present in 1998, but they didn't necessarily believe it themselves. Creating the circumstances whereby dialogue can take place was not just about persuading the adults that they should listen—it was also about reassuring the young people that they had something worthwhile to say.

Looked at from this perspective, a number of significant outcomes were achieved here. *Fare's Fair* is a well-written and balanced report. The new concessionary fare scheme itself is a considerable achievement. However perhaps the most important outcome has been the emergence of a group of young people able to take part in a political process as genuine participants. Many of the Transport Group continue to be involved with Investing in Children on different projects, where their experience and confidence is of great value not only to themselves, but to other young people.

The work of the Transport Group has been used as a model for other projects. For example, a group of young people are exploring the provision of leisure services in the county. They are following a similar pattern to the Transport Group. They are researching in detail the local arrangements. They then intend to look at how things are done elsewhere, so that, when they feel able to enter into a dialogue with the managers of the services, they will be able to participate fully, with confidence.

Put most simply, what the Initiative has tried to do is create opportunities for children and young people in County Durham to ask the question 'Why?' of public servants, whether they be police officers, GPs, teachers or youth workers etc. The result has been a series of questions, which the agencies involved have struggled to answer:

- Why did young people in Durham pay higher bus fares than other young people in the region?
- Why do some public leisure centres place restrictions on young people's access in the evenings?
- Why do the police move young people on if they are committing no offence?
- Why do some youth centres close during the summer holidays?

Workers have then been able to support young people to pursue answers to their questions. In doing this, they have asserted a different relationship between rights and responsibilities. Agencies have been reminded of their stated support for the Investing in Children Statement of Intent, and that, if children and young people have rights, adults have responsibilities to recognise these rights. The question then becomes one addressed to adults: Are you meeting your responsibilities?

What Have We Learned?

A number of points are key to what has been tried in Durham:

- *Start with a blank sheet.* The more discretion the young people themselves are able to exercise over the content and direction of the project, the richer will be the outcome.
- *Universal and inclusive.* We accept that all children and young people have rights. Campaigning with and on behalf of all children, i.e. your children and my children, provides more powerful arguments for change than concentrating on a small minority group. Indeed specific groups may well be empowered by making common cause with other young people.
- *Dialogue not consultation.* Children and young people want and have a right to a share of the action. This means that there needs to be a sharing of power:

  > *It is important to understand that visibility does not equal participation or empowerment.*

  (Woolcombe, 1998)

- *It takes time.* The Investing in Children Transport Group took nearly two years to achieve some change, but in the end, their persistence paid off. This approach '...constitutes a major threat to the status quo, and will therefore erect barriers...' (Feeney, 1998).
- *Children's rights, adult's responsibilities.* It has been important to be able to work at a number of different levels. Creating opportunities for children and young people to say what they need to say would have limited value unless the circumstances exist whereby some adults have to take notice.

Key Questions

1. Is anybody in your organisation responsible for ensuring that children's rights are respected and, if not, what can you do about it?

2. How do we work on rights issues with hard-to-reach young people?

Conclusions

Over the past three years a large number of young people and a significant group of adults have been working together to try to develop some new thinking about the way children and young people can become involved in shaping and improving the services they use. The approach in Durham has been based firmly within the UN Convention on the Rights of the Child, and much effort has gone into working out exactly what this should mean on the ground, where real young people live real lives.

I have tried to describe some of what were seen to be the key issues, and how they were addressed. We don't think what we have been doing is rocket science (quite the opposite, in fact), nor do we think that our approach is the only approach, but it does appear to be having some effect:

> *Investing in Children is a very ambitious initiative. It is innovative and visionary in what it is trying to achieve...It would appear that Investing in Children is influencing some agencies and individuals to encourage some children and young people's participation some of the time.*
>
> (Shenton, 1999)

It seems appropriate that the last word should go to a young person. In an interview with the National Children's Bureau, Helen Swanwick, a member of the Investing in Children Transport Group commented:

> *Just because they are younger and they haven't had experience...doesn't mean young people can't get involved. It's only experience they lack: they have ideas.*

And she went on:

> *This is just the beginning. There really is a lot more that can be done.*
>
> (Seeley, 2000)

References

Alderson, P. (2000). School Students Views on School Councils and Daily Life at School. In *Children and Society*, Vol. 14.

Ennew, J. (1998). Preface. In Johnson, et al. (Eds.). *Stepping Forward. Children and Young People's Participation in the Development Process.* Intermediate Technology Publications.

Feeney, M. (1998). Introducing Participation by Children and Young People into Local Public Services: First Steps, Early Mistakes and Lessons Learned. In Johnson, et al., above.

Lansdown, G. (1995). The Children's Rights Development Unit. In Franklin (Ed.), above.

National Youth Agency (1999). *Ethics in Youth Work.* NYA.

Seeley, K. (2000). Opinion. In *Children Now*, Summer.

Shenton, F. (1999). *Evaluation of County Durham Investing in Children Initiative.* University of Durham.

Woolcombe, D., and Olivier, A. (1998). The Peace Child Rescue Mission Experience. In Johnson, et al., above.

Further Reading

Franklin, (Ed.) (1995). *The Handbook of Children's Rights.* Routledge.

Johnson, et al. (Eds.) (1998). *Stepping Forward. Children and Young People's Participation in the Development Process.* Intermediate Technology Publications.

21 Using Information Technology in Youth Work

Paul Oxborough

Key Points

1. ICT is a tool to work with young people, remember to focus on the process and do not get wrapped up in using the equipment.

2. On-line communication such as the Internet needs to be used after prior consideration of the risks and dangers, pieces of work should be planned and staff should receive appropriate training.

3. Young people should always be aware of the boundaries when using ICT, ground rules are essential for any piece of work.

4. Never underestimate the skills young people have related to ICT.

5. Enjoy yourself: always give the fun element a high priority when developing ICT training sessions, it will make your job as a facilitator much easier.

Introduction

This chapter will look at how Information Communication Technology (ICT) or the newer term 'Telematics' can be used in a youth work educational setting. It will give examples of pieces of work as well as exploring the huge growth potential of using Information Technology as a modern youth work tool.

The Future of Information Technology

This is the early stage of a modern computer era. A few years ago people could take or leave computers. Now computers are integrated into every aspect of society. Everywhere computers are shaping the way things are done; for example:

- Supermarket loyalty cards: think about the use of these, they are gathering information about every item bought, so that managers know what stock to reorder.
- Card cash machines: an apparently simple way of dispensing money, these machines are appearing in shops like Boots, garages, McDonalds and even pubs. Each one reduces the need for a human cashier.
- Internet shopping: order your shopping and have it delivered 24 hours a day, all you need is a credit card and computer.

- Tele-conferencing: with a £60 camera you can talk to relatives in New Zealand and transmit videos of your family live at weekends for a little as 0.065p a minute, perhaps even for free soon.
- Close circuit television cameras: strategically placed around town centres, they are watching you and helping to monitor and record crimes 24 hours a day.
- Interactive Digital TV: giving access to 1000s of different channels at any one time.
- Access to the Internet and e-mail through mobile phones; new phones can track where you are and even tell you where the nearest hairdresser or garage is.

How Could This Affect The Way Society Functions?

There is always the scenario of gloom and doom, and of the world destroying itself through technology. What is more likely is that technology and use of computers will help people to live longer, through pushing science understanding to the limit. It will also mean better communication and less isolation felt by those who are elderly and live in rural areas, as they will communicate with families through the television. In theory, people's quality of life should improve, as services are tailored to meet the customer's needs. Already in some parts of the country you can go into a shop and a laser will scan your body and measure you up for perfect-fitting clothes.

We live in a consumer culture and in America big shops are giving away free computers if you spend a certain amount each month on-line shopping with them. Think about how much a month you spend at your supermarket! This sounds far fetched but it is surprisingly easy, quick and convenient, so it leaves you more time to do other things. Computers inevitably will make some people anti-social, as they have the potential to erode people's socialising skills. It will be very scary when socialising becomes a person's favourite hobby at a weekend. Make no mistake, computers will affect society in ways you cannot yet imagine. Think about touch screen exams in schools, with the ability to mark on the spot? Cars custom-made on-line to your exact specification, and then delivered to your doorstep. Virtual reality holidays where you can escape and go on holiday with your favourite film star? Who knows...

Many parents fear for the safety of their children, so will encourage children to stay in on an evening giving them access to the computers and the Internet so they know where they are. But there are chat rooms where young people can meet friends in a virtual world on the computer. Within these chat rooms anyone can talk about any topic imaginable, so many parents who have allowed this are now becoming painfully aware of some of the dangers of the internet: there is no censorship so people can access pornography, violent photos, information on how to make bombs etc. Reports are suggesting organised crime is thriving through using the Internet to sell drugs and weapons.

Whatever the future of computers it has to be understood that times are changing very quickly, and many of the older generation have missed out on the education that young people are now getting in schools, colleges and universities, even in nursery schools. It is important not to be blasé about how computers will change society. In ten years time the world may start to look very alien to those who aren't IT literate.

Let us embrace the positives of modern computers whilst at the same time being aware of the potential dangers of their misuse. To embrace we need to understand...

How Information Technology has been Used in Milton Keynes

One local authority that has strategically planned its youth work using Information Technology is Milton Keynes. It has a full time worker who is part of the Staff Development and Training team, and it is their role to offer staff opportunities to develop their IT skills so they can be used as a youth work tool. The IT youth worker also supports time-limited pieces of work with youth work staff and young people. One example of this has been working with the voluntary youth service to develop a state-of-the-art IT training centre in Central Milton Keynes library. This has been a partnership project involving six other key organisations:

1. Milton Keynes Council for Voluntary Organisations.
2. Milton Keynes and North Bucks. Economic Partnership.
3. Adult and Continuing Education.
4. Milton Keynes Library Service.
5. Milton Keynes Leisure, Youth and Community Service.
6. Milton Keynes Youth Council.

This approach has avoided a duplication of resources and led to a sharing of a whole wealth of skills across the partnership. By having one joint project, budgets can stretch so much further.

The commitment to IT is a very important one: society is becoming more complex and sophisticated because of IT, so young people need to be able to access projects in and out of school time. There is a danger that the Internet will become a middle class service only available to those with money therefore making the gap between rich and poor even wider. But even when resources have been established for everyone how then could ICT be used to work with young people? The model below shows two different ways:

Figure 1: How information technology can be used in youth work

Route 1
Formal training course teaching young people new skills which can be relevant and appropriate for future career choices.

Examples
Web site design, CD-ROM development, using Microsoft Office suites, using on-line communications systems, using presentation packages.

Overview

This a formal training session that is aimed at young people within the youth service catchment age group. It often appeals to specific focused groups, i.e. single gender or ethnic minority groups. Groups can be already established or come together specifically for the period of the training.

Outcome

Key skills developed
Accredited and certified training for School Record of Achievement folders. Hands-on experience of using IT equipment. Ability to demonstrate competence in using IT equipment. Ability to share learning with others.

Life skills developed
Peer education, passing on skills to others. Working together effectively as part of the team. Communication skills. Presentation skills. Increased confidence. Increased self-esteem.

Route 2
Using information technology as a tool for addressing a social issue such as bullying, sex education, racism, peer pressure etc. that is affecting the group.

Examples
Drugs/sex education, CD-ROM project; addressing homophobia, video project; dealing with racism, photo stories; looking at disability issues, teleconferencing project; social exclusion, internet/e-mail project.

Overview

These sessions, whilst often referred to as information education, need to be well planned in advance. As well as the user groups identified for Route 1, this type of training can also be used to engage those young people who are socially or educationally excluded. The contentious nature of some of the issues dealt with requires that youth workers are equipped with the skills to enable full participation by all the young people.

Outcome

Key skills developed
Ability to address or discuss issues objectively. Learning how to use IT equipment. Project develops a strategy for dealing with the social issue identified. Young person learns about the importance of informed decision-making and positive action strategies.

Life skills developed
Reassurance that others may have been in similar situations. Working together effectively as part of a team. Communication skills. Presentation skills. Increased confidence. Increased self-esteem.

Result
Young people are accessing new experiences that allow their personal development and increase their life opportunities.

The rest of this chapter will focus on new technology mainly using on-line communication (the Internet); working through different stages of developing this work with young people. But what is on-line communication? Figure 2 explains this.

This is not an exhaustive list it just shows the four main areas at the moment. All of these mediums can be very powerful tools in youth work, they can break down geographical boundaries therefore addressing access issues, provide a route

---

Figure 2: 4 Areas of on-line communication

E-mail

Electronic mail is fast, clean and very reliable. You can send attachments, i.e. photos, text files, spreadsheets, video clips, music etc. Research has shown people respond quicker to e-mails than any other office based medium such as the telephone, memos, faxes etc.

IRC

Internet Relay Chat is the on-line chatting tool. It can be text based where you have a live (real time) text based conversation. Or it can be done in a 3D virtual landscape where you assume the role of a character and wander around meeting up with other 3D characters across vast landscapes. Research has shown this is an area that (at the moment) is particularly of interest to young people. You can set up your own chat room, issue your friends/colleagues with the password and then set the computer to page them when they go on-line to invite them in for a chat.

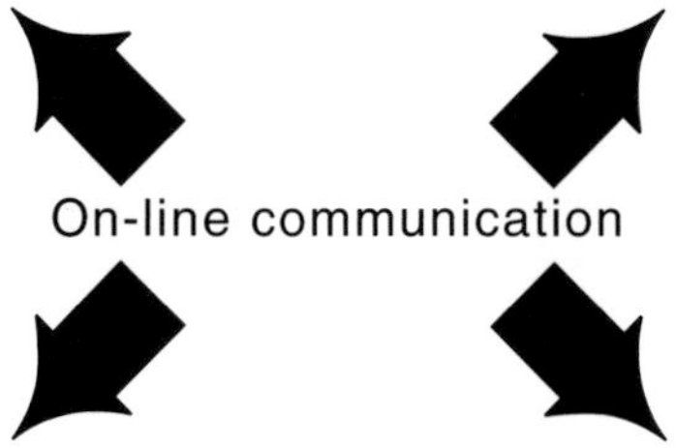

On-line communication

News Groups

These are specialist areas, there are 1000s of news groups covering every topic imaginable. You can subscribe to as many as you want or even create your own, covering your own specialist area of work. You can read or post questions to news groups and encourage other people to participate in your discussion or answer your questions. This area is particularly useful for help in gathering research and addressing something you are stuck on.

WWW

The WWW stands for the World Wide Web or the Internet. This is the 24-hours-a-day, 365-days-a-year reference library. Millions of web sites are at your disposal covering any topic imaginable. There is no censorship and there is a lot of useless content. The Internet is shaping the way people think and interact and will over the next few years change the way we obtain information.

to information, and be a way of selling and promoting your work. Most importantly on-line communications are an arena where young people can share issues that are affecting them; creating a web site gives them an instant public arena. This next section will explore step by step how new technology can be used in projects to enhance the services offered to young people, and to do so by a hypothetical scenario, allowing a discussion of the processes involved.

An Example Scenario

You are a manager of an active youth project. You have an over 17s drop-in centre where young people see the project as a way to chill out but also to talk to workers and get information about current issues like bullying, racism, drugs and sex education. The staff team are quite traditional but committed youth workers and the project has just invested in an Internet-ready computer. Young people respond to

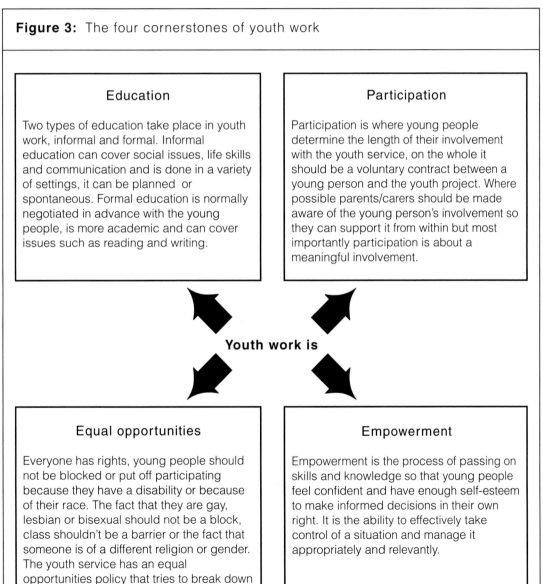

Figure 3: The four cornerstones of youth work

Education

Two types of education take place in youth work, informal and formal. Informal education can cover social issues, life skills and communication and is done in a variety of settings, it can be planned or spontaneous. Formal education is normally negotiated in advance with the young people, is more academic and can cover issues such as reading and writing.

Participation

Participation is where young people determine the length of their involvement with the youth service, on the whole it should be a voluntary contract between a young person and the youth project. Where possible parents/carers should be made aware of the young person's involvement so they can support it from within but most importantly participation is about a meaningful involvement.

Youth work is

Equal opportunities

Everyone has rights, young people should not be blocked or put off participating because they have a disability or because of their race. The fact that they are gay, lesbian or bisexual should not be a block, class shouldn't be a barrier or the fact that someone is of a different religion or gender. The youth service has an equal opportunities policy that tries to break down any barriers that prevent access to projects

Empowerment

Empowerment is the process of passing on skills and knowledge so that young people feel confident and have enough self-esteem to make informed decisions in their own right. It is the ability to effectively take control of a situation and manage it appropriately and relevantly.

this enthusiastically and over the following weeks they drift towards chat rooms and the staff are getting concerned about the types of conversations young people are having on-line. What makes it more frustrating for the workers is they are unsure as to how else they can use the computer with the young people because of their own confidence levels. When the staff challenge the young people they agree to tone down the conversations and things come to a head when some older members are caught downloading some instructions on how to make a bomb out of items found in a kitchen. Let us look at how this situation can be turned around.

Step 1: Ensuring staff are aware of the principles of youth work

See how Figure 2 can be linked to Figure 3 by:

Education:

- All projects should have clear aims and objectives agreed by all facilitating staff members.
- Training can be relatively formal and structured but should generate an element of fun into each session.
- Use the skills of the young people so that they can be peer educators.
- Work with young people so they can offer training opportunities away from the project teaching older generations.
- Don't be scared of charging for training courses as this will help generate income to keep equipment updated.
- Look at how you can accredit the learning by networking with your local school, college or Adult Education Centre.

Equal opportunities:

- ICT can be a powerful tool at breaking down geographical isolation. Facilitate an on-line youth club so that rural clubs can meet other young people; this is good for addressing access issues.
- Explore how ICT can help young people with a disability, network with Disability Forums and make changes if relevant and appropriate.
- Use the Internet to find out more about different cultures or religions and to promote anti-racist discussion.

Empowerment:

- Use the skills of young people to teach others, and work with the young people to document this.
- Never assume with ICT that an adult is the best trainer or person to promote work in a project.
- Explore innovative uses of ICT and support young people in setting up a small business.

Participation:

- Young people should be fully involved with projects using ICT.
- Young people should be instrumental in teaching others.
- Young people should determine the types of ICT projects the youth project takes on.

Step 2: Ensure the staff members are working cohesively together as a team

Through support from the training team the staff call a team meeting and identify a strategy that will allow them to use the Internet more constructively. One of the big issues they have identified with this group of young people, is that when a reactive stance is taken at addressing an issue, certain group members will work against the staff and it becomes an 'us and them' situation leading to confrontation and a testing of boundaries. Part of the reason for this is a lack of cohesion as a team of workers in saying and agreeing upon the same thing.

What issues does this meeting bring up?

- It allows staff members to discuss where they each stand on the issue of censorship.
- It identifies what current skills the group have around Information Technology.
- An IT training plan is identified, so staff can be more supportive and confident in offering young people help.
- It identifies the need for good clear ground rules when using the Internet.
- A session looking at the positives and negatives of having Internet access in the project takes place. Through this process staff become more aware of each other's strengths and weaknesses.
- Staff agree that if a young person is

challenged others will back up this decision and discuss whether they agree with the decision away from the young people, not in front of them.

Step 3: Creating some ground rules

The staff brainstorm some draft ground rules when young people are using the internet, and they agree that:

- The principles of youth work should be on display.
- Young people should not engage in activities that go against these youth work principles.
- Chat rooms won't be allowed if groups are involved in oppressive or anti-social discussions or language.
- Downloading of anti-social material is not acceptable.
- A steering group of staff and young people is formed so if there is a breech of ground rules this group deals with the issue together.
- Staff will be around to monitor access and support young people's learning positively.
- Access is time-limited so everyone gets a chance to use the facility.
- Young women have equal access to the equipment.

These draft ground rules are then shared with the young people and a period of consultation takes place:

- By discussing them with young people they develop an ownership of the draft ground rules.
- Young people have an opportunity to add or modify (through discussion) the current ground rules.
- A formal set of ground rules are established that are owned by the project, both staff and young people.
- It is a priority to value young people's contribution to this process.

Step 4: The final step on the development of ground rules

Work with young people to present and display these agreed ground rules in an attractive way near the computer:

- It will create an opportunity for the group to reflect further on the ground rules agreed.
- Workers can now explore more innovative uses of IT in the project with a way of challenging inappropriate use: these should be innovative, planned, relevant and appropriate.
- It's an opportunity for the young people's work to be valued and displayed in the project.

Having gone through this process the staff will be feeling more aware of the issues around using IT in their project and young people will be enthusiastic about getting involved.

How can the Internet be used more effectively? The above process is very important as it allows staff members to feel confident in dealing with serious issues if they arise. An example of this could be to create a curriculum of discussion groups or debates, which can involve the Internet for gathering information. Let us show this as a planned piece of work using the NAOMIE youth work model.

Example of Discussion Group

Need: young people are asking for a discussion about drugs and the legalisation of soft drugs, workers are aware there is a need to do more drugs-based discussion, so a piece of work is formulated.

Aim: To give young people access to information so they can make their own informed choices as to whether soft drugs ought to be legalised.

Objectives:

1. To involve the whole project in a vote about whether soft drugs ought to be legalised, everyone is given a voting form with the question and a yes/no tick box.
2. Once the voting forms have been filled out young people are invited to participate in a organised debate about the issue.
3. Staff encourage young people to use the internet and ten approved web sites about drugs for them to gather material to justify their stance on the issue (20 minutes per group).
4. Young people present their argument to the rest of the group.

5. Staff give out drugs information publicity and leaflets that are up to date and accurate at the end of the session.

Method: All youth project members are given a chance to participate at a simple level by voting on the issue; for those who want to take it further they can opt into a debating group. The role of the staff is to facilitate the session and remain impartial so remember this is about young people's views, and staff shouldn't influence these. The Internet is being used strategically to give broader access to information, after young people get the information the computer can be switched off.

Implementation: How did the session go? What actually happened? Was it successful, how many young people participated? What was the staff's role etc.?

Evaluation: This should be done as part of the session with young people and it could be a good opportunity to plan a similar session or ask the group what they would like to do at the next session. A separate evaluation should be done with staff to explore each other's role, deal with any conflict and make process recordings about the event.

This is just one of hundreds of different ways of using the Internet constructively in your youth work setting: below are some more ideas.

Ten Innovative Projects Using the Internet/E-mail

1. Safe chat room

Create a young person-led steering group which recruits 5–10 youth projects to participate in an on-line youth club. It is the steering group's job to co-ordinate the event. Using one of the big search engines such as Yahoo or Excite set up a private chat room. Issue all participants (prior to the event) with a password to access this room and set a date when you will all log on. Use the opportunity to have discussions, competitions, debates and a platform for developing other pieces of work. This is particularly useful for rural projects with poor transport links. It can lead to participants visiting each other's projects.

2. The great debate

This can involve all members in the club or project. Using a relevant current news story form a contentious question and open it up to a vote. You can split into teams to encourage users to surf the net to justify their points of view. This is more fun if you only allow each group 5–10 mins on the internet. It is also helpful to have identified before the session some useful sites covering the issue.

3. A club web site directory

If you have a regular group who use the internet get them to log down good web sites, to form a useful directory that can be copied to other members. You can introduce training on other programmes to show young people how to create a booklet, catalogue or database etc.

4. A club e-mail directory

If young people are on the Internet at home an e-mail directory could be a good way to keep in touch. Be aware of personal safety issues about sharing private information when entering into this.

5. A homework cyber-café

Develop an afternoon youth work session where young people can come to the club for light snacks, such as toasties or sandwiches etc., drinks, and access to the Internet to help with homework. There are 100s of sites set up for this purpose (BBC On-line/Bite Size Homework etc.) and it could attract young people you won't attract on an evening.

6. An internet treasure hunt

Young people, split into teams of four or five, are given cryptic clues, that have been planned beforehand. They have to find certain types of information by using the Internet and they have to find a site that fits the clue. It's a race against time as each group only has 10 minutes to solve as many clues as possible. Be aware that anti-social material may come up if young people are doing open searches on the Internet.

Key Questions

1. How can the youth work service come up with usable national policies related to ICT which are cohesive and fieldworker driven?
2. How do we utilise and accredit young people's far reaching ICT skills so that they can offer something back to others?
3. How can ICT and the internet be used as tools to deliver youth work, engage with young people, and respond to some governmental initiatives?
4. How do youth workers get appropriate levels of training so they aren't left behind?
5. Most importantly is it feasible and possible to do youth work on-line...?

7. Celebrating cultural diversity

In what is fundamentally an arts-based session, you can use the Internet to help make it more interesting. Young people have to find and print out 20 images and words that celebrate cultural diversity. These images are then used to form a collage that can be put on display in the project.

8. Mega-savings bulk-buying

If you have a regular membership explore with them what they buy on a regular basis (i.e. CDs, printer cartridges, computer games, stationery etc.) and if there are items that are similar use the net to bulk-buy on-line: you can save up to 50% on shop prices. This needs to be carefully planned and young people need to contract into the scheme so that someone isn't left out of pocket. This is easier to manage if you have a long term club membership and is a good idea to inform parents.

9. Pen-pals

Lots of young people are looking for pen-pals, and using the internet is a way of making contact. International youth work sites are a good starting point. Rather than using pen and paper you can use the Yahoo messenger service or ICQ programs to let you know when your new pen-pals are logged on, and you can then talk to them direct through a chat room or e-mail, you can even use sound files and photos.

10. Multimedia explosion

To set this up you need Internet access for two–four PCs, and a multimedia projector for each PC. These are projected onto empty walls, the bigger the image the better. You will also need some disco equipment, lights and a good DJ. Young people take responsibility for finding good web sites that go with the music that is being played, these can be set to loop throughout the evening. It makes sense to avoid high costs by downloading the sites to the computer's hard drive beforehand. Tickets are sold and the evening is a combination of intense sound, light and imagery projecting onto four walls. It creates a fantastic and very sophisticated night out.

Conclusion

At the time of writing there are massive changes in the world of IT, with WAP phones now enabling people to obtain information from the internet through their mobile phones. Society expects information to be available 24 hours a day and bearing in mind that a lot of youth work takes place on an evening, this is good, as it always used to be frustrating when doing some research with a group to the library being shut. Now this information can be accessed through the internet.

However we use the internet with young people, by remembering the four cornerstones of youth work we can plan new and innovative pieces of work. The Internet is a mind blowing resource but remember it is simply another tool that will enable you to respond to the needs of young people more effectively.

Further Reading
Other resources: MK Web Directory

Milton Keynes Leisure, Youth and Community service has since 1997 been developing a web directory of useful web sites. They are very specific to issues facing young people. There is an index with 150 categories that make finding a site very easy. To see a copy of this directory go to http://www.mkweb.co.uk/cth/webdirectory

Web links page

Title	URL	Description
Information Society	www.information-society.org.uk	An on-line database of UK based projects concerned with ICT/ telematics
Youth.Org	www.youth.org.uk	A comprehensive site that links 100s of youth projects nationwide
Youth Clubs UK	www.ukyouth.org	A wide reaching national youth work site which covers many voluntary groups
Telematics Centre	http://telematics.ex.ac.uk/home	Information about telematics in practice and other links
Youth FM Radio	www.youthfm.co.uk	Youth radio broadcast over the internet and run by young people
Up My Street Information	www.upmystreet.com	A useful database that gives you information about your street based on your postcode
The Young Persons Site	www.thesite.org.uk	A comprehensive sites dealing with many issues young people may face
The Childline web site	www.childline.org.uk	Comprehensive site which covers many child protection issues
Black issues site	www.blink.org.uk	A huge site giving access to many resources covering Black issues
Cyber reading materials	www.rheingold.com	Access to 100s of publications related to ICT, cyberspace and other new technology
Anti bullying information	http://bullybeware.com	Useful information and links about the issues of bullying
Drugs information	www.isdd.co.uk	Comprehensive drugs site giving accurate info and links to valuable anti-drugs materials
Eating disorders	www.eating-disorders.com	Centre for eating disorders main page with links to other web sites
Jobs on line	www.jobsite.co.uk	Use the internet to find the ideal job, with access to large national databases
National Youth Agency	www.nya.org.uk	The National Youth Agency's official web site with links section

Reader's Guide

This final section provides an opportunity to explore, in greater depth, the needs of young people characterised by particular experiences of exclusion. On some, much negative media attention has been focused, particularly asylum-seekers, travellers, young offenders, young people out of school, the unemployed and young women with children. Undoubtedly, such attention serves to perpetuate myths and stereotypes about these groups.

Unaccompanied Asylum-seeking Young People

Laurence Chester draws upon his own extensive experience of working with unaccompanied asylum-seeking young people to provide the reader with an insight into the lives of displaced youngsters who face racism in their day-to-day lives. Whilst advising upon the nature of specific service delivery, he is able to draw parallels in addressing the needs of these young people as with any other group, and identifies the potential effectiveness of the youth work intervention.

New Travellers Helping Themselves

Alan Dearling's contribution on the needs of young people within travelling communities offers an insider's view of how practitioners can offer a variety of services to young people once the initial prejudices are overcome. Creative suggestions are made, and again, the transferability of skills and methods is all too apparent.

Youth Crime, Youth Justice and Youth Work

Documenting the historical developments within youth justice from the 'welfarist' model, prevalent until the 1960s to a return to 'justice' in the 1970s, minimalist interventions in the 1980s through to the punitive policies of the 1990s and onwards, John Pitts questions the role and contribution of youth workers to the newly established Youth Offending Teams.

Young People Out of School

Hertfordshire Youth Service has been involved in the design and delivery of a programme for young people currently out of school. Dealing with those excluded, as well as school refusers, Pam Rogers reviews the progress of the work undertaken, also providing a useful background on the messages from research in this area.

Unemployed Young People

Howard Williamson's contribution on young people, who experience unemployment, assesses the impact of numerous government initiatives designed to promote re-integration into the workplace. Howard's involvement on the government's New Deal Task Force Advisory Group provides a rare insight into the potential for the initiatives championed by New Labour.

Working with Young Women with Children

The theme of recognising the needs of young people as individuals first is emphasised in this contribution from Julie Scurfield and Sue Stevens. Deliberately titled as such to reflect this group's identity as young women first, and parents second, it demonstrates the need for and potential of targeted service delivery that allows young women their own space and opportunity for personal growth and development.

Young People Sexually Exploited Through Prostitution

Margaret Melrose has extensively researched the services provided for young people sexually exploited through prostitution. From such a perspective she is able to identify good practice in this area, and is persuasive in her argument that not to view the young person as a victim of exploitation is misguided, and will therefore lead to inappropriate interventions.

Young Carers

Difficult to identify in the first place, between 20–50,000 young carers exist in the UK (National Strategy for Carers). Paul Adams and David Land's chapter identifies the multiple reasons for this, and offers practitioners an insight into the realities of the existences of this much ignored group of young people, and appropriate lessons for the design of services to meet their needs.

Youth Homelessness

Homeless young people never achieve a high media profile. The acknowledgement of their existence is often too unpleasant to consider, although the Social Exclusion Unit's Report, *Rough Sleeping* (1998) provides services with an opportunity to work together in this arena. Sybil Qasir gives a thorough account of the legal entitlements of this group to services, as well as examples of initiatives designed to work with young people experiencing homelessness.

Young People, Drugs and Youth Work

The government's 10 Year Strategy, *Tackling Drugs Together*, places young people centre-stage. Gerard Murray and Karen Shillitoe provide evidence to support the growing use of illicit substances in young people's lives, the shortfall in public policy and the difficulties in accessing relevant resources to support appropriate interventions. They give clear guidance to youth work practitioners on the positive contribution their unique approach can have in an increasingly normalised drug culture.

Young People and Mental Health

Rory Reynolds describes the more common mental health issues that affect young people during adolescence. Focusing upon depression, eating disorders and schizophrenia, he identifies symptoms, treatment options, support services and messages for practitioners who may be working with young people demonstrating some of these behaviour patterns.

22

Unaccompanied Asylum-seeking Young People

Laurence Chester

Key Points

1. Unaccompanied asylum-seeking young people are entitled to the full protection of the Children Act 1989.

2. Unaccompanied asylum-seeking young people, are especially vulnerable groups. Practitioners should never refuse a service to a young person on the basis of their immigration status.

3. It is extremely helpful for young people if they have a Refugee Council Children Panel Advisor allocated to them. Practitioners who work with unaccompanied asylum-seeking young people should ensure that the panel is advised as soon as possible.

4. Practitioners should ensure that a solicitor registered with the Legal Services Commission is legally representing the child or young person.

5. It is not advisable for practitioners to ask intrusive questions about the circumstances that have led to the exile of the unaccompanied asylum-seeking young person.

Background

The UNHCR regards one in every 115 people on earth as being forced to flee. There are 49 million people who have been forced to leave their homes and 23 million of these are internationally displaced. The majority are women and young people. These figures are rising rapidly. Each year at least 30,000 people seek refuge in Britain, not including dependants. Among this number are between 1,000 and 2,000 unaccompanied asylum-seeking young people (statistic from the Home Office and Refugee Council). This includes only those young people who are registered at port of entry, though in reality more arrive with adults to gain entry into the country and are then left to fend for themselves.

There are many teenagers who may be unaccompanied but are not included in this count, as those over the age of 18 are officially considered as adults. This would also apply to a young person below the age of 18 arriving with a brother or sister of 18. The younger sibling would not be viewed as unaccompanied.

Unaccompanied young people come to Europe from all over the world. Very often their parents are dead, missing or imprisoned or when the young people are particularly at risk, their parents have struggled to get them to safety. Some young people have been forcibly recruited into armies, of both government and opposition, and participated in violence.

Prejudice against immigrant children and young people is an issue that practitioners witness. It is reflected within the professions working with them and occasionally in the places where they are living. This along with other forms of institutional racism can act as an inhibitor to young people receiving the services they are entitled to. This may manifest itself in educational needs assessment, health care, the benefits system or the immigration process.

Much of the work with unaccompanied asylum-seeking young people is more time consuming and specialist than many social workers have time for. Some local authorities have set up specialist teams but it is not uncommon for the experience of these young people to be considered a low priority for a social worker dealing with a heavy case load of other child protection concerns.

Legal Framework and Definitions

The legislation affecting unaccompanied asylum-seeking young people in the UK is:

- International Convention on the Rights of the Child 1989.
- Immigration Act 1971.

- Asylum and Immigration Appeals Act 1993.
- Children Act 1989, specifically Section 17 and Section 20 (1) (3) 6, 2, 2 schedule 2, paras. 15 and 17.
- Children (Leaving Care) Act 2000.
- Immigration and Asylum Act 1999.

This legislation defines the following:

- *Illegal immigrant*: This definition is used to describe an applicant for asylum or residential status in the United Kingdom, who under the Immigration and Asylum Act 1999 has no right to apply.
- *Refugee*: A refugee is someone who leaves or remains outside their country of origin 'owing to a well founded fear of persecution through reasons of race, religion, nationality, member of a particular social group or political opinion' (UN Convention, 1951).
- *Unaccompanied*: The term unaccompanied refers to young people under the age of 18 years old who are '...separated from both parents and are not being cared for by an adult who by law or custom, is responsible to do so' (UNHCR, 1994).
- *Asylum*: Protection given to a refugee by a government i.e. permission to enter or remain as a refugee. In addition, an asylum-seeker may be granted residency if they meet the UN 1951 Convention definition of a refugee. To do so they must have a 'well founded fear of persecution' on the grounds of 'race, religion, nationality, membership of a particular social group or political opinion'. The UK has signed the UN Convention 1951 and the 1967 Protocol, and is therefore obliged to receive and formally recognise those fleeing persecution if they meet one of the five UN criteria.

The Children's Panel of Advisors

While most unaccompanied young people are in the age group of 15 to 17, there are significant numbers under 15 and some under 10 years of age. There are no accurate numbers for young people neither in the EU nor in Western Europe as a whole. Many states do not keep figures of unaccompanied young people who seek asylum.

Once it is established that a child is unaccompanied and seeking asylum and a responsible adult carer has been identified as willing to take charge of the child, a temporary admission document may be issued. When no responsible adult is available a referral is made to the local authority's social services department in which the port of entry is situated. Since the 1st April 1994 social services turn first to the Refugee Council Childrens' Panel of Advisors when responding to the needs of unaccompanied young people. These advisors are workers recruited by the Refugee Council (part funded by the Home Office) from the communities from which most young people would be expected to come. The panel is a non-statutory body and the advisors are chosen for their suitability for the role and are given training. Some, but not all, are social workers. When an unaccompanied asylum-seeking child comes to their attention the panel offers the services of an advisor.

Key roles for the advisor are to ensure that the child's wishes and cultural considerations are addressed by social services and that the child understands as far as possible what is happening.

Assessing need

Practitioners who work with asylum-seeking young people are working with a client group who are culturally and experientially diverse, and often from cultures of whom practitioners may have had little or no prior experience. The cultural differences may directly affect the assessment process. Language and cultural differences can distract from seeing the child as primarily a 'child in need'. Issues associated with child immigration become one amongst many issues to be addressed. An important initial task for any practitioner working with unaccompanied asylum-seeking young people is to explain clearly what their role is. Children and young people may have a mistrust of authority figures and before any trust is built they need to be reassured that the practitioner is not working to an agenda that is contrary to the child's interest. In addition, it is often unhelpful to ask intrusive questions about the circumstances that have led to the young person's being in exile as they will have gone through this process many times already with immigration officers and lawyers and often it will have been a wearing and traumatic experience.

Section 17 of the Children Act 1989 offers clear guidance for practitioners. It furthermore places unaccompanied young people firmly within the parameters of being 'in need'. When assessing need, this should be informed by the Welfare Checklist, in section 1 of the Children Act 1989. The use of interpreters helps in assessing need. When picking an interpreter it should not be assumed that because the interpreter is from the same country as the child that they speak the same language or dialect. The interpreter may in fact come from another ethnic, religious, cultural or political group that may hold views opposite to that of the child. An example would be where there are extreme divides in the child's home country due to civil war.

Care Plan and Reviews

Reference to the Department of Health publication *Social Work with Unaccompanied Asylum-seeking Children: A Practice Guide* (1991) should be consulted when formulating a care plan. It was prepared to:

> ...assist Local Authorities, Social Services Depts. and independent agencies in undertaking the task of caring for unaccompanied children who are asylum seekers, who have been granted exceptional leave to remain or who have been recognised as refugees.

For the initial stages of contact with unaccompanied asylum-seeking young people there are often pressing health or immigration issues that may need to be addressed, within the first 24 hours in some cases.

The clearest way to deliver and evaluate services to young people is to recognise that they fall within Section 17 of the Children Act 1989 and are therefore to be considered as 'children in need'. This should trigger a response informed by the Children Act 1989 and *Working together* (DoH, 1991). Agencies representing different aspects of the child or young person's life need to meet and formulate a care plan that considers the best interests of the child or young person. This is a process that should be reviewed at regular intervals. It is advisable to ensure that a representative from the Refugee Council's Children Panel of Advisors is present at the initial care plan meeting. Central to this process is listening to the child or young person. Except in exceptional circumstances, the child or young person should be present throughout the meeting and should be aware of all the discussion and

decisions made concerning their welfare. Time should be taken to ensure that at no stage does the young person feel left out of this process. Reinforcing the idea for the young person that they have some control over their own life is a central part of making the young person feel secure.

At care plan/review meetings, issues that should be included are: health, education, placement issues, immigration issues, legal orders and social orientation.

Health

This should be addressed as a top priority when delivering a service for young people who have arrived in this country unaccompanied. They come with no medical records and as discussed above, there may be injuries that are life threatening. A valuable task for practitioners working with unaccompanied asylum-seeking young people is to try and identify GPs who are sensitive to the needs of such people. There can be problems with some GPs accepting these young people on their registers. Some challenge their addresses as being impermanent due to their immigration status being undecided. The practitioner needs to consider the advantage of pressing the GP to accept their responsibility against the fact that they may be hostile to the child.

Accessing medical services is a decision that should be made at a strategic managerial level to ensure that young people do not slip thorough the net. Sometimes young people will be carrying injuries typically received by soldiers or other from their country of origin. The young person may be suffering the symptoms of trauma such as lack of sleep, stomach pains or even stress-related heart problems. Panic attacks are very frightening for young people. These needs should be attended to before any other tasks, as risk to life may be a real issue. They should be accompanied when seeing a medical practitioner and where necessary an interpreter provided. A request should be made for a written medical report from the doctor to keep on Social Services files. This may be usable as evidence in the Immigration Court, of any torture or trauma the young person has suffered. The Medical Foundation for the Care of Victims of War has their own team who offers therapeutic help and practical medical treatment and assessment. However they usually have a lengthy waiting list.

Education

Often, unaccompanied asylum-seeking young people arrive in this country without any education history. An important consideration of a care plan is to facilitate an accurate assessment of the child or young person's ability and achievements. Language may be an issue initially for a child or young person but this should not be seen as an overriding factor in blocking opportunities for pursuing other academic subjects. Many young people may need extra language teaching to improve their standard of English so that they can reach a level in other subjects that would meet academic requirements. This represents, for some, a challenge which requires understanding and extra support emotionally. For some young people school is an opportunity to concentrate on matters outside of their recent negative experiences and immigration issues. They welcome and enjoy the opportunity to regain a degree of normality in their lives.

Placement issues

Placement issues for unaccompanied asylum-seeking young people is a highly contentious issue within Social Services. They fall within the provisions of Section 20 of the Children Act, which sets out the relevant criteria for the accommodation of vulnerable children.

The considerations of the indigenous population of local communities has often hit national headlines and hostility shown by the residents of those towns or cities indicate the challenges many unaccompanied asylum-seeking young people face in their day-to-day lives. Unaccompanied asylum-seeking young people primarily should be placed close to their own community in exile and where possible be placed with people from that community, though many of the young persons' community in exile may not be in a sufficiently stable situation within this country to be able to offer that service. Although it is usual policy for social services and other agencies to place young people, with as close a cultural match as is possible, with unaccompanied asylum-seeking young people other considerations need to be taken into account. If a young person is coming from a situation where there is civil war in their home country, even though the placement on offer may be with a family from the same country, they may be on the other side of a political divide.

Immigration issues

It is a responsibility of practitioners to ensure that the unaccompanied asylum-seeking young person has appropriate legal representation, i.e. a solicitor registered with the Legal Services Commission. If the child or young person is due to be re-unified with their own family in their country of origin then preparations need to made as early as possible to prepare them. Progress should be regularly reviewed at each meeting.

Practitioners can work with other professionals in helping to relate objective information for immigration hearings in accordance with Paragraph 3 of the *Immigration and Asylum Rules* (House of Commons 395: 351) which refers to the value of objective information. A practitioner's report can offer an insight to the court into the background and progress of the young person in this country. The report may reflect a view about the likely impact deportation may have on the young person. Social services may request time to seek evidence regarding what circumstance the young person may be returning to.

Asylum-seeking young people have stated that the immigration process affects their sense of security and well-being. The object of the immigration process is frequently to determine a course of action, which is opposite to the wishes of the child and their family. The most useful role in these circumstances, is not to deny any deportation threat, but to become informed about the young person's individual circumstances, in consultation the panel advisor, and to offer an informed realistic view of how the immigration process will apply to the young person. A young person at risk of deportation will be more able to cope with the outcome if the professionals involved prepare the young person appropriately, rather than to enforce any denial of the reality of their circumstances.

Who will accompany the young person to court and other legal appointments should also be considered.

Legal orders

Unaccompanied asylum-seeking young people are entitled to the same protection as other young people. This means that in the eventuality of an unaccompanied asylum-seeking young person disclosing abuse by family members in their county of origin etc. appropriate legal orders should be considered. In situations where young people are under threat of returning to life endangering situations in their home countries, or to situations where they may suffer significant harm, the local authority should consider whether to seek a legal order to protect the best interest of the child or young person. As with any other allegations of abuse to young people, unaccompanied asylum-seeking young people are entitled to the protection of Section 47 of the Children Act 1989, which outlines the local authority's duty to investigate child protection concerns.

Social orientation

The social orientation of an unaccompanied asylum-seeking young person should be considerate of the child or young person's cultural background. They should be given the opportunity to meet their peers, within a setting where they can feel supported and safe. As they may not know what resources are available to them, practitioners should address this within the child or young person's care plan.

A professional youth and community approach can contribute in meeting the needs of unaccompanied asylum-seeking young people both on a group work basis and individually. A pro-active approach should be adopted to access the child or young person's own communities. Programmes designed at positively representing the experience and values of that community to indigenous populations can be helpful in integrating young people into the local community. Many unaccompanied asylum-seeking young people feel that they are part of an underclass. A social education programme that reinforces the message that their value as young people is not defined by their legal status, is an important message. There is a role in addressing life skills issues. Helping unaccompanied asylum-seeking young people learn to survive is obviously crucial but they also need to be supported in the development of a social life, e.g. how to book cinema tickets, find a local swimming pool, and helped to mix with young people who are linked into the local resources.

Social education in an informal environment provides unaccompanied asylum-seeking young people opportunities to learn how to adjust to their current environment both geographically and socially, to help find themselves. Including unaccompanied asylum-seeking young people in decision-making forums whether about their personal circumstances or as a particularly defined group encourages a sense of self-empowerment, essential in rebuilding the confidence of these young people, who have been dis-empowered in so many ways due to their refugee experience. There are clear benefits in consulting with young people when assessing what they want from a service. In addition, youth workers can utilise their skills in the areas of group work, family contact, life storybook etc.

Group Work

When I was working as a social worker in a specialist team in Croydon Social Services for unaccompanied asylum-seeking young people, the young people asked for weekly meetings for all unaccompanied young people within the area. They shared foods from their countries of origin, talked to peers in a common language and heard information about their home country and advice on how to survive in Britain from trusted adults. For some this was literally a 'life line' as the setting enabled the young people to identify unmet needs that they felt unable to express in other settings.

A strategic plan agreed with local services and concerned with representation from refugee or migrant communities may benefit from discussions about communal activities that can take place in 'community' settings. This can offer opportunities for young people to positively engage with peers from the indigenous local population in pro-active anti-discriminatory social education programmes. Issues around language and religious or cultural need should be central to this planning, e.g. if young people are Muslim by ensuring that their dietary laws are respected.

The organisation *Unaccompanied Children in Exile from Former Yugoslavia* organised a residential weekend for forty unaccompanied young people. These were young people across the political divide some with families on opposing sides of the civil war. This followed months of other activities that indicated that political difference was not the contentious issue for the group. They felt bonded by their refugee experience more than divided by their political backgrounds.

A concern the young people fed back to the facilitators of the weekend was that in every day life they feel frustrated by being defined as refugees and consequently suffered prejudice. The key benefit they expressed of the weekend, was the opportunity to socialise with their peers in a non-oppressive setting where they did not feel vulnerable to 'refugee prejudice'.

At this weekend the facilitators were supported by legal and therapeutic services which specialised in working with unaccompanied asylum-seeking young people. Their input proved essential at times in assessing previously unidentified 'needs'.

Family Contact

Unaccompanied asylum-seeking young people should be encouraged to maintain contact with their own families, whether in this country or abroad. Although there may be family in this country who are unable to care for them, they may be available for them in other ways. Where there is family abroad the child or young person should be enabled to maintain a regular communication with them. The Red Cross and International Social Services can assist with obtaining information about families abroad. The Red Cross keeps a register of unaccompanied children to help trace families.

Life Story Book

An adult best placed to undertake the role, e.g. a carer, should begin to put together a life story book for the child or young person at the earliest opportunity. It may be a way that the child or young person can talk about their past or they may just wish to start at the time their refugee experience began. It may, in later years, be of invaluable assistance in helping the child or young person understand their current experience, hopefully with a positive outcome to use as a perspective. A life story book may include any photographs of the child's home country including family photographs etc. It may be appropriate to assist the child or young person to either write or draw an account of their life prior to their refugee experience including the names of friends and relatives. This can then proceed to record the present experiences and people that affect their lives. Recording aspirations for the future may also be appropriate. Consideration must be given to any possible emotional impact this work could have on the child or young person.

Conclusion

Complaint procedures are an essential element of working with any client group. This is an especially

---

Key Questions

1. Am I aware of the immigration process?

2. Am I aware of the current political situation of the countries that are suffering the refugee experience? Not only knowledge of a country's current war status but also, a knowledge of the country's culture and pre-war history.

3. What assumptions am I making about this group of young people? It is very easy to make assumptions about the experiences of unaccompanied asylum-seeking young people. There is a clear benefit in addressing ones own assumptions and recognising the individuality of each young person and not defining them by their refugee experience.

4. As a practitioner working with unaccompanied asylum seeking young people have I reflected on whether the young person has access to services which they are entitled to, but may feel inhibited from accessing? This may be due to reasons associated with the dynamics of institutional racism and the inherent inhibitors that asylum-seeking people face when dealing with the support systems of this country.

5. What work can be done in partnership with other agencies, especially communities that have recently suffered the refugee experience?

vulnerable group of young people for whom complaints procedures which are pro-active and culturally appropriate may offer the only opportunity to voice concerns about the way they have been treated, in any aspect of their life. Some young people are afraid that if they complain about the service or their placement etc. everything will be withdrawn from them. There have been some reports of unaccompanied asylum-seeking young people being threatened by abusing adults that they will be deported and killed. Social services and youth work services should work together in offering support to asylum-seeking young people to enshrine the key principles of education, equality, empowerment and participation.

References

Department of Health (2000). *Children (Leaving Care) Act.* DoH.

Department of Health (1991). *Social Work with Unaccompanied Asylum-seeking Children: A Practice Guide.* DoH.

Department of Health (1991). *Working Together.* DoH.

General Assembly of the United Nations (1989). *Convention of the Rights of the Child.*

House of Commons (1984). *Immigration and Asylum Rules.* London.

UNHCR (1994). *Refugee Children: Guidelines on Protection and Care.*

Contacts

Refugee Council, tel: 0207 820 3000

Children Panel of Advisors, tel: 0207 820 3126

International Social Services, tel: 0207 582 6082

Immigration and Nationality Department, tel: 0870 606 7766

To contact a local social services call town hall or check telephone directory for Social Services.

British Red Cross, tel: 0207 235 5454

Legal Services Commission, tel: 0207 759 0000

Refugee Legal Centre, tel: 0207 827 9090

Medical Foundation for the Care of Victims of War, tel: 0207 813 7777

Further Reading

Community Care (1994). Risky Future. *Community Care*, November.

Community Care (1995). Gimme Shelter. *Community Care*, April.

Department of Health (1989). *The Children Act.* DoH.

Fahlberg, V. A Child's Journey Through Placement.

Herman, J., and Lewis, M.D. (1992). *Trauma and Recovery.* Basic Books.

Refugee Committee (1994). *Unaccompanied Asylum-seeking Children.* European Forum for Child Welfare. European Parliament Strasbourg, November 16th minutes.

Refugee Council (1994). *Helping Refugee Children in Schools.*

UNHCR/PTSS/Community Services *Working with Unaccompanied Minors in the Community.*

23

New Travellers Helping Themselves
Alan Dearling

Key Points

1. Offer only empathy and non-judgmental attitudes, confidentiality and voluntary rather than enforced relationship-building partnerships.

2. Aim to develop empowerment towards self-help and independence, rather than dependency.

3. Use only culturally appropriate materials and approaches which recognise and value diversity, rather than strategies which attempt to assimilate, obscure or destroy it.

4. Use techniques such as play, social action and experiential learning; network within the group and with external agencies for legal advice, education, benefits, health and other assistance and information.

5. Last, but by no means least: **Be yourself!**

Do you want to live in a Society, or in an Economy?

(Victor Bewley, friend of Travellers, Ireland, 1975)

Introduction: How I Got Involved

Each of us wears a number of 'hats' every day and through the course of our lives. Our 'hats' relate to many factors in our lives such as: family; community; tribe; race and ethnicity; skin colour; gender; age; education; religion; appearance and dress; language; economic and social status; employment or lack of it; behaviour; criminal record; lifestyle and interests. I'm sure I've missed some!

So, which 'hat' or 'hats' was I wearing when I started to get closely involved with the UK's New Travellers? It was a personal one. In this chapter I offer some insights into how that 'personal' involvement has been built on a bedrock of a number of youth and community work methods and perspectives. In turn it has helped me to establish contact with many New Travellers who are amongst the most vilified and demonised groups of people in the UK (Cohen, in Hetherington, 2000).

Despite the way in which the media and successive governments have tried to stereotype them as crusty, dirty, dole scroungers, begging on street corners with a can of Special Brew in one hand and a piece of string with a dog on the end of it, in the other, New Travellers are actually a very diverse group. Their history is one of evolutionary change and adaptation, starting from the late 1960s festival scene, through the period in the 1980s when the most visible group were known as the Peace Convoy, because of their involvement with the peace camps at Molesworth and Greenham Common, through to the almost re-invented 'tribes' of the 1990s and the present, which encompass many ex-road protesters, squatters, party people and even some traditional Gypsies and Irish and Scottish Travellers. What has remained constant is that New Travellers are largely youthful groups, and they have a lot of children travelling as part of their communities.

Thinking about classification, stereotyping and the process of marginalisation, I wrote in the introduction to *A Time to Travel? An Introduction to Britain's Newer Travellers* (Earle et al., 1994):

I lived for a couple of years, around 1989–1992 on a narrow boat around Worcestershire and Gloucestershire on the canals and rivers. My travelling brought me in much greater contact with Travellers, who the media dubbed as 'crusties', 'brigands' and 'New Agers'. As I travelled in my boat, pub and shop staff would stereotype me and say 'No Travellers wanted here'. At about that time, Fiona Earle and I were in contact about education and Travellers' children. (Slightly amended version)

Out of those meetings with Fiona, and together with people we knew and met, we put together the *A Time to Travel* book. It took nearly four years from a gleam in the eye to publication. A trained teacher, Fiona lives most of the time on the road and alternates between teaching drama and English in secondary schools, with working as a travelling teacher on 'new traveller' sites and at festivals. We have been involved with the Travellers' School Charity and the Educational Advice for Travellers, itself part of Friends and Families of Travellers Support Group, helping to develop a range of resources for Traveller children and their parents.

New Travellers: Who Are They?

To understand our involvement within the New Traveller communities, you need to understand a bit about the history of New Travellers in the UK and beyond; their lifestyles and the legislation and agency reactions to them. As successive researchers and commentators have found out, sometimes to their cost, it is very hard either to quantify the numbers of New Travellers, or to define them as a single group without acknowledging the diversity that exists (Kenrick and Clark, 1999).

Given that New Travellers are variably nomadic and purposely elusive, their numbers are hard to count. Organisations like Save the Children (SCF) and Friends and Families of Travellers (FFT), the Police and the Benefits Agency have all tried to estimate the numbers of people, vehicles and mobile homes involved at different times between about 1985 and now. The results are contradictory, ranging from the Benefits Agency figure of 1,425 registered with them on 27/10/93 to the Police figure of 'approximately 2,000 vehicles with about 8,000 people' (30/3/93 Minutes of Southern Intelligence Unit of the police, results of Operation Snapshot) through to FFT's figure of as many as '50–100,000' (FFT, 1996), presumably during the summer festival season.

Over ninety New Travellers were interviewed in a Children's Society survey and the findings certainly indicated a shift away from the more positive motivations of the 1970s and 1980s Traveller scene, in which many actively sought a travelling lifestyle and nomadism. Instead, many were forced into travelling because of issues such as homelessness, relationship breakdowns and leaving care (Children's Society, 1994).

After the police actions against the Traveller Peace Convoy, principally in Savernake Forest, in 1985, which became known as the Battle of the Beanfield, where the police loudspeaker on the helicopter urged the officers to 'take the bastards out' (reported in the *New Musical Express*, 8/5/93), and the evictions through Somerset and Dorset leading to Stoney Cross in Hampshire's New Forest 1986, Dennis Binns, the Head of Travellers Education in Manchester, compiled a collection of press cuttings entitled, *How to Decommission a Lifestyle*. These showed how efforts to provide education for Traveller children were being frustrated through lack of support by the authorities (Binns, 1986).

If you met New Travellers in the 1980s or 1990s, they never did conform to the stereotyped demonology portrayed in much of the media. Many New Travellers had previously made a living on the fringes of the summer festival circuit. Many acted as site crew, organised marquees and sound hire, were performers, sold craft goods and tat, or ran festival catering. Others have been involved in traditional Romany occupations, such as fruit and hop picking, dealing in scrap metal and even horse-trading. Finally, there were a number who have run kids' facilities and entertainment at festivals: indeed, working with children and young people has been a popular way of earning some income for many Travellers, especially young women.

In the 1990s, the New Traveller 'mix' included some new ingredients, particularly with an influx of dance-oriented ravers, mobile sound systems, and individuals and groups involved in environmental protest and street actions. And, outside of all these groups, some Travellers became semi-nomadic, still living in buses, benders, tipis and caravans for part of the year, sometimes seeking out isolated rural cottages as a base. These Travellers often refer to themselves as 'orbital' to a particular location, usually to increase employment and education opportunities.

To give a bit of reality to this description, here's Em (in a recent personal communication to me) talking about her current life and plans:

> *I'm doing a herbalism course based in Scotland, so I blat up there once each month. They don't burn witches any more, you know, they just try to ban, subvert or steal our knowledge... herbalism is getting really regulated and medicalised these days so I reckon it's important*

*for some of us witches /pagans to get the
qualifications they're bringing in before it gets
too hard (we're talking biochemistry degrees
here!) so that we can contrive to practise **our**
way and keep the old traditions alive, otherwise
they'll be sanitised to extinction... What else?
Been doing some anti-GM food campaigning
and plan to do a few festies this summer: Glasto,
Northern Green Gathering, Afro-Celt Explosion,
don't know where else yet. Getting a bit of a café
and fire show together with some friends and
busy whittling sticks for a dome.*

Legislation and Travellers

The legislation which the Conservative government
passed in attempt to outlaw Travellers and raves
was the Criminal Justice and Public Order Act
(CJPOA) 1994. It was something of a sledgehammer
to crack a small nut.

Amongst the most publicised intentions of the
Act were to give additional powers to local
authorities (Sections 77–80) and police (Sections
61, 63, 65, and 68–71), and to deal with
unauthorised campers and trespassers. This has
made evictions faster and made Travellers subject
to criminal proceedings if they obstruct the
eviction (see for instance Children's Society, 1996).
Traveller groups with more than six vehicles were
criminalised. It also removed the statutory
responsibilities on local authorities to provide sites
for Gypsies under the Caravan Sites Act 1968.

Now, it appears that it has had some unexpected
and arguably even positive effects, for the Traveller
community. Firstly, the passing of the CJPOA
brought about some new alliances between
squatters, the homeless, ravers, New Travellers,
Gypsies, environmental protesters and others
whose activities or lifestyles were now linked to
criminal behaviour. It created new interest in the
rights of Travellers, Traveller sites and consideration
of planning laws (e.g. DoE circular 1/94, *Gypsy Sites
and Planning*), which aimed to make proper
provision for people such as Travellers and others
with a nomadic lifestyles and also make it easier for
Travellers, Gypsies and people such as
permaculturalists to buy land on which they can
live sustainably and with low impact. The Land is
Ours, Chapter 7 and Groundswell are among the
organisations campaigning for sustainable human
settlement and development, often quoting Agenda

21, Chapter 7 from the 1992 Earth Summit (United
Nations, 1992), as grounds for planning
applications. Finally, the implementation of the
CJPOA brought with it new guidance. The Home
Office Guide (Bucke et al., 1998) to the Act for use
by the police suggests that before giving a directive
to leave, they take account of the personal
circumstances of the trespassers.

The DoE guide for local authorities, Circular
18/94, (DoE, 1994; and from FFT, 1996) again
identified the need to provide adequate facilities
for Travellers including the provision of skips,
toilets and drinking water.

The circular led to the now famous 'Wealden
Judgement' (reported in *The Times*, 1995), where
Judge Sedley ruled that before making a decision to
evict, councils must investigate the individual
circumstances of the people involved, and any
others that arrive during the eviction process. It
provided a further platform from which youth and
community workers and others can help to prevent
evictions, which are little more than 'social
cleansing'.

The Travellers' School Charity (TSC), the National Playbus Association and Other Social Welfare Agencies

Within the New Traveller community there exists a
powerful self-help ethic. They regard their lifestyles
as 'normal', settled even. They are embattled, tribal,
community-oriented but individualistic, idealistic;
one common factor being that New Travellers tend
to accept new people into their communities,
rather than exclude them. Obviously this causes
conflict, tensions, and frequent fragmentation on
sites. As already stated, New Travellers do not all
lead similar lifestyles. Some move around a lot,
others are virtually static. Quite a large number
have left England and Wales, either permanently or
temporarily, and moved to Scotland, Ireland or
further afield to Spain, Portugal, France, Germany
and even South Africa and Australia (Dearling,
1998b, 2000). Many see themselves in the classic
(sic) role of 'Gypsies' as re-defined by Section 80 of
the CJPOA (amended from Caravan Sites Act 1960)
as people with a nomadic life.

Vulnerable people are obviously suspicious of
'authority' figures, and with all too good reasons. In
terms of working with New Travellers, one of my

main contributions has been in creating enough trust with New Travellers using my specialisms such as group work; games, music, arts, crafts; outreach and detached work and so on. My work has also involved enabling Travellers to write their own histories in the two books and various articles and booklets which I've been involved in compiling. This has been much more than a simple 'oral history' project, and it has included:

- Nearly 200 New Travellers contributing their words, pictures and photos to the publications.
- My being able to help employ New Travellers as artists, photographers, proof readers, etc.
- Offering advice and support to over 100 students and researchers in their work with New Travellers.

Fiona Earle and Steve Witt in a recent publication for the National Playbus Association (2000) advocate guidelines for play, youth and community workers. The aim is to ensure that workers consider carefully the different cultures of the groups they may be working with. In the section on practical ideas on working with New Travellers, it mentions the need to pay attention at the point of first contact (e.g. if possible, go through someone who already visits regularly and has a good working relationship, such as a health visitor) to issues such as the use of language, i.e. avoid 'officialdom'. Consideration also needs to be given about **why** you are making a visit, what you hope to achieve, and what you have to offer in terms of resources or skills.

Returning to the TSC, its management and occasional staff are comprised of current and former Travellers. The TSC history is colourful (Dearling, 1998a). It started with a vision of running a mobile 'free school' for the New Travelling community. In 1987 they acquired a 23-foot long Bella Vega exhibition bus, after various fund raising benefits and 'bucketing' at festivals. Instantly recognisable, the School Bus acted as a magnet for kids on sites and at festivals, it provided fun and some educational recreation, but it was unwieldy, expensive to run, a difficult resource to move around, and without a permanent teacher on board, prone to abuse.

In 1989, the first qualified, paid teacher to work from the bus was appointed and the person was already a full time Traveller and known to the charity. The 1989–90 the TSC Annual Report

highlighted the internal tensions between the need for greater administrative efficiency and culture-friendliness at the heart of the TSC's operations (Dearling, 1998a). By 1993 the bus was finally abandoned as unworkable and since then the teachers have offered on-site and at-festival educational work for new Traveller children and their parents in 'caravan classrooms' and the 'geodesic dome'. A range of resources for Traveller parents and Traveller Education Service staff have also been developed and these publications are now at the heart of TSC's distance learning provision. Their production is a testimony to the commitment of members of the Traveller community to help themselves.

Members of the TSC team have now produced over forty workbooks for use from pre-school colouring books through to Key Stage 3. What makes the books very special is that they are culturally appropriate and Traveller-friendly. My own involvement has included working with about 200 New Travellers from around the world on the compilation of *A Time to Travel*, *No Boundaries* and a number of articles. Once again, the skills that I used were ones I see as very important in youth and community work, namely:

- networking
- relationship building
- listening and communication skills

And a commitment to helping Travellers' to speak for themselves, and only where necessary, trying too fairly represent people's diversity of opinions.

The TSC does not operate in a vacuum. It works with sister and brother charities and organisations to promote beneficial schemes such as the Woodland Skills Training courses, with the FFT, and Health and Safety and Education workshops with FFT and the Children's Society. It has had a hard struggle to compete for grants. Individuals have all brought their own personal style to each round of fund-raising applications. The problems of obtaining funding for Traveller education are very similar to many other youth projects. Registered as a charity since 1988, TSC has been able to apply for grants like any other charity, but the marginalised and demonised image of Travellers means that potential sponsors are in a small minority. Notably, money is available for a fixed term, often comes with strings attached, and is increasingly linked to 'problems', 'drugs prevention' and 'crime'. Also, there exists the 'Catch-22' where many trust bodies prefer to part-fund projects, which requires match funding. Furthermore, it can be hard to obtain the balance between capital and revenue funding, and almost impossible to gain funds for flexible use, administration and overheads.

Helping Traveller Parents

Just as in Youth and Community Work, commentators and practitioners argue over the relative value of different approaches, for instance, social action as compared with centre-based work, Travellers and those involved with them frequently debate the value of education as compared with schooling. It is because of the central importance for Traveller parents of either obtaining suitable state education or organising their own alternatives, that much input from youth-centred workers has focused on supporting what appears to be 'formal education' opportunities. In fact much of it is far from formal.

Of the New Travellers in the UK, the TSC believes that half are under sixteen years old (cited in Dearling, 1998a). Most other people in those children's lives are their own parents or parents of other children on site or at a festival. Travellers have therefore quite naturally asserted their right, under the 1944 Education Act to either demand inclusion of their children in local school or to provide 'education otherwise'. The work of TSC has helped provide one set of bridges which empower Traveller parents to make the best job of this process and help avoid the usual dependency culture.

Many Travellers argue that nomadism and the Travellers' lifestyle are an education in themselves. Individual schools often find it hard to cope with the temporary nature of Traveller and Gypsy children in their institutions dominated by the National Curriculum. The children frequently find the culture of the school threatening and intolerant of their own culture. For instance, how many schools possess books like the TSC 'Homes' series, which features narrow boats, benders, showman's wagons and tipis alongside flats and houses? Below is a sample from one of the *TSC Workbooks* designed for use by parents with their children.

The TSC and its workers cannot work with all Traveller children or their parents, so 'focus group' type discussions were run to identify what New

---

Compost

People living on their own land often build a compost heap. Materials which decay are allowed to break down and rot. The compost can then be used to help plants grow.

Colour green all the items below that could be added to a compost heap.

apple core   bread   peelings   tin can

cabbage leaves   bottle   cold tea   grass cuttings

banana   foil   cake   coin

Travellers prioritised as their needs either for their children or for themselves. This process produced a programme for funding, which features many aspects of youth work practice. The programme focuses on:

- The production of more imaginative and culturally-friendly distance-learning workbooks and activity books right up to GCSE level.
- Materials and play techniques for pre-school work with children and parents.
- Roadshow events aimed at training parents and other Traveller adults, which try to cram key elements of a teacher training course into two or three days. This would include an introduction to the concept of mentoring in education.
- Specific youth work activities at festivals and sites using small group work principles and focusing on the use of games, arts and crafts and creative activities such as magazine production, video work, music workshops, and use of portable computer equipment.
- Running youth clubs as drug-free zones at festivals.
- Mobile careers' advice and actual skills training courses for young Travellers. These might be specifically geared to the employment areas related to travelling, such

as circus and performance skills or environment and sustainability practice.
- Self-help and contact advice on dealing with authorities and legislation: evictions, planning, police, education, health and social work.

This is also linked to a proactive and strongly participative environmental youth work agenda whereby the practices link with other movements or groups involved in social change, environmental and global issues, low-impact lifestyles, human rights and protest (Dearling and Armstrong, 1997).

Questions for Youth and Community Organisations

Certain agencies have focused attention on marginalised and socially excluded groups such as Travellers. The National Playbus Association and the National Lottery have been especially supportive in terms of funding. Active at the policy level have been, NCVO, CRE, the Children's Society and universities such as Greenwich, Cardiff and Newcastle, and in Scotland, Moray House College, the Scottish Human Rights Centre and Save the Children. However, all Travellers, and New Travellers in particular, continue to evince attitudes of 'fear and loathing' from many social welfare agencies.

To end (in the spirit of listening to young people): a poem that Jacinta, a young Traveller sent to me.

Jacinta's rant

You call me a dreamer
A schemer
A slob
Say I'm not living in reality
Go get a job

You call me a waster
Of money and time
A waste of space
A doer of crime

You call me smelly
N' scruffy
N' weird

My views too stupid
Will never come true
But, I'd rather be like that
Than someone like **you**

Key Questions

1. How can youth and community work agencies move away from the view that Travellers are not 'workable' with?

2. In what ways can youth and community work empower Travellers?

3. How can more youth and community workers see working with such groups as an opportunity to act against social exclusion and for human rights in UK society?

4. Might it not be justifiable for youth workers to operate (rather like Festival Welfare Services) on the UK's festival circuit?

5. What sort of mobile or outreach opportunities would be culturally appropriate for work with Travellers?

References

Binns, D. (1986). *How to Decommission a Lifestyle.* Manchester: Traveller Education Service.

Bucke, T., and James, Z. (1998). *Trespass and Protest: Policing Under the Criminal Justice and Public Order Act.* Home Office.

Children's Society (1994). *Out of Site, Out of Mind.* Children's Society.

Dearling, A., with Armstrong, H. (1997). *Youth Action and the Environment.* Council for Environmental Education/ Russell House Publishing.

Dearling, A. (1998a). *Almost...Everything You Need to Know About the Travellers' School Charity.* TSC.

Dearling, A. (1998b). *No Boundaries: New Travellers Outside of Britain.* Enabler Publications.

Dearling, A., with Henley, B. (2000). *Alternative Australia: Celebrating Cultural Diversity.* Enabler Publications.

Department of the Environment (1994). *Gypsy Sites and Planning: Guidance.* Circulars 1/94 and 18/94. DoE.

Earle, F., Dearling, A. et al. (1994). *A Time to Travel? An Introduction to Britain's Newer Travellers.* Enabler Publications.

Earle, F., and Witt, S. (2000). *Working with Travellers.* National Playbus Association.

Friends and Families of Travellers Support Group (1996). *Confined, Constrained and Condemned: Civil Rights and Travellers.* FFT.

Hetherington, K. (2000). *New Age Travellers: Vanloads of Uproarious Humanity.* Cassell.

Kenrick, D., and Clark, C. (1999). *Moving On: The Gypsies and Travellers of Britain.* University of Hertfordshire Press.

Southern Intelligence Unit of the Police (30/3/93). *Minutes of the meeting, including Item 5, Operation Snapshot.* Police HQ, Devizes, Wiltshire.

The Times, 22/9/95. R v Wealden District Council: ex parte Atkinson and others.

United Nations (1992). *The United Nations Conference on Environment and Development, 1992.* Abridged version published by Regency Press.

Undercurrents. Ten alternative news videos about social and environmental action. Undercurrents, 16b Cherwell St, Oxford OX4 1BG.

Further Reading

Alex (1998). The Human Rights Act and Travellers. *FFT Newsletter,* Nov./Dec. Friends and Families of Travellers.

Advisory Council for Education of Romany and other Travellers (1993). *The Education of Gypsy and Traveller Children: Action-research and Co-ordination.* University of Hertfordshire Press.

Benefits Agency (1994). *Income Support Strategic Information Bulletin.* Benefits Agency.

Cemlyn, S. (1998). *Policy and Provision by Social Services for Traveller Children and Families.* Nuffield Foundation.

Clark, C. (1998). New Age Travellers: Identity, Sedentarism and Social Security. In Acton, T. (Ed.). *Gypsy Politics and Traveller Identity.* University of Hertfordshire.

Garrard, B. (1986). *The Children of the Rainbow Gathered in the Free State of Avalonia at the Christian Community of Greenlands Farm.* Unique Publications.

Kiddle, K. (1999). *Traveller Children: A Voice for Themselves.* Jessica Kingsley.

Liégois, J-P. (1998). *School Provision for Ethnic Minorities: The Gypsy Paradigm.* University of Hertfordshire Press.

Lowe, R., and Shaw, W. (1993). *Travellers: Voices of the New Age Nomads.* Fourth Estate.

McKay, G. (1996). *Senseless Acts of Beauty: Cultures of Resistance Since the Sixties.* Verso.

McKay, G. (1998). *DIY Culture: Party and Protest in Nineties Britain.* Verso.

Stone, C.J. (1996). *Fierce Dancing: Adventures in the Underground.* Faber and Faber.

Stone, C.J. (1999). *The Last of the Hippies.* Faber and Faber.

Watkinson, D. (1998). *Gypsies and Travellers.* Paper presented at Public Law Society/Shelter conference on the Human Rights Act.

Webster, L. (1996). *A Report for the Children's Society on the Impact of the Criminal Justice and Public Order Act, 1994 on the lives of Travellers and their Children.* Children's Society.

Williamson, H. (1995). *Social Action for Young People.* Russell House Publishing with SCF.

Resources

Videos for use in work with teachers, youth workers and young people include:

Just Like You. Traveller children speak out about their lives. Children's Society.

24

Youth Crime, Youth Justice and Youth Work

John Pitts

Key Points

1. In the UK, youth justice and youth work have usually expanded side by side and usually in response to similar concerns about the erosion of family values, discipline and crime and disorder. The period 1933 to 1969 saw the rise of 'welfarism', in which the needs of the child or young person in trouble came to assume a similar significance to their deeds. However this concern meant greater professional intervention which led to higher levels of institutionalisation. In the run-up to the Children and Young Person's Act 1969, the government was keen to involve the youth service in *Intermediate Treatment* but youth workers resisted on the grounds that their involvement with young people should always be voluntary.

2. The 1970s marked a backlash against 'welfarism', a return to a concern with due process and the emergence of a 'justice model' of work with young offenders. This was partly because the 1970s also saw an unprecedented rise in the numbers of young offenders confined in institutions. This precipitated a crisis throughout the penal system.

3. In the 1980s, the government, in partnership with academics, civil servants and professionals, pursuing a minimalist strategy, developed Multi-agency Diversion Panels. These panels aimed to steer youngsters away from the courts and penal institutions, towards activities and projects, many of which were run by youth workers. However, as youth justice grew in the 1980s, the youth service sustained successive waves of financial cuts and its significance as a preventive service was reduced.

4. From 1992 law and order was back on the political agenda and government and opposition strove to be 'tougher on crime' than one another. New Labour was elected on a law and order ticket. Its Crime and Disorder Act 1998 created Youth Offending Teams (YOTs) with the potential to offer a holistic response to youngsters in trouble. However, they were quickly flooded with young people on court orders, the supervision of which became the top priority for the YOTs. Several YOTs recruited youth workers who, once again, face the dilemma about working with young people as a requirement of a court order.

5. One area in which youth work appears to have been an effective crime prevention and community safety resource has been outreach and detached youth work. Despite this, these remain an underdeveloped area of youth justice and community safety.

Introduction

From its inception, youth work in the UK has been concerned with youth crime and its prevention. Indeed, youth work as we know it in this country has its origins in what Garland (1985) describes as the 'crisis of control' in the industrial cities in the final decades of the 19th Century (Garland, 1985; Lea, 1998). Then, as now, rapid social and economic change raised concerns amongst politicians, the media, the police and the clergy about the weakening of conventional family forms and values, the consequent erosion of informal social controls and the crime and anti-social behaviour which this was assumed to foster. Then, as now, the expansion of youth work occurred in parallel with the extension of the reach of the juvenile justice system (Factor and Pitts, forthcoming).

In 1908 a separate juvenile court was established in England and Wales. The legislation allowed for the supervision of juvenile offenders in the community by a probation officer. Although the advent of probation might be said to represent an acknowledgement of a young offender's right to help, it also placed them under obligatory surveillance, with the ever-present danger of harsher penalties if they did not abide by the conditions of the probation order. By 1920 over 10,000 people were under probation supervision, of whom 80% were under 21. The *Prevention of Crime Act* 1908 also introduced Borstals, penal institutions for 16–20 year olds which, unlike the adult prisons of the time, provided educational and vocational programmes and military training for their inmates. Although the Children Act 1908 placed strict limitations on the power of courts to consign juveniles to adult prisons, from 1908 the number of youngsters consigned to juvenile reformatories and Borstals rose steadily, topping 20,000 in the early 1920s. This expansion of institutional and community control occurred despite a steadily declining crime rate. As we were to re-discover in the 1970s and again in the 1990s, when additional penalties are created within justice systems, they will be used irrespective of the level of need or the threat posed by offenders.

Child-centred Justice

The second wave of juvenile justice reform in the UK occurred in the early 1930s. The Children and Young Person's Act 1933 established the principle that young offenders should be dealt with in ways which promoted their 'welfare' and that any necessary 'treatment', should be available to them. These policies were imbued with currently popular ideas of child development derived from Freudian psychoanalysis, which focused upon the underlying social and psychological origins of youthful criminality rather than crime itself (Klein, 1923; Bowlby, 1946). Over the next 15 years, a widening rift grew between those who favoured the traditional 'justice' model and those who maintained that young offenders should be taken out of the justice system and placed in the hands of experts in the care and welfare of children and young people. This argument was given greater power by research undertaken in the early 1960s which showed that the children who passed through the juvenile courts were overwhelmingly, poor, badly educated and, in many cases, victims of violence or abuse (see, for example, Titmus, 1968). By the mid-1960s, it appeared that the 'welfarist' argument would prevail.

The Rise of 'Welfarism'

The 1964 White Paper *The Child the Family and the Young Offender* stated the government's intention to replace the juvenile court with a family council in which lay people, and health and welfare professionals, would devise the most appropriate treatments for the problems which underlay young people's criminality. This radical proposal was bitterly attacked by opposition parties, some of the government's own MPs, lawyers, magistrates and probation officers. As a result, a significantly modified reform package was presented to parliament in the Children and Young Persons Act 1969. The 1969 Act retained the juvenile court but restricted the magistrate's power to impose Borstal sentences. It passed responsibility for the supervision of young offenders in the community and decisions about placement in Approved Schools (redesignated Community Homes with Education (CHEs)) to local authority social workers. The 1969 Act also introduced a new measure, Intermediate Treatment (IT), which could be utilised formally as a requirement of a Supervision Order, but also permitted local authorities to establish community-based schemes to 'prevent' youth crime amongst children and young people deemed to be 'at risk' of offending.

The big idea behind early IT was 'normalisation'. In practice, normalisation meant attempting to integrate children and young people at risk of, or involved in offending, into mainstream educational and recreational provision in order to steer them away from crime, and to minimise the stigma of involvement in formal justice systems. The government had hoped that the youth service and youth workers would 'buy into' IT. However, many youth workers, and the youth work trades union, the CYWA argued that to work with youngsters who were directed to them by the courts, or the social workers and probation officers who were supervising their court orders, constituted a violation of the profession's commitment to voluntary participation. 1969 represented the first skirmish in a sustained struggle between the government and youth work to involve youth workers in a more directive and controlling role in relation to young people who had broken the law. It is therefore significant that, from this point onwards, the expansion of 'youth justice', an area of work which attracted many trained youth workers, paralleled the contraction of the Youth Service (Pitts, 1988).

The Spreading of the Net of Control

1970 saw the election of a Conservative government which, while unwilling to limit the powers of juvenile court magistrates, nonetheless implemented many of the new provisions introduced by the 1969 Act. Thus, the new Care Orders, Supervision Orders and Intermediate Treatment were introduced alongside the fines, discharges, probation, attendance centre, detention centre and borstal orders of the existing system, rather than as an alternative to them. This gave both juvenile court magistrates and social workers more options than ever before for dealing with young offenders. What happened next had strong echoes of what had happened under similar circumstances between 1908 and 1920. By 1977, an estimated 12,000 youngsters were involved in Intermediate Treatment, of whom only about 1,500 were adjudicated offenders. At the same time the police had established specialist Juvenile Bureaux to deal more cost-effectively with petty juvenile offenders. Between 1965 and 1977 the numbers of 10–17 year olds cautioned by the police, that is, formally reprimanded by a senior police officer rather than being taken to the juvenile court, rose from 3,062 to 111,922 (Pitts, 1988). However, early informal intervention revealed a tendency to draw youngsters further into the system as the discovery of new needs and new problems appeared to necessitate the formalisation of these interventions. In consequence, larger numbers of children were appearing in the juvenile court and a higher proportion of these was receiving custodial sentences. Whereas in 1965, 21% of convicted young offenders were sentenced by magistrates to detention centres and Borstals, by 1977 this proportion had risen to 38%.

Delinquency Management

The Thatcher government, elected in 1979, recognised that it had a problem. Not only were residential and custodial institutions for juveniles chronically overcrowded, thereby placing additional strains on an equally overcrowded adult penal system, they were also costing a great deal of money. This was a particular concern for a government elected on a pledge to cut taxes, yet facing a fiscal crisis occasioned by rising state expenditure and a declining tax-paying population. Their response to this problem was shaped in crucial ways by contemporary intellectual and political developments in juvenile justice in the UK and the USA. By the mid-1970s, a growing body of Anglo-American criminological research was indicating that not only did rehabilitative programmes have only a minimal impact upon re-offending (Martinson, 1974; Wilson, 1975), they sometimes worsened the problem through processes of stigmatisation and 'labelling' (Becker, 1963; Matza, 1964). By the late 1970s in the UK, an increasingly influential juvenile justice lobby, composed of youth justice professionals, penal reform groups, progressive Home Office and Department of Health civil servants and academic criminologists was pressing for the replacement of a 'welfare'-oriented system by a 'justice'-oriented one which minimised intervention in the lives of young offenders. The promise of a cost-effective, 'slim-line juvenile justice system proved irresistible to a government under pressure.

The Rise of 'Progressive Minimalism'

In 1983, the Department of Health launched its Intermediate Treatment Initiative in which £15 million was granted to the voluntary sector to develop 4,500 alternatives to custody, over three years, in collaboration with the police and juvenile court magistrates. Between 1981 and 1989 the numbers of juveniles imprisoned in Young Offenders Centres fell from 7,700 to 1,900 per annum.

The radical reductions in custodial sentencing during this period are not solely attributable to changes in 'sentencing culture', although this clearly played a part. A major contributory factor was the reduction in the numbers of children and young people entering juvenile courts. Whereas in 1980 71,000 boys and girls aged 14 to 16 were sentenced by the juvenile courts in England and Wales, by 1987 this figure had dropped to 37,300, a reduction of over 52%. This was made possible by the development of local *Multi-agency Diversion Panels*, comprising representatives from the police, social services, education, the youth service and the voluntary sector. Many Multi-agency Panels attempted to fashion a non-stigmatising *shadow tariff* of robust informal intervention in the spheres of education, family relationships, use of leisure, vocational training and drug abuse. In many cases these interventions were undertaken by youth workers or the youth service on the basis of voluntary participation by the young offenders, into which those who had committed less serious offences could be 'diverted' from the formal youth justice process. This strategy had a remarkable impact upon the youth justice system. Between 1980 and 1987 the cautioning rate for girls aged 14 to 16 rose from 58% to 82%. For boys the figures were 34% and 58% respectively (Pitts, 1988). The implications for would-be reformers appears to be that diverting youngsters away from the justice system at an early stage may be more effective than attempts to change the attitudes and behaviour of sentencers.

The cost-cutting Conservative government was eager to build on the successes of the Multi-agency Diversion Panels and the alternatives to custody developed as part of its Intermediate Treatment Initiative. It therefore incorporated many of these practices into its Criminal Justice Act 1991, which was to introduce similar schemes for youngsters aged 18–21.

The Renaissance of Youth Imprisonment

Record rises in the crime rate at the end of the 1980s and youth riots on out-of-town housing estates in 1991 and 1992 were to force the Conservative government to defend its minimalist policies on youth crime. But it was the murder in 1993 of two-year-old James Bulger by two truanting ten-year-olds, which put juvenile crime unequivocally back on the 'front page'. As a result, the key reforms embodied in the Criminal Justice Act 1991 were abandoned. In March 1993, only five months after the newly implemented Act had abolished custody for children under 15, the Home Secretary promised to create 200 places for 12 to 15 year old persistent offenders in new 'Secure Training Centres'. This *volte-face* signalled a new era in which crime in general, and youth crime in particular, were to be moved back to the centre of the political stage. In 1994 Home Secretary Michael Howard, set about toughening the probation

service by allowing direct recruitment of junior officers from the armed forces and ex-police officers. He told the Conservative Party annual conference of that year that:

> *Prison works, it ensures that we are protected from murderers, muggers and rapists: and it makes many who are tempted to commit crime think twice.*

Clearly the courts were now being sent a very different message by the government and, between 1993 and 1998, the number of young offenders under sentence in penal establishments, rose from 5081 to 8,500.

1997 and All That

In 1997 the first Labour government for 18 years was elected in the UK, promising to revitalise the public services, including the youth service, hand power back to local authorities, and make good the social damage wrought by the neo-liberal experiment of the Thatcher and Major years. 'New Labour' has placed youth work at the centre of this endeavour. Thus, the professionals who will make New labour's policies work in the areas of vocational training, employment, drugs, citizenship, school exclusion, community safety and crime prevention, are youth workers. However, in the process the traditional youth service has been effectively sidelined and the role of youth work, and the task of the youth worker, have been re-described in crucial ways (Factor and Pitts, forthcoming). In this new policy environment, the roles to be played by youth workers, the problems to be addressed, the target groups for intervention and the methods of, and priorities for, intervention are defined by government rather than professionals or the young people they serve. It is in this political context that youth workers are becoming involved in youth justice.

The Crime and Disorder Act 1998

In the sphere of youth justice, New Labour's policies echo the hard line of their Tory predecessors. The measures introduced by the Crime and Disorder Act 1998 focus first and foremost upon the criminal deeds of young offenders rather than their social or psychological needs. Unlike earlier minimalist strategies, which aimed to divert younger children out of the system altogether, the provisions of the 1998 Act deliberately target younger juveniles on the edges of, or recently embarked upon, a criminal career in order to involve them and their parents in a formal intervention.

The Act requires chief executives of local authorities to bring into being Youth Offending Teams (YOTs), modelled on the multi-agency diversion panels of the 1980s, and staffed by personnel seconded from the police, the probation service, education, social services, the health service and, in several cases, the youth service. This raises practical and ethical questions about what it is that youth workers will actually do in the YOT and whether their involvement with the young people there will be voluntarily, as was the case with the Multi-agency Diversion initiatives of the 1980s, or whether they will be required to supervise court orders in the same way as the police and probation officers and social workers in the YOT.

The Act also created the Youth Justice Board of England and Wales which will oversee the development of the YOTs, specify the standards of efficiency and effectiveness to be achieved by them and, if necessary, assume control of them if they under-performed. The government hopes that, in this way, similar standards will be achieved throughout England and Wales. These changes represent a significant move towards a national system of juvenile justice. If it is successful, the Act promises to inject a greater degree of equity between regions into a system which has been characterised by significant variations in provision, quality of service and sentencing outcomes (ILYJS, 1995; Perfect and Renshaw, 1996). These, largely positive, developments stand in marked contrast with the propensity of the Act to draw into the youth justice system a new, younger and less problematic population of children and young people, and subject more serious young offenders to, usually counterproductive, custodial penalties.

The Potential and the Pitfalls of the YOT

The YOT brings together in one place what Robin Skynner (1974) calls the 'minimum sufficient network' of agencies, professionals and expertise necessary to make an effective, *holistic*, response to multiply-disadvantaged young people with complex needs. But responding effectively to these youngsters may take a long time and require sensitive networking with a range of agencies, plus regular follow-up contact. It also means allowing each professional to do what they do best and, in the case of youth workers, this may well mean allowing them to do what they do on the basis of voluntary involvement with the young people. The YOT also represents, potentially at least, a catalyst for positive change in the local authority and voluntary sector services and the police forces from which YOT personnel are seconded.

The YOT and its managers also face some important and potentially controversial choices. There is a real tension between the Crime and Disorder Act's (1998) perception of children and young people who break the law as 'offenders' and the Children Act (1989) and the United Nations Convention on the Rights of the Child (1990) which regard these youngsters as 'children in need'. This poses the YOT, and therefore the local authority the probation service and the police, with a question about whether, and to what extent, they should challenge the government's preferred perception of children and young people in trouble, and emphasise the YOT's role as a child care and educational resource.

In a similar vein, 'social exclusion' is high on the agenda of both local and central government, though the youth justice system when imposing stigmatising criminal penalties can serve as a major motor of social exclusion. Yet, if we wished to devise a professional service aimed specifically at preventing social exclusion amongst multiply-disadvantaged young people, by responding to their needs in all their complexity, the model which suggests itself would resemble a YOT.

As we have noted, the YOT places the Multi-agency Diversion Panels developed informally in the 1980s, on a statutory footing. However, whereas the Multi-agency Panels of the 1980s strove, wherever possible, to divert young people from the juvenile justice system, the YOTs will, as we have also noted, draw in a far larger number of children and young people, some of whom will have committed no offences at all. Indeed, the *Association for Youth Justice* has estimated that the new legislation will trigger a 150% increase in the throughput of YOTs (Pitts, 1999). One of the consequences of this hugely increased throughput is that the major task of the YOTs has become the supervision and completion of offence-focused programmes imposed by the courts. This means that the development of holistic responses to youngsters in trouble, in which the specialists, including youth workers, come together to devise programmes which will not only challenge their behaviour, but also meet their needs and enhance their competence and confidence, is jeopardised. The challenge for the professionals, including the youth workers who work in or with YOTs, is to reclaim the potential of the YOTs as a resource for youngsters in trouble and, indirectly, for their victims as well.

Youth Work and Youth Crime Prevention

As we have noted, the YOT also has a brief to promote youth crime 'prevention'. This is a field in which, from its inception, youth and community work has played a central role. The most comprehensive piece of preventive youth work undertaken in the UK was the Wincroft Youth Project which operated in Manchester in the late 1960s (Smith et al., 1972). Wincroft utilised techniques developed originally by the *New York City Youth Board* to target several hundred young people, identified by the police, social services, the probation service, schools and youth clubs as posing particular problems of behaviour and criminality. Wincroft worked with these young people in their peer groups over a three-year period. Broadly, the project offered young people a wider range of roles that they might play and alternative paths to adulthood. The project proved to be effective in engaging 'hard-to-reach' young people and enabling them either to stop offending or to reduce the frequency and seriousness of their offending.

In France, most urban neighbourhoods now have a *Specialised Prevention Team. Specialised Prevention* originally emerged in France in the 1960s in response to concerns about accelerated North and Central African migration into urban neighbourhoods, a consequent rise in inter-racial and racist violence, marked increases in youth unemployment and drug-taking, and the emergence of a flamboyant, oppositional youth subculture, the *blouson noire. Specialised Prevention* was originally modelled on North American models of 'street gang work', later

developing community development and educational functions. (Gazeau and Peyre, 1998). Whereas, in the UK, this approach to prevention went into steep decline in the 1980s, in France it is a model which continues to be refined and developed. With the advent of Francoise Mitterand's *Social Prevention Initiative* (SPI), in 1983, an expanded *Specialised Prevention* service became one of its the central props.

Pioneered originally by the voluntary sector, by the mid-1990s *Specialised Prevention* services were provided by 320 voluntary organisations deploying specialist teams in most medium and large French towns with a population of more than 10,000 people. These services were funded by French *Departments* on the basis of service agreements with the voluntary sector from *departmental* children's service budgets and the central government family benefits fund (CAF). At national level, a liaison committee promotes and supports *Specialised Prevention* services. *Specialised Prevention* is defined in law as a range of actions aimed at preventing social marginalisation and promoting the social integration of young people facing social problems (Article 45: *Code de la Famille et de l'Aide Sociale*). In practice *Specialised Prevention* provides:

- *Street social work*, with young people and some adults in targeted neighbourhoods.
- *Prevention clubs*, which offer support to families in crisis, access to legal advice and representation, health promotion, school homework support, advocacy and support for children facing exclusion from school.
- *Holiday play schemes and activity programmes*, the *ete jeunes*, for children in areas of poverty and high crime.
- *Training and employment*, helping youngsters access the best schemes, working with local employers to develop opportunities, working with young people to start their own businesses and co-operatives.
- *Working with mainstream agencies* to help local people gain access to them and helping the agencies to evaluate and enhance their impact locally.
- *Developing community problem-solving capacities* through the support of local people to develop residents and tenants associations and promote self-help networks, skills exchanges and purchasing collectives.

Specialised Prevention is rooted in the idea that some children and young people are denied the cultural and emotional experiences, and the social space, in which to grow to maturity. In consequence, they find it difficult, and sometimes impossible, to handle the adult world and its institutions. The task of the *Specialised Prevention team* is to undertake an analysis of local patterns of youth crime, violence and disorder and ascertain the location of young people believed to be at risk in a variety of ways. On the basis of this analysis, certain neighbourhoods or groups are targeted for intervention. The role of the worker on the street is to make and sustain contact with these young people, on their terms, in order to help them build a more positive self-perception, devise more satisfying, yet attainable, personal goals; to facilitate their contact with the agencies and individuals with the resources they need to achieve these goals and to support them through adversity. But the key to the apparent success of this strategy is time. Workers sometimes maintain relationships with the most troubled young people for five or six years.

Each member of *Specialised Prevention* teams will normally be assigned a particular *quarter* which can be covered easily on foot. The team in Bourg-les-Valence, for example, had four workers who served a population of 27,000, each team member having his or her own 'patch' (Walden-Jones, 1993). Teams undertook an analysis of local patterns of youth crime and disorder and the location of young people believed to be at risk in a variety of ways. In doing so they drew upon data supplied by the Education Department, the Mairie, the police and their own local knowledge. On the basis of these assessments, certain neighbourhoods or groups were targeted for intervention. One team identified a group of young drug users, hanging around the bus station, as their target. The *Service* gave the team 18 months to establish relationships with the targeted group and up to five years to locate and work with a broader network of around 300 opiate-using young people in that part of the city. The teams studied by Walden-Jones utilised a range of approaches to achieve their goal of shifting young people 'away from offending and disaffection and towards 'normal' social behaviour and integration'.

These initiatives appear to have had a considerable impact upon the nature and intensity of youth offending and there are indications that project participants tend to 'grow out of crime' at an earlier stage than non-participants. All the team's work was carried out with the agreement of the young people, and never as a condition of a sentence or a magistrate's directive. Furthermore, it is a normal and accepted practice that no information is passed on to the courts, other agencies or to their families, without the young person's permission.

Arguably, the prototype for all these forms of neighbourhood-based youth work described here was the *Chicago Area Project* (CAP) which began in the mid-1930s. In their 50-year follow-up study, Samuel Schlossman and his associates (1984) concluded that the evidence 'while hardly foolproof, justifies a strong hypothesis that CAP has long been effective in reducing rates of reported delinquency'.

Despite the fact that the youth service in general and 'detached' or 'street' youth work in particular has been contracting for the past two decades, there is currently renewed political interest in its preventive potential. In 1993 the DfEE launched its three-year GEST programme for the youth service, the *Youth Action Scheme*. The scheme supported 28 English local authorities to create 60 projects which aimed to enable youth workers to develop new ways of working which would reduce the risk of young people becoming involved in crime. These projects aimed to:

- Develop problem-focused approaches.
- Set up time-limited work with young people.
- Develop a monitoring and evaluation strategy.
- Establish structures to enable short-term financial management.
- Develop an exit strategy.

An evaluation undertaken by Alan France and Paul Wiles (1996) indicates that projects which accepted a crime-focused role, were largely successful in developing new ways of working with youngsters in trouble. In their first year, *Youth Action Scheme* projects worked with 4,322 young people, the bulk of whom were demonstrably at risk, or already involved in criminal activity. Despite problems of implementation and evaluation, it appears that these projects had a positive impact upon participant's involvement in crime. This is the more remarkable when we recognise that the bulk of them would have been unlikely to engage in conventional rehabilitative programmes.

Key Questions

1. What are the key areas of similarity and difference between the roles and responsibilities of youth workers and other youth justice system professionals?

2. To what extent, and under what circumstances, is it reasonable for youth workers to become involved in the statutory supervision of young offenders, or interventions in which a young person's participation is based on some degree of coercion?

3. What has youth work to teach YOTs about holistic interventions?

4. How might detached and outreach approaches to youth offending, based as they are upon a voluntary engagement between young person and worker, be promoted in the spheres of youth justice and community safety?

5. What are the principle differences between the French and UK histories of youth justice?

Conclusion

Medium-term youth work strategies of this kind are increasingly difficult to fund in the UK and this is unfortunate, not least because, as Elliott, Huizinga and Morse (1986) have shown, 84% of the serious violent offenders interviewed in the US National Youth Survey had no arrest record. Only an effective neighbourhood-based youth programme can make and sustain contact, and exert some influence over, such young people. There are young people who are currently in touch with nobody who can help them to contain their behaviour, and no one who can help them find alternative sources of status and self-esteem, and alternative routes to adulthood.

References

Becker, H. (1963). *Outsiders.* New York: Free Press.

Bowlby, J. (1946). *Forty Four Juvenile Thieves.* London: Balliere, Tindall and Cox.

Elliott, D., Huizinga, D., and Morse, B. (1986). Self-reported Violent Offending: A Descriptive Analysis of Juvenile Violent Offenders and their Offending Careers. In *Journal of Interpersonal Violence*, 1: pp. 472–514.

Factor, F., and Pitts, J. (forthcoming). *From Emancipation to Correctionalism? UK Youth Work and the Politics of the Third Way.* Paper presented to the Russo-Finnish Youth Strategy in the Baltic Region Conference, The Karelia Institute, Karelia, Russian Federation.

France, A., and Wiles, P. (1996). *The National Evaluation of Youth Action.* London: DEE.

Garland, D. (19885). *Punishment and Welfare.* London: Gower

Gazeau, J-F., Peyre, V., Mehlbye J., and Walgrave L. (Eds.) (1998). *Confronting Youth in Europe: Juvenile Crime and Juvenile Justice.* Denmark: AKF Forlaget.

Inner London Youth Justice Services (1995). *Statement of Principles and Practice Standards.* London: NACRO.

Klein, M. (1923). *Infant Analysis, Contributions to Psychoanalysis.* London: Hogarth.

Lea, J. (1998). *The Return of the Dangerous Classes: Crime Control in the 21st Century.* Inaugural professorial lecture, 10th December.

Martinson. R. (1974). What Works?: Questions and Answers About Prison Reform. In *The Public Interest*, Spring: pp. 22–54.

Matza, D. (1964). *Delinquency and Drift.* New York, Wiley.

Perfect, M., and Renshaw, J. (1996). *Misspent Youth: Young People and Crime.* London: Audit Commission.

Pitts, J. (1988). *The Politics of Juvenile Crime.* London: Sage Publishing.

Pitts, J. (1999). *Working With Young Offenders.* Basingstoke: Macmillan.

Schlossman, S., Zellman, G., and Shavelson, R., with Sedlak, M., and Cobb, J. (1984). *Delinquency Prevention in South Chicago: A Fifty Year Assessment of the Chicago Area Projects.* Santa Monica, CA: RAND.

Skynner, R. (1971). The Minimum Sufficient Network. In *Social Work Today*, August.

Smith, C., Farrant, M., and Marchant, H. (1972). *The Wincroft Youth Project.* London: Tavistock.

Titmus, R. (1968). *Commitment to Welfare.* London: Allen & Unwin.

Walden-Jones, B. (1993). *Crime and Citizenship: Preventing Youth Crime in France Through Social Integration.* London: NACRO.

Wilson, J.Q. (1975). *Thinking about Crime.* New York: Basic Books.

Further Reading

Mitchell, J., and Gelloz, N. (1997). Supporting Families and Strengthening Communities: The Role of the 'Specialised Prevention' Movement in France. In *Social Work in Europe*, Vol. 4: No. 3.

Pitts, J. (2001). *The New Youth Justice: Discipline or Solidarity.* Basingstoke: Macmillan.

25

Young People out of School
Pam Rogers

Key Points

1. The target group is vital in that it starts to define the curriculum and the likely initial relationship with the young people. What will be the age group? Will you have a statutory role with these young people?

2. It is important that workers are up-to-date in their knowledge of child protection recognition and procedures. Many of these young people are damaged through abuse.

3. Workers should know about the roles and responsibilities of other key agencies working with these young people. Many of these agencies are listed earlier in the chapter.

4. It is important that workers have support and supervision on a regular basis in order to enable them to work effectively, particularly if the nature of working, possibly in a more structured environment, is new to them.

5. Young people are often with youth workers for a short time. Knowledge about routes for moving on for young people will help workers to ensure that appropriate support is in place when that time comes.

Introduction

The youth and community service has had an input into working with young people out of school over many years. However this response had been ad-hoc and with no legislative base to inform the nature of the practice. It has varied from contact through generic youth clubs and projects and within the support network available to all young people who attend. In addition, there have been numerous projects geared at non or poor attenders, delivered in partnership with schools or jointly with the education welfare or careers service.

'Disaffection from school' is frequently used as an umbrella term within the education system although its manifestations are extremely varied (Parsons, 1999). It may therefore include; school refusers and truants, school phobics, and those who whilst attending school, are disengaged from the learning process and display either disruptive or withdrawn behaviour patterns. Statistical evidence for the numbers of pupils who may be categorised as such are not easy to gather.

The scale of truancy compared with that of exclusion constitutes a much more significant problem. DfEE research into truancy in England identified that in Years 10 and 11, 8.2 per cent of all pupils were frequent truants (at least once a week), rising to 9.9 per cent in Year 11 (O'Keefe, 1994). Again, the reasons for truanting are numerous, with 67 per cent of truants citing their reason being to avoid a particular lesson either because it was of no relevance to them, or because they did not like the teacher, or the subject. These facts continue to contribute to debates on the relevance of the national curriculum for all pupils (O'Keefe and Stoll, 1995).

There are as many reasons for being out of school as there are young people out of school. This range includes, but this is by no means exhaustive:

- young carers
- unaccompanied asylum-seekers
- those with unidentified special educational needs
- those moving into care placements
- offenders
- those who have been excluded or bullied
- those moving from another part of the country, or another country
- those with behavioural problems due to a wide range of emotional difficulties
- those with mental health problems

- those who have 'outgrown' the school environment and who want to be at work or college in an adult environment

The phenomenon of school exclusion is not new. Pupils have always been suspended or expelled from school. More recent interest has been generated by the increase in numbers of school exclusions during the late 1980s and 1990s. This trend ran concurrently with greater awareness of and concern about the disruptive and aggressive behaviour of some pupils becoming a more regular feature of the classroom, and the new arrangements under Local Management of Schools (LMS), coupled with the introduction of school league tables.

New laws, definitions and categories were introduced, and the Education Act 1993 (DfEE, 1993b), provided for two types of exclusion; fixed term (15 days in one term) and permanent exclusion. Research in this area has recently begun to distinguish between the different categories of exclusion, and undeniably there has been a marked increase in permanent exclusions at both primary and secondary levels. This trend demonstrated a year-on-year increase between 1993 and 1996/7, but with a decrease continuing into 1997/1998. 1995/6 recorded the number of permanent exclusions to be 13,581 whereas 1993 data shows the figure to be 8,636 (DfEE, 1993a). Whilst primary school exclusions constituted only 13.9 per cent of exclusions in 1997/8, the trend was demonstrating an increase whilst secondary level exclusions were slowing (Parsons, 1999).

Who Gets Excluded?

Certain pupils are particularly vulnerable to exclusion, and young men are four times more likely to be excluded than their female counterparts. Children from minority ethnic groups, particularly African-Caribbean males continue to feature disproportionately in the statistics, being over five times more likely to be excluded than white pupils (Parsons, 1999). Explanations for this discriminatory practice are difficult to ascertain; however, there are clear messages for the training of teachers with regard to the perceptions of what could be described as culturally-specific behaviour patterns.

Pupils with special educational needs are another group at risk of exclusion. This is particularly apparent in the area of emotional and behavioural difficulties. The lengthy statementing process, as well as reduced access to resources following the opting out from local authority control for some schools under LMS could indicate possible reasons here. However, such a trend would therefore require re-visiting the whole debate about integration of those pupils with different needs into the mainstream (Brodie and Berridge, 1996).

Young people who are 'looked after' by the local authority social services teams also feature prominently in the statistics. Not surprisingly, poverty, disadvantage, abuse and family breakdown are common characteristics of young people who have been excluded. For those young people in care, stigmatisation within the system, as well as disruption by constantly changing placements together with residential and foster environments not being conducive to educational achievement, perpetuate further disadvantage and potential exclusion from school (Brodie and Berridge, 1996).

Whether temporary or permanent, the peak is during Year 10. The likelihood of returning to mainstream education is far greater for the primary level than secondary pupils. In 1984, the proportion of secondary level pupils reintegrating into the system is recorded at 14.8 per cent compared with 27 per cent of primary pupils (DfEE, 1993).

The term 'exclusion' commonly implies poor or unmanageable behaviour; little attention however is given to groups vulnerable to exclusion, pregnant students and Travellers being identified additionally (Booth, 1996). Young carers may also be included here (see Paul Adams and David Land's Chapter 29). Minimal if any legal control exists over the grounds for exclusion used by schools.

The trend still seems to be that more young men than young women are excluded, but that amongst non-attenders there are more young women. The national concerns about the high numbers of exclusions amongst young men of African-Caribbean origin, have been partly addressed at a local level through the establishment in Hertfordshire of a mentoring scheme for pupils and their families where there is risk of exclusion.

Parsons subdivides these possible characteristics into three groups:

- socio-economic and cultural
- institutional factors
- individual factors

He further identifies 27 factors promoting or inhibiting exclusion.

The link between truancy and exclusion and for example, offending is unquestioned. In their study, *Young People and Crime Research Study*, Graham and Bowling (1995) claim that 75 per cent of those permanently excluded are engaged in offending.

Legislative Framework and Governmental Responses

Within the law, children's rights to education are poorly protected (Parsons, 1999). The Education Act 1996 has re-enacted Section 298 of the 1993 Act:

> *Each local authority shall make arrangements for the provision of suitable full-time or part-time education at school or otherwise for those children of compulsory age who, by reason of illness, exclusion from school or otherwise, may not for any period receive suitable education unless arrangements are made for them.*
>
> (Education Act 1993)

This provision has been subject to intense scrutiny in the courts. Definitions of terms, and interpretations in law have done nothing to further protect the rights of children in this area. The lack of congruence with the Children Act 1989 in terms of the protection of the child's welfare is all too obvious.

The outcome has been that inconsistent and piecemeal responses and provision are the norm for those young people who have failed in their appeal against exclusion. The amount of time taken to establish alternative educational opportunities are also a cause for concern, and have far reaching implications for the family and community within which the young person is located (Factor and Pitts, forthcoming).

Transitions into adulthood are increasingly complex and elongated (Macdonald, 1998), and young people now find themselves experiencing multiple disadvantage. The Labour Government's Social Exclusion Unit established in 1998 is attempting a 'joined up' response to young people's needs and a plethora of new policy initiatives has been introduced. Particular developments in the areas of post-16 education and training (DfEE, 1999c), include *Bridging the Gap* (SEU, 1999), *New Start* and the *Learning Gateway* as established within the Learning and Lifeskills Bill 1999 (DfEE, 1999b), and the development of a new Youth Support Service, now known as *ConneXions Service*. An acknowledgement of the broader picture of disadvantage becomes evident as the focus shifts:

> *...On those who are disadvantaged, have low aspirations, are at risk of dropping out, failing to achieve, or not making a successful transition to further education, training or employment.*
>
> (DfEE, 1998b)

Additionally, Stephen Byers, Schools Standards Minister announced the establishment of a Ministerial Taskforce in May 1998:

> *The Social Exclusion Unit has taken just four months to produce its first report which contains twenty nine recommendations and a clear practical and dynamic agenda for action. By reducing the levels of truancy and school exclusions we will effectively cut off one of the main supply routes to welfare dependency, joblessness and criminal behaviour.*
>
> (DfEE, 1998a)

Contained within his announcement is the intention by 2002 to reduce by one third the number of exclusions and the time lost to truancy. Other measures include; new mechanisms to record the statistics, publication of exclusion league tables, broken down by ethnic group, new grounds for appeal against exclusion, and targeted funds for preventative work with young people 'at risk' of exclusion, amongst other measures.

These initiatives for post-16 young people have acknowledged that many young people have not had a consistent educational experience and the proposal for the new *ConneXions Service* identifies support for pupils from 13 years onwards to enable them to take advantage of the new opportunities. Integral to the effective delivery of *ConneXions* is the role of the 'Personal Advisor'. The *ConneXions Strategy Document* states that:

> *The youth services, both statutory and voluntary, already perform a range of valuable support functions for young people, and often undertake excellent outreach and personal advisor work.*
>
> (DfEE, 2000)

The DfEE document *Social Inclusion: Pupil Support* (1999d) suggests a wide range of strategies for reducing the risk of disaffection from school, explicitly encouraging multi-agency partnerships and identifies that:

The Youth Service works with young people who are disaffected or who have dropped out of school or who have other behavioural problems.

Education Action Zones have been established often incorporating numerous homework clubs and summer universities, in an attempt to raise the educational achievements of young people in line with national targets. Alternative projects to identify those pupils at risk from either exclusion or refusing to attend are now widespread, and not operating solely within the Pupil Referral Units (PRUs), their traditional location.

Often such projects engage a wide variety of professional groups aiming to adopt a preventative and holistic approach to the needs of young people, acknowledging that the school alone cannot support all aspects of a young person's life. Whilst the Children Act 1989 placed a statutory duty on LEAs and health authorities to provide services for children defined as being 'in need', the Audit Commission noted in 1994, that although parents, health authorities, education and social services shared a common concern for the well-being of children, very few local authorities had effective inter-agency arrangements in place (Audit Commission, 1994):

> *Prevention, almost by definition, is a multi-agency affair. Unless children's or families' needs are addressed as a whole a preventative strategy can be sabotaged by one area of deficiency.*   (Hodgkin and Newell, 1996)

Planning and Delivery Considerations

In 1998 a Youth Programmes Unit, staffed by youth workers, of whom I am one, was established to address the needs of children out of school in Hertfordshire. It works with Key Stage 4 pupils (Years 10 and 11) who are not able to complete their education in school through non-attendance, exclusion or through coming into the system with no school place. All efforts are made to find a suitable school place for these young people before they are referred to the Unit. The Youth Programmes Unit buys-in formal education from Education Support Centres (Pupil Referral Units), colleges, training providers and individual tutors as appropriate to the young people. It also arranges work experience, both short and long-term. The

youth workers provide a programme of personal and social development through group-work and individual support.

Each young person has a nominated youth worker who offers individual support on a regular basis and who carries on through the transition to work or further education for a year after the ending of compulsory education should the young person choose. The Unit is developing good relationships with a wide range of agencies, the education welfare service, social services, the careers service, formal education providers, youth offending teams, educational psychologists and admissions departments, in order to facilitate the support offered to young people, this being essential to meet the wide range of needs identified.

Delivery is informed by both the needs of the young people and other stakeholders. Many participants have missed large parts of their schooling and this, combined with their varied abilities in different areas, means that there may be gaps in their education. It is also quite likely that special educational needs may not have been recognised. An example of this is a young man who would suddenly become disruptive and storm out of group-work sessions. After a short period of time it became clear that this happened every time he was expected to do any reading or writing. Delivery was then adapted to ensure that reading and writing were kept to a minimum and any handouts were read out loud by a worker. The disruptions then become minimal. At the same time extra help was offered with reading and writing outside of the group sessions. Had there been better access at the time, and longer with the young person, tests would have been arranged for dyslexia.

Another major consideration is the nature of the group, given that in a group whose members are excluded pupils, they are likely to be predominantly male with perhaps only one female in the group. If working exclusively with excluded pupils there is little that can be done in defining the make-up of the group in terms of gender or ethnicity. It is therefore important to have a range of experiences, which will appeal to all of the young people. For most of the time, this does not present a major problem as long as it is kept in mind when planning. Where it has become an issue, as far as young women are concerned, is in the area of outdoor education and physical activity where they are 'body conscious' and do not wish to undertake the activity in the presence of young men, or just don't like physical activity. Where possible it is helpful to ensure female individual support workers and group facilitators to provide relevant support. In terms of ethnicity it is important to have a cultural dimension to the programme and again, if possible, have appropriate workers who can support the young people effectively.

Issues for practice depend, to a large extent, on the way in which projects or programmes are targeted and set up. One of the major issues depends on the nature of young peoples' participation in the project: is the participation voluntary or compulsory? If the participation is voluntary in nature and the school retains the responsibility for the education of the young person, the relationship of the youth worker and the young person retains its traditional status. However, particularly in the case of youth workers working with young people who are excluded from school, the young people are sometimes with youth workers as their compulsory education and this changes the nature of the relationship significantly. This can also apply to poor and non-attenders who may be subject to Education Supervision Orders, or whose parents may have the threat of prosecution by the education welfare service to consider. Young people who are in this situation may attend youth work provision as a voluntary part of their education, but only as an alternative to school: the education is still compulsory.

Youth workers working with young people in this situation may have to report non-attendance and therefore are seen as part of the authority structure. This change in the dynamics of the relationship has an effect on delivery. Young people are often resistant to building relationships with 'authority' figures and this is a barrier to overcome. One of the challenges in building the relationship is to arrive at a stage where young people are coming because they want to, not because they have to. This is particularly important in the individual support relationship and the confidentiality available within this.

When planning work it is important to recognise that it can be very intensive: spending up to five days a week with a group for a year or more is very different from spending one night a week in a traditional youth work setting, but at the same time it is very rewarding, tangible results soon becoming apparent.

The other effect that being a part of the compulsory educational system has, is in terms of the curriculum offered. The overt curriculum may need to take account of the PHSE (Personal, Health and Social Education) curriculum for pupils in school. *Curriculum 2000, The Revised National Curriculum Guidelines* (DfEE, 1999a) has laid down certain topics, which must be included for young people in Key Stage 4 e.g. drug education, sexual health, and citizenship. Youth workers need to be aware of this when developing the curriculum for young people if they are the PHSE providers, particularly if they are to be part of the OFSTED inspection process. Other factors which may need to be built in are the key skills—communication, use of numbers, Information and Communication Technology (ICT), working with others, problem solving, improving own learning and performance. None of this is new to youth workers. What may be new is that the planning needs to be more explicit in terms of the learning outcomes to be achieved and relaying this to the young people so that they can recognise their learning.

In Hertfordshire it has been extremely useful to have outdoor education specialist youth workers in each team to provide a range of new and challenging activities for the young people. It is recognised that not all young people are willing to participate in these kinds of activities and alternatives such as arts also need to be available. Still and video cameras have been taken to outdoor education sessions for use by those who are unable or unwilling to participate. This way they still remain part of the group and are able to record valuable evidence for those undertaking the activity.

The less overt curriculum derives from the reasons why many young people are with the youth worker: behaviour and motivation. As I have said before, there are many reasons for young people being out of school. These are often tied up with personal and social development and these issues need to be incorporated into the topic-based curriculum.

Young people sign an agreement about behaviour, which includes respect for others as an integral element; they are aware that they will be challenged on attitudes, which are seen to be discriminatory. All are aware that they are on the programme because their circumstances are such that there are difficulties in their lives and others are in the same position, although not necessarily with the same difficulties. The aim of the programme is to help them to be successful in moving on to adult life. In practice this means planning opportunities for confidence building, developing self-esteem, learning to work with others and build relationships, anger management alongside other personal development issues.

Work with individuals is an important way of backing up what happens in the group. The youth worker can pick up on issues raised or observed in the group situation or can explore personal issues which are affecting the young person. They can also explore personal aspirations and develop education plans that will help the young person to reach their goals, whether these are in terms of behaviour, attitude or learning or moving on.

The other important aspect for young people in developing the curriculum is that of accreditation. There are several routes developed and in development. Some examples include The Duke of Edinburgh Award Scheme and the Award Scheme Development and Accreditation Network (ASDAN) Youth Awards, which follow a modular set of challenges for young people. Workers can write Assessment and Qualifications Alliance (AQA), formerly NEAB, Units on specific topics and at different levels for young people. The National Youth Agency is currently developing the Youth Achievement Award. There are many other routes available. For young people out of school, accreditation is particularly important in affirming their achievements.

Evaluation

Evaluation takes place in a number of ways. A group of workers is currently developing a matrix by which to measure personal and social development. It has taken account of matrices developed in other parts of the country and through the work carried out by the GEST funded Youth Action Schemes. It is at an early stage and will be tested over the next year. It covers the areas of motivation, self-awareness, relationships and communication. Personal and social development measurement has always been a challenge for youth workers and needs to be carried out with the individual involved. It is valueless unless the

young person is able to recognise their development.

With regard to the overt curriculum, by setting the knowledge, skills and concepts that workers wish young people to learn at the planning stages it is possible to measure whether these have been achieved, through 'testing' at the end of the sessions or modules or by building a portfolio. This also helps in planning the content of the delivery and evaluating whether aims have been achieved. This then can be formally accredited.

Recordings are vital in helping workers to recognise the developments young people have made and to plan for further development. They also act as a means of developing the programme— what has worked, and what hasn't. Evaluation by young people on a regular basis also helps in this process and can be carried out in a wide variety of ways.

Attendance is another tool of measurement. If young people do not feel they are gaining anything from a programme they will vote with their feet, although this measurement also needs to take account of the circumstances of young people. Young carers in particular are likely to have other priorities and need support in order to feel able to attend.

Resources and Funding

Given that many of the young people who are out of school have major difficulties in their lives, the best ways of working with them appears to be through small group and individual work. This is extremely resource intensive: needing two and sometimes three workers with each group, depending on their composition and needs. In addition much accredited work needs access to ICT equipment, which also develops skills and is an area in which youth work has received criticism for its lack of attention. If outdoor education is to be included this has resource implications. Transport for these young people can also be a major expense, since many of them have difficulty in accessing provision. It is therefore important that these costs are taken into account when planning such provision.

Funding for young people's compulsory education is usually devolved to schools. Schools do not often put money aside to pay for alternative provision for young people who do not engage

Key Questions

1. What is your legal status and responsibility in terms of delivering the programme as part of a young person's compulsory education: e.g. do you need to keep an official attendance register (which is a legal document)?

2. What is to be the referral process: are you working with an individual school? Are referrals to come from schools, or the education welfare service or the admissions service (if a child has no school place), or from social services? This needs to be clear from the outset, otherwise you may be swamped with enquiries and having to make judgements on an ad-hoc basis.

3. What are your criteria for working with young people? This will come partly from the target group but there is a need to be aware that even within this there will be young people for whom the provision might not be suitable.

4. Are your policies and guidelines for workers in this situation clear, appropriate and sufficient? Are the ones in place for generic youth work still applicable to this work or is there a need to write new ones?—e.g. are policies regarding confidentiality rigorous enough and are they congruent with those of other agencies with whom you may be working closely?

5. What are the alternatives for those who will not engage with your project/programme, particularly if they are no longer on the roll of a school?

with them and because the money is tied up in teacher salaries, buildings and resources which benefit the whole school community, it is not easily accessible. However, some schools are now recognising this need and are able to make some funding available to other services. Having said that schools also rely on economies of scale and even if they are able to release a young person's AWPU (Age Weighted Pupil Unit) it does not go far when working intensively with young people.

Other agencies, particularly the careers services, are able to work in partnership, both in terms of staffing and delivery and ICT resources (videos etc.). The same applies to voluntary agencies, such as drugs agencies and the Red Cross. Locally there will be a wide range of people who are able to support the programme.

Conclusion

The main principles of education, equality, empowerment and participation are all enshrined in work with young people who are out of school. The main focus of the work is the education of young people and the principal curriculum design is that of personal and social development.

Young people who are out of school are missing out on one of their basic rights; that of education. Working with these young people helps to redress

the balance, to re-engage them with learning, to enable them to access an education. The topics covered not only address a curriculum set out by the education system, but also those identified as being needed by the young people themselves. Part of the curriculum is helping them to make choices, including some of the issues and activities to be covered on the programme.

Experience, to date, is limited but we feel that we are beginning to have some success, particularly in the personal and social development of young people. Many of them have achieved GCSE and other accreditation, moving on to college, training or employment.

We are gradually developing a more systematic approach to measuring young peoples' progression and feel that this will be important in demonstrating our effectiveness. It is too early to draw conclusions about our achievements to date but feel that we are on the right track; feedback received from parents, young people and other professionals seems to suggest just that.

References

Audit Commission (1994). *Seen But Not Heard: Co-ordinating Child Health and Social Services for Children in Need.* London: HMSO.

Blythe, E., and Milner, J. (Eds.). *Exclusion from School.* London: Routledge.

Booth, T. (1996). A Perspective on Inclusion from England. In *Cambridge Journal of Education*, 26(1): pp. 67–99.

Booth, T., and Ainscow, A. (1998). *From Them to Us: An International Study of Inclusion in Education*. London: Routledge.

Brodie, I., and Berridge, D. (1996). *School Exclusion: Research Themes and Issues*. Luton: University of Luton Press.

DfEE (1993a). *National Exclusions Reporting System*. Press release. London: DfEE.

DfEE (1993b). *The Education Act*. London: HMSO.

DfEE (1998a). *Byers to Head Ministerial Taskforce on Truancy and Social Exclusion*. Press release. London: DfEE.

DfEE (1998b). *Morris Reveals Ambitious New Plan to cut Truancy and Exclusion from School*. Press release. DfEE.

DfEE (1999a). *Curriculum 2000, Revised National Curriculum Guidelines*. London: DfEE.

DfEE (1999b). *Learning and Lifeskills Bill*. London: DfEE.

DfEE (1999c). *Learning to Succeed: A New Framework for Post 16 Learning*. London: DfEE/DTI.

DfEE (1999d). *Social Inclusion: Pupil Support*. Circular 10/99. London: HMSO.

DfEE (2000). *ConneXions: The best start in life for every young person*. London: DfEE.

Factor, F., and Pitts, J. (forthcoming). *From Emancipation to Correctionalism? UK Youth Work and the Politics of the Third Way*. Paper presented to the Russo-Finnish Youth Strategy in the Baltic Region Conference, Karelia.

Graham, J., and Bowling, B. (1995). *Young People and Crime Research Study 145*. London: Home Office.

Hodgkin, R., and Newell, P. (1996). *Effective Government Structures for Children*. London: Calouste Gulbenkian Foundation.

Macdonald, R. (Ed.) (1998). *Youth, 'the Underclass' and Social Exclusion*. London: Routledge.

O'Keefe, D. (1994). *Truancy in English Secondary Schools*. London: DfEE/HMSO.

O'Keefe, D., and Stoll, P. (1995). Understanding the Problem: Truancy and Curriculum. In O'Keefe, D., and Stoll, P. (Eds.). *Issues in School Attendance and Truancy*. London: Pitman.

Parsons, C. (1999). *Education Exclusion and Citizenship*. London: Routledge.

Social Exclusion Unit (1998). *Truancy and School Exclusion*. London: Stationery Office.

Social Exclusion Unit (1999). *Bridging the Gap: New Opportunities for 16–18 Year Olds not in Education, Training or Employment*.

Useful addresses

ASDAN Central Office, 27 Redland Hill, Bristol BS6 6UX; Tel: 0117 923 9843

Assessment and Qualifications Alliance, Devon Street, Manchester M15 6EX

Further Reading

Clasen, J. (1997). *Long Term Unemployment and the Threat of Social Exclusion*. Bristol: Policy Press.

Corbett, J. (1990). *Uneasy Transitions: Disaffection in Post-compulsory Education and Training*. Basingstoke: Falmer Press.

Hyams-Parish, A. (1996). *Banished to the Exclusion Zone: School Exclusion and Law from the Viewpoint of the Child*. Colchester: Children's Legal Centre.

Kinder, K. (1996). *Talking Back: Pupil Views on Disaffection*. Slough: National Foundation for Educational Research.

Kinder, K. (1997). *Exclusion Who Needs It?* Slough: National Foundation for Educational Research.

Kinder, K. (1998). *Disaffection Talks: A Report for the Merseyside Learning Partnership Interagency Development Programme*. Slough: National Foundation for Educational Research.

Wheal, A. (1998). *Adolescence: Positive Approaches for Working with Young People*. Lyme Regis: Russell House.

26

Unemployed Young People

Howard Williamson

Key Points

1. Unemployed young people are a diverse group: with very different backgrounds and experiences, current lifestyles and circumstances, and motivations and aspirations.

2. Whatever our own personal and political 'agenda', we have a *duty to explain* the contemporary framework of possibility and opportunity (Williamson, 1983b).

3. It is imperative that, through individual and group work, a clear understanding is established of the social context, current circumstances, attitudes and behaviours of the young people concerned. Only then is it possible to build a vocational pathway, which corresponds with their needs.

4. Formal qualifications, academic and vocational, are the best passport to economic independence. Alternative qualifications are not a substitute. To disparage mainstream, formal, learning routes, even if they are less than ideal, is, ultimately, to collude with social exclusion.

5. The labour market is not renowned for its adherence to principles of equality, empowerment and participation. We may have to temper our ideals, and the principles upon which we base *our* work, with acknowledgement of the realities with which unemployed young people are going to be confronted.

Introduction

Unemployed young people have recurrently vacillated in the popular imagination between the folk devils at the vanguard of youthful resistance and rebellion and the unfortunate victims of the changing world. Punitive and sympathetic perspectives are often carried paradoxically and simultaneously in media and political stances towards the young unemployed. As I write, the New Deal for 18–24 year olds, the flagship programme in the government's welfare-to-work agenda which was heralded as a supportive initiative designed to meet the individual needs and aspirations of long-term unemployed young people, is about to invoke a 'three strikes and you're out' regulation (implemented in April 2000), whereby those who refuse a third reasonable opportunity within New Deal are at risk of having their entitlement to welfare benefits suspended for six months: the most punitive sanctions regime ever.

Not that any of this is especially new. Responses to youth unemployment throughout the twentieth century have routinely sought to magically encapsulate rhetorically person-centred philosophies (around personal and skills development), warehousing practices which in effect hold young people in limbo and conveniently massage the unemployment statistics, and controlling and scapegoating devices to demonstrate to young people that such a pathway to adulthood is best avoided and to others that the state will not tolerate profligate and 'idle' youth. Of course, programmes for the young unemployed are invariably proclaimed to be a quality and meaningful opportunity, which ironically serve to justify measures which establish *de facto* compulsion to participate. The counter view is that authentically good quality opportunities will be attractive to young people without the need for compulsion.

Historical Background

In juvenile justice, the distinction has long been made between the 'sad' and the 'bad', the 'deprived' and 'depraved'. Mary Carpenter and her contemporaries in the mid-nineteenth century saw the importance of ensuring that policy responses distinguished between the two: hence the Industrial Schools for the 'sad' and Reformatories for the 'bad' (Manton, 1979). Such distinctions have been less pronounced in policy responses towards the young unemployed, but they have clearly not been absent. The agenda of successive programmes has been about both *instruction* and *reform*. It has been concerned with developing vocational skills but it has also been preoccupied with engendering appropriate attitudes.

This applied as much to the Youth Opportunities Programme of the 1970s (Rees and Atkinson, 1982; Bates et al., 1984) as to the Juvenile Unemployment Centres, Junior Instruction Centres or 'dole schools' of the 1930s (Rees and Rees, 1982; Horne, 1983). Jeffs and Spence (2000) have argued that 'sympathy and understanding for the plight of the workless is time-limited, particularly in relation to young men who are often the most visible and threatening group amongst the unemployed'. They allege that there is a common *sequential* pattern to responses to youth unemployment:

> If the problem lingers, blaming the victim becomes a common-sense and attractive option for those unwilling to contemplate structural economic changes to promote full-employment. Blaming the unemployed for the conditions generated by unemployment has a pedigree which dates back directly to the Poor Laws and continues to inform policy today.
>
> (Jeffs and Spence, 2000)

My view is that the two positions run in parallel, albeit with a hardening of more punitive approaches as 'softer', more liberal ideologies fail to produce results sufficiently quickly and as a hard core of 'refusniks' are exposed as unwilling to participate voluntarily in such programmes. Many programmes expressly seek to deliver a practice which, *prima facie* at least, appears to resonate with the principles and purposes enshrined in youth and community work, although they may well turn out to be a corrupt version of this (Davies, 1979), and there is invariably a more containing and controlling side to the equation, captured in the observation of a YOP supervisor I once interviewed, who, when asked about the purpose of the programme said: 'let's face it, mate, life's a rat race, so you've got to learn 'em to be rats' (Williamson, 1982).

The essential point is that the young unemployed are not an homogenous group. Nor do the objectives of public policy interventions rest on a single track. The contemporary aspiration of New Deal, for example, is not just to equip unemployed young people with the 'skills for employability' but also to promote social inclusion. In launching the New Deal, the Chancellor of the Exchequer proclaimed, 'The age of exclusion is over and the era of economic prosperity has begun'. These, and other objectives, are directed towards a population of the young unemployed who have been crudely differentiated between those who are 'essentially confused, temporarily side-tracked, and deeply alienated' (Williamson and Middlemiss, 1999). I have argued recently that caution must be exercised in the application of the new draconian New Deal sanctions, particularly in distinguishing between the 'slow to motivate' and the 'spirited resisters' (Williamson, forthcoming). From a distance, it is easy to conflate and confuse the two, for both will appear to be dragging their heels in their willingness to participate. But in fact one group is displaying caution about the programme, while the other is trying to side-step it: both, almost certainly for quite rational reasons from their points of view.

A Way Forward

This example is symptomatic of what is, too often, the nature of the problem in responding to the needs and aspirations of the young unemployed: there is a failure to give sufficient time to establishing the bases of motivation and aspiration of *individual young people*, and tailoring responses accordingly. Institutional imperatives, governed by political and funding targets, drive a practice which is firmly detached from the kind of individualised, person-centred approach which informs the practice of youth and community work. As a result, youth and community work encounters difficulties in working alongside other agencies charged with, or seeking to respond to the 'needs' of the young unemployed. The inclination is to back off and to criticise from the sidelines. This does little for the credibility of youth work and does even less for the young people such programmes are intended to support. The challenge is to endeavour to establish person-centred practice, directly or indirectly, in the interventions directed at young people. It is *not* about colluding with undesirable practice. And it is certainly not about using young people as pawns in a wider ideological game (Williamson, 1987). Youth work and youth workers can engage at different levels of policy and practice, with the aspiration of creating a better—if not ideal—climate of opportunity for young people (especially those at the margins) and enabling those young people to make the best of the opportunities available to them. That is what *this* chapter is about.

Delivery and Evaluation

In practice, youth and community work has much to contribute to both the design, implementation and evaluation of programmes to advise and support the young unemployed. But the case has to be made. Flexible, organic and individualised approaches do not fit comfortably with large-scale, bureaucratic initiatives which usually end up with blinkered, straitjacketed methods of assessment and intervention, and measures of 'performance' which may well be 'reliable' but which are often of questionable validity. Bernard Davies (1986) warned us long ago that public policy had to win the consent of young people; it would not succeed if it sought to coerce their compliance.

The starting point must therefore be a serious and focused dialogue with the individuals concerned. Before it is possible to establish an appropriate 'action plan', one must be appraised of potential barriers to participation as well as the parameters of aspiration. Many programmes in the past failed to discover very much at all about individual circumstances and hopes: the simple fact of being unemployed within a certain age band governed the nature of the response. Other measures engaged in, usually cursory, 'assessments'—often by means of rather technical pro formas—which usually concealed more than they revealed and led to arbitrary and often inappropriate support and placement. As I argued vis-à-vis the Youth Opportunities Programme, there is not only a serious *objective* assessment to be done but there needs to be sensitivity to the *subjective* meanings and expectations attached to prospective interventions by the individuals concerned (Williamson, 1981). Various 'hidden' criteria may inform a young person's motivation to participate and not simply the formal criteria, which frame the nature and quality of provision. These may include factors such as wanting to be with your mates, or remaining close to home, as much as the probability of achieving, say, an NVQ level 2 qualification. It may take *time* for young people to be confident in divulging the full repertoire of issues of concern to them. This has been a problem with the New Deal Gateway, a commendable component in itself but one which has sometimes led to premature decisions. Issues which the Gateway was designed to deal with, such as literacy, or drug dependency problems, have not always surfaced as quickly as the planners of New Deal had, rather naïvely, anticipated.

This takes us back to the need for a calibrated response, according to the 'types' (not stereotypes) of young people who are being dealt with. Many unemployed young people are 'essentially confused'. Life has dealt them a shoddy hand. No one has paid much attention to their needs and circumstances. They will welcome support, guidance and opportunity provided that it squares with their own understanding of themselves. Others are what I have called 'temporarily side-tracked': currently unemployed but dealing with issues of more importance to them right now. This sub-group are not necessarily 'disaffected' from education and training opportunities, but require patience until they are ready to re-engage with them. Alternative support and intervention may be necessary before the central objectives of youth training and employment programmes are likely to be achieved. A third sub-group are those who might be considered to be 'deeply alienated'. Such young people are profoundly cynical about government programmes. Some are profoundly cynical about their futures in the round, and are inclined to 'live for today'; others have carved out alternative 'ways of living' which would be impeded by participation in planned provision. To leave them to it, or to impose sanctions too early when their strategies of resistance surface, is to collude with or reinforce their social exclusion. Theirs is not a romantic existence, though it has been wrongly celebrated as such by some sociologists and cultural commentators in the past. Previously, when labour markets were more buoyant and mainstream destinations more predictable, 'benign neglect' might have been the order of the day; today, it is tantamount to 'malign indifference' (Drakeford and Williamson, 1998). The evidence of the Social Exclusion Unit's Policy Action Team on Young People demonstrates how critical is retention (or re-integration) in formal learning, i.e. education and training, if the risks of exclusion are to be minimised and better prospects for adult futures are to be secured (Social Exclusion Unit, 2000). So there is clearly an imperative for youth and community work to acknowledge its responsibility to contribute to assisting and supporting unemployed young people in considering or re-considering engagement with the mainstream. What we know, but others have a tendency to overlook, is that attention to personal and social development is likely to be a fundamental pre-requisite before any vocational pathway can successfully be embarked upon.

The design of programmes therefore needs to acknowledge the importance of the capacity to respond positively to a range of more personal needs. Not only does this address some of the barriers to participation and progression but also, probably more importantly, an effective response on this front starts to establish trust on the part of young people and thereby secure some credibility for the programme. Without this starting point, unemployed young people will spot the credibility gap between an externally driven agenda and the rhetoric of person-centred provision.

This point is as pertinent to the evaluation of intervention. Programmes designed to address youth unemployment are naturally going to place 'employability' and jobs at the heart of performance measurement. Youth work and related practice has argued forcefully for the need for intermediary measures which are not concerned with jobs *per se* but with movement towards being able to compete effectively in the labour market. These would include attention to the ways in which interventions and opportunities had addressed the contexts, circumstances, attitudes and behaviour of the young people concerned (Adebowale, 1998). It may be tempting to project an academic argument that this is about 'remoralising' the young for exploitation in an unattractive and casualised labour market, but we always need to remind ourselves that the majority of young people wish to have a stake in mainstream social and economic life. 'Small step' progression to this end therefore remains important and the subjective and qualitative effects of programmes in this direction are an important component in evaluative judgements of their impact, even if quantitative outcomes around labour market success, or sustainable employment, remain paramount.

Theoretical Underpinning

Whether or not there needs to be a robust theoretical underpinning in work with the young unemployed, any more than work with young people in general, is debatable. Of greater importance, in my view, is the need to adopt a flexible and incremental approach with sufficient time for reflection and checking back.

By an incremental approach I mean that one cannot start with a focus derived from the status of the individual as 'unemployed' and policy targets preoccupied solely with labour market considerations, such as, job search, vocational qualifications, or employment outcomes. One has to start with the person within their social context. *Individual* and *social* considerations are critical barriers *or* catalysts in relation to labour market destinations, yet too often these are overlooked or ignored.

At an individual level, the core principles of Rogerian person-centred counselling serve well in guiding and framing our interaction and response (Mabey and Sorensen, 1995). *Empathy* is critical, requiring us to try to see the world through the eyes of the unemployed young person, and necessarily suspending our own pre-conceptions and assumptions about the reasons for them being unemployed and what may be 'good' for them. *Unconditional positive regard* is equally critical, for many unemployed young people have been knocked from pillar to post both by their families and the professional infrastructure around them on account of their 'inability' to get a job. And for further reasons, *congruence* is necessary: many unemployed young people rapidly conclude that those intervening in their lives are doing little more than processing them as 'cases' rather than dealing with them as individuals. Once this conclusion is reached, there is little likelihood of establishing the trust, which is essential for supporting positive trajectories towards the labour market.

At a social level (though the boundaries are blurred, for individuals are clearly embedded in their social worlds), the potential of group work (for example, Wright, 1989; Vernelle, 1994; Gibson and Clarke, 1995) needs to be fully acknowledged. Giving unemployed young people the space and opportunity to share their past experiences, current lifestyles and hopes for the future provides those working with them with a much more refined understanding of the wider *context* in which they are making their interventions. This carries major implications for a programme's capacity to deal with counter-pressures on young people, to provide appropriate levels of support, and to consider the *time* needed to address the barriers which may impede young people's prospects of engaging fully with vocational preparation. In many respects, the aspirations of the Gateway element of New Deal covered this territory, but there has clearly been an implementation gap in its operationalisation, largely because of the caseload pressures, bureaucratic requirements and skill levels of the personal advisers.

Only when these bridges are crossed effectively can programmes constructed to 'tackle' youth unemployment stand any real chance of being both credible to young people and realising the outcomes sought by public policy. With such preparatory work, and reflection and checking back with young people that their perspectives have been properly understood, it becomes possible to place young people in appropriate learning and work experience settings and to provide them with commensurate levels of support. Without such preparatory work, the outcome is more likely to be resistance and high-levels of drop-out, which have characterised youth unemployment interventions, and indeed school inclusion initiatives in the past (for example, Humphries, 1981; Horton, 1985; Humphries and Gordon, 1994).

Integrating Principles of Youth and Community Work into the Practice

This is a tough one! The history of youth unemployment programmes is one of inequalities, disempowerment and an absence of participation. The general disadvantages faced by unemployed young people, such as their usually lower educational qualifications, or postcode prejudice, have, too often, been compounded in terms of ethnicity, gender and disability. This has certainly not been intentional, but the *de facto* allocation of young people *within* youth employment programmes has often resulted, for a variety of reasons, in the reinforcement of wider inequalities, rather than their amelioration (Jones et al., 1983; Williamson, 1983a).

Nevertheless, it is imperative to endeavour to embed the key principles of youth and community work, precisely because they are the effective principles of *work with young people*, within strategies and practice in relation to *unemployed* young people. Where they are not adopted, practice is likely to be less than effective. Young people who feel railroaded into programmes are hardly likely to feel motivated to make the most of the learning opportunities presented: thus undermining the wider government agenda of lifelong learning. Similarly, a failure to establish equality of opportunity within

such programmes will lead to disproportionate drop-out by those groups who are discriminated against: thus undermining the wider government agenda around social inclusion. The same applies if principles of empowerment and participation are not taken seriously—which undermine the government's wider agenda around active citizenship. And all four principles are essential building blocks for the development of a capacity for 'life management' by young people, which is deemed to be central in contemporary academic analysis of the changing nature of youth transitions (Helve and Bynner, 1996).

To optimise the potential of interventions with unemployed young people, therefore, programmes need to engage actively with those young people, ensure that provision is constructed on a transparent and level playing field, and seek to provide pathways which are considered to be meaningful and relevant to the young people concerned. Only then will this ensure that young people are motivated to both stay the course and gain the most from that participation. This represents a significant challenge to the design and implementation of programmes and requires flexibility and choice, but it is not a policy impossibility and, indeed, will be essential if those most firmly at the margins are going to be persuaded to re-engage (Bentley and Gurumurthy, 1999).

Resource Implications

There are many funding sources for 'social inclusion' programmes, including those which focus on unemployed young people. These are, of course, constantly changing, but currently they comprise a range of UK government initiatives (New Deal, New Start, Learning Gateway), initiatives supported by the European Commission (Youthstart, and the new European Union 'Youth' programme), and charitable sources (notably the National Lottery Charities Board).

Many initiatives require inter-agency partnership and collaboration which, in and of itself, demands professional sensitivity and reflection, since successful partnerships ultimately rest on a 'precarious equilibrium' of personal, professional and institutional relationships (Williamson and Weatherspoon, 1985). Partnership activity always carries the risk of co-option by more powerful players and subordination to their agendas. Youth and community work practice must stand its ground, while recognising that its objectives, methodologies and practice will not necessarily have a place in those of others around the table. An absence of total complementarity does not infer that there cannot be co-operation, so long as each partner acknowledges the distinct contribution that each has to play at different points in the planning and delivery of intervention. The new *ConneXions* strategy and service for England (DfEE, 2000) will provide a vital test for youth and community work on this front. It will *require* much closer collaboration with other agencies as the new support service for young people is developed. Focused on 13–19 year olds, it is explicitly concerned with maintaining young people in learning and therefore, by implication, pre-empting their becoming unemployed. Now being piloted in a number of areas, it may be years before *ConneXions* becomes fully operational, and there are many questions about it which have still to be answered. Not least, there are concerns about it being 'over-individualised' (apparently taking little account of the peer and community context of young people's lives) and that there is a strong undercurrent around the 'policing of participation' rather than the extension of entitlement to those young people who cannot access support and opportunity from elsewhere. Nonetheless, *Connexions* holds the promise of considerable extra resources for young people and stronger political support, evidenced by the establishment of a Youth Unit within government and a Cabinet Committee on children and young people's services chaired by the Chancellor of the Exchequer. In principle, there is a profound logic to the *Connexions* initiative; in practice, it is likely to generate precisely the same concerns and dilemmas for youth and community work as previous government initiatives directed overtly or covertly at disadvantaged and excluded young people, including the young unemployed.

The critical issue is the extent to which funded programmes seek to, or permit applicants to dovetail the structural objectives of inclusion and employment with the individual needs of unemployed young people. There must be sufficient space, and adequate resourcing, for the personal and social support of young people prior to, and sometimes in parallel with, the learning and vocational pathways which necessarily lie at the heart of youth unemployment initiatives.

Conclusion

Working with unemployed young people in any context (from informal drop-in provision and local projects, to national programmes such as New Deal) presents a complex array of challenges and is likely to be, often simultaneously, rewarding and frustrating. Some young people will be motivated and receptive; others will be sceptical and resistant. Some will be seeking a fairly direct route into vocational activity, which will prepare them better for competing in the labour market; others will convey that a host of personal and social difficulties require resolution being they feel capable of engaging with strictly vocational activity. Some will require short-term support; others may need sustained intervention.

A simple message underpins this complex picture: these are individual young people first, they are 'unemployed' young people second. Their unemployment may be the presenting reason for contact (or targeting), but it remains central and critical to relate to them 'in the round', for they will have developed a range of strategies to 'cope' with

Key Questions

1. With young people, has sufficient time been given to assessing their needs and circumstances, in order to identify a suitably tailored vocational pathway?

2. Are appropriate levels of support going to be available prior to, and if necessary throughout, a young person's engagement with a programme?

3. With partner agencies, are role boundaries, mutual respect and an acceptable level of 'complementarity' properly in place to ensure clarity and consistency of practice?

4. To what extent have both final and intermediate 'outcomes' been considered: has a defensible argument concerning small-step achievement and progression be developed?

5. What mechanisms have been put in place for recording both the quantitative and qualitative impact of intervention?

the experience of unemployment, drawing on their personal resilience and their personal and social networks. These strategies will represent both threats and opportunities for addressing the fact that they are unemployed. Until those factors are carefully unpicked, through dialogue and negotiation with the young people concerned, and any apparent barriers to participation in training and employment overcome, it is unlikely that vocational pathways will be trodden successfully. The converse is, of course, also the case. Where professional intervention takes individual circumstances and aspirations seriously, and thereby builds trust and credibility with the individuals concerned, the prospect of successful engagement with vocational pathways to economic independence and adulthood will be greatly enhanced.

References

Adebowale, V. (1998). *New Deal for Disadvantaged Young People, A Report of the New Deal Task Force.* London: Department for Education and Employment.

Bates, I., Clarke, J., Cohen, P., Finn, D., Moore, R., and Willis, P. (Eds.) (1984). *Schooling for the Dole? Against the New Vocationalism.* London: Macmillan.

Bentley, T., and Gurumurthy, R. (1999). *Destinations Unknown: Engaging with the Problems of Marginalised Youth.* London: DEMOS.

Davies, B. (1979). *In Whose Interest? From Social Education to Social and Life Skills.* Leicester: National Youth Bureau.

Davies, B. (1986). *Threatening Youth: Towards a National Youth Policy.* Milton Keynes: Open University Press.

DfEE (2000). *ConneXions: The Best Start in Life for Every Young Person.* London: DfEE.

Drakeford, M., and Williamson, H. (1998). From Benign Neglect to Malign Indifference? Housing and Young People. In Shaw, I., Lambert, S., and Clapham, D. (Eds.). *Social Care and Housing, Research Highlights in Social Work,* 32. London: Jessica Kingsley.

Gibson, A., and Clarke, G. (1995). *Project-based Group Work Facilitator's Manual: Young People, Youth Workers and Projects.* London: Jessica Kingsley.

Helve, H., and Bynner, J. (1996). *Youth and Life Management: Research Perspectives.* Helsinki: Helsinki University Press.

Horne, J. (1983). Youth Unemployment Programmes: A Historical Account of the Development of 'Dole Colleges'. In Gleeson, D. (Ed.). *Youth Training and the Search for Work.* London: Routledge and Kegan Paul.

Horton, C. (1985). *Nothing Like a Job: A Survey of Unemployed School Leavers (1983-84) Who Could Have Gone on the Youth Training Scheme but Did Not.* London: Youth Aid.

Humphries, S. (1981). *Hooligans or Rebels? An Oral History of Working-class Childhood and Youth 1889-1939.* Oxford: Blackwell.

Humphries, S., and Gordon, P. (1994). *Forbidden Britain.* London: BBC Publications.

Jeffs, T., and Spence, J. (2000). New Deal for Young People: Good Deal or Poor Deal? In *Youth and Policy,* 66: pp. 34-61.

Jones, P., Williamson, H., Payne, J., and Smith, G. (1983). *Out of School: A Case Study of the Role of Government Schemes at a Time of Growing Unemployment.* Special Programmes Occasional Paper No. 4. Sheffield: Manpower Services Commission.

Mabey, J., and Sorensen, B. (1995). *Counselling for Young People.* Buckingham: Open University Press.

Manton, J. (1979). *Mary Carpenter and the Children of the Streets.* London: Heinemann.

Rees, G., and Rees, T. (1982). Juvenile Unemployment and the State between the Wars. In Rees, T., and Atkinson, P. (Eds.). *Youth Unemployment and State Intervention.* London: Routledge and Kegan Paul.

Rees, T., and Atkinson, P. (Eds.) (1982). *Youth Unemployment and State Intervention.* London: Routledge and Kegan Paul.

Social Exclusion Unit (2000). *National Strategy for Neighbourhood Renewal: Report of Policy Action Team 12: Young People.* London: The Stationery Office.

Vernelle, B. (1994). *Understanding and Using Groups.* London: Whiting and Birch.

Williamson, H. (1981). *Chance Would be a Fine Thing.* Leicester: National Youth Bureau.

Williamson, H. (1982). Client Responses to the Youth Opportunities Programme. In Rees T., and Atkinson P. (Eds.). *Youth Unemployment and State Intervention.* London: Routledge and Kegan Paul.

Williamson, H. (1983a). WEEP: Exploitation or Advantage? In Fiddy, R. (Ed.). *In Place of Work: Policy and Provision for the Young Unemployed.* Lewes: Falmer.

Williamson, H. (1983b). A Duty to Explain. In *Youth in Society,* Nov: pp. 22-23.

Williamson, H., and Weatherspoon, K. (1985). *Strategies for Intervention: An Approach to Youth and Community Work in an Area of Social Deprivation.* Cardiff: University College Cardiff, Social Research Unit.

Williamson, H. (1987). Youth Workers, the MSC and the Youth Training Scheme. In Jeffs, T. and Smith, M. (Eds.). *Welfare and Youth Work Practice.* London: Macmillan.

Williamson, H., and Middlemiss, R. (1999). The Emperor's got no Clothes: Cycles of Delusion in Community Interventions With 'Disaffected' Young Men. In *Youth and Policy,* 63: Spring; pp. 13-25.

Williamson, H. (forthcoming). Status Zero: From Research to Policy and Practice. In Parsons, C., and Walvaren, G. (forthcoming). *Combating Social Exclusion Through Education: Laissez Faire, Authoritarianism or Some Third Way?* EERA Network CAYAR and Urban Education.

Wright, H. (1989). *Groupwork: Perspectives and Practice.* Harrow: Scutari.

Further Reading

Williamson, H. (1997). *Youth and Policy: Contexts and Consequences, Young Men, Transition and Social Exclusion.* Aldershot: Ashgate.

27

Working with Young Women with Children

Julie Scurfield and Sue Stevens

Key Points

1. Clarity about the focus of the work is essential. Taking a holistic approach to their needs as young people and not only in their roles as young parents is critical.

2. Spending times talking to other agencies, gaining their support, understanding and trust for the work is crucial. This will ensure that referrals are forthcoming and young women gain support and encouragement to participate in what is being offered. Maintain inter-agency contacts so that the young women's needs can be referred to, e.g. housing, social services, education etc.

3. Areas of funding and researching for the project need to be determined early on, for example human, financial, buildings etc.

4. A crèche facility is fundamental to allowing the development of a social education focus for the group. It also maintains the project's separate identity from parent and toddler groups.

5. Be clear about how and when young women will need to move on from the project. We found it useful to develop a group contract with the young women which incorporated endings and moving on. Consideration should be given and research undertaken to identify appropriate opportunities for young people to move on to.

Introduction

The subject of teenage pregnancy and parenthood is an emotive one. Constant media attention seems to focus solely on the issue being problem-oriented and unacceptable in modern British society. When we established our first project for young women with children in 1993 we did so amidst a furore of media attention on the issue, which promulgated many myths. For example, young women's motives for becoming pregnant were to secure their own accommodation or receive benefits; teenage parenthood equalled lone parenthood; choosing pregnancy was an alternative to education or employment; or even that sex education itself had encouraged their own sexual activity and thus was to blame.

Little, if any, attention is ever paid to the possible reasons why these young women had become pregnant in the first place, or on the support networks available to them as they commenced their journey into parenthood. The underlying message is that the situations reported in the media are the 'norm' for all teenage parents, rather than any attempt to consider the individual nature of each young woman's situation. We feel sure that there could be as many, if not more, positive examples presented where young women have become parents and have been able to cope as well as any mother at any age with their first child.

Clarke and Coleman state:

> Early parenthood stems from a complex social and psychological process with many factors both individual and environmental, contributing to the actual circumstance that leads to conception. (1991)

The young women with whom we worked each had varying and individual reasons for choosing to have their babies. Whilst some had not planned to conceive, others had made that conscious decision and all had made a positive choice to keep their babies. Most of the young women were living in poor and cramped housing conditions, isolated from family and friends, a far cry from being attractive alternatives to living at home. The vast majority were living with their partners and most had a strong desire to pursue their education, albeit given the vast constraints their childcare needs imposed on their ability to do so. Young parents often feel victimised by bad press and society's lack of acceptance of young mothers in particular.

Whilst not wishing to undermine the difficulties early parenthood poses, and the financial constraints experienced by the young women, it is not all as negative as the media would have us believe. Working in a supportive way with this target group is very rewarding, not least because the young women themselves so appreciate non-judgmental space and opportunities to be themselves and explore their own needs.

This chapter will examine current government legislation and initiatives surrounding this issue, and we will share our practice experiences in working with this target group, identifying key factors to consider before embarking upon establishing work with young parents. We feel it important to acknowledge here that all our work to date has been with young women with children and therefore this forms our main reference point. We do also recognise the need to develop initiatives with young fathers, but, this should not be at the expense of the work with young mothers, as it is the young women who in the vast majority of cases, bear all of the childcare responsibility.

Government Initiatives

The report on teenage pregnancy (Social Exclusion Unit, 1999) has far-reaching implications and recommendations for working with this group of young people. The report is shrouded in negative terminology about the issue of teenage pregnancy and parenthood. Tony Blair, the Prime Minister, talks about Britain having the 'worst' record of teenage pregnancy in Europe, about our 'failure' to tackle the 'problem' and about our not being able to ignore this 'shameful record'. It is not therefore surprising that the government has stated its commitment to halve the rate of conceptions among under 18s by the year 2010, and this provides much of the focus of the report.

What is encouraging about the document is its acknowledgement of the support needs of teenage parents and its commitment to get more teenage parents into education, training or employment, thereby reducing their risk of long term social exclusion. There is a recognition that many young parents would like to go back to work and an identification of the significant barriers they face: child care, poor educational achievement due to inability to finish school, benefit dependency, and isolation from peers and supportive adults who can

encourage their personal development. Later on in this chapter, we will record the experience of young women with whom we worked who did manage, with great determination, to put themselves through college courses, but who were unable to proceed to employment due to the prohibitive costs of childcare.

The first project we established was with funding from the government's GEST Youth Action Scheme. This was primarily established as a short term funded initiative (three years), to work with young people deemed 'at risk'. Although the focus was primarily on young people at risk of offending, this was not explicit. We were therefore able to convince the funding body that the young women with whom we worked were at risk from social exclusion by factors such as isolation, lack of support, lack of educational and employment opportunities, limited financial resources and poor quality accommodation. In this way, they were as much in need of support as others targeted by the scheme, who were in the main young men. The project was able to secure funding for a further three years from the National Lottery.

Current initiatives include the Sure Start Plus programme which aims to co-ordinate services and support for pregnant teenagers and teenage parents, to include pregnancy advisors and support around housing, health care, parenting skills, education and child care. An Education Maintenance Allowance, payable in term time only is currently being piloted in 15 Local Education Authority areas. This will make up to £40 per week the amount available to 16–19 year olds on low incomes. In addition, the new national Student Support arrangements for post-16s will give increased funding to further education colleges for help with childcare costs.

New Start and Excellence in Cities initiatives are both concerned with young people of secondary school age, and aim to provide support, funding and resources to young people who are having difficulty in engaging in the formal education system: both initiatives identify young mothers as one of their target groups. The government is also investing £2 million in pilot childcare schemes, to enable 16 and 17 year old parents to return to education or training. Young mothers receiving Income Support or the Education Maintenance Allowance mentioned above will be eligible. Additionally, £10 million is committed for the provision of semi-independent housing with support for under-18 lone parents. Also, the New Opportunities Fund, in their provision of grants for Healthy Living Centres, have identified projects for young parents as one of the focus areas to be supported under the scheme. One of the projects mentioned herein was funded from the European Social Fund and of course the National Lottery is another source of revenue for such work.

Needs Analysis

Youth service provision for young parents in Hertfordshire has largely been in response to the contact youth workers have made with young women who are pregnant or who are young parents. When we first started to look at provision in existence for young women with children it became apparent that services were generally planned for expectant mothers or parents regardless of age group.

Research carried out shows that young women make less use of antenatal care services than other groups of women (Chisholm, 1989). Both studies found that more than a quarter of teenagers did not consult doctors to confirm the pregnancy until they were more than three months pregnant. For many this was due to fear or embarrassment and for a few, because they feared being talked into abortion (Simms and Smith, in Combes and Schonveld, 1989). Furthermore, higher than average numbers of young women under 17 years old were found to be late attending antenatal clinics, after 20 weeks. This resulted in missing out in parent education in the early part of the pregnancy.

As youth work practitioners our experience has confirmed these findings. A high proportion of young women did express concerns in using antenatal classes. Reasons were varied but generally included lack of confidence in speaking out in groups, feeling stigmatised by other older women, fear of facing the issues surrounding giving birth, not knowing anyone of the same age group.

This feeling of 'not belonging' is often transferred to baby clinics and to parent and toddler groups and other early childhood services. The experience can leave some young women feeling isolated and unsupported. Many young women do not have the confidence to use groups

populated by older mothers. One young mother said she had tried to go to a parent and toddler group but had felt the other mothers were giving her what she termed as 'the sly eye' she did not feel happy to return. These feelings are often exacerbated for young women from minority ethnic cultures and feelings of lack of acceptance can often be increased by possible racist attitudes (Hertfordshire County Council, 1996).

Because young parenthood is often accompanied by low income this accentuates the social divide often experienced by young women with children. Age itself frequently puts young parents in a different social class as they have not had time to save, develop career paths or become homeowners. Many families in the Hertfordshire study were on benefit but those dependent on partners' wages reported that these were very low as they were still in junior positions. One young woman made the following comment:

> *It's not very easy to join in with a group when other mums turn up in their flash cars and talk about holidays. If they know you live on a council estate they don't want to know.*
>
> (Hertfordshire CC, 1996)

The skills and expertise of youth workers puts the youth service in an almost unique position to be able to respond to this area of need by providing the young women with space of their own in which they can share the dual issues of being young and being parents, without feeling they will be judged.

Planning and Delivery

In the early stages of our particular project, we targeted areas that had a lack of mainstream Early Years services and where there was statistical evidence of high deprivation and clusters of young families in rented or in public housing accommodation. Analysis of census material and research with other agencies in contact with young parents gave us the data needed to target provision and position resources effectively. Primary agencies contacted included health visitors, Social Services children and family teams, Social Services family centres and antenatal clinics. We found the key professionals to be the health visitors. They were most likely to be in regular contact with young parents through antenatal care and baby clinics.

They played a fundamental role in linking young women into this new provision and supported us by gaining consent from the young women for us to make contact.

Developing appropriate provision required considering the following:

1. Access

A maximum age limit of 25 years ensured the focus would be on young parents. Additional support was given to younger members of the group (under 21 years) to help with transport, although predominantly young women accessed the group from the local neighbourhood. The youth centre used was situated in one of the highest wards of deprivation in the area. The local hostel for homeless families was situated around the corner and the area itself, from our research, was home to many young parents.

One of the key issues of access was funding and whilst there was no weekly charge the young women were aware of the need to fundraise to subsidise events and activities in order to make them affordable.

2. Outreach and referral mechanisms

When planning provision for this target group of young women with children, a key consideration was the need for home visits. We were often introduced to the young women by another agency. They would check with the young women that they were comfortable with us making contact. As the project evolved, referrals would often be made by the young women themselves. They were in a prime position to identify other young women with children who would benefit from this level of support.

3. Providing a welcoming environment

The home visit would give us the opportunity to set the scene and give information and an introduction to the group. This usually put the young women at ease and relieved worries that they would not know anyone when they walked into the building. This was often a major concern particularly for those young women who were housed on their own away from their families with little or no friendship

group: their isolation had diminished much of their self confidence. We always offered transport for a young woman's first visit to ensure she did not have to walk into the setting alone. Time was provided to settle their children into the crèche before joining the group.

4. Crèche provision

Provision of a crèche was an essential feature of the project and played a critical role in enabling the young women to take 'time out' for their own personal growth. Developmental group work could flourish where the young women were not constantly concerned with responding to their children's needs within the sessions. The young women had a key role in determining how the crèche was managed and were fully involved in recruitment of crèche workers, methods of operation and purchase of equipment.

Hertfordshire County Council Social Services 'Notes of Guidance for applicants wishing to provide crèche facilities' states the following:

> *As it is difficult to determine the exact number and age of children attending, an overall ratio of 1:4 must be adhered to. Higher ratios will be expected if under 2s attend.*

(Undated)

The document states further that at least one of the staff members must be qualified to NNEB and should have a minimum of three years experience of looking after or working with young children.

Key Principles and Theoretical Underpinning for the Work

Education, equality and empowerment were the key principles underlying the work with the young women. Giving them responsibility for the direction, content and aspirations of the project was the central aim. A contract was agreed with the group that focused on respect for individuals, commitments to the group and the boundary management issues for the crèche, i.e. nappy changing, behaviour management. The young women took responsibility for financial decisions and managed the project's accounts. They regularly reviewed how they operated as a group and how individual commitments were followed. Group ownership and identity were paramount.

Issues that evolved within the project focused on the support needs of individuals, managing relationships as parents and with their families, taking responsibility and encouraging partners to take their share of the parenting role.

We also encountered discriminatory attitudes and anti-discriminatory practice was a key element of our work. We were always clear that racist and homophobic comments would be questioned and challenged. We had many a heated debate around these issues and the young women were encouraged to consider their attitudes or language and the impact this had on others around them, on their children and on those against whom society discriminated. How they felt about the stereotypes and judgements made about them as young mothers, could be used as a means of developing their understanding around these issues.

Anti-discriminatory practice was important again when considering access to the project for new young women with children. The development of 'cliques' and an unwillingness to have the make up of the group change was an issue that we regularly addressed with the group. This included identifying and responding to the need for young women to move on when appropriate, to alleviate dependency and make space for new young women. Keeping these issues on the agenda is important. We found it helped if the young women were involved in recruiting new members and often one of them would accompany us on a home visit.

Accessing further education or employment was an aspiration for many. Arrangements for suitable and affordable childcare were a constant barrier. Support was given to individuals to apply for funding for their educational development. One young woman was successful in gaining funding for a part-time child-minding place to enable her to undertake a window dressing course at a local college. She was subsequently offered employment from the employer at her college placement. However, full-time childcare costs were prohibitive, and she was unable to take up the offer of full time employment after successfully completing the two-year course.

Evaluation

Evaluation of this work with young women with children has taken many forms. Self-assessment and sharing progress and difficulties were a regular feature of the group sessions, whereby the young women supported each other, discussed achievements and identified ways forward. Consistent recordings of the work took place, which ensured clear communication between the workers, allowed for the exploration of emerging issues, determined cause and effect, and agreed any appropriate action.

External reviews of one of the projects were undertaken through discussion with focus groups and observation of the group work. One such example of this was through the University of Sheffield's national evaluation of Youth Action Projects for the Department for Education and Employment (France and Wiles, 1996).

The young women were accustomed to giving feedback as to the benefit and value of the Young Women with Children's Support Group. Hertfordshire Youth Service internal quality assurance inspection in 1996, focused specifically on the Young Women with Children Group, for more in-depth analysis. The findings reinforced the positive aspects of the work and reaffirmed the importance of targeted work with this client group.

The project eventually managed to obtain more permanent funding through a National Lottery bid that was successfully put together by the young women. This promoted the benefits they saw of the mutual support gained and their wanting to extend the opportunity to other young women in a similar position over a longer term.

More recently an OFSTED Inspection of Hertfordshire Youth Service was undertaken and they made the following comment in the report about the project:

> *Young women showed empathy and sensitivity listening to the weekly account of others in the group, offering supportive advice and sharing well-placed humour. The programme of visits, discussions, local development issues and healthy living initiatives were fully developed by the group and a contract of commitment to the group was being agreed.*   (OFSTED, 1999)

Training Initiative

In a response to the educational aspirations of young women with children, a project was established in another part of the County to support young parents into further education through a specifically designed training programme. Funding was secured through the European Social Fund for young people 16 to 25 years old, who had been unemployed for over six months.

Match funding was met from different sources to enable this initiative to take place. This consisted of central funding from the LEA anti-poverty initiative, staffing and accommodation through the youth service and the young women's benefit allowances were included.

The basis of the programme was built around a social skills package delivered by the youth service complemented by basic skills training and a work experience placement at a local further education college. Childcare and travel costs were met up to an agreed limit on the programme. The young women were also given individual tutorials by youth workers to support their development and explore any difficulties they were experiencing.

Recruitment onto the project was difficult, even with childcare support. A number of negative articles in the national press about child-minders' care of children had made such a strong impression on some of the young women, they felt very wary about leaving their children in the care of 'strangers'. Those that managed to make suitable arrangements used known individuals or extended family members. The provision of suitable crèche places in the area were non existent. Although the further education college had a crèche on site, there was a waiting list and full-time students took preference.

Outcomes from the project were measured through individual and group evaluations of their progress. They recognised how they had moved on in both skills development and increased confidence and self esteem. As young mothers many of the young women found the experience liberating by giving them the opportunity to value themselves, to make choices without other people influencing their decisions and to learn how to handle themselves in new and challenging circumstances.

Follow up training or employment was still difficult for this group because of the ongoing child care costs. From the initial group of six only two of the young women managed to engage in further education and one managed to get part-time employment. This shows the lack of initiatives available to assist women into further education or employment by providing affordable childcare.

Through both projects for young parents in Hertfordshire, there have been difficulties identified in supporting young women moving on to long-term education or employment. Although the young women have undoubtedly made steps towards their own personal development, building confidence in their ability to take on new challenges, opportunities to move on have been restricted and are largely dependent upon the amount of support they can get from families or friends to assist with childcare. Young women who are isolated or without family support are particularly disadvantaged. The government initiatives outlined earlier, should go some considerable way towards addressing some of these difficulties provided they are targeted effectively and efficiently to support those young women who do wish to pursue education or employment.

Resource Implications

It is vital to consider the reality of the resourcing implications before commencing work with this target group. This should include giving specific thought to the following:

1. Crèche facilities

These are fundamental to running a project for young women with children and are by far the most costly aspect of the work. The young women we worked with so appreciated the space. Although only two hours per week, the crèche was valuable to them as it enabled them to consider, identify and address their specific needs without distraction. Sometimes that two hour break was a lifeline and was certainly something all looked forward to every week. With this comes the other consideration of suitable space. Social services departments have guidelines for setting up crèche facilities which identify health and safety implications and other considerations which should be followed. Again, expenditure may be needed to bring a particular space to the required standard for a crèche. Alongside this is the need to purchase adequate equipment and to employ suitably qualified staff. The numbers for the group will be restricted by the amount of crèche staff you are able to employ as there is a strict criteria for staff-to-child ratios which must be adhered to.

Key Questions

1. Who is my target group: young mothers, young fathers, mixed sex, single sex? What evidence is there to support the need for this work?
2. What avenues of funding are available and what support can the host organisation provide?
3. What methods will I use to make contact with and engage the young parents?
4. How will I support the young people moving on to access training or employment where appropriate?
5. How will I enable young parents to determine their own agenda and ensure the appropriate balance between worker and peer support?

2. Transport

Many of the young women lived in areas or estates where access to public transport was limited or difficult. We offered transport to and from the project for young women who lived over one mile away from the project in order that distance was not a prohibitive factor for them in attending the group. Often we transported the young women regardless of their proximity to the project for their first visit as many lacked the confidence to enter the group on their own for the first time.

3. Outreach

Again, because of the extreme sense of isolation and lack of social confidence of many of the young women, we found an initial home visit was often not enough. We regularly followed up an initial visit two or three times before the young woman felt able to take the first steps towards the group. This is a time-consuming aspect of the work and sufficient consideration should be given to how this will happen including allocation of time to pursue referrals.

References

Clarke, E., and Coleman, J. (1991). *Growing Up Fast: Adult Outcomes of Teenage Motherhood*. Brighton: Trust for the Study of Adolescence.

Combes, G., and Schonveld, A. (1989). *Life Will Never Be The Same Again*. London: Health Education Authority.

Hertfordshire County Council (1996). *Review of Day Care and Educational Services for Young Children*. Hertfordshire County Council.

Hertfordshire County Council Social Services Department (undated). *Notes of Guidance for Applicants Wishing to Provide Crèche Facilities*. Hertfordshire County Council.

Hertfordshire County Council Youth and Community Service (1996). *Internal Quality Assurance Review, Broxbourne Team*. Hertfordshire County Council.

OFSTED (1999). *Inspection of Hertfordshire Youth Service*. OFSTED.

Social Exclusion Unit (1999). *Report on Teenage Pregnancy*. Social Exclusion Unit.

University of Sheffield (1996). *Review of Youth Action Projects*. University of Sheffield.

Further Reading

Social Exclusion Unit (1999). *Report on Teenage Pregnancy*. Social Exclusion Unit.

Working With Men have useful resources around working with young fathers, 320 Commercial Way, London; Tel/Fax: 0181 308 0709

Trust for Study of Adolescence, 23 New Road, Brighton, East Sussex BN1 1WZ; Tel: 01273 693311; website address: www.tsa.uk.com

28

Young People Sexually Exploited through Prostitution

Margaret Melrose

Key Points

1. Young people who are involved in prostitution are not 'villains'; they are young people who are being sexually abused and exploited, who may be difficult to access and reluctant to accept help.

2. Many young people involved in prostitution come from difficult family backgrounds and may have experienced abuse early in their lives, consequently they may suffer a whole range of problems and emotional needs.

3. Some young people involved in prostitution have no plan to quit prostitution because of its income-generating potential and workers should be prepared to support them whatever their decision.

4. There are many complex reasons why some young people may remain in prostitution, such as 'belonging', drug-dependency. Youth workers might provide opportunities to attempt alternatives and support in undertaking them.

5. The multiple and complex problems experienced by young people involved in prostitution require long term solutions; there is no 'quick fix' and young people will need long term support.

Introduction

This chapter reflects, from the perspective of a researcher, on provisions made by projects across the country for young people who are sexually exploited through their involvement in prostitution. The projects were visited during the course of researching young people's involvement in prostitution (Melrose et al., 1999). The discussion hopes to illustrate examples of good practice and indicate what may be learned for practitioners in this field in the future. The research employed a retrospective approach to young people's involvement in prostitution and although the majority of participants were over 18 at the time of the interviews, they had all become involved in prostitution before they were 18. At the time of the interviews, 32 of the 50 participants were still involved in prostitution.

Some Definitions

Young people are defined in terms of the Children Act 1989 as anyone under 18.

'Prostitution' is usually understood to mean the provision of sexual services in exchange for some kind of payment: payment may involve monetary exchange or it may take the form of drugs, other consumer goods 'or even a roof over one's head for the night' (Green, 1992). 'Prostitution' describes a range of activities that may be performed under different terms and conditions (O'Connell-Davidson, 1995) but at the core of the phenomenon is 'the treatment of the human body as an asset, that is, as a means to seek subsistence' (Sangera, 1997). To avoid the pejorative connotations associated with the word 'prostitute' or 'prostitution', some commentators in this field now prefer the term 'sex worker' or 'workers in the sex industry'. However, when we are talking about juveniles involved in prostitution, this terminology only serves to 'obscure the enormity of the violation' (Pitts, 1997) and is 'most inappropriate' when we are talking about children and young people (Barrett, 1997). It is now widely accepted that when we are talking about young people's involvement in prostitution we are talking about vulnerable young people who are sexually abused and exploited by adults (Lee and O'Brien, 1995; Barrett, 1997; Home Office/Department of Health, 1998; Melrose et al., 1999). They are young people 'who suffer at the hands of men who desire, fantasise and buy sex with children' (Green et al., 1997).

The Projects

In the course of the research, six projects were visited in different towns and cities across England and Wales. There is an enormous gap in service provision for young people involved in prostitution (Green et. al., 1997) and only one of the projects specifically targeted its services to *young* people (i.e. under 18). One project focused its provision on men and boys. All the projects were working within very tight financial constraints and, for many, funding arrangements were insecure. Consequently, many found it difficult to plan for future development of the services on offer.

It is believed that up to 5,000 young people are involved in the sex industry at any one time (Thomson, 1995; Crosby and Barrett, 1999). There is, therefore, an obvious need for more securely funded projects specifically to target young people if they are to be supported and helped to get out of prostitution.

Recent government guidelines require that statutory and voluntary agencies work in conjunction with each other and respond to young people involved in prostitution as 'children in need who may be suffering or likely to suffer significant harm' (Home Office/Department of Health, 1998). It is therefore to be hoped that resources will be forthcoming to develop more of the much needed projects described below.

Delivery and Evaluation

Young people who are sexually exploited through prostitution often face a number of interconnected difficulties. In the course of their work they are often subject to violence from 'punters', partners, 'pimps' and other people who make their living on the street (Melrose et al., 1999). This means that they may need protection and support from those working with them in order to cope with problems of bullying, violence and peer pressure. However, because of the clandestine nature of their activities these young people can be a very difficult group to access. As a result of their past negative experiences in the public care system, the juvenile justice system or the education system, they may be suspicious and mistrustful of those who seek to support or help them (Melrose et al., 1999). The most appropriate form of provision is therefore 'street-based': that is, provision that is located in the vicinity in which young people are working and

which offers outreach and drop-in facilities. Such provision has been discussed elsewhere as offering examples of good practice and it has been suggested that young people respond better to this form of service delivery than more traditional forms (Browne and Falshaw, 1998; Crosby and Barrett, 1999).

The workers contacted in the course of the research described here had all worked extremely hard to establish contact with the young people and to build relationships of trust over a period of time. These relationships were highly valued by those who took part in the research. Most of those with whom agencies were in touch were 'street workers': that is, they were not working from 'off-street' premises such as houses, flats or saunas. It has been argued that the law circumscribes the activities of street workers in ways denied those working in other parts of the sex industry (Edwards, 1997) and that this group is amongst the most vulnerable and exploited of all sex industry workers (O'Connell-Davidson and Layder, 1995). Because of their visibility, agency workers are also more likely to come across 'street workers' than those involved in other parts of the sex industry (Brain et al., 1998).

Project workers were aware that young people who are sexually exploited in prostitution often have a variety of complex and interrelated needs. Many have been sexually abused in their families before becoming involved in prostitution and many have been looked after in the public care system (Melrose et al., 1999; O'Neill et al., 1995). These young people are usually poor and turn to prostitution as 'a viable alternative to no or low income' (Green et al. 1997; q.v. Melrose, 2000a; Melrose, 2000b). In the sex industry there is a premium on youth and, where young people are faced with insufficient incomes or inadequate or even non-existent welfare support, the financial incentive to become involved at a young age is high (Melrose et al., 1999; Melrose, 2000a; Melrose, 2000b). In addition to these difficulties, such young people may be facing problems with housing, drugs, court cases, child-rearing, losing their children to the care system, violent relationships, lack of qualifications and training, and low self-esteem (Melrose et al., 1999; Crosby and Barrett, 1999; Browne and Falshaw, 1998; O'Neill et al., 1995; Green, 1992). There may even be language barriers and difficulties (Kelly and Regan, 2000).

Some of the projects visited in the course of the research were better equipped to deal with these various needs than others were. Some for example, were primarily health focused and had fairly narrow remits. One project, for example, funded by the local health trust to promote sexual health, was unable to intervene to support a young person who was homeless. In the view of the project funders, tackling *social* rather than *health* problems was beyond the remit of the project. Workers were therefore left feeling that their efforts to help the young person exit from prostitution were undermined by their inability to help with the housing problems the young person faced. This demonstrates an urgent need for 'joined up' thinking and practice when responding to the needs of these vulnerable young people.

Other projects offered a wide range of integrated services where the client group was able to access juvenile justice workers, drugs workers, health services (where condoms were provided free), legal advice and advocacy (where women could be accompanied to court), welfare benefits advice and one-to-one counselling services. One such project offered drugs counselling and a methadone treatment programme. The young people were not disqualified from the programme if they tested positive for other drugs. This is a useful approach to adopt and one from which young people will feel less alienated compared to those where use of other drugs results in automatic disqualification from the treatment programme. A young woman of nineteen told us she had been 'thrown off' two methadone programmes in the past because she had tested positive for other drugs. She had consequently 'given up' the idea of a methadone treatment programme and continued to inject street heroin. Her drug dependence further entrenched her involvement in prostitution.

Previous research has established that, especially amongst those working at street level rather than from private flats, saunas or massage parlours, drug use is fairly widespread (May et al., 2000; Melrose et al., 1999; Crosby and Barrett, 1999). It is not uncommon for young people to become involved in prostitution to support their own or another's drug habit (O'Neill et al., 1995; Melrose et al., 1999). Those working with these young people therefore have to be prepared to respond to the young person's needs at this level and also to be aware that it may be drug dependence that

prevents the young person from getting out of prostitution (Melrose et al., 1999).

In the project specifically targeted at young people, outreach workers in conjunction with youth services and educational welfare officers, offered young people support with drug problems, counselling, emotional and practical support and help with child rearing. In addition, there were opportunities to resume their studies through the provision of educational outreach facilities. The project provided outreach and drop-in facilities where provision was made for the children of clients using the project. Toys and a play area were provided together with a relaxed lounge where young people could drop in for a cup of coffee. Private rooms for counselling sessions were also available if a young person wanted to speak in confidence with any of the workers.

The young people who made use of it valued the project a great deal: they were grateful for the emotional and practical support they had received and for the opportunity to return to study that the imaginative project had provided. One seventeen year old said she thought the project had been 'great' and that it had made her realise that there was 'more to life than working'. She had successfully exited from prostitution, was settled down in a relationship and had a new baby at the time of the interview. She was still receiving support from the project and would often pop in with her baby.

There is obviously a need for more of these projects that take a holistic view of young people 'at risk'. There is a need to provide them with a range of integrated services and opportunities (Browne and Falshaw, 1998; Crosby and Barrett, 1999).

Theoretical Underpinning

The projects visited in the course of this research were funded from different sources (voluntary or statutory) and as a result of this had quite different remits. Many were running on very small, and even temporary budgets and could not necessarily rely on the same funding for the next year. This obviously makes planning and development of future work extremely problematic and results in the provision of short term, rather than long term solutions. Those projects that were more securely funded could plan and develop the services they provided and increase the range of their provision over time. Secure funding is also vital to ensure consistency of delivery. A worker in a project whose funding arrangements for the coming year were uncertain was concerned that after establishing relationships of trust with vulnerable young people in the sex industry the project might just fold and the young people would be left to flounder again.

All the projects were concerned to support and empower those with whom they were in contact so that they might feel ready to exit from prostitution, or, if they had already made the decision to get out, to support them in that decision. Workers however, were non-judgmental in their approach to their clients, they did not 'preach' to them and they respected the choices their clients made. Clients were equally supported whether they chose to continue in prostitution or had decided to exit. Many workers kept in touch with those who had exited and they were still able to drop in at the projects. Many participants found the support of project workers extremely helpful. They felt that they were not judged negatively by project workers as they were by the 'straight' world beyond the project and found the emotional support they received important in restoring their sense of self-esteem. Projects were also important in countering feelings of social isolation. The research found that this was often an important factor in preventing people from getting out of prostitution once they had become involved (Melrose et al., 1999).

Principles of Youth and Community Work and Integration into Practice

It has been argued that the youth service is in a position to become 'the integral lynch pin in the development of multi-agency working and multi-agency outcomes for young people working in prostitution' (Green et al., 1997). The majority of agency workers encountered in the course of the research, although not youth service workers did indeed seem to share many of the central principles of youth work. That is, young people were viewed holistically and in many cases, there was an appreciation of the fact that the difficulties the young person faced were interrelated. All the projects worked to minimise the harm that might result from a young person's involvement in prostitution and all workers were committed to

promoting the well-being and safety of those with whom they worked. This, for example, involved raising awareness around issues of personal safety, women were advised to always let a friend know when they were going off in a car and to make sure that she recorded the registration. Descriptions of 'Ugly Mugz', that is, men who have attacked women, and descriptions of the cars they drive, were circulated. Safe sex practices were promoted by supplying condoms. One of the projects also offered a needle exchange scheme. Project workers were concerned to equip the people with whom they worked to make informed choices in relation to their circumstances. When they had made the decision to exit from prostitution, clients were assisted as much as possible in this choice. When they remained in prostitution clients were supported until, and if, they made the decision to quit.

The projects offered a confidential service to their clients and most explained fully to their clients the conditions under which such confidentiality would be broken. At one project, workers agreed that if they were to breach a client's confidentiality they would first of all inform the client of their intention to do so. This allowed those making use of the projects to trust the workers and to feel that they could be honest with them about the circumstances of their lives. It also enabled workers to understand what was the most appropriate support and help to offer each client.

Most of the projects offered their services to women in the sex industry and just one targeted provision on men and boys. Those providing services for women employed female outreach workers while a male outreach worker was employed by the project providing services for men and boys. In some projects, the ethnic mix of staff teams was more varied than in others: this may be a reflection of the local populations served by the projects and from which workers were often drawn. Obviously, greater diversity, in terms of gender and ethnicity, in project teams, will facilitate access to more diverse groups of young people.

The youth service can play an important role in developing preventative work with young people who are at risk of becoming involved in prostitution. Youth workers may act as role models or mentors for vulnerable young people and may encourage the development of peer education by training and supporting young people to work with other young people around the issues of concern to them. The youth service may also work in partnership with other agencies to intervene when a young person is in a crisis situation: that is when they are involved in prostitution or facing problems of homelessness or drug abuse. It has been suggested that, in conjunction with other agencies, youth workers can work to meet the immediate needs of these vulnerable young people and, while doing so, 'work through peer education and harm minimisation to prevent further harm' (Green et al., 1997).

Some Considerations for Other Projects

Young people who are involved in prostitution are being sexually abused and exploited. The goal of workers must be to protect them from further abuse and exploitation (Department of Health/Home Office, 1998). Even if young people assert that they have 'chosen' to be involved in prostitution or if they persist in their involvement in prostitution, workers should understand that this is not a 'free' choice. Entry into prostitution results from 'past negative experiences and dire circumstances that lead young people to act in ways that are inimical to their best interests' (Pitts, 1997). Theirs are 'structured choices' (Pettiway, 1997; Melrose, 2000a; Melrose, 2000b) that result from a highly constrained agency.

Because of the difficulties of their family backgrounds and in other areas of their lives such young people are likely to be confronting a whole range of problems and may be emotionally needy (O'Neill et al., 1995). The problems they confront might range from homelessness and poverty to drug dependence. Additionally, or alternatively, they may be experiencing problems with relationships and with childrearing. Their education may have been disrupted or interrupted and they may not have the skills required in the formal labour market. Their relative poverty and lack of opportunities may make it difficult for them to make the transition from prostitution to the formal economy. Some young people may be experiencing any or all of these problems and projects should be geared up to respond to them in a holistic manner, and should provide them with opportunities to explore their own victimisation (Shaw and Butler, 1998) and offer emotional support to allow them to restore their self-esteem

(Browne and Falshaw, 1998; Crosby and Barrett, 1999).

Because of its income-generating potential, some young people may have no immediate plans to exit from prostitution and workers should be prepared to support them whatever their decision. The decision to exit from prostitution may be triggered by a variety of factors. Personal trauma, such as the vicious rape of a friend, the death of a child, or changing personal circumstances, such as having a baby or establishing a new relationship, and the wider social policy context all play their part (Melrose et al., 1999). The young people involved should be approached and supported in a non-judgmental way until, and if, they make the decision to get out of prostitution.

There are a variety of complex reasons why some young people may remain in prostitution. Primarily they need the money or have insufficient incomes from welfare benefits, but also because they feel they 'belong' and are concerned about being isolated, or having no friends, in the world beyond prostitution (Melrose et al., 1999). In these circumstances, youth workers might provide them with opportunities for developing positive peer associations, for example, through sporting or leisure pursuits. Others may be drug dependent and remain in prostitution to finance their drug use. In such circumstances, support through detoxification programmes or drug substitution programmes may be necessary before a decision to exit from prostitution may be contemplated.

There is no 'quick fix' and young people will need long term support in order to move their lives in another direction. Things may be additionally complicated by the presence of a violent partner or pimp. When a partner is violent or taking her money a young woman may still think this is because he loves her and she may feel that she still wants to stay with him.

Resource Implications

The resource implications of providing the sorts of facilities outlined above are obviously huge. Projects require adequate numbers of staff who are appropriately qualified to respond creatively and imaginatively to a range of complex and interrelated needs. There is a great deal of potential for inter-agency co-operation between youth services, the education service, health services, social services and voluntary sector projects. It is possible that by

Key Questions

1. What is the young person's situation: i.e. how old are they, are they forced into prostitution by another, are they drug dependent?

2. Are other appropriate agencies aware of the young person's situation? If not, do they need to be informed?

3. What is the young person's decision in relation to remaining in or getting out of prostitution and how might they be provided with support, care and protection in the light of that decision?

4. What does the young person define as their immediate needs? For example, they may be more concerned about a drug problem, about being homeless, about a violent partner, or being socially isolated or unemployed than they are about working in prostitution. As a professional, what steps can I take to respond to these immediate needs?

5. What sources of support (if any) does the young person have beyond the world of prostitution? Can these be called on to support the young person in any way?

pooling resources such inter-agency initiatives might be established on a long-term basis and staffed with workers who can draw on a wide range of skills to provide the sorts of interventions that young people would find effective. Projects may be able to access charitable grants and even money from the European Union as well as statutory funding to develop local initiatives to respond to the problem and to prevent it from arising in the first place.

References

Barrett, D. (1997). Introduction. In Barrett, D. (Ed.). *Child Prostitution in Britain: Dilemmas and Practical Responses.* London: The Children's Society.

Brain, T., Duffin, T., Anderson, S., and Parchment, P. (1998). *Child Prostitution: A Report on the ACPO Guidelines and the Pilot Studies in Wolverhampton and Nottinghamshire.* Gloucestershire Constabulary.

Browne, K., and Falshaw, L. (1998). Street children in the UK: A case of abuse and neglect. In *Child Abuse Review,* 7: pp. 241–253.

Crosby, S., and Barrett, D. (1999). Poverty, Drugs and Youth Prostitution: A case study. In Marlow A., and Pearson, G. (Eds.). *Young People, Drugs and Community Safety.* Lyme Regis: Russell House Publishing.

Edwards. S.M. (1997). The Legal Regulation of Prostitution: A Human Rights Issue. In Scambler, G., and Scambler, A. (Eds.). *Rethinking Prostitution: Purchasing Sex in the 1990s.* London: Routledge.

Green, J., Mulroy, S., and O'Neill, M. (1997). Young People and Prostitution from a Youth Service Perspective. In Barrett, D. (Ed.). op. cit.

Home Office/Department of Health (1998). *Guidance on Children Involved in Prostitution.* London: Home Office/Department of Health.

Kelly, L., and Regan, L. (2000). *Stopping Traffic: Exploring the Extent of, and Responses to, Trafficking in Women for the Purpose of Sexual Exploitation in the UK.* Police Research Series Paper 125. London: Home Office.

May, T., Edmunds, M., Hough, M., with the assistance of Harvey, C. (2000). *Street Business: The Links Between Sex and Drug Markets.* Police Research Series Paper 118. London: Home Office.

Melrose, M. (2000a). *Globalisation and Child Prostitution in Britain in the 1990s.* Paper presented at The Globalisation of Sexual Exploitation Conference. London, July 10th.

Melrose, M. (2000b forthcoming). *Ties that Bind: Young People and the Prostitution Labour Market in Britain.* Paper to be presented at the 4th European Feminist Research Conference, Bologna, 28th September–1st October.

O'Connell-Davidson, J., and Layder, D. (1994). *Methods, Sex and Madness.* London: Routledge.

O'Connell-Davidson. J. (1995). The anatomy of 'free choice' prostitution. In *Gender, Work and Organisation,* 2(1): pp. 1–10.

O'Neill. M., Goode. N., and Hopkins. K. (1995). Juvenile Prostitution: The Experience of Young Women in Residential Care. In *Childright,* 113: pp. 14–16.

Pettiway, L. (1997). *Workin' It: Women Living Through Drugs and Crime.* Philadelphia: Temple University Press.

Pitts. J. (1997). Causes of Youth Prostitution, New Forms of Practice and Political Responses. In Barrett, D. (Ed.). Op. cit.

Sangera, J. (1997). *In the Belly of the Beast.* Discussion Paper for South Asia Regional Consultation on Prostitution. Bangkok, February 17th–18th.

Shaw. I., and Butler. I. (1998). Understanding Young People and Prostitution: A Foundation for Practice? In *British Journal of Social Work,* 28: pp. 177–196

Thomson. A. (1995). Abuse by Another Name. In *Community Care,* 19th–25th October, pp. 16–18.

Useful contacts

Handbook of Sexual Health Services

Europap (European Project for AIDS Prevention in Prostitution) (UK)
c/o Academic Department of Public Health
St Mary's Hospital Medical School
Norfolk Place
London W2 1PG
Tel: 0207 723 1252
This provides a list of projects working with sex workers and details of specific groups at whom services are targeted

Genesis Project

Oxford Chambers
Oxford Place,
Leeds
Tel: 01132 430036; ask for Sue or Carol.
Provides services for all women involved in the sex industry

Male Safe
(Men's Sexual Health Project)

Southern Birmingham Community Health Trust
St Patrick's Centre for Community Health
Highgate Street,
Birmingham
Tel: 0121 446 4747; ask for Morton Stanley or Darrell Gale
Provides services for men and boys working in the sex industry

The Safe Project

St Patrick's Centre for Community Health
Highgate Street
Birmingham
Tel: 0121 440 6655/0121 446 4747; ask for Carole Lennox
Provides services for all women working in the sex industry

Street Reach Project

28 Copley Road
Doncaster
Tel: 01302 328396; ask for Marilyn
Provides services to juveniles involved in the sex industry

MASH
(Manchester Action on Street Health)

Unit 110, Ducie House
37 Ducie Street,
Manchester
Tel: 0161 228 3433; ask for Sarah Crosby
The project provides services to sex industry workers

Safe in the City
(The Children's Society)

354 Waterloo Road,
Cheetham Hill
Manchester
Tel: 0161 740 4183; ask for Mark Lee
The project works with young people of 17 and under

The Harbour Centre

Ermington Terrace
Plymouth
Tel: 01752 267431; ask for Julie Prentice
The project works with women involved in the sex industry

Street Matters (NSPCC)

38 Wager Street
London E3
Tel: 020 8981 5583/020 8983 3555/0771 206 9430; ask for Nasima, Marian, Christina
The project works with women of 17 and under who are at risk or involved in prostitution

Breaking Free (NSPCC)

Tel: 020 7700 6260; ask for Lucy or Nora
The project works with young women of 17 and under

NSPCC Helpline

Tel: 0800 800 500

Childline

Tel: 0800 1111

London Refuge

Tel: 020 7700 7541

Further Reading

Barnardos (1998). *Whose Daughter Next?* Essex: Barnardos.

Barrett, D. (Ed.) (1997). *Child Prostitution in Britain: Dilemmas and Practical Responses.* London: The Children's Society.

Green, J. (1992). *It's No Game: Responding to the Needs of Young Women at Risk or Involved in Prostitution.* Leicester: National Youth Agency.

Lee, M., and O'Brien, R. (1995). *The Game's Up: Redefining Child Prostitution.* London: The Children's Society.

Melrose, M., Barrett, D., and Brodie, I. (1999). *One Way Street? Retrospectives on Childhood Prostitution.* London: The Children's Society.

29

Young Carers
Paul Adams and David Land

Key Points

1. Young carers can be any young people; often difficult to identity and target young carers frequently do not define themselves as young carers and can remain isolated and unrecognised.

2. Young carers need opportunities for personal development in an informal and supportive environment as they are often subject to pressures other than their direct caring role, from school, and family and may suffer bullying.

3. Effective work with young carers will involve a long term commitment to creating a supportive and trusting environment, that is valued by young carers, in partnership with other agencies.

4. Young carers have the legal right to an assessment of their situation by social services. One function of work with young carers is to encourage and support young people and their families to take up the opportunity of an assessment and gain any support to which they are entitled.

5. Developing work with young carers will take a good deal of energy and commitment and may be very time consuming.

Introduction

In this chapter we shall consider the roles and responsibilities that define a young person as a young carer and how youth workers can target this group and offer effective interventions. We will also identify some of the key principles relating to work with young carers, outline important issues that should be addressed when targeting young carers and conclude with questions for youth work professionals to consider.

The youth worker has a responsibility to liaise closely with social services, schools and education welfare services to advocate on behalf of young carers, representing their interests, as they define them. This can involve providing informal learning opportunities that complement those of the school setting, but equally importantly enhance the personal development of young carers with their peers, in a supportive social environment. Programmes and activities aimed at young carers including 'one-to-one' interventions and small group work have been effective in encouraging young carers to share their experiences, identify their own needs and develop personal and social life skills. Practitioners must remember that the caring role has implications for a young carer throughout their life, not solely through the time they are fulfilling that role, but on into adulthood.

Young carers have been defined as:

> ...children or young people under the age of 18 years, who carry out significant caring tasks or assume a level of responsibility for another person, which would usually be carried out by an adult. They may be caring for adults, usually their parents, or sisters or brothers.
>
> (Laming, 1995)

Young carers may be involved in performing a diverse range of tasks for instance:

- domestic tasks: cleaning, cooking, shopping
- personal care: washing, dressing and toileting their relative
- family responsibilities: caring for younger siblings, managing the household budget
- medical care: administering medication, injections, dressing wounds, lifting and handling
- emotional support: for other family members, including their cared-for relative

The government's *National Strategy for Carers* (1999), estimates that there may be between 20,000 and 50,000 young carers in the UK. It is difficult to judge the number of young carers because of the problems associated with identifying and contacting them. There are a number of possible reasons for this, in particular:

- The fear and stigma attached to young people contacting Social Services.
- The 'normalising' of the role of the young carer in the family, young carers are therefore unaware they are young carers. It is very uncommon for young people to identify themselves as a young carer and then seek assistance; often they will not know there are specific services available to them.
- Young carers may be embarrassed to disclose their caring role to a teacher or other adult.
- Young carers may be unwilling to contact anyone for help because they consider their caring role to be private.
- Young carers may be unaware that anyone will listen to them, let alone help them, especially if they have had negative experiences with welfare professionals in the past.

Legislation and Government Initiatives

There are a range of directives that relate to young carers. Current frameworks that directly affect young carers include:

- The Children Act 1989 and the Children (Scotland) Act 1995 both entitle young carers to support from local authority social services departments and health authorities. Under this legislation, and the Carers (Recognition and Services) Act 1995, young carers can receive support from local and health authorities. Using Section 17 of the Children Act social services departments can help young carers, by considering whether their welfare or development might suffer if support is not provided.
- The Carers (Recognition and Services) Act 1995, which states that young carers are legally entitled to an assessment of their home situation by social services, including their caring responsibilities. This is their most significant right as a carer and is not generally known. The 'National Strategy' outlined below has suggested that local authorities do not promote this entitlement due to concern about raising expectations

which they will be unable to meet due to lack of resources.

- The *National Strategy for Carers* 1999 has given caring a major national focus and signifies a commitment by the government to support all carers. It contains specific advice on working with young carers for all agencies.
- Department for Education and Employment (DfEE) *Pupil Support Circular* 10/99 to all head teachers gives guidance to schools on identifying young carers, and offers advice on having a designated member of staff in each school with a responsibility for supporting young carers.

The Needs of Young Carers

The Young Carers Research Group has undertaken research into the needs of young carers, a substantial amount by Loughborough University. It has been suggested that voluntary projects, alongside statutory agencies, are best placed to provide resources that meet the needs of young carers. Youth workers have a significant role to play in meeting these needs as young people they currently work with may be carers, and are therefore in good position to attract the voluntary attendance of young people to services. It is in this context that young carers have identified that they need:

1. Someone to talk to

Young carers need someone with whom they can share their concerns. This is a key role for youth workers. It can also be useful to work with existing counselling services to meet this need. However young carers can be reluctant to access such services due to lack of understanding of what counselling might involve and negative associations of being 'treated'.

2. Recognition of their role as a carer

It is important for professionals to recognise and respect the effort, knowledge and commitment of young carers. Young carers have something to bring to any encounter with a professional, as their experience forms a key part of who they are and contributes to the dynamics of the family group. The lack of recognition of a young carer's experience can lead to inappropriate and potentially damaging interventions. As in all work with young people, young carers should be treated as individuals with specific needs.

3. Information about the medical condition of the person they are caring for

This information needs to be clear and accessible. When a young carer understands why the person they care for behaves as they do, e.g. due to pain or mental illness, it will create a basis for them to make informed decisions about their caring role and their relationship.

4. Practical assistance and support

Young carers need practical assistance and support in the care of their relative, and this support should allow them space to be children and to develop emotionally and socially. This could take the form of additional or respite care for their relative e.g. a sitting service which allows the young carer free time to socialise with their peers.

Any support that is offered should not take the form of 'special' treatment for young carers, that solely tackles the presenting symptoms of their role (e.g. late or non attendance at school), rather than the cause, i.e. the day-to-day practicalities of caring. The core problem of their caring responsibilities needs to be addressed.

A young carer may first be identified through the school environment by the education welfare service. An educational welfare officer may be in a good position to create a support structure designed to lessen the caring responsibilities of the young person. This structure will rely on input from other professionals, i.e. a multi-agency approach. This may include social and personal development programmes and strategies to ensure that they are regularly attending school and meeting their educational targets and commitments

5. Time for themselves

Young carers need to have free time away from their caring responsibilities. Youth workers are able to support young carers by providing specific groups and activities for and with young carers or by targeting young carers to attend existing programmes. Research has suggested that young carers find it useful to talk with other young carers about what they all do and to take part in social activities together.

Case Studies
Kimberly

Kimberly is fourteen and lives at home with her mother and two younger brothers. Her mother experiences clinical depression and spends long periods of time in bed or sitting in front of the television. Kimberly does all the shopping and cleaning and cooks for the family. Her brothers are very demanding, and every morning she gets them up and takes them to school. This makes her late for her own classes and means she is constantly in trouble with her teachers. Some girls make fun of her because she is always with her younger brothers and doesn't have time for boyfriends.

Jason

Jason is ten years old and lives with his mother and father. His father suffers from Multiple Sclerosis and his mother works as an office cleaner early in the morning. Jason has to help his father wash and dress and ensure he takes his medication before preparing breakfast and getting ready for school. Jason loves his father but he does not like having to wash him and finds it embarrassing to talk about it and resents his mother leaving him to do this.

Education

Young carers may not attend school or may be constantly late. This can lead to sanctions and the escalation of the problem, creating poor relationships with teaching staff. This situation can be exacerbated if the young person is unwilling to tell anyone at the school they are caring for someone. In some cases non-attendance can be endorsed by parents, especially if they consider that their caring responsibilities take priority.

Some young carers may not have the opportunity or the time to join in social clubs or after-school activities. This can lead to isolation and bullying by other young people and a lack of contact with teachers outside the classroom, thereby affecting the development of longer-term relationships.

Additionally, some young carers can be subject to bullying by other young people both within the school environment and outside, because they are seen as different and are often isolated from social circles due to the lack of time created by their caring responsibilities. Consequently bullying can add pressure to the life of the young carers and in some cases lead to further low attendance at schools in an attempt to avoid encounters with the perpetrators. Support on how to deal with this issue should form a part of any service or programme.

These factors can lead to poor primary and secondary education in turn creating a lack of higher education opportunities and limited career prospects, not necessarily due to lack of an individual ability.

The Department for Education and Employment circular (DfEE, 10/99) recommends the use of a designated member of school staff to support young carers. In one example a member of staff was identified and this led to every pupil completing a questionnaire as they entered the school, regarding their social activities and home life. The member of staff analysed these in an attempt to identify signs of caring or non-participation in social activities. Pupils were then asked about their questionnaire on a one-to-one basis. Young carers identified in this way can be well supported by the designated member of staff in the school, with the opportunity to call home during breaks to check on the cared-for relative and with the opportunity to attend lunch time clubs. The teacher is also able to refer them to a local young carers project. Schools are a key arena for the support of young carers and it is imperative that any youth work initiative has good relationships with local schools in order to support, advise and guide them to be able to undertake this function.

Health

A young carer's physical health can be affected by a variety of influences including the lifting and manual handling of the cared-for relative, as well as lack of sleep, exercise and balanced diet due to limited opportunities and awareness. Young carers can experience emotional and mental health problems related to their circumstances, such as feelings of guilt and resentment towards the one cared for or loss of role and identity following the death of the person they are caring for, or if that person is moved into residential care or a hospice. Young carers may continue to care into their adult life and this will restrict the development of social and emotional relationships.

Primary Care Groups can provide access to local doctors' surgeries and health centres. Surgeries are required to 'tag' patient's notes if they have a carer or are a carer. The surgery can target carers with information about local carers projects which will allow the carer to make an informed choice about whether to access this support or not. This also applies to young carers and means they can be supported by their own GP's, who should make sure the young person's health needs are taken into account.

Identifying Young Carers

Traditionally 'care' has been seen as an adult function carried out either in the home or by another adult relative or in the nursing or health-related professions. Young people are often unrecognised as carers and it is important to be clear that the responsibilities of a young carer are beyond those that could usually be expected of a child. Therefore shopping and other household 'chores' are not in themselves evidence of a young carer. In a number of cases young carers may not be the primary carer, as this role is performed by an adult member of the family. The role of young carer only exists within the context of a family and a balance needs to be found between supporting the needs of the young person alongside the family.

Whilst this means that the young carer may perform other domestic functions it can also mean that they are more difficult to identify and target within resources and support. Many projects across the country have identified resources for work with young carers. The government has also allocated funds for the support of 'breaks' for young carers e.g. day trips, holidays or weekend residential activities. There is a danger that without effectively identifying young carers, grant aid and the resources that are available will not benefit those most in need.

Race and Ethnicity

It has been suggested that some ethnic minority communities have well-developed support structures that play a central role in caring for family members, particularly in the extended families of the Asian community. This reality of self-reliance in Black and ethnic minority communities is partly the result of 'cultural' factors of religion and tradition, but it is also likely to be the result of experience of life in UK society. Many families have had to become self reliant as a result of the lack of provision of appropriate facilities, services and resources. For some, it is the obvious choice to care for family members with little or no intervention from welfare services, for others it has been less a matter of choice and more a case of doing the best for the family with the limited resources available.

In a society where Black young people are disproportionately more likely than their white counterparts to be excluded from school, sent to prison or psychiatric institutions, Black and ethnic minority communities often have negative experiences and perceptions of predominately white welfare professionals and social services. Some of the reasons for this are based on prejudiced and racist perceptions about some Black and minority ethnic groups, their background, culture and family lifestyles. This can put barriers in the way of accessing resources and services. Therefore services and resources need to be made available in culturally appropriate ways. This may involve producing materials in a variety of languages and providing targeted programmes of outreach work. Whilst it may be that caring in the extended family is more established and acceptable in some ethnic minority cultures for example Asian or Chinese communities, it should not be assumed that young people from these families are better equipped for the role of a young carer.

A comprehensive survey of young carers published by *Community Care* magazine also showed that 90 per cent of young carers, in contact with young carers projects, were white (Sanchez, 1995).

Whatever the expectations are of the family, or community and welfare services, it does not mean that a young person will be supported, will cope well or will be happy with the caring role. For example in families with adults whose first language is not English it can be difficult to access appropriate services and resources. In this context

young carers will often be used as interpreters by agencies visiting families. However it is inappropriate to expect a child to interpret a relative's personal intimate details, interpret specific medical knowledge or terms and to operate under this pressure:

> ...If young carers are hidden, black young carers are more so, as racism is endemic in society... until racism is challenged and professionals take on a preventative approach then many young carers will remain hidden.
>
> (Waul, 1998)

The youth worker should be prepared to tackle racism in its different forms, both on behalf of the young carers themselves, their families and the specific services they are providing. Other agencies and youth and community work managers may ask why Black and ethnic minority young carers require specific interventions and services, and the youth and community worker may well need to lobby for resources and to make a case to justify this approach.

In many cases people's understanding of the term 'care' can differ from background and culture. Within the family some people may perceive caring for someone as a duty based on love and respect, whilst others may experience resentment at the tasks they have to undertake. Therefore we must ensure that we do not over-generalise about cultures and religions and their attitudes to caring; families differ and attitudes will differ also. For instance it has been suggested that:

> ...with the breakdown of extended family support structures there is an issue of young Asian carers not wanting to care despite outside and familial expectations, and the idea somehow they're being 'groomed' for the caring role.
>
> (Gill; 1998)

Any work with young carers needs to be undertaken in close liaison with the family and an understanding and non-judgmental approach should be adopted, whilst being clear that the focus for involvement is the young person's welfare. Often it will not be possible to divorce this from the welfare of the family as a whole, so it is essential that youth and community workers talk to families and other professionals to share concerns and information, and make appropriate interventions.

Gender

The assumption that girls and young women should take the main caring role has implications for girls and young women from ethnic minority backgrounds as in wider society, i.e. historically, girls and young women have been expected to undertake the role of carers in the family. Youth workers, and in indeed all welfare professionals, should be wary of reinforcing the notion of young women as better and more acceptable carers by using the justification that this it is endorsed and determined by the race, religion and culture of families.

Whilst youth workers should strive to demonstrate a respect for culture and religion, these should not become the determining factors of their work with young people that override all others, in particular if they are detrimental to the well-being of the young people they are working with.

These can be challenging issues to work with but the responsibility of youth and community workers should be with the needs of the young person and the family. A large part of work with Black and ethnic minority young carers may involve questioning and working with welfare professionals and family expectations.

If caring for someone in the home puts undue pressure and stress on children and young people, in particular girls and young women, then these need to be addressed. For instance, this may involve developing programmes of single-sex activities for girls and young women, which are acceptable to parents and of benefit to girls and young women, recognising the specific needs of this target group in a supportive environment.

Youth Work with Young Carers

Youth work has been defined in the following way:

> *To work with young people to facilitate their personal, social and educational development, and to enable them to gain a voice, influence and place in society in a period of dependence to independence.*
>
> (NYA, 1999)

The focus on work with young carers is on their personal, social and educational development. It is not to enable young people to be better carers. It is to allow them the space to develop as children and young people in the transition to adulthood and independence, and to enable young carers to gain equal access to the same educational opportunities as experienced by their peers.

A number of principles underpin quality youth work with young carers, and as such the following issues should be considered:

- *Participation*: any programme should be decided with the young carers themselves, encouraging them to play an active role in any decision-making processes. This will promote ownership of the project by the young people themselves, encourage personal development and enable more appropriate activities to be developed.

- *Voluntary attendance*: young people have a choice about their free time, they are not obliged to attend and if they do not have a sense of ownership of the project and its activities they may decide not to attend.

- *Informal education*: any work needs to enable young people to develop skills, knowledge and feelings that help them to develop as individuals, and to play a active role in society as they choose.

- *Equal opportunities and challenging inequality*: any work with young carers needs to be developed within a framework of equal opportunities, ensuring the participation of young carers from all backgrounds. In practice this will mean that particular communities and groups of young people will need to be targeted. Any information and materials should be produced to be appropriate for the age and culture of the young carers you are working with and targeting. Structures should be created to enable young people to influence any activities they become involved in. Similarly any programme should be monitored to ensure it does not exclude particular groups. Good practice would suggest that working in partnership with other existing community and voluntary groups and statutory services can be an effective approach. Consideration should be given to whether specific services, information or groups may be required to meet the needs of young carers from distinct communities.

- *Diversity*: young carers exist in all sections of the community and as such will have different needs. Work with young carers needs to start from the reality of life for them as young people, whilst taking in to account their specific needs.

Working in Partnership

Local voluntary agencies are taking the lead in supporting young carers. However these projects must work in a multi-agency environment to ensure that young carers are identified and targeted and that their needs are met. A range of statutory agencies have contact with, and responsibility for, work with young carers. These include social services, education welfare, schoolteachers, health, youth, and community and play services. Multi-agency working should aim to ensure that all professionals in an agency are aware of young carers issues, ways of identifying young carers, and, most importantly, which agency to refer young carers to.

A number or organisations support national programmes of work with young carers; including the Princess Royal Trust for Carers, NCH Action for Children, the Children's Society and the Carers National Association. This support tends to be in the form of research, financial aid to projects, national conferences and networking events. The Carers National Association performs a lobbying role with government departments and other key agencies on the behalf of all carers. In spite of, and perhaps because of, the diverse range of agencies involved in work with young carers there are currently no nationally agreed standards for working with young carers in either the statutory or voluntary sectors.

Referrals, Disclosures and Confidentiality

Young carers may be referred to a local project or service from all of the agencies mentioned above. In most cases this means young carers will be in contact with social services who will be aware of their home situation. Young carers are children in need and social services have a responsibility to ensure support is available for them.

However if a young carer refers themselves to a service or project, as a result of out reach work or publicity, social services may not know of their situation. Therefore a youth worker may be the first professional to become aware of the young carer's situation. If this is the case the youth worker will need to contact social services to inform them of the young carer in order to provide help and support to the young person and their family.

This can be a potentially difficult area if the young person wants their situation to remain confidential. Therefore when providing any activities or services for young carers, it is essential to have clear ground-rules and procedures in place to ensure young people are aware that should certain issues be disclosed these will have to be acted on and referred to social services in line with standard Child Protection guidelines. This may result in them being identified as 'children in need': Children Act 1989.

Resource Implications

Working alongside other agencies, in particular schools, social services, education welfare, health authorities, NHS trusts and the voluntary sector will present opportunities for accessing funding from different sources and making joint funding bids to grant-making bodies, although attempting to bring together different agency agendas and professional approaches can be time-consuming and challenging.

Experience has shown that the best agency to host a group of young carers is one that already has operating procedures for working with vulnerable young people; there is no need to

---

Key Questions

1. How can caring responsibilities affect young people's lives?
2. How do we identity and target young carers?
3. What issues do we need to consider when planning a programme of work with young carers?
4. What might be some of the potential blocks to developing work with young carers?
5. What statutory provisions are there for young carers?

're-invent' the wheel and any project aimed at young carers needs to operate within 'safe practice' guidelines.

Work with young carers will require a high ratio of adults to young carers e.g. one adult to eight young people. An intense level of 'face to face' support may be required, often involving small group work and counselling.

Any young carers group will need an accessible and suitable venue in which to meet as, well as the other practical considerations associated with a youth group meeting on a regular basis. Separate quiet areas for 'one to one' support and counselling may be needed.

In addition, transporting carers to and from any group meeting or activity will be an important consideration as it can remove any potential barriers to young carers attending, such as lack of access to transport, and can also encourage attendance, allowing young carers to feel more comfortable about leaving their cared for relative.

Any service should aim to be free at the point of delivery to young carers enabling equal access for all that want to attend.

References

DfEE (1999). *Pupil Support Circular 10/99*. London: DfEE.

Department of Health (1995). *Carers Act (Recognition and Services)*. London: HMSO.

Department of Health (1989). *Children Act*. London: HMSO.

Gill, S. (1998). *The National Handbook of Young Carers Projects*. Carers National Association and Young Carers Research Group.

Laming, H. (1995). *Letter to Directors of Social Services on Young Carers*, 28th April. Social Services Inspectorate.

NYA (1998). *Occupational Standards in Youth Work*. NYA.

Sanchez, D. (1995). The Needs of Black Young Carers. In *Young Carers: Back Them Up*. London: Community Care and Carers National Association.

Waul, D. (1998). *The National Handbook of Young Carers Projects*. London: Carers National Association and Young Carers Research Group.

Key agencies

Carers National Association
20–25 Glasshouse Yard,
London EC1A 4JS
Tel: 020 74908818
CarersLine: 0345 573369 lo-call
www.carersnorth.demon.co.uk
E-mail: info@ukcarers.org

The Princess Royal Trust for Carers
142 Minories
London EC2N 1LB
Tel: 020 74807788
www.carers.org
E-mail: info@carers.org

NCH Action for Children
85 Highbury Park
London N5 1UD
Tel: 020 72262033
www.nch.afc.org.uk

Barnados
Tanners Lane
Barkingside
Ilford
Essex 1G6 1QG
Tel: 020 85508822
www.barnados.org.uk

h Homelessness

Qasir

---

1. 'Homeless young people' means the 'hidden homeless' (those living with friends or relatives) as well as those sleeping rough.

2. Homelessness is more than just a housing problem; homeless young people are at risk and often require other services such as support, advice and counselling.

3. Family conflict, violence and abuse are the most common reasons for leaving home but those leaving care are up to 60 times more likely to become homeless than other young people.

4. Youth homelessness is a rural as well as a city problem.

5. A homeless young person may be assessed for housing if they are:
   - 'vulnerable' and in 'priority need' (Housing Act 1996)
   - a 'child in need' (Children Act 1989)

   but restrictions on the nature and cost of housing, severely reduces accommodation options.

Introduction

Youth homelessness, while not a new phenomenon, first came to public notice in the UK in the 1960s when Ken Loach's drama-documentary *Cathy Come Home*, focused national attention on the homelessness problem. The squalid conditions in which Cathy and her children were shown to be living created the impetus for the creation of Shelter, the homelessness pressure group, while the Ministry of Housing was galvanised into improving conditions in temporary accommodation. The 1975 television documentary *Johnny Go Home* was instrumental in exposing the risks of homelessness for young people going to London and placed the problem of youth homelessness onto the public agenda. It was this concern for young people sleeping on the streets in the West End of London that led to the opening of the Centrepoint Night Shelter in the 1970s. Centrepoint was the first charity to raise youth homelessness as a specific issue and campaign about it.

The advent of youth homelessness must be understood in the context of the expectation in western culture that young people will live independently when they become adults. Once they leave school they are expected to make their own way in the world by seeking employment or going

to college. Leaving home is regarded as the next logical step in this process of growing up. However, for some young people, leaving home is not planned and is very often precipitated by a particular negative event or chain of events which leads to them running from or being 'thrown out' of their parental homes, foster homes or residential care. It is important to understand the distinction between normal patterns of adolescent development and growth towards independence, and the experiences of the young people who find themselves homeless.

Partly as a result of the Thatcher administration's housing policies, the 1980s and 1990s saw a dramatic rise in youth homelessness in the UK. Large-scale youth unemployment led to fears in government circles that the benefits paid to young people would put the social security budget under stress. This concern was expressed in the right-wing media by describing young people who were living off the state as being on the 'Costa del Dole' and the furore whipped-up around this issue culminated in the Social Security Act 1988 which withdrew state benefits from under-18s living away from the parental home. Responsibility for young people was now shifted from the state, to the family. However, the failure to clarify what 'parental responsibility' actually meant for this group of young people and the acute pressures this legislation placed upon the most vulnerable, contributed to a significant increase of youth homelessness.

A survey conducted by Centrepoint in the eight months following the implementation of the Social Security Act 1988 found that the numbers of 16–19 year olds without proper accommodation in London had increased by 35 per cent. Their predicament was made even worse by major changes to the board and lodgings regulations in 1989, and changes in the funding arrangements for housing association hostels in the Housing Act 1989. Of the young people entering Centrepoint nightshelter in 1994/5, 41 per cent had no source of income and 43 per cent were receiving no state benefits (Pitts, 2001). As a result, the age of economic independence for most young people was effectively raised to somewhere in the mid-20s. Subsequent minimum wage legislation introduced by New Labour established a 'transitional' wage to be paid to under-22s with adult levels of social security benefits only being paid at 25 years.

A Problem of Definition

It is difficult to get a true picture of the extent of the problem, as there is little agreement about what constitutes youth homelessness. In the UK the term is usually taken to refer to homelessness among young single people between the ages of 16 and 25 years. However, it has been in the interest of governments to define homelessness as narrowly as possible, and they have usually employed the term to describe rooflessness, the state of having no accommodation whatsoever or 'sleeping rough'.

In 1981 a Department of the Environment study suggested a very broad definition incorporating the notion of the 'hidden homeless' (hidden in so far as they are not officially recognised as homeless), as well as the 'visible' homeless. The study defined homelessness as involving persons:

- Being without immediate shelter.
- Facing the loss of shelter within one month.
- Living in a situation of no security of tenure and being forced to seek alternative accommodation, e.g. potential dischargees from institutions of all types, living temporarily with friends or relatives in overcrowded conditions, illegal tenancies.

- Living in reception centres, derelict buildings, squats, hostels, bed and breakfast hotels.

The Scale of the Problem

Due to the inaccuracy of official statistics, the exact number of young people who are homeless in Britain is unknown; however a number of organisations have tried to estimate the extent of the problem. *The National Inquiry into Youth Homelessness* estimated that in 1995 33,000 16–21 year olds and 246,000 16–25 year olds were homeless. Their findings suggest that 1 in 20 of the young people in the age range are likely to experience homelessness at some point. It is estimated that in one year alone 25,900 young people were homeless in central London. (Smith, 1996).

A Social Exclusion Unit report *Rough Sleeping* (1998) found that young people are over-represented among those who sleep rough. It estimated that approximately 25 per cent of the 10,000 people who sleep on the streets in England, in the course of a year, are aged between 18 and 25. In recent years, there has been a considerable increase in homelessness among 16 and 17 year olds. One third of all the homeless young people in a national survey undertaken in 1996 were aged below 18. Of young people admitted to the Centrepoint night shelter, 41 per cent were aged 16 and 17 and, as such, they had no automatic right to welfare benefits.

The Characteristics of the Young Homeless

London generates its own homeless young people but it also attracts many young people from other parts of the UK. In 1998–99, the London borough in which young people from Centrepoint's Berwick Street emergency shelter had most commonly slept rough in, was Westminster in which the 'West End' is situated. 51 young people with an average age of 18.5 years had slept rough for between three and four nights. The next most common boroughs were Hackney and Lambeth. An increasing proportion of the young homeless are female. Of those currently entering Centrepoint, 44 per cent are young women; a substantial majority is under 18.

Homelessness amongst Black and Asian young people tends to be less visible because unlike white young people, they tend not to end up sleeping rough. *Discounted Voices*, the first national survey into homelessness amongst young Black and Asian people, found these young people are disproportionately over-represented in hostels and bed and breakfast accommodation. Of young people entering Centrepoint, 43 per cent are Black or of mixed parentage.

Gay and lesbian young people are a group at particular risk of homelessness. One in nine gay and lesbian young people are evicted from their homes by their parents when they disclose their sexuality. These young people are also vulnerable to homelessness as a result of harassment by landlords and neighbours.

Running away from home may be a precursor to homelessness: 53 per cent of homeless young people interviewed had run away from home or care before the age of 16, and 85 per cent of these had done so more than once. (Craig et al., 1996). There are approximately 50,000 young people in the care of, or 'looked after' by local authorities in the UK at any given time and approximately 8,000 young people leave care each year. Despite the fact that 1 per cent of young people, under the age of 18, have been in care, between 20 per cent and 50 per cent of young homeless people have been 'looked after' by or in local authority care. Care leavers are up to 60 times more likely to become homeless, and are particularly over-represented among those sleeping rough or living in temporary accommodation (Evans, 1996).

A survey by the youth homelessness charity Centrepoint (1995) revealed that in 1994/95, 28 per cent of young people entering their nightshelter had previously been in care. Of these, 51 per cent had run away before they were 16. In a subsequent study of 39 care leavers, Centrepoint found that over half had been homeless immediately after leaving care, that nearly all of them had 'slept rough', and that 30 per cent had become homeless when social work help was withdrawn. In his study of 1,158 first admissions to the 'safe house' referred to above, Matthew Pitts (1992) noted that 36 per cent of first admissions had run from local authority with 75 per cent of 17 year olds having 'run' at least once before. The Centrepoint study of care leavers estimated that within six weeks, most young people living on the street would resort to crime, drugs or prostitution as a survival strategy.

Youth homelessness is not restricted to London and other big cities. Centrepoint's work around the country shows that there is serious incidence, including rough sleeping, in areas such as Devon, Cumbria and Warwickshire.

The Causes of Homelessness

In 1999, Safe in the City, the first pan-London initiative aimed at preventing youth homelessness, produced a homelessness study entitled *Taking Risks* (Bruegel and Smith, 1999). 195 homeless young people in London hostels aged 20 and below were interviewed. The study highlights the young people's negative experiences in their families and in school as key links in the chain of events, which leads to homelessness. The report notes that the routes into homelessness constitute an 'unhappily familiar set of landmarks; poverty, family instability and stress, problems at school and school exclusion'. The following factors have been linked at different times with a range of causes:

- low self-esteem
- poor literacy
- youth crime
- mental health problems
- teenage pregnancy
- unemployment

Research by Centrepoint in London in 1987 found that 52 per cent of the homeless young people approaching them for help had left their home for 'pull' reasons, like moving to find work or needing to establish their independence. However, by 1995 only 14 per cent had left for these reasons. The majority, 86 per cent, had been forced to leave due to 'push factors' such as violence, abuse, family breakdown and being thrown out. Some parents ask their children to leave when poverty means they have difficulty in supporting them. There is some evidence that same-gender step-relationships can be more problematic than the average adolescent relationship. Moreover, opposite-sex step-relationships are more likely to be abusive and there is evidence that step-relationships are significantly associated with running away and youth homelessness (Russell, 1986). The most stressful areas are divided loyalties and discipline. The conflicts that arise can lead stepchildren to leave home (Smith et al., 1997). In 1999, 40 per cent of homeless young women in touch with Centrepoint had experienced sexual or physical abuse in childhood (Centrepoint, 1999).

The Dangers of Homelessness

The homeless population is an unhealthy population and chest respiratory problems are *most* common amongst them. Homelessness often precipitates deterioration in young people's mental health in the form of the onset, or deepening of, anxiety and depression. One third of young people interviewed by the Mental Health Foundation in 1998 had attempted suicide at some point in their lives. Homeless young people experience loneliness, a loss of self-esteem and feelings of worthlessness. They are disproportionately prone to alcohol and drug misuse; 39 per cent of young people sleeping rough under the age of 25 had a drugs problem (DoE, 1993). As we have noted, after a relatively short time on the streets, a disproportionate number of homeless young people will turn to crime or prostitution. On the other hand, homelessness puts these young people at far greater risk of violence, and physical and sexual abuse. Lack of money, leads to hunger, which may lead on to begging or the commission of committing petty offences. Of the young homeless interviewed for a study in 1996, 52 per cent had committed some form of crime, mainly involving theft or violence.

Homelessness Legislation

The Housing Act 1996 places a duty on local authorities to provide information about homelessness and the prevention of homelessness. However a number of barriers exist which must be overcome if a homeless young person is housed. They must first satisfy local authorities that they are:

- Homeless or threatened with homelessness within 28 days.
- In 'priority need' i.e. families with children, pregnant women, victims of fire or flood, or those vulnerable by reason of illness, disability or age (S.189).
- They are not 'intentionally homeless'.
- They do not have a 'local connection' with another area: if there is a connection elsewhere that other authority will have responsibility (S.198).

Discretion in interpreting *these* guidelines resides with individual local authorities and there are significant variations in their decisions about what constitutes a priority case. As many as one in five Social Service Departments do not assess 16 and 17 year olds for housing need. Similarly, housing departments will not accept 16 and 17 year olds as being in 'priority need' because of their age. Section 14.10 states that vulnerability should not 'automatically be judged on age alone' and this has allowed housing departments considerable room for legal and administrative manoeuvre. Even if a local authority accepts that a young person is homeless and in 'priority need' it may nonetheless refuse to house them on the basis that they are 'intentionally homeless' if they may have outstanding rent arrears.

For many homeless young people the transition to independent living includes a number of 'false starts'. These young people need advice and support in following correct tenancy procedures if they are not to jeopardise their chances of gaining access to 'social housing'. Although social services and housing departments operate under different legislative frameworks, the Housing Act 1996 places a duty on them to work together in the case of young care leavers. The Labour government amended the Act in 1997 by taking away the guidance placed on the housing authority to provide suitable temporary accommodation for a minimum period of two years (Section 193(3)), and further extended their duties to include young people leaving care up to 21 years of age. The DETR, (Department of the Environment, Transport and the Regions) will shortly issue guidance to local housing authorities, making clear that with very few exceptions, all care leavers and homeless 16 and 17 year olds, without back-up support, should be regarded as 'vulnerable' and have priority rights to be housed in suitable accommodation. Also, the Rough Sleepers' Unit and the DoH will be setting up a special team to look at the effectiveness of care-leaving packages in place across London.

The Act has also introduced important housing benefit changes, which has had an impact on young people's ability to access decent accommodation in the private rented sector. Young homeless people are traditionally highly dependent on the private rented sector, and are competing for an increasingly scarce resource. Housing benefit is linked to income support and meets the rent if it is assessed to be at, or below the 'local reference rent'. The local reference rent is the average rent for mid-priced accommodation in the area but such an assessment takes no account of the quality of the accommodation. Those whose rents are considered to be above a reasonable market rent have to make up the shortfall. This is a particular problem for young people because of the reduced level of benefit they receive. Those aged 16 or 17 are not generally entitled to benefits as they are expected to go on a training scheme. At 16 years they are paid a Job Seekers' Allowance of £29.50. Those without a training place are paid discretionary payments known as Severe Hardship payments, awarded to young people for a period of 8 weeks at a time. Young people have to prove estrangement from their parents to be awarded this. At 17 years it rises to £35 and to £37.50 for those aged between 18 and 24 years. With an estimated subsistence level of £134.84 (excluding housing costs) for a single person over 25 in 1995, it is clear why many socially disadvantaged young people are likely to fall into arrears and face eviction and why landlords are reluctant to let properties to those under 25 years. Young people under the age of 25 are further disadvantaged as they are only eligible for housing benefit to meet the cost of **shared** accommodation. This has raised issues of safety for some very vulnerable young people, with few social skills, and who find sharing difficult. Making them share increases the risk of tenancy breakdown.

The Children Act 1989 was, among other things, designed to offer a safety net for homeless young people in need. The Act placed the onus on social services departments to assess the needs of young people and, in certain circumstances, to accommodate them. This was an important innovation, designed to prevent the drift into homelessness, which characterised so many young people's experience of leaving local authority care. In practice, however, young people continue to be passed between departments with nobody accepting responsibility. Recent reports from the CHAR (The Campaign for the Homeless and Roofless) found that only three-quarters of councils had a policy of assessing all 16 and 17 year olds who approached them for accommodation under the Children Act. Yet, section 24 of the Act makes it clear that the social services department has responsibility for young people leaving care and outlines their duty to give 'advice, assistance and befriending until the young person is 21'. However, disproportionate numbers of care leavers and those who have spent time in care continue to end up as homeless, indicating that the state, in its role as guardian of these young people, is failing to meet their needs.

Government Initiatives

The government's *Rough Sleepers Initiative* (RSI), was launched in 1991, with a remit to provide emergency accommodation, including winter shelters, and access to 'move-on' accommodation for an estimated 1–3,000 people sleeping rough in London. In 1996 this was extended to other towns and cities designated as action zones. The RSI and the subsequent increase in the number of London hostel places has decreased the incidence of rough sleeping in London, but it has done nothing to stem the flow of newly homeless young people onto the streets. This is because the RSI does not target homeless or potentially homeless young people; just rough sleepers.

In response to the Social Exclusion Unit's 1998 report, the government has established the Rough Sleepers Unit so as to address the high incidence of young people sleeping rough. The DETR has also launched a Youth Homelessness Action Partnership to bring together representatives of central government, local government and the voluntary sector. Its aims are to produce an agreed definition of youth homelessness and an estimate of the numbers involved; to identify what works in tackling and preventing youth homelessness, to disseminate good practice, and to contribute towards the evaluation of the impact of government policies on youth homelessness.

The young person's Safe Stop project is part of the Rough Sleepers Unit's strategy to reduce the numbers of people sleeping rough to as near to zero as possible and by at least two-thirds by 2002. The aim of the Safe Stop project is to provide an emergency safety net for young vulnerable rough sleepers in a secure and safe environment, with the intention of providing opportunities to return home or securing access to accommodation or other specialist services as appropriate.

New Initiatives

The Supporting People Programme will offer housing support services to a wide range of vulnerable people. It promotes housing-related services which are cost effective and reliable, and

which complement existing care services.
Supporting People is a working partnership of local government, service users and support agencies. The programme is a key element in the government's drive against social exclusion, and will be developed in a way which complements the Modernising Social Services agenda, the Crime Prevention agenda, and the recently announced proposals of the Housing Green Paper. The aim is to improve the quality and effectiveness of these support services by:

- Focusing provision on local need.
- Improving the range and quality of support. In particular the previous link of support services to tenure will be broken, so that more 'floating support' may be introduced where appropriate.
- Integrating 'support' with wider local strategies, particularly within health, social services, housing, and neighbourhood renewal and community safety.
- Monitoring and inspecting quality and effectiveness in a more structured way.
- Introducing effective decision making and administration. This will include changing the arrangements for funding.

The Transitional Housing Benefit Scheme has now started. After 2003 the new scheme will continue to develop in partnership with the Department of Social Security and other government departments.

Delivery and Evaluation

The range of accommodation available to homeless young people currently includes:

- Emergency short stay accommodation, which may include the provision of free meals, clothing, showers, laundry, advice and medical facilities. Some projects now have a range of on-site facilities, including an IT room, resources room, life skills kitchen and counselling facilities.
- Hostels offering medium to long-term accommodation.
- Shared housing which usually offers a single room with shared facilities.
- Supported lodgings for young people with mental health and drug problems.
- Independent living projects which offer assistance with budgeting, cooking, and

sustaining a tenancy.
- Bed and breakfast hotels.
- Private rented accommodation, although high market rents mean that this is generally of poor quality with few facilities and little security of tenure.
- Permanent accommodation from local authority housing departments and housing associations. It is unusual for single young people under 25 years of age to be offered this type of accommodation.

In addition, specialist or separate provision and support are available for young people from black and other minority ethnic communities, young women and young lesbians and gay men. The Ashiana Project provides safe accommodation for women from the South Asian, Turkish and Iranian communities, who have experienced physical, sexual, mental or emotional abuse. Support includes short term crisis counselling, advice on benefits, health care, education, employment, and applications for re-housing and accessing legal advice.

The Foyer movement, a model based on the French network of *foyers pour jeunes travailleurs* (hostels for young workers), is running projects alongside the government's New Deal programme for unemployed 18–24 year olds. This usually takes the form of a partnership between government, the private sector, the voluntary sector and a number of housing associations. These projects provide easy access to relatively cheap accommodation, which is linked to training or employment. Centrepoint's Camberwell Foyer is an example of this integrated approach, where residents meet with a vocational guidance worker to draw up an action plan within two weeks of moving in, and are given on-site training in 'job ready' skills. However, Youth Aid's evaluation of the foyer experience (Chatrik, 1994) found that the foyers they reviewed offered little more than the unpopular government training schemes. The report also expressed concerns about the capacity of foyers to provide the types of intensive support required by more vulnerable young people. Drop-in services offered by agencies such as CLASH (Central London Action for Street Health) and The London Connection, while not offering accommodation, provide excellent facilities and services during the day which homeless young people are able to utilise. CLASH focuses its work on harm minimisation. 'Works', syringes, condoms etc., can be purchased here, and there is a drugs advice team on hand. Doctors and nurses are available for service users and to advise and support other staff. The London Connection offers 'drop-in' sessions throughout the week for specific target groups such as homeless women and young men selling sex.

Preventative Work

Safe in the City is an independent charity set up by Centrepoint and the Peabody Trust and partially funded through the government's Single Regeneration Budget. Over a six year period the organisation will work closely with, and invest in, 30 charities and eight London local authorities (Lambeth, Waltham Forest, Newham, Hackney, Tower Hamlets, Brent, Greenwich and Islington) to provide support for over 12,000 young people and their families. Together, they will identify successful models of service delivery to prevent young people from becoming homeless. Each service will be monitored and evaluated for its effectiveness. The programme aims to provide a joined-up and structured support pathway for young people at risk which includes three important interconnected elements:

- *Skills and employability*: mentoring projects will assist in basic literacy and numeracy skills, and peer education schemes where young people can learn from their own and other's experiences.
- *Personal development*: a focus on confidence building, acquiring social communication skills as well as skills in budgeting, prioritising and advice on hygiene, nutrition, benefits, tenancy rights and how to maintain a tenancy.
- *Family support*: this will offer individual support as well as solutions focused on family interventions. Family conflicts can be addressed and managed by using mediation techniques. The NCH project, Turnaround, is one such service which works with young runaways and is based at the London Refuge, a certified 'safe house', under Section 51 of the Children Act 1989, for young runaways under the age of 16. Family mediation addresses family conflict in a safe environment in which all parties have an opportunity to express their views. The project aims to facilitate negotiations in

order to arrive at an agreement which all family members can live with. In this way it is hoped communication will be restored and conflict resolved, thus preventing young people running away again. In certain circumstances, of course, a return home would not be in the young person's best interests and staff are ever mindful of the child protection dimensions of their task.

Safe in the City recognise that multiple and connected problems experienced in childhood consistently put young people at risk in early adulthood. Therefore in order to turn crisis intervention to crisis prevention, a co-ordinated and holistic response to the reasons why young people become disaffected, excluded and homeless is required.

Responses to Youth Homelessness

Clearly, the model of intervention adopted by agencies and individual workers in their work with homeless, or potentially homeless young people, will influence the experience and outcome for those young people. Harding (1999), in a study examining the relationship between beliefs about youth homelessness and the steps being taken by local authorities to tackle the problem, has identified five models of response:.

- *The Individual Culpability Model* arises from a school of thought which sees recipients of welfare services as deviant and undeserving. A young person is regarded as selfish, in opting to become destitute, and so evading their obligations.
- *The Social Pathology Model* takes a more sympathetic view in regarding the homeless young person as 'socially inadequate, maladjusted and psychologically disturbed'. They are believed to be acting in a pathological manner as a result of their background or genetic make-up.
- *The Child Model* sees the young person as a child and their homelessness as arising from immaturity and naïveté.
- *The Spiritual/Religious Model* regards the homeless person as 'a sinner to be saved' and homelessness as a symptom of the spiritual poverty of society.

- *The Political Model* identifies the causes of youth homelessness as political, social and economic rather than personal. Individuals are believed to have a right to accommodation and the factors which bring about homelessness are those which prevent them from exercising this right, e.g. shortage of suitably priced accommodation, job scarcity, and inadequate benefits levels.

Youth homelessness is currently high on the political agenda. New policies are still in the early stages of implementation and development but it appears that both central and local governments are beginning to identify more closely with Harding's *Political Model*. This policy focus will hopefully shift the apparently ingrained tendency amongst moral commentators, elements of the media and sections of the British public who exclude socially, pathologise and punish the young homeless 'for not fulfilling their citizenship obligations, even though the state fails to fulfil its duties of nurturance and protection towards them' (Carlen, 1996).

Partnership and Empowerment

The principle of partnership should be paramount in any 'inclusionary' strategy for the young homeless. Consulting young people on a particular issue or proposal allows them to express their views and to have an effective voice. This has the advantage of gathering new perspectives and increases the sense of ownership of an idea or project amongst its intended beneficiaries. Partnership can take the form of *representation* as is the case in Centrepoint's 'Real Deal' programme,

in which young people's views are gathered, listened to and acted upon where appropriate. Alternatively, participation can be in the form of *joint decision-making* or *self managing* where young people have effective control over finances and forward planning, thus allowing them to change, influence, direct or control their own activities. Greater participation allows greater responsibility for the decisions. This has benefits of educating and empowering young people, increasing their self-confidence and self-esteem and improving young people's communication skills.

Participation can also give organisations a new impetus and an opportunity to work beyond established ways of doing things. Advisory Group Meetings are a good example of joint working, where many different organisations and agencies come together to feed in their ideas and viewpoints on a particular issue or project. Joint decision making can ensure a more creative approach to problem solving which will reflect what young people really want or really need. This more open style of education is based on equality, trust and mutual respect for each other and is based upon 'continual dialogue' which 'ensures that both play an active part in the process' (Rosseter in Jeffs and Smith, 1987).

Resource Implications

By adopting a multi-disciplinary approach, local authorities can ensure that their education, leisure, economic development, social services and housing policies mesh into an integrated and coherent strategy for prevention of youth homelessness.

Key Questions

1. Have you consulted and encouraged each young person to participate in making decisions and finding solutions?

2. Are you working in partnership with other agencies in a holistic way?

3. Has a full assessment of youth housing need and support required under the criteria of the Housing Act 1996, and the Children Act 1989 taken place in your local authority area?

4. Are you offering basic life skills training, including budgeting skills and benefits advice, in order to support young people in their accommodation?

5. Can early support to young people in their schools and communities prevent them running away and becoming homeless?

Councils are in a good position to take the lead in co-ordinating coherent complementary programmes. Central government needs to re-direct money out of traditional professional streams and into local partnership work, focusing on 'outcomes' rather than more narrowly defined 'outputs'. Corporate policies and clear departmental procedures will ensure an up-to-date inter-agency network of information about agency policies, procedures and services. A common register of information and support services, and a daily up-dated listing of accommodation vacancies can be shared via the Internet.

References

Bruegel, and Smith (1999). T*aking Risks: An Analysis of the Risks of Homelessness for Young People in London*. London: Safe in the City.

Carlen, P. (1996). *Jigsaw: a Political Criminology of Youth Homelessness.* Open University Press.

Centrepoint (1995). *Statistics: April 1995–March 1995.* London: Centrepoint.

Centrepoint (1999). *Statistics: April 1998–March 1999.* London: Centrepoint.

Centrepoint (2000). *Annual Report 1998–1999.* London: Centrepoint.

Chatrik, B. (1995). *Taking their Chances: Education, Training and Employment Opportunities for Young People.* London: Youth Aid.

Craig et al. (1996). *Off to a Bad Start.* The Mental Health Foundation.

DoE (1993). *Rough Sleepers Initiative: An Evaluation Report.* London: DoE.

Evans, A. (1996). *We Don't Choose to be Homeless: Report of the National Inquiry into Preventing Youth Homelessness.* London: CHAR.

Fawcett, J. (2000). Youth Homelessness: Invaluable Lessons. *Housing Today.*

Harding, J. (1999). Explanations of, and Responses to, Youth Homelessness in Local Authority Housing Departments. In *Local Government Studies,* 25(3) pp. 58–69.

Hutson and Liddiard (1994). *Youth Homelessness: The Construction of Social Issues.* Basingstoke: Macmillan.

Jeffs, T., and Smith, M. (1987). *Youth Work.* Basingstoke: Macmillan.

Pitts, J. (2001). *The New Politics of Youth Crime: Discipline or Solidarity.* Basingstoke: Macmillan.

Pitts, M. (1992). *Somewhere to Run.* BA dissertation. Exeter University.

Russell, D. (1986). *The Street Trauma.* New York: Basic Books.

Smith, et al. (1997). *Young Homeless People and their Families.* York: Joseph Rowntree Foundation.

Smith, J. et al. (1996). *Bright Lights and Homelessness.* London: YMCA.

Social Exclusion Unit (1998). *Rough Sleeping Report.* London: HMSO.

Further Reading

Evans, A. (1996). *We Don't Choose to be Homeless: Report of the National Inquiry into Preventing Youth Homelessness.* CHAR.

Hutson, S., and Liddiard, M. (1994). *Youth Homelessness: The Construction of a Social Issue.* Basingstoke: Macmillan.

McCluskey, J. (1994). *Breaking the Spiral: Ten myths on the Children Act and Youth Homelessness.* CHAR.

Nistala, H., and Dane, K. (2000). *Staying Safe.* Safe in the City.

Safe on the Streets Research Team (1999). *Still Running: Children on the Streets in the UK.* The Children's Society.

Smith, J. (2000). *Hidden Statistics.* London: Centrepoint.

Young People, Drugs and Youth Work

Gerard Murray and Karen Shillitoe

31

Key Points

1. Prevalence rates for youth drug use in the UK remains the highest in the EU, with that use, and the cultures around it, remaining a 'normal' part of the lives of many young people, despite the government's emphasis on crime-control-oriented prevention.
2. Only a small minority of drug users, mainly heroin and crack users, experience major and lasting health or social problems directly related to their drug consumption.
3. Of drug users, both the unproblematic majority and the problematic minority remain out of contact with existing drug agencies.
4. Whilst existing social and health care agencies need to refocus their efforts to meet the needs of the problematic minority, youth and community work may be the most appropriate agency to engage with the great number of young people participating in 'normalised' drug use.
5. Youth and community workers need to make closer links with existing statutory and non-statutory agencies as a way of improving their own practice, and to inform those agencies about the needs of their young people.

Introduction

Youth workers will be aware that drug use is widespread and a growing feature of the lives of the young people with whom they have contact. They will also be aware that given its hidden, necessarily secretive, nature, it is also a feature of young people's lives which crime control, social welfare and youth serving agencies have limited access to or information about. There is a resultant tendency for this area of adolescent behaviour to be surrounded with a slight air of mystery.

This chapter will try to demystify drug use by young people by outlining the patterns of that use, highlighting the responses of the agencies (primarily those in the fields of health, social services and criminal justice) to the spread of drug use and suggesting some ways that youth and community workers can develop strategies to engage constructively with young drug users.

For the purposes of this chapter, our argument relates primarily to the consumption of illicit substances, although it is understood that the use of licensed substances, such as tobacco and alcohol and others such as solvents may pose an equal or greater risk of harm to their consumer.

Recent surveys have shown that not only are the number of young drug users increasing, their drug use also appears to be starting at an earlier age. This is particularly so for heroin use, for whom the average age of onset has fallen from around 17 or 18 in the late 1980s, to around 15 in the most recent surveys. Moreover, there is a growing trend towards the use of crack cocaine . The use of crack and heroin raises particular concerns because of the serious health and crime problems associated with the pursuit and administration of these highly addictive substances (HAS, 1996; Hough, 1995). Yet, despite the critical social problems associated with heroin and crack, to which we shall return, practitioners should be aware firstly that users of these substances retain a largely discrete identity within a broad and complex spectrum of drug users as a whole and that the patterns of use or 'drug careers' within that spectrum, the movement from cannabis to heroin use for example, is neither as predictable nor as inevitable as some media and government commentators would have us believe.

Patterns of Illicit Substance Use

Statistics point to a pattern of drug use across the EU in which the UK figures prominently in a number of areas. Whereas in EU-wide terms, the proportion of under 25s having 'ever' used cannabis was between 20 per cent and 30 per cent, in the UK that figure ranged from 25 per cent to 50 per cent. This disparity is repeated across a range of substances. Amphetamine use amongst 15 to 16 year olds is 2–4 per cent) in the EU as a whole and 8–9 per cent in the UK. For LSD use amongst school children this data shows, 13–14 per cent in the UK, 5–6 per cent in Spain and Italy and 2 per cent or less in the other states. Ecstasy use, is 1 per cent in Finland, 5–6 per cent in Belgium and Spain and 8–9 per cent in the UK (EMCDDA, 1999). Whilst there are no EU figures to compare with the most recent UK study on young heroin and crack users, we can safely assume that Britain's disproportionately problematic situation will remain constant despite the otherwise relatively low estimate of 1 per cent of under 24s using either crack or heroin (Home Office, 1998). The statistics outlined here are interesting in two respects. Firstly they show that the UK, despite adopting a strongly punitive line on substance misuse, continues to report increasing and significantly higher rates of drug use than other EU states. Secondly, it is evident that within the broader picture there is a clear demarcation between the numbers using what are commonly considered to be 'soft' drugs and the far smaller numbers reported to be using 'hard' drugs like heroin and crack. This suggests that a large number of young drug users in the UK are making choices about the substances they consume and that this drug use is becoming 'normalised'.

The Normalisation Thesis

The normalisation thesis, presented most cogently by Parker et al., (1998), builds upon the evidence of the growing consumption of 'soft' drugs by young people. Normalisation refers to a growing acceptance within youth culture of the 'recreational' use of soft drugs, mainly cannabis, but also nitrites, amphetamines and, more equivocally, LSD and Ecstasy, and the ways in which these young drug users draw a clear distinction between themselves and the users of heroin and crack. This distinction is akin to that conventionally drawn between social drinkers and alcoholics. Parker et al. point to 'vibrant and informed drug cultures', linked in large part with dance cultures, in which participants indulge in essentially recreational, situational, drug use, which is generally relatively unproblematic in terms of their health and social and professional lives. Parker et al. write:

Abstainers, former users and prospective tryers are able and willing to recount drugs stories
based on drugs episodes involving siblings, friends, acquaintances and the local pub, club, party scene. Drugs are real to them, they no longer belong to an unknown subcultural world.
                                                    (1998)

This normalisation of drug use, presented by Parker et al. (1998) is a phenomenon which youth and community workers will probably be aware of amongst the young people with whom they have contact. Whilst it is a thesis which we largely accept, it does present certain difficulties to the practitioners. Firstly, as Shiner and Newburn (1996) argue, the normalisation thesis tends to underplay the prevalence of negative opinions about drug use amongst young people, particularly in those instances where the respondents may accept substance use as an inevitable, but not wholly acceptable, aspect of their peer relations. Secondly the implicit notion of an informed market of young people 'clued-up' about the health aspects of the largely unmonitored substances they are consuming is one which conflicts with the evidence of many Ecstasy- and other drug-related deaths. It is not so much the active chemicals in the drug that lead to fatality, but rather the user's misguided response to the drug's side effects, as in the kidney failure from the over-intake of water in the case of Ecstasy. Thirdly, whilst the normalisation thesis correctly highlights the moral dimension of drug use by, for example, demonstrating that there is no inevitable pathway from cannabis use to heroin consumption, there remains the fact that one of the central features of almost all drug use is its illegality. The necessity for young people to become involved with illegal dealer networks is, perhaps, one of the most hazardous aspects of drug use. Parker et al.'s assert that:

...drug dealing...is perceived by most young users as a sign of trust and friendship. 'Sorting' friends and acquaintances is rarely perceived as a serious criminal offence.   (1998)

Nevertheless, it is evident that this picture of a drug market characterised by mutuality and solidarity will not pertain far beyond ground level. Beyond the network of 'friends and acquaintances' lies a relatively flat criminal hierarchy, which quickly connects with global drug traffickers.

The dangers here are, in our view, two-fold. Firstly it is our belief that the proximity of one illegal market for 'soft' drugs to the other for 'hard' drugs will lead inevitably to a certain degree of cross-over, whether that be from an individual tendency to experiment or from other pressures associated with the heroin and crack market. Secondly, despite the moral codes of the street-level market, the reality is that the consumption of all substances under discussion in this paper is to some extent illegal and, as such, subject to legal sanction. Indeed, possession of Ecstasy, a 'Class A' drug, may well lead to the imposition of lengthy custodial sentences, similar to those imposed upon heroin users or suppliers. The response of the criminal justice agencies will be discussed in the following section, but this discussion will conclude on the patterns of substance misuse with a brief look at two of the most criminogenic substances, heroin and crack (Hough, 1995).

Heroin and Crack

Heroin and crack users constitute a small proportion of all drug users and an infinitesimal proportion of the population as a whole. However, the highly addictive qualities of these substances create social and health problems out of all proportion to the numbers using the drug. These problems can only increase because, as already noted, greater numbers of younger users are now becoming opiate users. Users experience physical and psychological dependence quicker and remain dependent for longer than for any other illicit substance. Moreover, in an attempt to minimise the negative side effects of opiates, many users become consumers of other substances like benzodiazepams or methadone on which they may well also become dependent, thus compounding the initial problem of opiate use. Such multi-dependency will, of course, bring more health problems in its wake (HAS, 1996).

The 'moreish' nature of these substances leads quickly to high levels of use and with it all the problems associated with getting sufficient cash to finance the habit. Young people tend to start by smoking heroin but this is quickly abandoned in favour of the more cost-effective method of intravenous use as the habit takes hold. This carries a number of major additional risks.

For example, young people out of contact with needle exchanges, often share needles and place themselves in danger of contacting HIV or Hepatitis, both of which can be transmitted through dried blood present in shared spoons or the residue of blood traces in a filter. Intravenous users also place themselves at risk of the loss of blood vessels, the development of abscesses and ultimately the loss of limbs through damage caused by frequent and commonly inaccurate use of needles etc. Whilst it is

not our intent to rehearse the problems associated with these substances at great length, it is our view that one of the factors in the spread of heroin and crack use is the fact that, in order to enter the market for 'soft' drugs, the consumption of which is being increasingly regarded as a relatively innocuous cultural phenomenon, young people become exposed to the sales techniques of the 'hard' drug market. Although it may be that the two markets maintain discrete identities at ground level, the organisational connections are often little more than a dealer away. The 'soft' drugs culture remains fertile ground for dealers who see themselves as being 'in business' and employ advanced sales techniques: free samples, short-term interest free credit deals etc., in an attempt to extend their pitch.

Drugs Policy

Most statutory and voluntary agency approaches to the 'drug problem' occur under the banner of the 'Tackling Drugs' policy initiatives (Home Office, 1995; Home Office, 1998). Launched as an innovative Conservative flagship Policy, Tackling Drugs, which promotes a co-ordinated approach at local, regional and national levels, reads in places as an almost verbatim copy of the European Union drugs policy presented in the Maastricht Treaty (Kaminski, 1997). This is not, it appears, something which governments have been keen to publicise. The policy was developed on the basis of evaluations of pilot schemes, which indicated that local action tended to be uncoordinated, with agencies either overlapping or actively working against each other at ground level. The proposal was therefore that local policy should be co-ordinated by Drug Action Teams (DATs), made up of agency Chief Executives who would gather information from, and direct policy back to, Drug Reference Groups, (DRGs), made up of agency managers or senior practitioners who would be charged with implementing action. This, essentially, is how policy is currently structured, the government having appointed a drug 'tsar', currently Keith Hellawell, to co-ordinate policy at a national level.

Tackling drugs was, and remains, a controversial and contradictory policy. It attempts to reconcile two conflicting demands: the first for treatment and prevention through tolerance and 'harm reduction'; the second for 'law and order' through the suppression of drug use, a characteristic of UK drugs policy for four decades. This conflict is reflected in the official policy remit to:

...increase community safety from drug related crime...Reduce the susceptibility of young people to drug use and...reduce the health risks and other damage associated with drug misuse...this is to be achieved by vigorous law enforcement, accessible treatment and a new emphasis on education and prevention. (Home Office, 1995)

Action in general, but action on youth drug use in particular, a central tenet of the new policy, was slow to arrive. The 1996 report, *Children and Young People: Substance Misuse Services: The Substance of Young Needs* (HAS, 1996), indicated that services for young people were, in general, 'ad-hoc and patchy'. More damning, perhaps, was a later report on services provided by local authority social services departments, which found that 90 per cent of them had no budget for young people's drug services. Indeed, one third of them had not begun to address the issues, despite the fact that local authorities had, by that time, signed up to tackling drugs. This, despite the fact that children, either using or at risk of using drugs, are entitled to social work assistance under Section 17 of the Children Act 1989 implemented in 1991 (HAS, 1995). The election of New Labour and the high profile given to Keith Hellawell and his remit to tackle drugs, gave fresh impetus to what was essentially the same policy.

The SCODA Guidelines and Agency Responses

A major influence on the planning and implementation of young people's drug services has been the SCODA guidelines to working with young people. SCODA propose a five-tiered approach, ranging from basic advice-giving, health awareness, campaigns through school or youth-work-based 'peer education' schemes, onto the higher levels of Child and Adolescent Mental Health (CAMH) or medical services for more problematic users. The success of SCODA's approach depends upon close collaboration and co-ordination between agencies in order that a drug-using young person coming to the attention of one agency which is unable to provide an adequate response is referred on to an agency which can. For example, a drug-using young person who comes to the attention of a local authority child care social work team, may be referred to a voluntary sector service more attuned to that individual's specific needs. Whilst the local DRG would appear to be the ideal forum for such collaboration it has been our experience in three local authorities that inter-agency co-operation to implement the SCODA

model remains patchy. Such co-operation is hampered by lack of structured agreements for client exchange and, consequently, reliance as before on the willingness of caseworkers to initiate interventions.

Exceptions to this rather dismal picture are to be found in the criminal justice field where Arrest Referral Teams and Youth Offending Teams are both directly engaged in multi-agency work. Young people who have been arrested for drug-related offences, whether for possession or more serious offences like drug-related robbery are, as Arrest Referral schemes expand, likely to be seen by a drug worker, responsible for steering drugs-related offenders towards treatment under the Tackling Drugs initiative. If their offence leads to a community or custodial sentence the young person may be seen by a member of the multi-agency Youth Offending Teams (YOTs). Created under the Crime and Disorder Act 1999, YOTs represent a major innovation in dealing with youth crime. YOTs are intended to target not only the consequences, but also the broad contribution to offending behaviour, of substance misuse, using the expertise of seconded health, education, police, probation, social and community workers. YOT drug workers have tended to be either health-based or seconded in from existing local substance misuse agencies. However, treatment provision remains circumscribed by the reluctance of health authorities to provide the standard methadone service available to adult heroin addicts. Moreover, local authorities have proved unwilling to provide funding for residential rehabilitation placements; the former based on concerns about issuing highly addictive substitutes to people at an early stage of their using career and the latter based on the fact that most young people have yet to develop the motivation necessary to complete the highly intensive programmes of residential intervention.

Some Pointers to a Youth and Community Response

The patterns of treatment for young people tend to coalesce around the lower and higher ends of problem severity: education and advice for those experimenting with or contemplating drug use; and essentially behavioural, non-medical, interventions for those whose substance misuse has begun to create social problems. The middle-ground of drug use, for those 'normalised' recreational users whose drug behaviour, whilst not yet problematic, presents clear risks of social or self-harm would, we believe, be the most appropriate area for youth and community intervention.

Many young users remain, for various reasons, out of contact with existing services and remain untouched by the formal, often medicalised, language of harm-reduction publications. If these users are in contact with any agency outside of education, where confidentiality remains a barrier to effective intervention, it will be with youth and community workers whose central task is to meet young users on their own terms, in their own communities and, crucially, in their own language. This is a task yet to be achieved by the treatment agencies.

On a practical basis, in our own locality, the debate on youth and community intervention with young users has focused on whether the agency should recruit specialised drugs workers and integrate them into youth and community teams or whether specialist drugs workers should be 'borrowed' from existing drugs agencies as needed. We would disagree with the former approach on the basis of practicality. The difficulty of recruiting appropriately trained workers and integrating them into a generic team is formidable. Our reservations about the latter approach is that the specialised 'one off' event tends to ghetto-ise the issue of drug use, separating it from the other concurrent realities of the client's life, thus replicating the problems experienced by drug agencies in this domain. Our favoured approach pursues a broader line in which youth and community workers should avail themselves of drugs knowledge from specialist workers in the drugs field and use this to inform their daily work with their contact group. This approach should be supported by regular links with the various treatment agencies in their area, most of which would welcome a youth and community presence at their team meetings in order that when a young person appears with a clear difficulty they may be referred quickly to the most appropriate specialist worker.

The youth and community service is ideally placed to deal with the issue of the broad acceptance of recreational drug use amongst young people. A well-informed, well-connected youth and community work team can meet young people on their own territory, speak to them in their own language and, crucially, not treat the issue of drug use as something separate from, and necessarily problematic within the total context of the young person's life.

References

Drug Prevention Advisory Service (1999). *Doing Justice to Treatment.* London: Home Office.

European Monitoring Centre for Drugs and Drug Addiction (1999). *Annual Report on the State of the Drugs Problem in Europe.* Lisbon: EMCDDA.

Health Advisory Service (HAS) (1996). *Children and Young People: Substance Misuse Services: The Substance of Young Needs.* London: Department of Health.

HAS (1996). *Drug Misuse and Dependence: Guidelines on Clinical Management.* London: The Stationery Office.

Home Office (1995). *Tackling Drugs Together.* London: HMSO.

Home Office (1998). *Tackling Drugs to Build a Better Britain.* London: HMSO.

Hough, M. (1995). *Drug Misuse and the Criminal Justice System.* London: Drugs Prevention Initiative.

Kaminski, D. (1997). The Transformation of Social Control in Europe: The Case of Drug Addiction and its Socio-penal Management. In *European Journal of Crime, Criminal Law and Criminal Justice*, 5/Z: pp. 122–133.

Parker, H., Aldridge, J., and Measham, F. (1998). *Illegal Leisure, The Normalisation of Adolescent Recreational Drug Use.* London: Routledge.

Shiner, M., and Newburn, T. (1996). *Young People, Drugs and Peer Education.* London: Drugs Prevention Initiative.

Key Questions

1. What are the needs of the drug using young people in your contact? Are you informed enough about drug behaviour to understand those needs?
2. Have you developed any strategies to allow young people to participate in their own drug prevention education programmes?
3. How will you manage the tension of illegality and criminalisation in working with drug-using young people? Have you developed a coherent workable and legal policy around confidentiality?
4. Do you have regular contact or liaison with existing drug agencies? Do you have a named worker for them to contact?
5. What plans do you have to incorporate a drugs education/information programme into the work of the youth and community team in a consistent and holistic way?

32

Young People and Mental Health
Rory Reynolds

Key Points

1. Mental health problems affect some 10 per cent of young people.
2. Depression is not always easy to spot in teenagers and may present itself as disruptive behaviour or aggressiveness.
3. Eating disorders such as anorexia nervosa and bulimia affect girls more than boys. Although relatively uncommon, many more youngsters show some of the signs of anorexia or bulimia at times of stress and may require support and help.
4. Early onset schizophrenia affects about 1 per cent of the population. It usually has a slow onset but over time the changes in the individual are very marked. Common symptoms include auditory hallucinations, bizarre beliefs and train of thought 'derailments', where the person makes strange connections in their speech.
5. Professional support is available through the education system and the NHS, via the client's GP.

Introduction

Over the last few years there has been an increased awareness about the mental health needs of young people among professional workers. We might see this as part of a greater concern for young people generally within our society as well as recognition that adolescent experiences are likely to have an enduring effect into adult life. Many of the problems of troubled young people are attributable to changing economic circumstances, to acute poverty among the most needy sections of society and to stresses that affect families such as divorce, death of a family member or abuse.

In this chapter I shall provide information about some common disorders and pre-disposing risk factors that should alert professionals that preventative work might be necessary. I shall also briefly review the range of services available to young people and their families.

There is a general perception that adolescence is a time of stress and uncertainty. The adolescent, poised between childhood and the adult world, is deemed by many older people to be in an unenviable position. This view is supported by the writings of therapists like Erikson (1985) who formulated a lifespan theory of human development. He characterised adolescence as a period of conflict between the search for a meaningful identity and of role confusion as the ego attempts to adjust to the obvious physical, social and psychological changes that signify the move from being a child to being an independent adult.

The end of childhood is a stressful time in other ways too: education is taken seriously and GCSE and higher exams demand a great amount of time and focused work. Further there are negotiations with the family, parents or caregivers, about how increasing independence should be given. With all this stress, it isn't surprising that adolescence can be a time of great trauma as well as discovery and excitement. At a time of life when experimenting with extremes is fairly normal, the task of identifying where things are going wrong enough to warrant some sort of intervention may be difficult. What is 'normal' anyway? Here are some pointers that may help you decide.

Putting Young People's Behaviour in Context

Behaviour that looks odd or even downright bizarre can make more sense if you know something of its background. In therapeutic work with adolescents, assessments are often made with the whole family present. Within the context of a particular family, the presenting behaviour can often appear quite appropriate. This *systemic* approach to behaviour is frequently used by adolescent therapists. For example:

> *Eric is 14 years old and totally refuses to go to school. When his father attempts to take him in the car, he has to be dragged from the vehicle and runs back home as soon as he can. The school have reassured the parents that he has not been bullied at school as far as they are aware and Eric himself says that he feels anxious all the time he is at school although he doesn't know why. In a family meeting, Eric's mother says that she too found school difficult when she was a girl and now can only leave the house when Eric or her husband accompanies her. Since his father works, Eric has a real decision to make: go to school or stay at home and help his mother. In many ways he is being a good child rather than a disobedient one. The subsequent family work aims to help Eric's mother to make it clear to him that she can cope if he is not around during the day.*

The Duration of Troubling Behaviour

It has already been mentioned that adolescence is a time for extremes. The pressures of exams, the trauma of the loss of a boyfriend or girlfriend, taking drugs or alcohol, all have transient affects. Grief at the loss of a loved one may last much longer but is, in this context, quite a natural reaction and its effects too diminish (or at least become less evident) with time. While someone may grow out of feeling sad, it is less likely that depression will get better over time: in fact untreated it will probably get worse (Carr, 1999). Similarly, teenagers may react to a brief episode of stress by becoming less partial to food and eating very little. This is probably not going to be a problem unless the behaviour does not return to normal once the stress is relieved. For example:

> *Parveen is 17 years old and was admitted to hospital after taking an overdose of her mother's sleeping tablets. She would not readily speak to staff at the hospital and an adolescent psychiatrist was asked to assess whether it would be safe to discharge her once she was physically recovered. The psychiatrist managed to engage with Parveen and although she did not say much, she told him that she hated*

school, disliked her family and had no real friends. She also said that she saw no future for herself and wanted to die. Her parents told the psychiatrist that Parveen had been getting gradually lower in mood over the last 4 months although they were not sure why. She had been a bright and eager student but now her results were mediocre and she did not appear to care either for herself or anyone else. Her friends now rarely called to see her because she would often not speak to them. The duration of the problem and the deterioration in her mood over time indicated a major depressive episode that required urgent intervention. In this case, Parveen was admitted to a young adults mental health unit so that she could receive appropriate treatment.

The Concept of Mental Wellness and Resilience

In 1995, the HAS review of child and adolescent mental health services *Together We Stand* identified these components of mental health:

- The ability to develop psychologically, emotionally, intellectually and spiritually.
- The ability to initiate, develop and sustain mutually satisfying personal relationships.
- The ability to become aware of others and to empathise with them.
- The ability to use psychological distress as a developmental process, so that it does not hinder or impair further development.

Within this broad framework which incorporates the developmental nature of both body and mind in adolescents, mental health in young people is indicated by:

- A capacity to enter into and sustain mutually satisfying personal relationships.
- Continuing psychological development.
- An ability to interact in ways that are appropriate for age and intellectual level.
- Developing a moral sense of right and wrong.
- The ability to recover from setbacks and distress.

The HAS report is at pains to distinguish between those transient and common life experiences that can cause short-term worry, anxiety, upset and even distress which, while unpleasant, are unlikely to contribute to long-term harm and those factors that are known to increase the risk of chronic trauma, such as sexual abuse. It is accepted by most writers that adverse life events are necessary to build up resilience which will give protection against the stresses of life (Collins, 1997). There is evidence that people who are well supported through trauma in childhood and adolescence are more mentally resilient as adults (Tiet and Bird, 1998). The Mental Health Foundation's publication, *Bright Futures* (1999), endorses this view and draws a parallel between learning to become resilient, and emotional literacy: the ability to accept and recognise emotions in oneself and others and react to them constructively.

Emotional literacy is much more likely to come about when a youngster has a caring home life, good relationships with peers and attends a well run and encouraging school, college or place of work.

The same report points out that there have been a number of changes for the better and some for the worse for children and young people since 1945. They are on the whole physically healthier, have greater life expectancy, are better educated and have more spending power compared to earlier generations. Less positively they are more likely to experience spells of unemployment, take drugs, suffer psychological disorders, experience parental separation and become engaged in criminal behaviour.

While the problems of poverty, family disruption, poor educational attainment and lack of basic social skills have existed for centuries, the social context is now very different and the increasing pace of social change may be paradoxically exacerbating the stress of growing up in modem Britain.

Table 1 shows a list of the mental health risk factors and protective factors for young people. Essentially these fall into four main categories: intra-personal factors (within the person themselves), family factors, social factors and school, college and work factors.

Treating Adolescent Ill-health

Most treatment in adolescent psychiatry is carried out on an outpatient basis, either in a hospital unit or in clinics in the community, but inpatient units are also necessary especially for the more seriously

disturbed youngster. There is a need for the workers from the different teams (say, mental health team, local authority workers and Education) to co-operate with one another and for the therapists to be able to use a number of different methods of treatment and theoretical models.

Drug treatment is not widely used in adolescent psychiatry but where prescribed, should not be stopped without medical agreement and planning.

Talking therapies are the most common form of intervention.

Systemic therapy focuses on relationships within the family or home network. It aims to produce small changes within key areas of the network that can profoundly alter the context for the youngster. For example:

> *Jude is 18 years old and lives at home with his parents. His parents complain that unlike his older brother, Jude is aggressive, defiant and 'out of control'. Jude regularly makes an unnecessary amount of noise, comes home late and irritates his father by rarely taking part in family events. In a family meeting with therapists, it becomes clear that Jude's parents have very high expectations of him and Jude is clearly failing to fulfil their hopes. A vicious circle of criticism leading to even more aggressiveness by Jude had developed. Using a systemic approach, the therapists encouraged some cognitive re-framing by the parents: what did they appreciate about their son? Could they look for opportunities to recognise what he was doing right e.g. he was getting very good grades at school. At the same time Jude was asked to think what small changes he could start to make to his own behaviour at home. This led to an immediate small improvement in relationships at home that was gradually developed in further sessions into a sustained change.*

Cognitive-Behavioural Therapy (CBT) can be effective in cases of anxiety and depression. CBT attempts to change the automatic negative thought patterns that underlie anxious or depressed feelings. This is combined with an entirely practical homework component that gives the client the

Table 1: Chart summarising mental health **protective** and **risk** factors for adolescents

Protective factors		Risk factors
Confidence Good self esteem Good physical health	**Intra-personal factors**	Genetic predisposition Chronic illness Physical or sensory disability Poor social skills Learning difficulties Low achievement Low self esteem
Clear boundaries Consistent parenting Secure attachment to parent/caregiver Relatively stable home life Parent feels able to cope Good diet Emotional needs met	**Intra-family factors**	Unclear boundaries Poor parenting Insecure attachment to parent/carer Divorced or rowing parents Parents feel unable to cope Physical, sexual or emotional abuse Poor diet Parent with mental health problem Looked after children
High standard of living Safe neighbourhood Feel part of a community Access to caring adults Good peer network Culture/ethnicity valued	**Social factors**	Poverty Urban environment Unsafe neighbourhood Feel isolated from neighbourhood No access to caring adults Poor relationships with peer group Culture/ethnicity not valued or abused Sudden trauma Being a refugee

Consistent and clear rules
Positive day-to-day environment
Effective anti-bullying policy in place
Lots of chances to succeed
Recognition of skills
Encouragement to reflect on
   development
Treated with respect
	School/college/work factors	Inconsistent or unclear rules
		Punitive environment
		Bullying not acknowledged
		Low morale environment
		Skills not valued
		Lots of chances to fail
		Values not clear or promoted
		No health or mental health promotion
		   programme in place
		Poor student-tutor relationships

chance to rehearse behaviour that enables them to lead a more normal life. For example:

Shana is a 19-year-old hostel resident who found it difficult to settle down after her arrival at the placement some two months earlier. She complained to staff that none of the other residents like her although this does not appear to be true. In reality, Shana avoids them and is anxious in their company. In CBT sessions, Shana learns to identify and challenge the negative thoughts that sustain her nervous feelings. At the same time she gradually builds up the periods spent with her fellow residents: so a few minutes are extended over time to 10, then 20 and then 30 minutes. Graded exposure in this way allows Shana to get to know them and so start to build up a network of relationships.

Serious Disorders in Adolescence

Depression in adolescence has emerged as a disturbingly common phenomenon with some estimates putting the incidence as high as one in four youngsters aged between 17 and 19 years. The government has recently set targets for a reduction in the level of suicide by 17 per cent by the year 2010 (from the 1996 baseline) in the White Paper, *Our Healthier Nation* (1999). While there has been a drop in successful suicides overall, the figure for young men aged 15-30 has shown little change.

The Department of Health document, based on a study from the Office of Population, Census and Surveys, *The Health of Our Children* (1995) presents statistical evidence of a decline in young people's mental health. About 10 per cent of young people reported internal feelings of 'misery and worthlessness' and suicides had risen by 40 per cent over 15 years among young males aged 15 to 19. In his book *So Young, So Sad, So Listen*, Philip Graham (1995) estimates that one in a hundred 12 to 16 year olds will attempt suicide at some time. Twice as many girls appear to suffer from depression and will go on to attempt suicide compared to boys. However, the statistics confirm that young men are much more likely to succeed. While the common symptoms of depression are fairly easy to spot (irritability, withdrawal, sleep disturbance) others are more difficult to discern. Doyle (1996) points out that 'attention deficit' and 'hyperactivity', exhibitionism and aggressiveness are hidden signs of depression that frequently get put down to temperament or are diagnosed as conduct disorders. These symptoms are often a reaction to a particular experience or set of circumstances which may include suffering physical, sexual or verbal abuse, rowing or divorcing parents, living in a hostile environment, family financial pressure or having a family member chronically ill or disabled. Doyle goes on to argue that since these factors frequently affect generations of the same family, depression tends to be handed down. Depression has been linked by a number of studies to an increased risk of drug and alcohol abuse, early sexual experience and pregnancy, as well as other high-risk behaviours including criminal activity (e.g. Fombonne, 1998; Hall, 1995). Once depression has occurred in teenage years, studies have shown that

there is a high likelihood of reoccurrence in later life (Goodman, 1997).

Indicators of depression

The DSM-IV indicators, the standard North American diagnostic scale commonly used by doctors/psychiatrists, suggests that 5 or more of the following symptoms indicate severe depression:

- Depressed mood which in adolescents sometimes presents as irritability.
- Diminished interest or pleasure in daily activities.
- Significant weight loss or gain (5% per month).
- Insomnia or excessive sleeping.
- Slowing of responses or hyperactivity.
- Complaints about fatigue, loss of energy.
- Feeling worthless or unloved.
- Poor concentration and indecisiveness.
- Over-anxiety to please.
- Thoughts about self-harm or suicide.

Treatment

Severe depression requires expert intervention. Young people with this condition are unable to 'snap out of it', 'look on the bright side' or respond to the observation that they are 'luckier than most people their age'. Their feelings of poor self worth and, often, self-anger are being fuelled by repetitive thoughts which may have their origin in childhood experiences and negative family patterns of coping. These thoughts are not easily controlled and the resultant depressed state affects appetite, appearance, sleep patterns, relationships with others, concentration and the ability to see tasks through.

Recent comprehensive studies (Roth and Fonagy, 1999) have highlighted the effectiveness of both cognitive-behavioural therapy (CBT) and medication, where severe depression is diagnosed. CBT encourages the youngster to challenge the negative thoughts in a structured way and gradually increase the level of activity. Medication also helps most people but it must be carefully monitored by the GP, psychiatrist or specialist nurse and gradually reduced as the mood improves.

Where serious self-harm is a feature, a careful risk assessment needs to be undertaken by a specialist mental health worker in order evaluate how best to keep the person safe. Contrary to the received wisdom that people who threaten to harm themselves rarely do so, statistics show that many successful suicides have given clear warnings of what they intend to do. Consequently threats of self-harm made by someone who you consider to be depressed should always be taken seriously.

Eating Disorders

Eating disorders, in particular anorexia nervosa and bulimia, are commonly considered to afflict adolescent girls and young women. However, boys sometimes show signs of the condition and they should not be excluded from consideration because of their gender.

It is far from clear how prevalent eating disorders are amongst adolescents. Bryant-Waugh (1993) points out that a formal diagnosis of one of the eating disorders is quite rare but at least one study showed that about 5 per cent of all teenage girls develop a mild form of anorexia at some point in their adolescence (Button and Whitehouse, 1981). This high incidence of unreported eating problems is supported by other studies (e.g. Johnson-Sabine et al., 1988) and means that those who work and care for adolescent girls in particular should be alert to the signs. Detection is made difficult by the secret nature of the condition and sufferers (particularly of anorexia) rarely complain, and frequently strongly deny, that they are having any problems with food and eating.

Anorexia nervosa is variously defined in the literature but DSM-IV gives 4 indicators of the condition:

1. Refusal to maintain body weight over the minimum normal weight for age and height (body weight over 15 per cent lower than expected weight).
2. Intense fear of gaining weight or getting fat even though underweight.
3. Disturbance in the experience of body weight, size or shape (e.g. claiming to feel fat although emaciated).
4. The absence of at least 3 menstrual cycles when they are expected to occur (amenorrhoea).

Bulimia is an eating disorder characterised by out-of-control behaviour regarding food. Food avoidance may alternate with over-eating and the cycle of bingeing and starvation is common among youngsters with this condition. The exaggerated dread of being fat (also found in anorexia) persists and episodes of overeating may be counterbalanced by stringent methods of weight reduction using laxatives and frequent vomiting.

Eating disorders are more common among the affluent social groups, 67 per cent being from social classes I or II. There is a growing incidence of these disorders amongst teenage girls from an African-Caribbean or Asian background in the UK (Bryant-Waugh, 1993). Paradoxically it appears to be more prevalent in families that maintain their own practices and beliefs and socialise mainly with people of the same racial origin. This high incidence may reflect the strain on youngsters who straddle a wide cultural divide.

Treatment should be offered as early as possible. If weight loss is severe, health care staff initially concentrate on building up body mass because of the severe effects on physical well being both in the short and long term. Bryant-Waugh (1993) points out that there is no preferred treatment model and overall about three-quarters of patients recover to some extent. The remaining 25 per cent continue to struggle with weight and a proportion of these will continue to do so throughout their lives. Most large towns or Health Trusts offer some specialist help in the form of dedicated staff and clinics. Inpatient care in specialist residential units is indicated where weight has fallen to a dangerously low level. For example:

Susan is a 17-year-old girl who was referred to the Family Clinic by her GP because of her reducing weight. The GP had seen Susan and her mother several times and had even offered to weigh her regularly at the surgery to keep an eye on her weight. However, Susan had failed to turn up to a number of these appointments and things appeared to be getting worse. During the initial family session at the Clinic, we learned that Susan was a keen amateur athlete and had formed a close relationship with another female athlete who was very slim. As an athlete Susan had always been careful about her diet and now she started to take in less fat and carbohydrate as she tried to match her friend's physique. Her parents described Susan as a very determined girl who was something of a perfectionist. She began to take over the cooking of most of the meals in the house in order, she said, to completely in control of her food intake. She told us that she realised logically that her weight loss was dangerous (she was at the time 5 per cent below the normal minimum weight for her height and age) but that she felt she had only limited control over the urge to continue to be obsessive about food. Despite some CBT and systemic family work at our clinic, Susan was unable to achieve her target weight and she was eventually admitted to a specialist residential clinic where more intensive group and psychotherapy work was undertaken. Under this regime she has sustained some weight gain for the first time in two years and is beginning to spend some time at home and school in preparation for her discharge.

Schizophrenia

Schizophrenia is a seriously debilitating condition that affects nearly 1 per cent of the population aged 18 years and over. Among teenagers there are more male cases than females with a slightly earlier average age of onset at about 15 years for boys and 17 for girls (Asarnow, 1994). About a quarter of cases will have a single relapse with a good chance of complete recovery. Another quarter will have multiple relapses but will function well between breakdowns while the remaining 50 per cent will have a poor outcome with a need for frequent hospitalisations and careful and sustained follow-up (Asarnow, 1994). For reasons not completely understood, there is an over-representation of young African-Caribbean men and women in the UK diagnosed with this disorder. It has been suggested that the diagnostic criteria used e.g. DSM-IV, are Eurocentric and so discriminate against people from non-European cultures (Fernando, 1991).

The DSM-IV criteria are shown below:

- Delusions (erroneous beliefs).
- Hallucinations (errors of perception, usually auditory: 'voices in my head').
- Disorganised speech (incoherence of train of thought 'derailments').
- Grossly disorganised behaviour or catatonia (frozen position).
- Negative symptoms include inability to concentrate, poor personal hygiene and indifference to strong stimuli, e.g. pain.

Only one symptom from the above list is required for diagnosis if delusions are bizarre or if hallucinations consist of a voice keeping up a running commentary on the person's behaviour or thoughts. There is also gross disturbance in the person's ability to work or attend school, keep up interpersonal

relationships and look after themselves. Over time there is a clear deterioration in all these areas.

In practice, the boundaries between schizophrenic disorders and some other disorders such as deep depression, autism and a drug-induced psychosis are difficult to define clearly. About a third of the young people who meet the diagnostic criteria for schizophrenia also meet the criteria for depression (Asarnow, 1994) and so may not be initially identified as having a schizophrenic condition.

There is some evidence that schizophrenia may have a genetic component. It is the case, that the more genes one shares with a schizophrenic parent (or parents), the greater one's chance of developing the disorder (Carr, 1999). Studies of identical and non-identical twins show that where the genetic material is identical, there is a 48 per cent probability that if one twin suffers from schizophrenia, the other will too. For non-identical twins the figure is 17 per cent (Gottesman, 1991). However, the majority of sufferers have no relative with the disorder, therefore other factors such as social stress, environment and early experience must play their part in the development of schizophrenia.

Some personality and social factors appear to confer protection against the disorder. A young person who is clearly successful, happy and well supported prior to their first breakdown is more likely to make a complete recovery (Carr, 1999). High IQ, an easy-going temperament and high self-esteem also confer protection and such youngsters are more likely to recover faster and stay well longer. Family attitudes that are positive and optimistic about the future are protective as well. Finally, it is crucial for the family and the teenager to have access to accurate information about managing the disorder so that intervention is offered speedily if a further breakdown appears to be occurring. Organisations such as MIND and the National Schizophrenia Fellowship publish a large number of booklets responding to this need and should be read by anyone working with young people where severe mental health problems are likely to be an issue.

NHS and Educational Services for Young People with Mental Health Problems

All NHS services must be accessed through the client's GP who will make a written referral to the relevant clinic. Residential placements within the

NHS require a referral from a consultant adolescent psychiatrist based at the Child and Adolescent Mental Health Service Clinic.

Education based services

Schools have access to a range of services for children and young people who appear to be struggling in the education system. Young people with mental health problems or behavioural difficulties frequently come to light because of the disruption they cause in the classroom. Such students are also often failing academically (Sutton, 2000).

Educational psychologists

Offer a wide range of services including assessment for Statement of Need, counselling and offering strategies to teachers who are working with youngsters who may have a range of mental health problems.

College/university based counselling services

All colleges should have a pastoral or counselling service that is available to students to offer support and, if necessary, referral to other support services.

Health-based services

Child Development Centres (CDC)

This is a community-based service aimed at assessing youngsters of school age with a range of genetic and neurological problems that may impede their normal development including Attention Deficit/Hyperactivity disorder, Asperger's

Syndrome and some specific sensory disorders. Staff include community paediatricians, clinical psychologists, occupational therapists and community psychiatric nurses (CPNs).

Child and Adolescent Mental Health Service (CAMHS)

CAMHS is the specialist community resource mainly involved in working directly with youngsters and parents on a wide range of presenting disorders. They also offer support to professionals such as GPs and social workers who are dealing with troubled young people. CAMH clinics (often called Family Consultation Clinics) are staffed by a multi-disciplinary team including adolescent psychiatrists, social workers, clinical psychologists, family therapists, community psychiatric nurses, drama therapists and child psychotherapists.

Residential units

In some areas there are in-patient facilities that may be used for young people who require treatment that cannot be safely offered while they are in the community, say for severe eating disorders where the client's safety may be an issue or for acting out behaviour that puts either themselves or others at risk.

Conclusion

Given the prevalence of mental disorders among young people, what action can be taken to ensure that their problems can be identified early on and interventions sought when they are likely to prove most effective?

Key Questions

1. Am I aware of the major symptoms of depression, eating disorders and schizophrenia? Would I recognise when someone is presenting with some of the indicators?

2. Is there training available through my organisation that can increase my skills in this area?

3. Bearing in mind that low-key skills are important in helping young people with possible mental health problems, what other techniques can I identify that might be useful (e.g. listening skills)?

4. If the family of a youngster who is having problems asks for help, where could I refer them?

5. What practices in my organisation are unhelpful to young people who have mental health problems?

It is often the case that low-key strategies applied early on are more effective than trying to deal with a major crisis. Thus the key actions below mainly focus on preventative approaches.

Key actions

- Create a relaxed relationship in which it is OK for the youngster to tell you about their difficulties.
- Don't be afraid to offer guidance based on your own experience of life and explore with them some simple strategies for solving their problems themselves which will reduce their level of stress and increase their self-esteem.
- Give clear feedback to youngsters about how they are doing. Recognise their strengths and ensure that criticism is given in a way they will find acceptable: e.g. 'I've noticed that sometimes you...' rather than 'you always...'
- It is important for the adult worker to model mature ways of coping with difficult situations. You are being watched and copied more than you may think.
- Have very clear and explicit boundaries about behaviour, especially how you expect people to interact. This is particularly important for youngsters with conduct problems, anxiety and schizophrenic disorders.
- Be optimistic in your work with those who have mental health problems. This is a major factor in offering effective support and will help the youngster feel positive.

References

Button, E., and Whitehouse, A. (1981). Subclinical Anorexia Nervosa. In *Psychiatric Medicine*, 11: pp. 509–516.

Carr, A. (1999). *A Handbook of Child and Adolescent Clinical Psychology*. London: Routledge.

Collins, A. (1997). Use of Family: A Care-giving Model to Articulate the Role of the Public Health Nurse in Infant Health Promotion. In *Comprehensive Pediatric Nursing*, 20: pp. 207–216.

Erikson, E. (1985). *Life Cycle Completed*. New York: Norton.

HAS (1995). *Together We Stand*. London: DoH.

Useful organisations

MIND
15–19 Broadway
London E15 4BQ
www.mind.org.uk

National Schizophrenia Foundation
28 Castle Street
Kingston-on-Thames
Surrey KT1 1SS
www.nsf.org.uk

Young Minds
102–108 Clerkenwell Road
London EC1M 5SA
www.youngminds.org.uk

Further Reading

Asarnow, J. (1994). Childhood Onset schizophrenia. In *Journal of Child Psychology*, 35: pp. 345–371.

Bryant-Waugh, R. (1993). *Childhood Onset Anorexia Nervosa*. Hove: LEA.

Doyle, C. (1996). The Hidden Signs of the Depressed Child. In *Daily Telegraph*, 26th October: p. 21.

Fernando, S. (1991). *Mental Health: Race and Culture*. London: MIND.

Fombonne, E. (1998). Suicidal Behaviours in Vulnerable Adolescents. In *British Journal Psychiatry*, 173: pp. 154–159.

Goodman, R. (1997). Child Mental Health: Who is Responsible? In *BMJ*, 314: p. 813.

Graham, P. (1995). *So Young, So Sad, So Listen*. London: Gaskell.

Gottesman, I. (1991). *Schizophrenia Genesis: The Origins of Madness*. New York: Freeman.

Hall, C. (1995). Children Becoming Healthier in Body but not in Mind. In *Daily Telegraph*, 22nd September, p. 18.

HMSO (1999). *Our Healthier Nation* (White Paper). London: HMSO.

Johnson-Sabine, E. (1988). Abnormal Eating Attitudes in London Schoolgirls. In *Psychiatric Medicine*, 42: pp. 615–622.

Linsey, A. (1996). *Lifespan Journey*. London: Hodder and Stoughton.

Mental Health Foundation (1999). *Bright Futures*. London: Mental Health Foundation Press.

Roth, A., and Fonegy, P. (1999). *What Works for Whom*. London: Guilford Press.

Sutton, C. (2000). *Helping Families with Troubled Children*. London: Wiley.

Tiet, Q., and Bird, H. (1998). Adverse Events and Resilience. In *Journal of American Child & Adolescent Psychiatry*, 37: pp. 1191–1200.

Index

The art of youth work

By Kerry Young

What is youth work? What do youth workers do?

As youth work has become the flexible friend of New Labour, able apparently to promote school inclusion, reduce youth crime, contribute to health gain and so on, it has been at serious risk of losing any distinctive identity, co-opted by others' agendas. Young endeavours in this book to restore its distinctive value base and principles...I commend her effort... Young People Now

Young's description of the way in which good youth work can instil the key features of critical thinking that underpin educational attainment and the sense of citizenship is about as good as it gets...an eloquent, poetic and philosophical reassertion of the unique contribution of the youth work purpose... Rapport

Whilst acknowledging that the task can sometimes seem exceedingly hard, Kerry Young enables us to engage in the continuous process of reflection that is essential to success... whether the young people we are working with are 'in trouble', at risk, disaffected, socially excluded... or just young people in the process of creating themselves, their identity, and the meanings and values which shape their lives and guide their actions in the world.

...teachers see young people as pupils. Doctors see young people as patients. Probation officers and social workers see young people as clients. Whereas youth workers see young people as people. Three Cheers for that. www.trainingzone.co.uk

144 pages   1-898924-49-X   £11.95

Kids at the door revisited

By Bob Holman

What do youth workers do? This book tells the story of a community youth work project in Bath through interviews with young people who were involved. It also tells their stories over the decade that followed.

...its core message must not be overlooked: effective support for young people at risk cannot be built in a vacuum and must be developed organically in the context of the cultures and communities to which they belong.   Young People Now

It has been said of author Bob Holman that few people can have provided more thoughtful and personal a testament to the value of working with, and living in, local communities. Now living and working in Easterhouse, Glasgow, Holman suggests that we:

...finance residents in deprived areas so that they can appoint teams who will live locally and long-term to promote the well-being of youngsters into teenage years and adulthood. It can be done.

His book supports this claim and, whether you fully accept his argument, or not, it presents a vivid picture of what youth workers do, which is well worth reading and sharing.

112 pages   1-898924-58-9   £9.95

Delivering good youth work
A working guide to surviving and thriving
By Gina Ingram and Jean Harris

Written in plain English, this book offers anyone who works with young p
strategies to survive and thrive in a fast changing world.

Delivering good youth work helps with:
- Understanding the world of young people
- Understanding youth work
- Why we need it more than ever
- How good youth work works
- Planned approaches to delivery
- Managing yourself and others effectively
- How to manage you manager!
- How to supervise well and develop staff
- Building support
- Looking after yourself, your co-workers and young people
- Best practice in partnership working
- Reflecting on your work and learning from experience

And above all...helping young people.

Packed with case studies, *Delivering good youth work* offers effective and tested ways of putting theory into practice. It is an essential support to you and your work with young people.

Big claims for a small book? Written by two experienced youth workers, one of whom now manages a Connexions team, *Delivering good youth work* incorporates advice and comments from students, lecturers and co-workers from a broad spectrum of practice who have read their work and encouraged its publication. Why not judge for yourself?

160 pages   1-898924-97-X   £11.95

th and safety in youth and community work

Doug Nicholls

Full of specific peculiarities, traps, tricks and tips that cannot be found in generic guides to health and safety.

...genuinely must-have resources for both employers and employees. They can liberate professionals so they can get on with their educational work, free from danger and harm.

Young People Now

The books cover: policy and practice checklist; useful contacts; model forms; regulations; rights; responsibilities; risk assessment; representatives; reporting; rest; implementing a strategy; stress; violence and aggression; minibuses; harassment and bullying; staffing ratios; pregnant at work; outdoors, trips, visits; smoking; fire precautions; injuries and claims; support and information.

The pocket guide is a daily companion that can be used away from base and the resource manual is a reference and planning tool to implement strategies for systematic introduction of new and improved practice.

Resource Manual: 168 pages   (A4 wirebound)   1-898924-02-3   £29.95
Pocket Guide: 128 pages   1-898924 03-1   (Only available as pack of 3)   £17.95

Employment practice and policies in youth and community work
Second Edition
By Doug Nicholls

For managers and workers, in both statutory and voluntary sectors, of youth work, community work and play work, this comprehensive and practical guide to issues of employment has now been thoroughly updated to take account of:

- changes in the delivery and organisation of youth, community and play work
- new ideas about best practice
- the completely new trade union and individual employment rights legislation introduced since 1997.

The first edition was acclaimed:

All the information you could possibly need is somewhere between these covers.

NYCVS Clipboard

...straightforward and easy to understand...   Young People Now

A comprehensive and inspiring resource...   Youthwork

It will ensure that those employed in the youth and community services can get on with the task with which they are charged, confident in the structures behind them and competent to make the professional interventions ahead of them.   Howard Williamson

The second edition is even better. It covers: Part time youth and community workers. The Joint Negotiating Committee. Health and safety issues. Equal opportunities. Legal responsibilities. Us and them. Financial problems. Employment law. Being managed. Redundancy, re-organisation and redeployment.

176 pages   1-898924-63-5   £16.95

Doug Nicholls is General Secretary of CYWU: the union for everyone working with people.

Working with young people in Europe
What we can learn from our neighbours
Edited by Brigitte Volond and David Porteous

In this important book for practitioners, managers and students you will find factual information about the history, organisation and delivery of services in France, Spain, Netherlands, UK. Separate chapters describe in generic terms the structure and organisation of: youth and social work, health-care, youth justice, housing, education, training and employment. They situate recent changes in policy within a broader historical framework and give particular attention to the issues of social exclusion.

There are also critical commentaries on contemporary issues and debates, which set out not merely to describe but also to evaluate the effectiveness of particular aspects of youth and social work with socially excluded young people, and to speculate upon alternative approaches as we enter the 21st century.

Based on a collaborative research project between academics and practitioners in the four countries, comparative analysis of this kind is still relatively rare. So the book also asks how such comparisons can assist our work. While we can learn from our neighbours, we must do so on the basis of a sound knowledge of different approaches and methods deployed by professionals in very different cultural settings, as presented here.

160 pages   1-898924-74-0   £14.95

Anti-racist work with young people
European experiences and approaches
Edited by Anna Aluffi-Pentini and Walter Lorenz

...thought-provoking...excellent practical activities... Youthwork

...interesting, practical and important... Professional Social Work

A good book, ranging from a theoretical overview to practical possibilities...reflected in practical case studies of anti-racist work in Britain, Germany and the Netherlands...23 activities are suggested ranging in duration from 10 minutes to a whole day. Young People Now

...the basis for developing a wide range of strategies... Kids Club Network

220 pages   1-898924-01-5   £14.95

Adolescence
Positive approaches to working with young people
By Ann Wheal

Designed for use by anyone who works with young people.

Based on extensive interviews with young people and those who work with them:
- *provides advice and practical suggestions on ways of achieving success in work with young people aged 12–16*
- *presents strategies for creating the right environment, guidelines for training the people involved and ways of dealing with hiccups, obstacles and pitfalls*
- *covers working with parents, successful communication, care and control, encouraging positive behaviour, education, health, promoting equality and young people's rights and the law.*   Social Action Today

...draws on contemporary thinking, writing and experience as well as taking on board the opinions of young people themselves...useful and up-to-date...   Community Care

184 pages   1-898924-19-8   £14.95

Having their say
Young people's participation: European experiences
Edited by David Crimmens

This fascinating and important book looks at how various European countries have gone beyond incorporation of the UN Convention on the Rights of the Child into their legislation to:
– foster participation by children and young people in political processes
– involve them in making decisions about how to improve services provided for them.

Each chapter addresses common themes. So, taken as a whole, the book builds a picture of how the voice of the child is becoming more influential, not just in the search for more effective services, but also reflecting a fundamental change in the status of children and young people in their relationships with wider adult society. But read individually each chapter provides a snapshot of particular and diverse developments, including:

- how young people are participating in the design and delivery of the new Connexions service in England and Wales
- the experiences of young people meeting with MEPs to discuss 'An Agenda for Young People'
- the struggle to establish the rights of children in state care in Scotland
- a major consultation exercise in Ireland
- political disenchantment and the development of 'Learning Democracy' in German local government
- young people researching young people's involvement in formal politics in Amsterdam and Rotterdam
- how young people are changing the nature of their own educational experiences in Norway
- the children's parliament in Slovenia
- how approaches to the development of children's rights vary from city to city in Spain
- the struggle between participation and traditional emphasis on the primacy of the family in Italian social policy.

About 160 pages   1-898924-78-3   £14.95

Making a difference
Practice and planning in working with young people in community safety and crime prevention programmes
Edited by Alan Dearling and Alison Skinner

Effective ways of working with young people at risk and in trouble are in demand at present, at neighbourhood level, as well as more formally through the courts and police final warning referral programmes. Changes in legislation and the development of new multi-agency youth offending teams are providing new contexts in which such work can take place.

Making A Difference reviews this new context and offers a range of practice based approaches for working more informally with young people in trouble in a variety of settings, many of which can enable more intangible issues of need and aspiration to emerge and be addressed.

This book is full of 'hands-on' practice based material which can provide effective and tried and tested methods for all those involved with young offenders and young people at risk. These techniques and activities are appropriate for youth workers, members of youth offending teams, community-based projects, teachers, indeed, almost anyone working with young people.

There are ideas, guidance and examples in this book that will guide, encourage and provoke. At a time when it sometimes appears that novelty is all-important, it is vital that we are reminded that we should not lightly cast away the lessons of prior experience. 'Making a Difference' is that reminder and I recommend it highly.　　　Professor Tim Newburn, Goldsmiths' College, London

About 160 pages　　　1-898924-39-2　　　£14.95

The new youth games book

By Alan Dearling and Howie Armstrong

Over 40,000 copies sold.

A classic resource for training with young and old with over 200 practical activities and guidance on how to use them.

Excellent. There is only one other book to compare with it.

A compendium resource of the first order.

Encourages interaction between people to:
- have fun
- develop positive relationships
- learn literacy and numeracy skills
- increase creativity and imagination
- improve communication skills
- cope with tension and stressful situations
- break down barriers and ease the getting-to-know new people process
- identify problems and help find solutions
- build trust, sensitivity and understanding
- develop self-awareness
- improve social skills
- increase confidence

232 pages   1-898924-00-7   £9.95

Youth prostitution in the new Europe
The growth in sex work
Edited by David Barrett

...that youth prostitution is widespread is not in doubt. What is less clear is how this problem should be addressed...There is also the issue of wider social causes and of the appropriate agency response...the rise of economic inequalities, easier cross border movements, the growth of international crime syndicates and the lack of sophistication amongst intervention services...the problem is 'joined up' to a range of other problems... Childright

...a timely contribution, not least in view of increasing evidence of the growing global trend in the trafficking of humans, highlighting some of the complexities associated with attempts to define and measure the phenomenon and provide adequate protection for the young people concerned... Community Care

176 pages 1-898924-61-9 £14.95

Fixing it?
Young people, drugs and disadvantage
By Margaret Melrose

...interventions will only be effective when young people's motivations for using drugs are better understood...the different ways in which young people perceive their drug misuse and (therefore) their different views about the help they might need or want.

This is an interesting book...Melrose has brought to the surface the complexities of drug use by vulnerable young people, testified to the 'rationality' of that use (from their perspective) and made more prominent the motivations which are often more likely to sustain their use of drugs rather than find the reasons to stop...

In particular, Melrose seeks to uncover the gender-blindness which has so often characterised the drugs debate.

'Fixing It?' is enriched by case studies which run throughout the text. They remind us repeatedly of the human condition of drug misuse — an important corrective to the daily diet of strategy documents and political pronouncements.   Young People Now

128 pages   1-898924-79-1   £11.95

After Macpherson
Policing after the Stephen Lawrence Inquiry
Edited by Alan Marlow and Barry Loveday

This bridge building book, written by senior police officers and by former officers now working as criminologists, together with their colleagues in community and social studies, looks at ethnic minorities' experience of policing and the criminal justice system: who is stopped and who is searched; developments in police/community relations; effective partnerships.

Chapters include:
- Black people and discrimination in criminal justice *Anita Kalunta-Crumpton*
- 'Dirty Babylon': reflections on the experience of racism *Lana Burroughs*
- The concept and context of institutional racism *Gurchand Singh*
- Must do better: the state of police race relations *Barry Loveday*
- Policing ethnic minorities *Jayne Mooney and Jock Young*
- Being realistic about stop and search *Peter Kennison*
- Developing locally responsive information systems in the post-Macpherson era *Robin Fletcher*
- Principled policing *John Alderson*

144 pages   1-898924-71-6   £14.95